Fodor's 2002

W9-CTE-282

Washington, D.C.

CONTENTS

MAPS

Circled letters in text correspond to letters on the photographs. For more information on the sights pictured, turn to the indicated page number Ⓐ> on each photograph.

DESTINATION
WASHINGTON, D.C.

It's hard to anticipate the impact of Washington, D.C. As you enter town, buildings you've seen on a thousand postcards, icons of America, stand firmly before you, larger than life: the Washington Monument, the Lincoln Memorial, the White House, the Capitol. Rising majestically from the low city, often flanked by sweeping lawns, they inspire awe. Just as striking, almost palpable, is the energy that comes from Washington's being the nation's center of government. Congressional staff rush around Capitol Hill, motorcades speed down side streets, politicians jockey for position on the Senate floor. After working hours, the city turns quiet and reflective. Take a stroll on the Mall one night when moonlight washes over the monuments. Pause to contemplate the grandeur of it all. Ready or not, you will be moved.

OFFICIAL WASHINGTON

A 52

The soul of the nation takes tangible form in stone as you walk the streets south, east, and west of Union Station, the grand beaux-arts rail terminal that even today welcomes thousands to Washington. The city's power grid is focused on the Ⓐ **White House**; a guided tour is obligatory and enlightening despite the tight format. Across the street and a heartbeat away is the vice president's office in the wedding-cake Ⓕ**Old Executive Office Building.** Another *tour de rigueur* is the glorious Ⓓ**Capitol** with its grand and inspiring rotunda. Other Washington monuments will move you to tears—notably the Ⓒ**Vietnam Veterans Memorial,** a quietly shining black wall, half sunk into the lawn and inscribed with the names of those who died for their country. Opposite, another wall remembers the hundreds of thousands of

B 111

C 41

American and United Nations troops who perished in the Korean conflict. Daniel Chester French's statue of Abraham Lincoln gazes down from his vigil inside the Parthenon-like Ⓔ**Lincoln Memorial,** providing solace in troubled moments to Washingtonians great and small. Another venue for contemplation is Ⓑ**Arlington National Cemetery,** where John F. Kennedy and his brother Robert are entombed along with so many other fallen heroes, known and unknown. For causes noble or murky, those interred here died in fealty to that which Washington gathers unto itself: America.

Ⓔ▷ 39

Ⓕ▷ 49

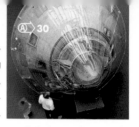

If, by way of sci-fi fantasy, every government building were whisked off to the moon, the city would remain a first-class destination for its museums alone. So often their names include the word "national," as if to proclaim that the very best of America is inside. Many are part of the Ⓔ**Smithsonian Institution,** also known as the nation's attic. In its Ⓐ**National Air and Space Museum** you can touch a moon rock and see Charles Lindbergh's *Spirit of St. Louis* and numerous sparkly, spiky spacecraft—

MUSEUMS

there's no collection of things airborne that is more persuasively curated. The Smithsonian's B **National Museum of Natural History** houses more than 120 million specimens, plus an insect zoo. The National Museum of American History has George Washington's false teeth and the original Star-Spangled Banner. Elsewhere, the city's art makes the senses reel. Among the masterworks in the D **National Gallery of Art** is Leonardo's pensive *Ginevra de' Benci*. The cozier C **Phillips Collection** houses Degas's *Dancers at the Bar* and other treasures. Close by but a world away in mood is the F **United States Holocaust Memorial Museum,** a shattering testament to man's inhumanity to man.

GREEN SPACES

You come to Washington *expecting* to see government buildings and national landmarks. What you might not expect—but will be delighted by—is the space that the city devotes to greenery. Small parks are everywhere, decked out with flowers in season. On a grander scale, great swaths of green such as Rock Creek Park cut through the town and line the rivers that frame it. The Ⓐ Ⓔ **East and West Potomac Parks,** two halves of one park, really, divided by a few yards of water, are verdant refuges, a rosy blizzard of the city's famous Japanese cherry blossoms in spring. Between them in a crook of the Tidal Basin sits the many-columned Jefferson Memorial. The parks also include miniature golf and a 100-times-life-size statue of a reclining man known as the *Awakening*. The Ⓑ **Hillwood Museum and Gardens** and Ⓒ **Dumbarton Oaks,** grand homes and once private parks, beckon those who love beautiful gardens. The houses are

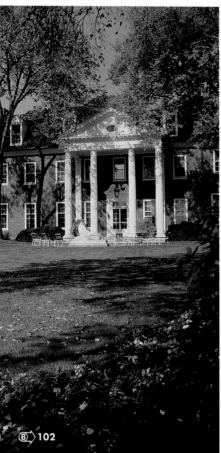

Ⓑ 102

Ⓒ 83

also museums, with exceptional collections of *objets* and artifacts. And although the Fabergé eggs at Hillwood and the Byzantine artifacts at Dumbarton Oaks might not entertain every member of the family, the live show at the sprawling Ⓓ**National Zoological Park** surely will.

Ⓐ 78

NEIGHBORHOODS

You can have a film-gobbling stay in Washington without ever realizing that people live here. But the city's neighborhoods are definitely worth a look. Toniest of all is Ⓐ**Georgetown,**

Ⓑ 70

where the university of the same name stands high on a hill. Power and wealth reside here—along with Washingtonians enchanted by either or both. Georgetown is pricey, chic, yuppie, inarguably pretty. Kalorama, not far north, is leafy, peaceful, and exclusive. Down-to-earth and ethnically diverse, Ⓒ**Adams-Morgan** can be crowded but it's never dull. The same can be said of vibrant, fashionable Dupont Circle and the trendy U Street area. A world away is tiny Ⓑ**Chinatown,** where designer coffee—refreshingly, in the opinion of many—is a tough find.

Ⓒ 104

DINING

Ⓐ⟩ 139   Ⓑ⟩ 126

Washington's food scene is as vibrant and varied as you'd expect in a melting-pot city, the sophisticated capital of the most diverse nation on earth. Ambassadors, politicians, and immigrants find the delicacies and comfort food of home, whether home is Chicago or Kansas City or Tangier. Ethiopian *injera* bread and West African tomato soup with goat; collard greens and Turkish kabobs; sushi and steak frites; Jamaican jerk chicken and all-American meat loaf—it's all here. Asian-food lovers have a chic café to call their own, Ⓐ**Teaism,** where the bento boxes are as sublime as the featured beverage. The Middle Eastern Ⓑ**Lebanese Taverna** transports you halfway around the world. Ⓒ**Vidalia** showcases the best of America—its seafood, its seasonal vegetables, and the creativity of its chefs.

Restaurants such as Galileo, Gerard's Place, Citronelle, and Kinkead's sum up the state of culinary art in America's restaurant cuisine today. Meander through the city, read what's posted on menus in the windows, and let your instincts be your guide—then pick up a fork and dig in.

Ⓒ⟩ 134

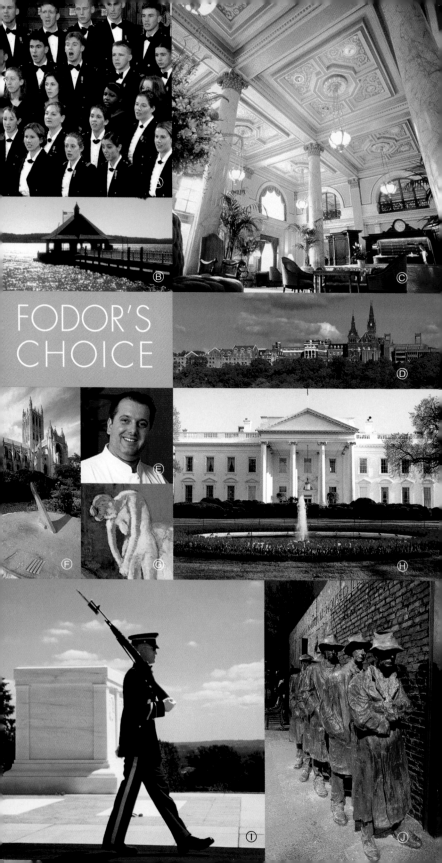

FODOR'S
CHOICE

Even with so many special places in Washington, D.C., Fodor's writers and editors have their favorites. Here are a few that stand out.

MEMORABLE SIGHTS

U.S. Capitol. Home of the Senate and the House of Representatives and reminiscent of the Roman Pantheon in design, the marble Capitol is a fresco- and statue-filled architectural marvel. ☞ p. 55

Ⓙ **Franklin Delano Roosevelt Memorial.** With its waterfalls, sculptures, wide walkways, and inspirational messages, this rambling memorial is ideal for contemplation. ☞ p. 37

Ⓓ **Georgetown University.** The Gothic spires of Georgetown's older buildings make the country's oldest Jesuit school look almost medieval. ☞ p. 84

Lincoln Memorial. Many people consider the Lincoln Memorial the city's most inspiring monument. The somber Daniel Chester French statue of the seated president, in the center of the memorial, gazes out over the Reflecting Pool. ☞ p. 39

Ⓑ **Mount Vernon.** Here you can tour the plantation workshops and reconstructed slave quarters as well as the kitchen, the carriage house, the gardens, and the tomb of George and Martha Washington. The sweeping Potomac views are a bonus. ☞ p. 236

Ⓘ **Tomb of the Unknowns.** At this moving shrine in Arlington National Cemetery, soldiers from the Army's U.S. 3rd Infantry keep watch around the clock. ☞ p. 112

Ⓐ **United States Naval Academy.** Crisply uniformed midshipmen populate this institution on 329 scenic acres alongside the Severn River in Annapolis. ☞ p. 227

Vietnam Veterans Memorial. This black-granite memorial is a moving tribute to those who died in this war. ☞ p. 41

Ⓕ **Washington National Cathedral.** Like its 14th-century counterparts, this 20th-century cathedral has a nave, flying buttresses, transepts, and vaults that were built stone by stone. ☞ p. 86

Ⓗ **White House.** If you think about it, it really is extraordinary that the president opens his house most mornings to throngs of visitors who peer past ropes at his family's dining rooms and living rooms. ☞ p. 52

MUSEUMS

National Air and Space Museum. At the most-visited museum in the world, you'll find displays of the airplanes and spacecraft that have made history. The flight-simulating IMAX movies are not to be missed. ☞ p. 30

National Gallery of Art. John Russell Pope's domed West Building and I.M.Pei's East Building house one of the world's finest collections of paintings, sculptures, and graphics. ☞ p. 30

National Museum of Natural History. Filled with bones, fossils, stuffed animals, and more, this is one of the great natural history museums of the world. ☞ p. 33

Ⓖ **Phillips Collection.** It's as beloved for its well-known paintings as for its relaxed atmosphere and knowledgeable guards. ☞ p. 93

United States Holocaust Memorial Museum. In a clear and often graphic fashion, this moving museum tells the stories of the 11 million people killed by the Nazis. ☞ p. 35

FLAVORS

Citronelle. In this embodiment of California chic, the kitchen's glass front lets you watch the chefs scurrying to and fro as they prepare, say, leek-encrusted salmon steak topped by a crisp fried-potato lattice. $$$$ ☞ p. 142

Gerard's Place. The focus is on the intriguing. Entrées such as poached lobster with ginger, lime, and Sauternes sauce are every bit as exquisite as the lovely desserts. $$$$ ☞ p. 135

Ⓔ **Galileo.** A spacious, popular Italian restaurant, Galileo makes everything in house, from bread sticks to mozzarella. $$$–$$$$ ☞ p. 136

Ⓘ **Ricchi.** Critics and upscale crowds praise the earthy Tuscan fare, offered on seasonal menus—one for spring and summer, one for fall and winter. $$$–$$$$ ☞ p. 136

Jaleo. At this lively Spanish bistro you can make a meal out of the many hot and cold tapas (appetizer-size dishes), although such entrées as grilled fish and paella are just as tasty. $$–$$$ ☞ p. 138

COMFORTS

Hay-Adams Hotel. Part Italian Renaissance, part English Tudor, the Hay-Adams has brightly decorated rooms with views of the White House. The afternoon tea is renowned, the staff dignified and friendly. $$$$ ☞ p. 155

Ⓒ **Willard Inter-Continental.** An opulent beaux arts hotel with a fascinating history, the Willard has hosted U.S. presidents and foreign heads of state. $$$$ ☞ p. 155

Jefferson Hotel. The style is federal in this small, luxurious charmer. Original art, antiques, and reproductions furnish the rooms. High-ranking politicos and film stars favor the Dining Room, the hotel restaurant, for its refined cuisine. The high staff-to-guest ratio ensures outstanding service. $$$–$$$$ ☞ p. 156

Hotel Washington. In this Edwardian hotel, reproductions of antiques fill the rooms. Washingtonians bring their out-of-town friends to the rooftop bar here for cocktails and a view of the White House grounds and the Washington Monument. $$$ ☞ p. 157

Morrison-Clark Inn. This unusual small inn is Victorian with an airy, modern twist. The fireplaces are marble and the rooms are filled with antiques. $$$ ☞ p. 157

1 EXPLORING WASHINGTON

From the stateliness of the Capitol and
the monuments to the funkiness of Adams-
Morgan, and from spaceships to Renoirs and
the National Zoo to the White House, the
capital has enough to keep visitors of all ages
and interests on the go for days and days.

THE BYZANTINE WORKINGS of the federal government; the sound-bite–ready oratory of the well-groomed politician; murky foreign policy pronouncements issued from Foggy Bottom; and $600 toilet seats ordered by the Pentagon cause many Americans to cast a skeptical eye on anything that happens "inside the Beltway." Washingtonians take it all in stride, though, reminding themselves that, after all, those responsible for political hijinks don't come *from* Washington, they come *to* Washington. Besides, such ribbing is a small price to pay for living in a city whose charms extend far beyond the bureaucratic. World-class museums and art galleries (nearly all of them free), tree-shaded and flower-filled parks and gardens, bars and restaurants that benefit from a large and creative immigrant community, and nightlife that seems to get better with every passing year are as much a part of Washington as floor debates or filibusters.

The location of the city that calls to mind politicking, back-scratching, and delicate diplomatic maneuvering is itself the result of a compromise. Tired of its nomadic existence after having set up shop in eight locations, Congress voted in 1785 to establish a permanent "Federal town." Northern lawmakers wanted the capital on the Delaware River, in the North; Southerners wanted it on the Potomac, in the South. A deal was struck when Virginia's Thomas Jefferson agreed to support the proposal that the federal government assume the war debts of the colonies if New York's Alexander Hamilton and other Northern legislators would agree to locate the capital on the banks of the Potomac. George Washington himself selected the site of the capital, a diamond-shape, 100-square-mi plot that encompassed the confluence of the Potomac and Anacostia rivers, not far from his estate at Mount Vernon. To give the young city a head start, Washington included the already thriving tobacco ports of Alexandria, Virginia, and Georgetown, Maryland, in the District of Columbia. In 1791, Pierre-Charles L'Enfant, a French engineer who had fought in the Revolution, created the classic plan for the city.

It took the Civil War—and every war thereafter—to energize the city, by attracting thousands of new residents and spurring building booms that extended the capital in all directions. Streets were paved in the 1870s, and the first streetcars ran in the 1880s. Memorials to famous Americans like Lincoln and Jefferson were built in the first decades of the 20th century, along with the massive Federal Triangle, a monument to thousands of less-famous government workers.

Despite the growth and the fact that blacks have played an important role in the city's history (black mathematician Benjamin Banneker surveyed the land with Pierre-Charles L'Enfant), Washington continues to struggle for full racial and ethnic equality. It's a city of other unfortunate contrasts: citizens of the capital of the free world couldn't vote in a presidential election until 1964, weren't granted limited home rule until 1974, and are now represented in Congress by a single nonvoting delegate. Homeless people sleep on steam grates next to multi-million-dollar government buildings. Violent crime, although it still exists, is way down (as it is in many other big cities) from the drug-fueled violent days of the late 1980s and early 1990s. Though it's little consolation to those affected, most crime is restricted to neighborhoods far from the areas visited by tourists.

Still, there's no denying that Washington, the world's first planned capital, is also one of its most beautiful. And though the federal government dominates many of the city's activities and buildings, there are places where you can leave politics behind. The walks that follow take you through the monumental city, the governmental city, and the residential city. Washington is a city of vistas—pleasant views that shift and change from block to block, a marriage of geometry and art. Unlike other large cities, Washington isn't dominated by skyscrapers, largely because in 1910 Congress passed a height restrictions act to prevent federal monuments from being overshadowed by commercial construction. Its buildings stretch out gracefully and are never far from expanses of green. Like its main industry, politics, Washington's design is a constantly changing kaleidoscope that invites contemplation from all angles.

WHAT'S WHERE

It's often said that Washington doesn't have any "real" neighborhoods, the way, for example, nearby Baltimore does. Although it's true that Washingtonians are not given to huddling together on their front stoops, each area of the city does have a clearly defined personality.

The Mall

With nearly a dozen diverse museums ringing an expanse of green, the Mall is the closest thing the capital has to a theme park—but here, almost everything is free. Lindbergh's *Spirit of St. Louis,* the Hope Diamond, the Fonz's leather jacket, dinosaurs galore, and myriad other modern and classical masterpieces await you. Of course, the Mall is more than just a front yard for all these museums: it's a picnicking park and a running path, an outdoor stage for festivals and fireworks, and America's town green.

The Monuments

Punctuating the capital like a huge exclamation point is the Washington Monument—at 555 ft 5 inches one of the world's tallest masonry structures. The Jefferson Memorial's rotunda rises beside the Tidal Basin, where you can rent paddleboats and admire more than 200 cherry trees, gifts from Japan and the focus of a festival each spring. The Lincoln Memorial has a somber statue of the seated president gazing out over the Reflecting Pool. The Vietnam Veterans Memorial is one of the most visited sights in Washington, its black granite panels reflecting the sky, the trees, and the faces of those looking for the names of loved ones. The popular Franklin Delano Roosevelt Memorial is on seven parklike acres near the Jefferson Memorial.

The White House Area

In a city full of immediately recognizable images, perhaps none is more familiar than the White House. In the neighborhood are some of the city's oldest houses and two important art galleries: the Renwick Gallery—the Smithsonian's museum of American decorative arts—and the Corcoran Gallery of Art, known for its collections of photography, European Impressionist paintings, and portraits by American artists.

Capitol Hill

Anchoring the neighborhood is the Capitol, where the Senate and the House have met since 1800. But the Hill is more than just the center of government. There are charming residential blocks here, lined with Victorian row houses and a fine assortment of restaurants, bars, and shops. Union Station, Washington's train depot, has vaulted and gilded ceilings, arched colonnades, statues of Roman legionnaires, and a modern mall–movie complex with food for every palate and pocketbook. Also in this area are the Supreme Court, the Library of Congress, and the Folger Shakespeare Library.

Exploring Washington, D.C. *(Boxes Refer to Detail Maps)*

Cleveland Park and the
National Zoo

Adams-Morg

Dupont Circle

Georgetown

Massachusetts Ave.

Columbia Rd.

18th St.

California St.

T St.

S St.

R St.

Decatur Pl.

R St.

Sheridan
Circle

New Hampshire Ave.

Corcoran

Florida Ave.

S St.

R St.

S St.

Wisconsin Ave.

32nd St.

31st St.

31st St.

30th St.

29th St.

28th St. N

27th St.

Q St.

Massachusetts Ave.

22nd St.

21st St.

20th St.

19th St.

Dupont
Circle

Church St.

P St.

17th St.

P St.

O St.

O St.

N St.

Rock Creek

New Hampshire Ave.

M St.

M St.

M St.

US 29

C&O Canal

Whitehurst Fwy.

26th St.

25th St.

L St.

L St.

Washington
Circle

29

K St.

Pennsylvania Ave.

Francis Scott
Key Bridge

George Washington Memorial Pkwy.

I-66

24th St.

23rd St.

22nd St.

The White
House Area

17th St.

Theodore
Roosevelt
Island

G St.

F St.

Virginia Ave.

E St.

D St.

C St.

50

Constitution Ave.

NW

Foggy Bottom

SW

50

Lincoln
Memorial

Reflecting Pool

Independence Ave.

Kutz
Bridge

Tidal Bas

George Washington Memorial Pkwy.

Arlington Memorial
Bridge

Columbia
Island

West Potomac Park

Ohio Dr.

W. Basin Dr.

Potomac River

FDR
Memorial

Memorial Dr.

Ladybird Johnson Park

ARLINGTON
NATIONAL
CEMETERY

Arlington

V I R G I N I A

To
Old Town
Alexandria

The Monuments

NW ◆ NE

Florida Ave.

U St. Ⓜ

16th St.
15th St.
14th St.

T St.

Vernon Ave.

S St.

Ⓜ

Rhode Island Ave.

Florida Ave.

St.
St.
St.

R St.

R St.

Q St.

Lincoln Rd.

Church St.

Logan
Circle

Q St.

9th St.

O St.

3rd St.

1st St.

O St.

Scott
Circle

13th St.
12th St.

Rhode Island Ave.

11th St.
10th St.
8th St.
7th St.
6th St.
5th St.
4th St.

P St.

New Jersey Ave.

New York Ave.

North Capitol St.

M St.

3rd St.

Thomas
Circle

Massachusetts Ave.

N St.
M St.
L St.

50

15th St.

16th St.

Mt. Vernon
Square

New Jersey

Capital
Children's
Museum

H St.

Ⓜ

I St.
Ⓜ

Ⓜ
50

Ⓜ
50

**Old Downtown and
Federal Triangle**

**Capitol
Hill**

New York Ave.

H St.

Union
Station

The White
House

Ⓜ

G St.
Ⓜ

G St.

2nd St.

I-395

Columbus
Memorial
Fountain

15th St.
14th St.

F St.

E St.

Pennsylvania

D St.

Louisiana Ave.

Stanton
Park

The
Ellipse

Ave.

Ⓜ

Constitution Ave.

Ⓜ

US
Capitol

NE ◆

National Gallery
Sculpture Garden
Madison Dr.

National Gallery
of Art

Washington
Monument

Smithsonian
Institution

THE   MALL

Jefferson Dr.

National
Air and Space
Museum

E. Capitol St.

SE ◆

Independence Ave.

Ⓜ

Maryland Ave.

Canal St.

Folger
Park

C St.

Ⓜ

The Mall

Ⓜ

Outlet Bridge

D St.

New Jersey Ave.

E St.

Jefferson
Memorial

395

Southwest Fwy.

395

Virginia Ave.

395

Francis Case
Memorial
Bridge

G St.

I St.

0   500 yards

Water St.

Maine Ave.

Ⓜ

0   500 meters

Washington Canal

N ↑

Ⓜ

SW ◆ SE

Old Downtown and Federal Triangle

In Old Downtown—the area within the diamond formed by Massachusetts, Louisiana, Pennsylvania, and New York avenues—are Chinatown, Ford's Theatre, and several important museums. The National Building Museum, formerly known as the Pension Building, has the largest columns in the world as well as displays devoted to architecture. Other museums include the National Museum of Women in the Arts, the National Portrait Gallery, and the Smithsonian American Art Museum. The Old Post Office Pavilion is also located here, with its shops and restaurants. You can tour the J. Edgar Hoover Federal Bureau of Investigation Building, with exhibits illustrating famous past FBI cases. And at the National Archives, the original Declaration of Independence, the Constitution, and the Bill of Rights are on display.

Georgetown

Georgetown, the capital's wealthiest neighborhood (and a haven for architecture buffs), is always hopping: trendy restaurants, bars, nightclubs, and boutiques line the narrow, crowded streets. Originally used for shipping, the C&O Canal today is a part of the National Park system: walkers follow the towpath and canoeists paddle the calm waters; you can also go on a leisurely mule-drawn trip aboard a canal barge. Washington Harbour is a postmodern riverfront development that includes restaurants, offices, apartments, and upscale shops; Georgetown Park is a multilevel shopping extravaganza; and Georgetown University is the oldest Jesuit school in the country. Dumbarton Oaks's 10 acres of formal gardens make it one of the loveliest spots in Washington.

Dupont Circle

Fashionable, vibrant Dupont Circle has a cosmopolitan air and many restaurants, offbeat shops, and specialty bookstores; it's also home to the most visible segment of Washington's gay community. The exclusive Kalorama neighborhood (Greek for "beautiful view") is a peaceful, tree-lined enclave filled with embassies and luxurious homes. For a glimpse of the beautiful view, look down over Rock Creek Park—1,800 acres of green—which has a planetarium, an 18-hole golf course, and equestrian and bicycle trails. The Phillips Collection is also here; its best-known paintings include Auguste Renoir's *Luncheon of the Boating Party,* Edgar Degas's *Dancers at the Bar,* and a Paul Cézanne self-portrait. At the National Geographic Society's Explorers Hall, you can learn about the world in an interactive way.

Foggy Bottom

Foggy Bottom—an appellation earned years ago when smoke from factories combined with swampy air to produce a permanent fog along the waterfront—has three main claims to fame: the State Department, the Kennedy Center, and George Washington University. Watergate, one of the world's most legendary apartment–office complexes, is notorious for the events that took place here on June 17, 1972. As Nixon aides sat in a motel across the street, five men were caught trying to bug the headquarters of the Democratic National Committee.

Cleveland Park and the National Zoo

Tree-shaded Cleveland Park, in northwest Washington, has attractive houses and a suburban character and is popular with professionals. Its Cineplex Odeon Uptown is a marvelous vintage-1936 art deco movie house. The National Zoological Park, part of the Smithsonian Institution, is one of the foremost zoos in the world. Star denizens include Komodo dragons and two new giant pandas.

Adams-Morgan

Adams-Morgan is one of Washington's most ethnically diverse and interesting neighborhoods, home to a veritable United Nations of cuisines, offbeat shops, and funky bars and clubs. The neighborhood's grand 19th-century apartment buildings and row houses as well as its bohemian atmosphere have attracted young urban professionals, the businesses that cater to them, and the attendant parking and crowd problems.

Arlington, Virginia

Two attractions here—both linked to the military and accessible by Metro—make Arlington a part of any complete visit to the nation's capital: John F. Kennedy, Jacqueline Bouvier Kennedy Onassis, and Robert Kennedy are buried in Arlington National Cemetery along with 200,000 veterans; and the U.S. Marine Corps War Memorial is a 78-ft-high statue based on the Pulitzer Prize–winning photograph of five marines and a navy corpsman raising a flag atop Mt. Suribachi on Iwo Jima. The Newseum is the world's first museum dedicated to the history of news gathering and dissemination.

Alexandria, Virginia

Alexandria's history is linked to the most significant events and personages of the Colonial, Revolutionary, and Civil War periods. This colorful past is still alive on the cobbled streets; on the revitalized waterfront, where clipper ships dock and artisans display their wares; and in restored 18th- and 19th-century homes, churches, and taverns. The history of African-Americans in Alexandria and Virginia from 1749, when the city was founded, to the present is recounted at the Alexandria Black History Resource Center, near Robert E. Lee's boyhood home.

GREAT ITINERARIES

You could easily spend two weeks exploring Washington, D.C., but if you're here for just a short period, you'll need to plan your time carefully. The following suggested itineraries (one set is geared specifically for those traveling with children) can help you structure your visit efficiently.

If You Have 1 Day

Head directly to the **Mall.** Start at either end—the Capitol or the Lincoln Memorial—and walk leisurely to the opposite end. You won't have time to see everything along the way, but you'll walk past or have in sight most of the attractions Washington is famous for: the **Lincoln Memorial,** the **Korean War Veterans Memorial,** the **Vietnam Veterans Memorial,** the **Tidal Basin** and **Jefferson Memorial,** the **Washington Monument** (and, to the north, the **White House**), most of the **Smithsonian museums,** the **National Gallery of Art,** and the **Capitol.**

If You Have 3 Days

Spend two of them on the **Mall.** Visit all the museums that interest you—a few don't-misses are the **National Museum of Natural History,** the **National Air and Space Museum,** and the **United States Holocaust Memorial Museum.** Take time out for a leisurely paddleboat ride in the **Tidal Basin.** Your third day can be spent exploring trendy **Georgetown.** There are sights to see, but people come here mainly to watch other people, shop, eat, and bar-hop.

If You Have 5 Days

Follow the three-day itinerary above and spend your fourth day at the **National Zoo.** Split your last day between **Adams-Morgan** and **Dupont**

Circle. Although not as upscale as Georgetown, these two neighborhoods have unusual shops, restaurants, and clubs. Ethnic food and crafts abound, especially in Adams-Morgan; both areas also have an assortment of commercial art galleries.

If You Have 1 Day with Children

Head right to the **Washington Monument,** where children can enjoy a breathtaking view—in both directions—of the mall. From here head to the **National Air and Space Museum**; on the way, you can stop to ride a painted pony at the **carousel** near the Smithsonian castle and/or take a few minutes to wander through the **Hirshhorn Museum and Sculpture Garden.** If you still have time, visit either the **National Museum of American History** or the **National Museum of Natural History**; both have hands-on rooms for little ones that are open most afternoons.

If You Have 3 Days with Children

Spend two days on the **Mall,** visiting museums and monuments that interest you. Even children who can't read the Gettysburg Address etched on the walls of the **Lincoln Memorial** can recognize the building on the back of a penny. At the **Vietnam Veterans Memorial,** children old enough to hold a pencil can make rubbings of the names (paper and pencils are available at the site). Consider investing in Tourmobile tickets for a respite from walking while still seeing the attractions. For breaks, ride the **carousel** on the Mall or a **paddleboat** in the **Tidal Basin.**

On the third day, older children may enjoy morning tours of the **Bureau of Engraving and Printing** and the **Capitol** before heading off to the **National Zoo.** If you have younger children, start and end the day at the zoo. On cold or hot days, take advantage of the numerous indoor animal houses. If little ones wear out, you can rent strollers.

If You Have 5 Days with Children

Follow the three-day itinerary above and start your fourth day at the **Capital Children's Museum,** where you can expect to spend at least three hours. If you and your children still have stamina, grab a bite to eat at **Union Station** on your way to the **National Postal Museum.** Older children may enjoy touring the **Federal Bureau of Investigation,** followed by a trip to the **Washington Navy Yard,** the **Newseum,** or the **MCI Sports Gallery.** With younger children, see creatures of the deep at the **National Aquarium,** followed by a trip to **Glen Echo** for a play or puppet show.

THE MALL

Revised by
Maureen
Graney

The Mall is the heart of almost every visitor's trip to Washington. With nearly a dozen museums ringing the expanse of green, it's the closest thing the capital has to a theme park (unless you count the federal government itself, which has uncharitably been called "Disneyland on the Potomac"). As at a theme park, you may have to stand in an occasional line, but unlike the amusements at Disneyland, almost everything you'll see here is free. You may, however, need free, timed-entry tickets to some of the more popular traveling exhibitions. These are usually available at the museum information desk or by phone, for a service charge, from Ticketmaster (☎ 202/432–7328).

Of course, the Mall is more than just a front yard for these museums. Bounded on the north and south by Constitution and Independence avenues and on the east and west by 3rd and 14th streets, it's a picnicking park and a jogging path, an outdoor stage for festivals and fireworks, and America's town green. Nine of the Smithsonian Institution's 14 museums in the capital lie within these boundaries.

THE CITY'S ARCHITECT

THE LIFE OF Pierre-Charles L'Enfant, architect of the city of Washington, has all the elements of a television miniseries: handsome, idealistic, 22-year-old Parisian volunteer in the American war for independence; rises to rank of major of engineers; becomes popular with fellow officers (and their wives); becomes toast-of-the-town architect in New York City; is selected by President George Washington to plan the new Federal City; gets fired amid controversy; dies bitter and broke; is vindicated posthumously.

L'Enfant was educated as an architect and engineer in France. At least two of his teachers had profound influence on his career and, ultimately, his plan for Washington. He learned painting from his father, who was a battle-scene and landscape painter, and he studied landscape architecture with Andre LeNotre, who designed the gardens at Versailles. After Congress voted in 1785 to create a permanent Federal City, L'Enfant enthusiastically wrote to George Washington in 1789 with an offer to create a capital "magnificent enough to grace a great nation." He got the job, and arrived in Washington in 1791 to survey the land with black mathematician Benjamin Banneker.

L'Enfant's 1791 plan borrowed much from Versailles, with ceremonial circles and squares, a grid pattern of streets, and broad, diagonal avenues. He described Jenkins Hill, the gentle rise on which he intended to erect the "Congress House," as "a pedestal waiting for a monument." He envisioned the area west of the Congress House as a "Grand Avenue, 400 ft in breadth, and about a mile in length, bordered with gardens, ending in a slope from the houses on each side." (This is the area we now know as the Mall.)

Pennsylvania Avenue was to be a broad, grand, uninterrupted straight line running from the Capitol to the site chosen for the Executive Mansion. (The con-

struction of the Treasury Building in 1836 ruined this straight sight line.) The area just north of the White House was to be part of "President's Park" (it was basically the president's front yard). But in yet another change to L'Enfant's plans, Thomas Jefferson, concerned that large, landscaped White House grounds weren't befitting a democratic country, ordered that the area be turned into a public park (now Lafayette Park).

Congress authorized a monument to George Washington in 1783. L'Enfant chose a site at the spot where a line drawn west from the Capitol crossed one drawn south from the White House. But marshy conditions at his original site required moving the position of the monument 100 yards southeast to firmer ground. A stone marker just north of the monument denotes L'Enfant's original site.

THOUGH SKILLFUL at city planning, the headstrong L'Enfant had trouble with the game of politics. Things went slightly awry early on when L'Enfant had difficulty with the engravers of the city plan, they got worse when he expressed his resentment at dealing with Secretary of State Thomas Jefferson rather than the President, and they hit rock bottom when he enraged the city commissioners by tearing down a manor house being constructed where he had planned a street. The house belonged to Daniel Carroll—one of the commissioners. Only 11 months after his hire, L'Enfant was let go by Jefferson. L'Enfant continued to work as an architect, but when he died in 1825, he was poor and bitter, feeling he hadn't been recognized for his genius. His contributions to the city were finally recognized when, in 1909, amid much ceremony, his body was moved from his original burial site in Maryland to Arlington Cemetery at the request of the Washington, D.C., board of commissioners.

In the middle of the 19th century, horticulturist Andrew Jackson Downing took a stab at converting the Mall into a large, English-style garden, with carriageways curving through groves of trees and bushes. This was far from the "vast esplanade" L'Enfant had in mind, and by the dawn of the 20th century the Mall had become an eyesore. It was dotted with sheds and bisected by railroad tracks. There was even a railroad station at its eastern end.

In 1900 Senator James McMillan, chairman of the Committee on the District of Columbia, asked a distinguished group of architects and artists to study ways of improving Washington's park system. The McMillan Commission, which included architects Daniel Burnham and Charles McKim, landscape architect Frederick Law Olmsted, and sculptor Augustus Saint-Gaudens, didn't confine its recommendations just to parks; its 1902 report would shape the way the capital looked for decades. The Mall received much of the group's attention and is its most stunning accomplishment. L'Enfant's plan was rediscovered; the sheds, railroad tracks, and carriageways were removed; and Washington finally had the monumental core it had been denied for so long.

Numbers in the text correspond to numbers in the margin and on The Mall map.

A Good Walk

Start your tour of the museums on the Mall in the **Smithsonian Institution Building** ① (also known as the Castle), where the Smithsonian Information Center can orient you and help you plan your time. Walk east on Jefferson Drive to the **Arts and Industries Building** ② and its changing exhibits—mostly cultural—from the Smithsonian and other institutions. The **Hirshhorn Museum and Sculpture Garden** ③, which exhibits modern and contemporary art and has outdoor sculpture gardens, is the next building to the east on Jefferson Drive.

Cross 7th Street to reach the **National Air and Space Museum** ④, one of the most visited museums in the world with more than 9 million visitors a year. Continue east on Jefferson Drive to 4th Street past the construction site bounded by 3rd and 4th streets and Independence Avenue and Jefferson Drive SW, where the Smithsonian's National Museum of the American Indian is scheduled to open in 2004. Turn left on 4th Street and head across the Mall (be sure to check out the view of the Capitol to your right and the Washington Monument to your left). Cross Madison Drive to get to the two buildings of the National Gallery of Art. The **National Gallery of Art, West Building** ⑤ exhibits works from the 13th to the 20th centuries, and the **National Gallery of Art, East Building** ⑥ generally displays 19th- and 20th-century works. If you're visiting in winter and would like an active museum break, cross 7th Street and don skates in the National Gallery Sculpture Garden Ice Rink. Walk west on Madison Drive to the **National Museum of Natural History** ⑦, which has some 124 million objects in its collection. The next building to the west is the **National Museum of American History** ⑧, which explores America's cultural, political, technical, and scientific past.

Go south on 14th Street, crossing the Mall and Independence Avenue, to the **United States Holocaust Memorial Museum** ⑨, a powerful reminder of the human capacity for cruelty. One block to the south is the **Bureau of Engraving and Printing** ⑩, the source of all U.S. paper currency, stamps, military certificates, and presidential invitations. Head back north up 14th Street, cross Independence Avenue, and turn right, passing below overpasses connecting the two buildings of the **Department of Agriculture** ⑪. Just across 12th Street is the **Freer Gallery of Art** ⑫ and its collection of Asian treasures. East of the Freer, off Independence Avenue, are the winding brick paths and wooden benches of the 4-acre Enid Haupt Memorial Garden. The garden sits mostly on two underground museums, the **Arthur M. Sackler Gallery** ⑬, sister museum to the Freer, and the **National Museum of African Art** ⑭, with objects representing hundreds of African cultures.

TIMING

Don't try to see all the Mall's attractions in a day. Few people have the stamina for more than a half day of museum or gallery going at a time; children definitely don't. To avoid mental and physical exhaustion, try to devote at least two days to the Mall. Do the north side one day and the south the next. Or split your sightseeing on the Mall into a walking day, when you take in the scenic views and enjoy the architecture of each museum (the Mall museums are free, so a quick peek inside doesn't cost anything), and a museum day, when you go back to spend time with the exhibits that catch your interest. Afterward, plan something relaxing that doesn't require more walking—picnicking or enjoying a snack in one of the many museum cafeterias may make more sense than, say, shopping.

Sights to See

⑬ **Arthur M. Sackler Gallery.** When Charles Freer endowed the gallery that bears his name, he insisted on a few conditions: objects in the collection could not be loaned out, nor could objects from outside the collections be put on display. Because of the latter restriction it was necessary to build a second, complementary museum to house the Asian art collection of Arthur M. Sackler, a wealthy medical researcher and publisher who began collecting Asian art as a student in the 1940s. Sackler allowed Smithsonian curators to select 1,000 items from his ample collection and pledged $4 million toward the construction of the museum. The collection includes works from China, Southeast Asia, Korea, Tibet, and Japan. Articles in the permanent collection include Chinese ritual bronzes, jade ornaments from the 3rd millennium BC, Persian manuscripts, and Indian paintings in gold, silver, lapis lazuli, and malachite. The lower level connects to the Freer Gallery of Art. ⊠ *1050 Independence Ave. SW,* ☎ *202/357–2700; 202/357–1729 TDD,* WEB *www.si.edu.asia.* ▣ *Free.* ☉ *Daily 10–5:30. Metro: Smithsonian.*

🖐 ❷ **Arts and Industries Building.** This was the second Smithsonian museum to be constructed. In 1876, Philadelphia hosted the United States International Exposition in honor of the nation's Centennial. After the festivities, scores of exhibitors donated their displays to the federal government. To house the objects that had suddenly come its way, the Smithsonian commissioned this redbrick-and-sandstone structure. Designed by Adolph Cluss, the building was originally called the United States National Museum, the name that's still engraved in stone above the doorway. It was finished in 1881, just in time to host President James Garfield's inaugural ball.

The Arts and Industries Building housed a variety of artifacts that were eventually moved to other museums as the Smithsonian grew. It was restored to its original appearance and reopened during Bicentennial celebrations in 1976. Today, the building is home to changing exhibits, a working fountain in the rotunda surrounded by a horticultural exhibit and geometric stencils in rich Victorian colors, a museum shop, and the Discovery Theater for children. The Smithsonian carousel is right outside. ⊠ *900 Jefferson Dr. SW,* ☎ *202/357–2700; 202/357–1500 Discovery Theater show times and ticket information; 202/357–1729 TDD,* WEB *www.si.edu.ai.* ▣ *Free.* ☉ *Daily 10–5:30. Metro: Smithsonian.*

The Mall

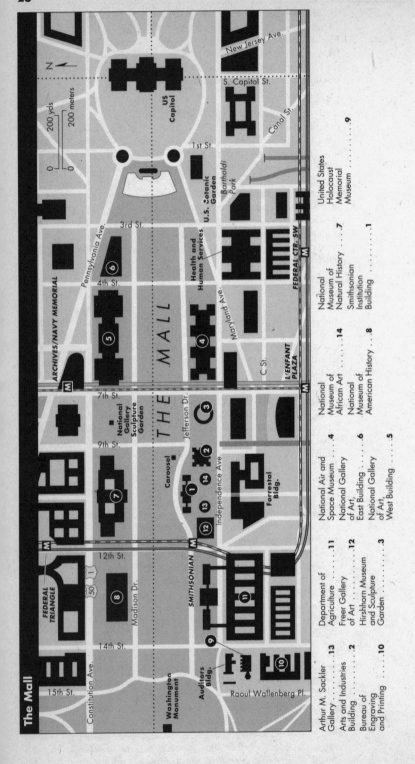

New Jersey Ave.

S. Capitol St.

US Capitol

1st St.

Canal St.

U.S. Botanic Garden

Bartholdi Park

3rd St.

Pennsylvania Ave.

ARCHIVES/NAVY MEMORIAL

4th St.

Health and Human Services

Maryland Ave.

THE MALL

C. St.

L'ENFANT PLAZA

FEDERAL CTR. SW

7th St.

National Gallery Sculpture Garden

THE

Jefferson Dr.

9th St.

Carousel

Independence Ave.

Forrestal Bldg.

12th St.

FEDERAL TRIANGLE

Madison Dr.

SMITHSONIAN

14th St.

Washington Monument

Auditors Bldg.

Raoul Wallenberg Pl.

15th St.

Constitution Ave.

200 yds
200 meters
0
0

N

🔁 ⑩ **Bureau of Engraving and Printing.** Despite the fact that there are no free samples, the guided tour of the bureau—which takes you past presses that turn out some $38 million a day—is one of the city's most popular. Paper money has been printed here since 1914, when the bureau relocated from the redbrick-towered Auditors Building at the corner of 14th Street and Independence Avenue. In addition to all the paper currency in the United States, stamps, military certificates, and presidential invitations are printed here, too. The tour lasts 35 minutes; the wait to get in, however, can be twice that long. ✉ *14th and C Sts. SW,* ☎ *202/874–3188,* WEB *www.bep.treas.gov.* 🎫 *Free.* ☉ *Sept.–May, weekdays 9–2; June–Aug., weekdays 9–2 and 5–6:30. Mar.–Sept., same-day timed-entry passes issued starting at 8 AM at Raoul Wallenberg Pl. SW entrance. Metro: Smithsonian.*

⑪ **Department of Agriculture.** Although there's little of interest inside, this complex is too gargantuan to ignore. The home of a major governmental agency responsible for setting and carrying out the nation's agricultural policies, it comprises two buildings. The older, white-marble building, on the north side of Independence Avenue, begun in 1903, was the first to be constructed by order of the McMillan Commission on the south side of the Mall. The cornices on the north side depict forests as well as grains, flowers, and fruits—some of the vegatation the department keeps an eye on. The newer building (built between 1930 and 1936) south of Independence Avenue covers two city blocks. ✉ *Independence Ave. between 12th and 14th Sts. SW,* WEB *www.usda.gov Metro: Smithsonian.*

⑫ **Freer Gallery of Art.** One of the world's finest collections of masterpieces from Asia, the Smithsonian's Freer Gallery of Art was made possible by an endowment from Detroit industrialist Charles L. Freer, who retired in 1900 and devoted the rest of his life to collecting art. Opened in 1923, four years after its benefactor's death, the collection, dating from Neolithic times to the 20th century, includes more than 27,000 works of art from the Far and Near East, including Asian porcelains, Japanese screens, Chinese paintings and bronzes, Korean stoneware, and Islamic objects.

Freer's friend James McNeill Whistler introduced him to Asian art, and the American painter is represented in the vast collection. On display is the Peacock Room, a blue-and-gold dining room decorated with painted leather, wood, and canvas and designed by Whistler for a British shipping magnate. Freer paid $30,000 for the entire room and moved it from London to the United States in 1904. The works of other American artists Freer felt were influenced by the Far East also are on display. A lower-level exhibition gallery connects the building to the Arthur M. Sackler Gallery. ✉ *12th St. and Jefferson Dr. SW,* ☎ *202/ 357–2700; 202/357–1729 TTD,* WEB *www.si.edu.asia.* 🎫 *Free.* ☉ *Daily 10–5:30. Metro: Smithsonian.*

③ **Hirshhorn Museum and Sculpture Garden.** An architecturally striking round building that opened in 1974, the Hirshhorn manages a collection that includes some 12,000 works of art donated and bequeathed by Joseph H. Hirshhorn, a Latvian-born immigrant who made his fortune in this country running uranium mines. American artists such as Edward Hopper, Willem de Kooning, Andy Warhol, and Richard Diebenkorn are represented, as are modern European and Latin masters, including Francis Bacon, Piet Mondrian, Jean Dubuffet, and Joan Miró.

The Hirshhorn's impressive sculpture collection is displayed throughout the museum, as well as on the lawns and granite surfaces of the fountain plaza and across Jefferson Drive in the sunken Sculpture Garden. Indoors and out, the display includes works by Henry Moore, Alexander Calder, and Alberto Giacometti. In the garden, Henri Matisse's *Backs I–IV* and Auguste Rodin's *Burghers of Calais* are highlights.

Dubbed by detractors "the Doughnut on the Mall," the cylindrical, reinforced-concrete building designed by Pritzker Prize–winning architect Gordon Bunshaft is a fitting home for contemporary art. The severe exterior lines of the museum were softened a bit in 1992 when its plaza was relandscaped by James Urban. Grass and trees provide a soft setting for such recent work as Juan Munoz's *Conversation Piece*, an intriguing ensemble of five beanbag-like figures in bronze. ⊠ *Independence Ave. and 7th St. SW,* ☎ *202/357–2700; 202/633–8043 TDD,* WEB *hirshhorn.si.edu.* ☎ *Free.* ☉ *Museum daily 10–5:30, sculpture garden daily 7:30–dusk. Metro: Smithsonian or L'Enfant Plaza (Maryland Ave. exit).*

★ ☺ ❹ **National Air and Space Museum.** Opened in 1976, this museum attracts more than 9 million people each year. Its 23 galleries tell the story of aviation from the earliest human attempts at flight. Suspended from the ceiling like plastic models in a child's room are dozens of aircraft, including the *Wright 1903 Flyer,* which Wilbur Wright piloted over the sands of Kitty Hawk, North Carolina; Charles Lindbergh's *Spirit of St. Louis*; the X-1 rocket plane in which Chuck Yeager broke the sound barrier; and an X-15, the first aircraft to exceed Mach 6.

Other highlights include a backup model of the Skylab orbital workshop that you can walk through; the *Voyager,* which Dick Rutan and Jeana Yeager flew nonstop around the world; and the Lockheed Vega piloted by Amelia Earhart in 1932 in the first solo transatlantic flight by a woman. You can also see a piece of the moon: a 4-billion-year-old slice of rock collected by *Apollo 17* astronauts.

Don't let long lines deter you from seeing a show in the museum's Samuel P. Langley Theater. IMAX films shown on the five-story-high screen—including *Cosmic Voyage, To Fly!,* and *SolarMax*—usually feature swooping aerial scenes designed to make you feel as if you've left the ground. Purchase tickets up to two weeks in advance or as soon as you arrive (prices vary); then tour the museum. Upstairs, the Albert Einstein Planetarium projects images of celestial bodies on a domed ceiling. A multi-year renovation of the main-floor galleries was completed in 2001, including a new permanent exhibition on the history of the scientific study of the universe, "Explore the Universe." ⊠ *Independence Ave. and 6th St. SW,* ☎ *202/357–2700; 202/357–1686 movie information; 202/357–1729 TDD,* WEB *www.nasm.si.edu.* ☎ *Free, IMAX $6.50, planetarium $4.* ☉ *Daily 10–5:30. Metro: Smithsonian.*

NEED A BREAK?   A cafeteria-style restaurant at the eastern end of the National Air and Space Museum, the **Flight Line** (☎ 202/371–8750), open daily from 10–5, is a welcome self-service cafeteria with hamburgers, hot dogs, pizza, soda, and ice cream. At peak times lines can be long.

★ ☺ ❻ **National Gallery of Art, East Building.** The atrium is dominated by Alexander Calder's mobile *Untitled,* and the galleries display modern and contemporary art, though you'll also find major temporary exhibitions that span years and artistic styles. Permanent works include Pablo Picasso's *The Lovers* and *Family of Saltimbanques,* four of Matisse's cutouts, Miró's *The Farm,* and Jackson Pollock's *Lavender Mist.*

The East Building opened in 1978 in response to the changing needs of the National Gallery. The awkward trapezoidal shape of the building site, which had been taken up by tennis courts and rosebushes planted during Lady Bird Johnson's spruce-up campaign, prompted architect I. M. Pei's dramatic approach: two interlocking spaces shaped like triangles provide room for galleries, auditoriums, and administrative offices. Although the building's triangles contrast sharply with the symmetrical classical facade and gentle dome of the West Building, both structures are constructed of pink marble from the same Tennessee quarries. Despite its severe angularity, Pei's building is inviting. The axe-blade-like southwest corner has been darkened and polished smooth by thousands of hands irresistibly drawn to it.

To reach the East Building from the West Building, take the underground concourse, lined with gift shops, a café, and a cafeteria. But to appreciate Pei's impressive, angular East Building, enter it from outside rather than from underground. Exit the West Building through its eastern doors, and cross 4th Street. (As you cross, look to the north: seeming to float above the Doric columns and pediment of the D.C. Superior Court are the green roof and redbrick pediment of the National Building Museum, four blocks away.) ⊠ *Constitution Ave. between 3rd and 4th Sts. NW,* ☎ *202/737–4215; 202/842–6176 TDD,* WEB *www.nga.gov.* ⊠ *Free.* ☉ *Mon.–Sat. 10–5, Sun. 11–6. Metro: Archives/Navy Memorial.*

★ ❺ **National Gallery of Art, West Building.** The two buildings of the National Gallery hold one of the world's foremost collections of paintings, sculptures, and graphics. If you want to view the museum's holdings in (more or less) chronological order, it's best to start your exploration in the West Building. The rotunda, with its 24 marble columns surrounding a fountain topped with a statue of Mercury, sets the stage for the masterpieces on display in more than 100 galleries. A tape-recorded tour of the building's better-known holdings is available for a $5 rental fee on the main floor adjacent to the rotunda. If you'd rather explore on your own, get a map at one of the two art information desks; one is just inside the Mall entrance (off Madison Drive), and the other is near the Constitution Avenue entrance on the ground floor. The Micro Gallery, near the rotunda, offers computerized information on more than 1,700 works of art from the permanent collection. Touch-screen monitors provide access to color images, text, animation, and sounds to help you better understand—and appreciate—the works on display.

The National Gallery's permanent collection includes works from the 13th to 20th centuries. A comprehensive survey of Italian paintings and sculpture includes *The Adoration of the Magi,* by Fra Angelico and Filippo Lippi, and *Ginevra de'Benci,* the only painting by Leonardo da Vinci in the western hemisphere. Flemish and Dutch works, displayed in paneled rooms, include *Daniel in the Lions' Den,* by Peter Paul Rubens, and a self-portrait by Rembrandt. The Chester Dale Collection comprises works by Impressionist painters such as Edgar Degas, Claude Monet, Auguste Renoir, and Mary Cassatt. Salvador Dalí's *Last Supper* is also in this building.

The **National Gallery of Art Sculpture Garden** is between 7th and 9th streets along the Mall. Granite walkways take you through the garden, which is planted with shade trees, flowering trees, and perennials. Sculptures on display from the museum's permanent collection include Roy Lichtenstein's playful *House I,* Alexander Archipenko's *Woman Combing Her Hair;* Miró's *Personnage Gothique, Oiseau-Eclair;* and Isamu Noguchi's *Great Rock of Inner Seeking.* The huge central fountain is used as a skating rink during the winter.

Opened in 1941, the domed West Building was a gift to the nation from financier Andrew Mellon. (The dome was one of architect John Russell Pope's favorite devices. He designed the domed Jefferson Memorial and the National Archives, with its half-domed rotunda.) A wealthy financier and industrialist, Mellon served as secretary of the treasury under three presidents and as ambassador to the United Kingdom. He first came to D.C. in 1921 and lived for many years in a luxurious apartment near Dupont Circle, in a building that today houses the National Trust for Historic Preservation. Mellon had long collected great works of art, acquiring some on his frequent trips to Europe. In 1930 and 1931, when the Soviet government was short on cash and selling off many of its art treasures, Mellon bought more than $6 million worth of old masters, including Raphael's *The Alba Madonna* and Sandro Botticelli's *Adoration of the Magi*. Mellon promised his collection to America in 1936, the year before his death. He also donated the funds for the construction of the huge gallery and resisted suggestions it be named after him. ⊠ *Constitution Ave. between 4th and 7th Sts. NW,* ☎ *202/737–4215; 202/842–6176 TDD,* WEB *www.nga.gov.* ▦ *Free.* ☼ *Mon.–Sat. 10–5, Sun. 11–6. Metro: Archives/Navy Memorial.*

NEED A BREAK?

For a quick, casual meal, try the **Cascade Café**, in the concourse between the East and West buildings of the National Gallery of Art. Open 10–3 on Monday to Saturday and 11–4 on Sunday, it has a selection of sandwiches and salads, as well as an espresso bar and homemade *sorbetto* (sorbet). The **Garden Café** (☎ 202/215–5966), in a picturesque spot on the ground floor of the National Gallery's West Building, gracefully combines food and art by presenting a menu of dishes related to current exhibitions, as well as traditional American fare. It's open 11–3 Monday to Saturday and noon–6:30 on Sunday. The **Pavilion Café** offers indoor and outdoor seating and views of the National Gallery of Art Sculpture Garden to those enjoying its specialty pizzas and sandwiches. It's open 10–5 Monday to Saturday and 11–6 on Sunday.

🖐 ⑭ **National Museum of African Art.** Opened in 1987, this unique underground building houses the museum's galleries, library, photographic archives, and educational facilities. The museum's rotating exhibits present a wide variety of African visual arts, including sculpture, textiles, photography, archaeology, and modern art. Long-term installations explore the sculpture of sub-Saharan Africa, the art of Benin, pottery of Central Africa, the archaeology of the ancient Nubian city of Kerma, and the artistry of utilitarian objects. The museum's educational programs include films showing contemporary perspectives on African life, storytelling programs, festivals, and hands-on workshops for families, all of which bring Africa's oral traditions, literature, and art to life. Workshops and demonstrations by African and African-American artists offer a chance to meet and talk to practicing artists. If you're traveling with children, look for the museum's free printed family guide to the permanent "Images of Power and Identity" exhibition. ⊠ *950 Independence Ave. SW,* ☎ *202/357–2700; 202/357–1729 TDD,* WEB *www.nmafa.si.edu.* ▦ *Free.* ☼ *Daily 10–5:30. Metro: Smithsonian.*

🖐 ⑧ **National Museum of American History.** Opened in 1964 as the National Museum of History and Technology and renamed in 1980, the museum explores America's cultural, political, technical, and scientific past. The incredible diversity of artifacts helps the Smithsonian live up to its nickname, "the Nation's attic." This is the museum that displays Muhammad Ali's boxing gloves, the Fonz's leather jacket, Judy Garland's ruby slippers from *The Wizard of Oz,* and the Bunkers' living-room furniture from *All in the Family.*

You can wander for hours on the museum's three floors. Exhibits on the first floor emphasize the history of science and technology and include farm machines, automobiles, and a 280-ton steam locomotive. The permanent "Science in American Life" exhibit shows how science has shaped American life through such breakthroughs as the mass production of penicillin, the development of plastics, and the birth of the environmental movement. Another permanent exhibit looks at 19th-century life in three communities: industrial-era Bridgeport, Connecticut; the Jewish immigrant community in Cincinnati, Ohio; and African-Americans living in Charleston, South Carolina. Also here are Lewis and Clark's compass and Abraham Lincoln's life mask. The second floor is devoted to U.S. social and political history and has an exhibit on everyday American life just after the Revolution. A permanent exhibit, "First Ladies: Political Role and Public Image," displays gowns worn by presidential wives, but it goes beyond fashion to explore the women behind the satin, lace, and brocade. The third floor has installations on money, musical instruments, and photography.

Be sure to check out Horatio Greenough's statue of the first president (near the west-wing escalators on the second floor). Commissioned by Congress in 1832, it was intended to grace the Capitol Rotunda. It was there for only a short while, however, since the toga-clad likeness proved shocking to legislators who grumbled that it looked as if the father of our country had just emerged from a bath. If you want a more interactive visit, check out the Hands on History Room, where you can try some 30 activities, such as pedaling a high-wheeler bike or plucking an old stringed instrument. In the Hands on Science Room you can do one of 25 experiments, including testing a water sample and exploring DNA fingerprinting. ⊠ *Constitution Ave. and 14th St. NW,* ☎ *202/357–2700; 202/357–1729 TDD,* WEB *www.si.edu/nmah.* ⊠ *Free.* ☉ *Daily 10–5:30; call for hrs of Hands on History and Hands on Science rooms. Metro: Smithsonian or Federal Triangle.*

★ ☾ ❼ **National Museum of Natural History.** This is one of the great natural history museums in the world, filled with bones, fossils, stuffed animals, and other natural delights—124 million specimens in all. It was constructed in 1910, and two wings were added in the 1960s.

The first-floor rotunda is dominated by a stuffed, 8-ton, 13-ft-tall African bull elephant, one of the largest ever found. (The tusks are fiberglass; the original ivory ones were far too heavy for the stuffed elephant to support.) Off to the right is the popular **Dinosaur Hall.** Fossilized skeletons here range from a 90-ft-long diplodocus to a tiny thescelosaurus neglectus (a small dinosaur so named because its disconnected bones sat for years in a college drawer before being reassembled).

Beyond the Dinosaur Hall is the newest permanent exhibition, **African Voices.** It shows the influence of Africa's peoples and culture with refreshingly up-to-date displays, including a Somali camel herder's portable house, recreations of markets in Ghana (featuring vendors of housewares, cola nuts, and yams), a Tunisian wedding tunic, and artifacts showing the Yoruba influence on Afro-Brazilian culture.

The west wing, which houses displays of birds, mammals, and sea life, is closed for renovation through 2003. If you've always wished you could get your hands on the objects behind the museum's glass windows, stop by the **Discovery Room,** in the northwest corner of the first floor (but scheduled to move to larger quarters during 2002). Here elephant tusks, petrified wood, seashells, rocks, feathers, and other items can be handled.

The highlight of the second floor is the **Janet Annenberg Hooker Hall of Geology, Gems and Minerals.** Objects on display include a pair of Marie Antoinette's earrings, the Rosser Reeves ruby, spectacular crystals and minerals, and, of course, the Hope Diamond, a blue gem found in India and reputed to carry a curse (though Smithsonian guides are quick to pooh-pooh this notion).

Also on the second floor is the **O. Orkin Insect Zoo** (named for the pest-control magnate who donated the money to modernize the exhibits), featuring a walk-through a rain forest. You can view at least 60 species of live insects, and there are tarantula feedings Tuesday through Friday at 10:30, 11:30, and 1:30.

The second IMAX theater on the mall—the other is in the National Air and Space museum—is the Samuel C. Johnson IMAX theater, which shows two- and three-dimensional natural-history films, such as *Galapagos.* The theater is also open Friday evenings from 6:30 to 9 for the "IMAX Jazz Café," an evening of live entertainment, food, and special IMAX films not shown during the day. Tickets for the theater can be purchased at the museum box office. ⊠ *Constitution Ave. and 10th St. NW,* ☎ *202/357–2700; 202/357–1729 TDD,* WEB *www. mnh.si.edu.* ⧉ *Free, IMAX $6.50; free passes required for entry into the Discovery Room.* ⊙ *Museum daily 10–5:30, Discovery Room Tues.–Fri. noon–2:30, weekends 10:30–3:30; Discovery Room passes distributed starting at 11:45 weekdays, 10:15 weekends. Metro: Smithsonian or Federal Triangle.*

❶ **Smithsonian Institution Building.** The first Smithsonian museum constructed, this red sandstone, Norman-style building is better known as the Castle. It was designed by James Renwick, the architect of St. Patrick's Cathedral in New York City. Although British scientist and founder James Smithson had never visited America, his will stipulated that should his nephew, Henry James Hungerford, die without an heir, Smithson's entire fortune would go to the United States, "to found at Washington, under the name of the Smithsonian Institution, an establishment for the increase and diffusion of knowledge." The museums on the Mall are the Smithsonian's most visible example of this ideal, but the organization also sponsors traveling exhibitions and maintains research posts in such places as the Chesapeake Bay and the tropics of Panama.

Smithson died in 1829, Hungerford in 1835, and in 1838 the United States received $515,169 worth of gold sovereigns. After eight years of congressional debate over the propriety of accepting funds from a citizen of another country, the Smithsonian Institution was finally established on August 10, 1846. The Castle building was completed in 1855 and originally housed all of the Smithsonian's operations, including the science and art collections, research laboratories, and living quarters for the institution's secretary and his family. The statue in front of the Castle's entrance is not of Smithson but of Joseph Henry, the scientist who served as the institution's first secretary. Smithson's body was brought to America in 1904 and is entombed in a small room to the left of the Castle's Mall entrance.

Today the Castle houses Smithsonian administrative offices and, to help you get your bearings or decide which attractions you want to visit, the **Smithsonian Information Center.** A 24-minute video provides an overview of the Smithsonian museums and the National Zoo and monitors display information on the day's events. Interactive touch-screen displays provide more detailed information on the museums as well as other attractions in the capital. The center opens at 9 AM, an hour before the other museums, so you can plan your day without wasting valuable sightseeing time. ✉ *1000 Jefferson Dr. SW,* ☎ *202/357–2700; 202/357–1729 TDD,* WEB *www.si.edu.* 🎟 *Free.* ☉ *Daily 9–5:30. Metro: Smithsonian.*

★ ❾ **United States Holocaust Memorial Museum.** Museums usually celebrate the best that humanity can achieve, but this James Ingo Freed–designed museum instead illustrates the worst. A permanent exhibition tells the stories of the millions of Jews, Gypsies, Jehovah's Witnesses, homosexuals, political prisoners, and others killed by the Nazis between 1933 and 1945. Striving to give a you-are-there experience, the graphic presentation is as extraordinary as the subject matter: upon arrival, you are issued an "identity card" containing biographical information on a real person from the Holocaust. As you move through the museum, you read sequential updates on your card. The museum recounts the Holocaust with documentary films, video- and audiotaped oral histories, and a collection that includes such items as a freight car like those used to transport Jews from Warsaw to the Treblinka death camp, and the Star of David patches that Jewish prisoners were made to wear. Like the history it covers, the museum can be profoundly disturbing; it's not recommended for visitors under 11, although "Daniel's Story," in a ground-floor exhibit not requiring tickets, is designed for children ages 8 and up. Plan to spend two to three hours here. After this powerful experience, the adjacent Hall of Remembrance provides a space for quiet reflection. In addition to the permanent exhibition, the museum also has a multimedia learning center, a resource center for students and teachers, a survivors registry, and occasional special exhibitions. Same-day timed-entry passes (distributed on a first-come, first-serve basis at the 14th St. entrance starting at 10 AM or available through Protix) are necessary for the permanent exhibition. ✉ *100 Raoul Wallenberg Pl. SW (enter from Raoul Wallenberg Pl. or 14th St. SW),* ☎ *202/488–0400; 800/400–9373 tickets.com,* WEB *www.ushmm.org.* 🎟 *Free.* ☉ *Daily 10–5:30. Metro: Smithsonian.*

THE MONUMENTS

Revised by
Maureen
Graney

Washington is a city of monuments. In the middle of traffic circles, on tiny slivers of park, and at street corners and intersections, statues, plaques, and simple blocks of marble honor the generals, politicians, poets, and statesmen who helped shape the nation. The monuments dedicated to the most famous Americans are west of the Mall on ground reclaimed from the marshy flats of the Potomac. This is also the location of Washington's greatest single display of cherry trees, gifts from Japan.

Numbers in the text correspond to numbers in the margin and on The Monuments map.

A Good Walk

Start with the tallest of them all, the 555-ft **Washington Monument** ①, at the western end of the Mall. Then walk diagonally southwest past Independence Avenue to the **Tidal Basin** ②. The path that skirts the basin leads to the Outlet Bridge and the **Jefferson Memorial** ③, which was inspired by the Pantheon in Rome. Continue along the sidewalk that hugs the Tidal Basin. Cross Inlet Bridge, bear right, and enter the **Franklin Delano Roosevelt Memorial** ④; you'll be going through the park in reverse, but this won't spoil your enjoyment of the memorial's drama. Exit the memorial through its entrance and bear right on West Basin Drive. At the next traffic light, cross Independence Avenue and walk left toward the **Korean War Veterans Memorial** ⑤, in a grove of trees called Ash Woods.

Your next stop is the **Lincoln Memorial** ⑥, the most inspiring monument in the city. After visiting it, walk down its steps and to the left to the **Vietnam Veterans Memorial** ⑦, one of the most popular sites in Washington, and to the **Constitution Gardens** ⑧ (taking the path that passes the **Vietnam Women's Memorial** on the way). Walk north to Constitution Avenue and head east to the stone **Lockkeeper's House** ⑨ at the corner of Constitution Avenue and 17th Street, the last remaining monument to Washington's unsuccessful experiment with a canal.

TIMING

Allow four or five hours to tour the monuments. This includes time to relax on a park bench and to grab a snack from either a vendor or one of the snack bars east of the Washington Monument and near the Lincoln Memorial. If you're visiting during the first two weeks in April, take some extra time around the Washington Monument and the Tidal Basin to marvel at the cherry blossoms. From mid-April through November, you might want to set aside an hour for a relaxing paddleboat ride in the Tidal Basin. In summer, if it's an extremely hot day, you may want to hop a Tourmobile bus and travel between the monuments in air-conditioned comfort.

Sights to See

🕭 **The Awakening.** J. Seward Johnson Jr.'s colossal aluminum sculpture of a bearded giant with head and limbs breaking through the ground near Hains Point in East Potomac Park is beloved by children and adults. ⊠ *Hains Pt., East Potomac Park.*

❽ Constitution Gardens. Many ideas were proposed to develop a 50-acre site that was once home to "temporary" buildings erected by the navy before World War I and not removed until after World War II. President Nixon is said to have favored something resembling Copenhagen's Tivoli Gardens. The final design was a little plainer, with paths winding through groves of trees and, on the lake, a tiny island paying tribute to the signers of the Declaration of Independence, their signatures carved into a low stone wall. In 1986, President Reagan proclaimed the gardens a living legacy to the Constitution; in that spirit, a naturalization ceremony for new citizens now takes place here each year. ⊠ *Constitution Ave. between 17th and 23rd Sts. NW,* WEB *www.nps. gov/coga. Metro: Foggy Bottom.*

NEED A BREAK? At the circular **snack bar** just west of the Constitution Gardens lake you can get hot dogs, potato chips, candy bars, soft drinks, and beer at prices lower than those charged by most street vendors.

🕭 **East Potomac Park.** This 328-acre finger of land extends from the Tidal Basin between the Washington Channel to the east and the Potomac River to the west. Facilities include playgrounds, picnic tables, tennis courts, swimming pools, a driving range, two 9-hole golf courses, and an 18-hole golf course. Double-blossoming cherry trees line Ohio Drive and bloom about two weeks after the single-blossoming variety that attracts throngs to the Tidal Basin each spring. *The Awakening* sits on Hains Point, at the tip of the park. ⊠ *Maine Ave. SW heading west, or Ohio Dr. heading south (follow signs carefully),* ☎ *202/619– 7222. Ohio Dr. closed to traffic on summer weekends and holidays 3 PM–6 AM.*

★ 🕭 **❹ Franklin Delano Roosevelt Memorial.** This monument, designed by Lawrence Halprin, was unveiled in May 1997. The 7½-acre memorial to the 32nd president features waterfalls and reflection pools, four outdoor gallery rooms—each symbolizing one of his four terms as president—and 10 bronze sculptures. The granite megaliths that connect the galleries are engraved with some of Roosevelt's most famous quotes, including, "The only thing we have to fear is fear itself." Although today the memorial is one of the most popular in the District, a delight to toddlers as well as to those who remember FDR firsthand, the FDR Memorial has had its share of critics. Roosevelt is not portrayed with his omnipresent cigarette nor is he pictured in a wheelchair, which he used for the last 24 years of his life, after he contracted polio. However, a wheelchair that FDR used is now exhibited in the visitor center and it's the first D.C. memorial purposely designed to be wheelchair accessible. It is also the first to honor a first lady; a bronze statue of Eleanor Roosevelt stands in front of the United Nations symbol. ⊠ *West side of Tidal Basin,* ☎ *202/619–7222,* WEB *www.nps.gov/fdrm.* 🎟 *Free.* ☉ *24 hrs; staffed daily 8 AM–midnight. Metro: Smithsonian.*

❸ Jefferson Memorial. The monument honoring the third president of the United States incorporates his own architectural taste in its design. Jefferson had always admired the Pantheon in Rome—the rotundas he designed for the University of Virginia were inspired by its dome—

MEN ON HORSEBACK

HOME TO MORE equestrian statues than any other city in the nation, Washington can truly be called a city of men on horseback. You can find them everywhere, green-streaked men atop their steeds watching the city from traffic circles, squares, and parks. The statues proliferated in the 19th century; Civil War generals who went into politics seemed virtually assured of this legacy—regardless of their success in either endeavor. Some of the statues reveal more than stories of men in battle.

Author Henry James wrote of America's first equestrian statue, "the most prodigious of all Presidential effigies, Andrew Jackson, as archaic as a Ninevite king, prancing and rocking through the ages." Standing in Lafayette Square across from the White House, the statue of Jackson is by sculptor Clark Mills, who had never seen an equestrian statue, much less created one. In order to get the proportions of the rearing horse correct, Mills had a horse trained to remain in an upright position so he could study the anatomy of its muscles. Though the statue is much acclaimed, some critics have argued that it's too small for the park, and should be replaced with Mills' statue of George Washington that currently stands in Foggy Bottom's Washington Circle.

Directly up 16th Street from Lafayette Square at Massachusetts and Rhode Island avenues is a statue of Lt. Gen. Winfield Scott, in the circle bearing his name. "Old Fuss and Feathers" was to be shown atop his favorite mount, a lightweight mare. That is, until right before the statue was cast, when some of Scott's descendents decided that a stallion would be a more appropriate horse to ride into battle (regardless of historical accuracy). Sculptor H. K. Brown was forced to give the horse a last-minute "sex change."

Farther up Massachusetts Avenue, at 23rd Street, is a statue of Civil War Gen. Philip Henry Sheridan, also in a circle bearing his name. The piece is by Gutzon Borglum, who completed more than 170 public statues, including the head of Abraham Lincoln in the Capitol Rotunda, and whose final work was the presidential faces on Mount Rushmore. The statue of the leader riding Rienzi (who was later renamed "Winchester" for Sheridan's victory there) stands in the type of circle Pierre-Charles L'Enfant envisioned in his plan for Washington—a small, formal park where avenues come together surrounded by isolated houses and buildings.

The statue of Gen. William Tecumseh Sherman at 15th Street and Treasury Place is often overlooked—in the summer, the general's head is obscured by trees, and all year long he presents his back and his horse's hindquarters to most people walking by. He's positioned where he is thought to have stood while reviewing the Union troops on their victorious return from Georgia. The bar at the Hotel Washington, which affords some of the best views of the city, is the best place for a good look at Sherman.

A long-held theory says that the number of raised legs on the mount of an equestrian statue reveals how the rider died: one leg raised means the rider died of wounds sustained in battle, two legs raised means the rider died in battle, and four feet on the ground means the rider died of natural causes. Actually, though, it isn't true. Of the more than 30 equestrian statues in Washington, only about a third (including Scott, Sheridan, and Sherman, but not Jackson) are true to the "code."

— Lisa Greaves

so the memorial's architect, John Russell Pope, drew from the same source. In the 1930s Congress decided that Jefferson deserved a monument positioned as prominently as those in honor of Washington and Lincoln, so workmen scooped and moved tons of river bottom to create dry land on this spot directly south of the White House. Dedicated in 1943, it houses a statue of Jefferson, and its walls are lined with inscriptions based on the Declaration of Independence and his other writings. One of the best views of the White House can be seen from its top steps. ⊠ *Tidal Basin, south bank,* ☎ *202/426–6821,* WEB *www.nps. gov/thje.* ⊡ *Free.* ☉ *Daily 8* AM*–midnight. Metro: Smithsonian.*

❺ **Korean War Veterans Memorial.** Dedicated in 1995, this memorial to the 1.5 million United States men and women who served in the Korean War highlights the high cost of freedom. The 19 statues in the triangular Field of Service depict multi-ethnic, poncho-clad soldiers on patrol in rugged Korean terrain heading toward an American flag. To the south of the soldiers stands a 164-ft-long granite wall etched with the faces of 2,400 unnamed service men and women with a silver inlay reading "Freedom is Not Free." The adjacent Pool of Remembrance honoring all who were killed, captured, wounded, or missing in action provides a spot for quiet contemplation. ⊠ *West end of Mall at Daniel French Dr. and Independence Ave.,* ☎ *202/619–7222,* WEB *www.nps.gov/kwvm.* ⊡ *Free.* ☉ *Daily 8* AM*–midnight. Metro: Foggy Bottom.*

★ ❻ **Lincoln Memorial.** Many people consider the Lincoln Memorial to be the most inspiring monument in the city. This was not always the case. Although today it would be hard to imagine Washington without the Lincoln and Jefferson memorials, both were criticized when first built. The Jefferson Memorial was dubbed "Jefferson's muffin"; critics lambasted the design as outdated and too similar to that of the Lincoln Memorial. Some also complained that the Jefferson Memorial blocked the view of the Potomac from the White House. Detractors of the Lincoln Memorial thought it inappropriate that the humble Lincoln be honored with what amounts to a modified but nonetheless rather grandiose Greek temple. The white Colorado-marble memorial was designed by Henry Bacon and completed in 1922. The 36 Doric columns represent the 36 states in the Union at the time of Lincoln's death; the names of the states appear on the frieze above the columns. Above the frieze are the names of the 48 states in the Union when the memorial was dedicated. (Alaska and Hawaii are represented with an inscription on the terrace leading up to the memorial.)

Daniel Chester French's somber statue of the seated president, in the center of the memorial, gazes out over the Reflecting Pool. Although the 19-ft-high sculpture looks as if it were cut from one huge block of stone, it actually comprises 28 interlocking pieces of Georgia marble. (The memorial's original design called for a 10-ft-high sculpture, but experiments with models revealed that a statue that size would be lost in the cavernous space.) Inscribed on the south wall is the Gettysburg Address, and on the north wall is Lincoln's second inaugural address. Above each inscription is a mural painted by Jules Guerin: on the south wall is an angel of truth freeing a slave; the unity of North and South are depicted opposite. The memorial served as a fitting backdrop for Martin Luther King's "I Have a Dream" speech in 1963.

Many visitors look only at the front and inside of the Lincoln Memorial, but there is much more to explore. On the lower level is the Lincoln Museum, a small exhibit that was financed with pennies collected by schoolchildren. There's also a set of windows that overlooks the huge structure's foundation. Stalactites (hanging from above) and stalagmites (rising from below) have formed underneath the marble tribute to Lincoln. Although visiting the area around the Lincoln Memorial during the day allows you to take in an impressive view of the Mall to the east, the best time to see the memorial itself is at night. Spotlights illuminate the outside, and inside light and shadows play across Lincoln's gentle face. ⊠ *West end of Mall,* ☎ *202/426–6895,* WEB *www.nps.gov/linc.* 🎫 *Free.* ◷ *24 hrs; staffed daily 8 AM–midnight. Metro: Foggy Bottom.*

❾ Lockkeeper's House. The stone Lockkeeper's House is the only remaining monument to Washington's unsuccessful experiment with a canal. The stone building at this corner was the home of the canal's lockkeeper until the 1870s, when the waterway was covered over with B Street, which was renamed Constitution Avenue in 1932. It's not open to visitors. ⊠ *Constitution Ave. and 17th St. Metro: Federal Triangle, 5 blocks east on 12th St.*

❷ Tidal Basin. This placid pond was part of the Potomac until 1882, when portions of the river were filled in to improve navigation and create additional parkland, including the land upon which the Jefferson Memorial was later built. At the **boathouse** (☎ 202/479–2426), on the northeast bank of the Tidal Basin, you can rent paddleboats during the warmer months. Rental cost is $8 per hour for a two-person boat, $16 per hour for a four-person boat. The boathouse is open from mid-March through October, weekdays from 10–6 and weekends from 10–7.

Two grotesque sculpted heads on the sides of the Inlet Bridge can be seen as you walk along the sidewalk that hugs the basin. The inside walls of the bridge also sport two other interesting sculptures: bronze, human-headed fish that spout water from their mouths. The bridge was refurbished in the 1980s at the same time the chief of the park—a Mr. Jack Fish—was retiring. Sculptor Constantine Sephralis played a little joke: these fish heads are actually Fish's head.

Once you cross the bridge, continue along the Tidal Basin to the right. This route is especially scenic when the cherry trees are in bloom. The first batch of these trees arrived from Japan in 1909. The trees were infected with insects and fungus, however, and the Department of Agriculture ordered them destroyed. A diplomatic crisis was averted when the United States politely asked the Japanese for another batch, and in 1912 Mrs. William Howard Taft planted the first tree. The second was planted by the wife of the Japanese ambassador, Viscountess Chinda. About 200 of the original trees still grow near the Tidal Basin. (These cherry trees are the single-flowering Akebeno and Yoshino variety. Double-blossom Fugenzo and Kwanzan trees grow in East Potomac Park and flower about two weeks after their more-famous cousins.)

The trees are now the centerpiece of Washington's Cherry Blossom Festival, held each spring since 1935. The festivities are kicked off by the lighting of a ceremonial Japanese lantern that rests on the north shore of the Tidal Basin, not far from where the first tree was planted. The once-simple celebration has grown over the years to include concerts, fashion shows, and a parade. Park-service experts try their best to predict exactly when the buds will pop. The trees are usually in bloom for about 10–12 days in late March or early April. When winter refuses to release its grip, the parade and festival are held anyway, without the presence of blossoms, no matter how inclement the weather. And when the weather complies and the blossoms are at their peak at the time of the festivities, Washington rejoices. ⊠ *Bordered by Independence Ave. and Maine Ave. Metro: Smithsonian.*

If you've worked up an appetite at the Tidal Basin, head four blocks down Maine Avenue to the **Maine Avenue Seafood Market,** where vendors sell fresh fish and shellfish. Seven restaurants stretch along the avenue, including local seafood powerhouse Phillips Flagship. All have terraces overlooking the Washington Channel and the motorboats, houseboats, and sailboats moored here.

★ ❼ **Vietnam Veterans Memorial.** Renowned for its power to evoke poignant reflection, the Vietnam Veterans Memorial was conceived by Jan Scruggs, a former infantry corporal who had served in Vietnam. The stark design by Maya Ying Lin, a 21-year-old Yale architecture student, was selected in a 1981 competition. Upon its completion in 1982, the memorial was decried by some veterans as a "black gash of shame." With the addition of Frederick Hart's realistic statue of three soldiers and a flagpole south of the wall, most critics were won over.

The wall is one of the most-visited sites in Washington, its black granite panels reflecting the sky, the trees, and the faces of those looking for the names of friends or relatives who died in the war. The names of more than 58,000 Americans are etched on the face of the memorial in the order of their deaths. Directories at the entrance and exit to the wall list the names in alphabetical order. (It was discovered that because of a clerical error the names of some two dozen living vets are carved into the stone as well.) For help in finding a name, ask a ranger at the blue-and-white hut near the entrance. Thousands of offerings are left at the wall each year: letters, flowers, medals, uniforms, snapshots. The National Park Service collects these and stores them in a warehouse in Lanham, Maryland, where they are fast becoming another memorial. Many visitors also bring paper and crayons or charcoal to make rubbings of the names of their loved ones. Tents are often set up near the wall by veterans groups; some provide information on soldiers who remain missing in action, and others are on call to help fellow vets and relatives deal with the sometimes overwhelming emotions that grip them when visiting the wall for the first time. ⊠ *Constitution Gardens, 23rd St. and Constitution Ave. NW,* ☎ *202/634–1568,* WEB *www.nps.gov/vive.* 🔲 *Free.* ⏱ *24 hrs; staffed daily 8 AM–midnight. Metro: Foggy Bottom.*

Vietnam Women's Memorial. After years of debate over its design and necessity, the Vietnam Women's Memorial, honoring the women who served in that conflict, was finally dedicated on Veterans' Day 1993. Sculptor Glenna Goodacre's stirring bronze group depicts two uniformed women caring for a wounded male soldier while a third woman kneels nearby. The eight trees around the plaza commemorate each of the women who died in Vietnam. ⊠ *Constitution Gardens, southeast of Vietnam Veterans Memorial,* WEB *www.nps.gov/vive/commem.htm. Metro: Foggy Bottom.*

★ ☝ ❶ **Washington Monument.** At the western end of the Mall, the 555-ft, 5-inch Washington Monument punctuates the capital like a huge exclamation point. Visible from nearly everywhere in the city, it's truly a landmark.

In 1833, after years of quibbling in Congress, a private National Monument Society was formed to select a designer and to search for funds to construct this monument. Robert Mills's winning design called for a 600-ft-tall decorated obelisk rising from a circular colonnaded building. The building at the base was to be an American pantheon, adorned with statues of national heroes and a massive statue of Washington riding in a chariot pulled by snorting horses.

Because of the marshy conditions of L'Enfant's original site, the position of the monument was shifted to firmer ground 100 yards southeast. (If you walk a few steps north of the monument you can see the stone marker that denotes L'Enfant's original axis.) The cornerstone was laid in 1848 with the same Masonic trowel Washington himself had used to lay the Capitol's cornerstone 55 years earlier. The National Monument Society continued to raise funds after construction was begun, soliciting subscriptions of $1 from citizens across America. It also urged states, organizations, and foreign governments to contribute memorial stones for the construction. Problems arose in 1854, when members of the anti-Papist "Know Nothing" party stole a block donated by Pope Pius IX, smashed it, and dumped its shards into the Potomac. This action, a lack of funds, and the onset of the Civil War kept the monument at a fraction of its final height, open at the top, and vulnerable to the rain. A clearly visible ring about a third of the way up the obelisk testifies to this unfortunate stage of the monument's history: although all of the marble in the obelisk came from the same Maryland quarry, the stone used for the second phase of construction came from a different stratum and is of a slightly different shade.

In 1876 Congress finally appropriated $200,000 to finish the monument, and the Army Corps of Engineers took over construction, thankfully simplifying Mills's original design. Work was finally completed in December 1884, when the monument was topped with a 7½-pound piece of aluminum, then one of the most expensive metals in the world. Four years later the monument was opened to visitors, who rode to the top in a steam-operated elevator. (Only men were allowed to take the 20-minute ride; it was thought too dangerous for women, who as a result had to walk up the stairs if they wanted to see the view.)

The view from the top takes in most of the District and parts of Maryland and Virginia. You are no longer permitted to climb the more than 800 steps leading to the top. (Incidents of vandalism and a disturbing number of heart attacks on the steps convinced the park service that letting people walk up on their own wasn't a good idea.)

To avoid the formerly long lines of people waiting for the minute-long elevator ride up the monument's shaft, the park service now uses a free timed-ticket system. A limited number of tickets are available at the kiosk on 15th Street daily beginning at 8 AM Memorial Day to Labor Day and 9 AM Labor Day to Memorial Day, with a limit of six tickets per person. Tickets are good during a specified half-hour period. In 2000, the steel scaffolding and transparent-fabric sheath that covered the monument during a long renovation were removed, and by 2002 the monument should once again be open to visitors year-round. ⊠ *Constitution Ave. and 15th St. NW,* ☎ *202/426–6840,* WEB *www.nps.gov/wamo.* ⊠ *Free.* ☉ *Memorial Day–Labor Day, daily 8 AM–11:45 PM; Labor Day–Memorial Day, daily 9–4:45. Metro: Smithsonian.*

West Potomac Park. Between the Potomac and the Tidal Basin, West Potomac Park is best known for its flowering cherry trees, which bloom only two weeks in late March or early April. During the rest of the year, West Potomac Park is just a nice place to relax, play ball, or admire the views at the Tidal Basin.

THE WHITE HOUSE AREA

Revised by
Maureen
Graney

In a world full of recognizable images, few are better known than the whitewashed, 32-room, Irish country house–like mansion at 1600 Pennsylvania Avenue. The residence of arguably the single most powerful person on the planet, the White House has an awesome majesty, having been the home of every U.S. president but, ironically, the father of our country, George Washington. This is where the buck stops in America and where the nation turns in times of crisis. In the wake of past political scandals, however, America has been reminded that for all the power and majesty that come with the title and the address, the house is still inhabited by imperfect humans. After joining the more than 1.5 million people who visit the White House each year, strike out into the surrounding streets to explore the president's neighborhood, which includes some of the city's oldest houses.

Numbers in the text correspond to numbers in the margin and on The White House Area map.

A Good Walk

Your first stop should be the **White House Visitor Center** ① at 14th and E streets. Walk north one block on 15th Street, and then turn left to the **White House** ②. Across Pennsylvania Avenue is **Lafayette Square** ③, with its statues, trees, and flowers. Beyond the park, on H Street, is the golden-domed **St. John's Episcopal Church** ④, the so-called Church of the Presidents. Head west on H Street to Jackson Place and the federal-style **Decatur House** ⑤, built for naval hero Stephen Decatur and his wife, Susan, in 1819. Walk down Jackson Place to Pennsylvania Avenue and turn right to the **Renwick Gallery** ⑥, another member of the Smithsonian family of museums, and its neighbor Blair House, used as a residence by visiting heads of state. Go south on 17th Street past the **Old Executive Office Building** ⑦, once home to the War, Navy, and State departments. At the corner of 17th Street and New York Avenue is the **Corcoran Gallery of Art** ⑧, one of the few large, non-Smithsonian museums in Washington. Proceed one block west on New York Avenue to the unusually shaped **Octagon** ⑨, with exhibits on the architecture and history of Washington. A block south on 18th Street is the **Department of the Interior** ⑩, decorated with 1930s murals illustrating the department's work as overseer of most of the country's federally owned land and natural resources.

Walk back east on E Street to 17th Street to the three buildings of the American Red Cross, one of which has three Tiffany stained-glass windows. A block south is Memorial Continental Hall, headquarters of the Daughters of the American Revolution and home to the **DAR Museum** ⑪, which has 33 period rooms decorated in a variety of styles. Just across C Street to the south of Continental Hall is the headquarters of the **Organization of American States** ⑫, in the House of the Americas. Behind the House of the Americas is the **Art Museum of the Americas** ⑬, a small gallery that features works by 20th-century Latin American artists. Head east on Constitution Avenue and take the first left after 17th Street, following the curving drive that encircles the **Ellipse** ⑭. Take E Street east to 15th Street; then turn left and pass between the mammoth **William Tecumseh Sherman Monument** ⑮ on the left and **Pershing Park** ⑯ on the right, a quiet, sunken garden honoring General John J. "Blackjack" Pershing. Continue north up 15th Street to admire the impressive **Treasury Building** ⑰, the largest Greek Revival edifice in Washington.

TIMING

Touring the area around the White House could easily take you a day, depending on how long you visit each of the museums along the way. But now that the White House uses a timed-ticket system, you won't have to waste precious hours waiting in line to get in, and the walk described above could take half a day. If you enjoy history, you may be more interested in spending that extra time at Decatur House, the

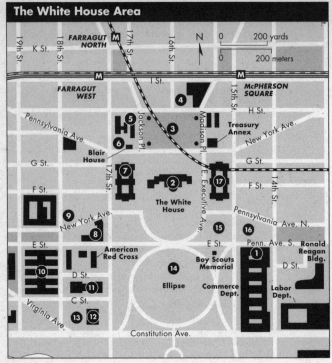

The White House Area

DAR Museum, and the Octagon. If art is your passion, devote those hours to the Corcoran and Renwick galleries instead.

Sights to See

American Red Cross. Although it hosts occasional art exhibits, the American Red Cross national headquarters is mainly of passing interest. It's composed of three buildings. The primary one, a neoclassical structure of blinding-white marble built in 1917, commemorates the service and devotion of the women who cared for the wounded on both sides during the Civil War. Its Georgian-style board-of-governors hall has three stained-glass windows designed by Louis Comfort Tiffany. The building at 1730 E Street NW, dedicated to the women of World War I, is closed for renovation during 2002, after which it will house a museum and visitor center. ⊠ *430 17th St. NW,* ☎ *202/639–3300,* WEB *www. redcross.org.* 🎟 *Free.* 🕑 *Weekdays 9–4. Metro: Farragut West.*

⓭ Art Museum of the Americas. Changing exhibits highlight 20th-century Latin American artists in this small gallery which is part of the ☞ **Organization of American States.** The museum also screens documentaries on South and Central American art. A garden, open to the public, connects the Art Museum and the OAS building. ⊠ *201 18th St. NW,* ☎ *202/458–6016,* WEB *www.oas.org.* 🎟 *Free.* 🕑 *Tues.–Sun. 10–5. Metro: Farragut West.*

Blair House. A green canopy marks the entrance to Blair House, the residence used by heads of state visiting Washington. Harry S. Truman lived here from 1948 to 1952 while the White House was undergoing much-needed renovations. A plaque on the fence honors White House policeman Leslie Coffelt, who died in 1950 when Puerto Rican separatists attempted to assassinate President Truman at this site. ⊠ *1651 Pennsylvania Ave. Metro: McPherson Square.*

Boy Scouts Memorial. Near the Ellipse stands this statue of a uniformed Boy Scout flanked by a male figure representing Patriotism and a female figure who holds the light of faith. ⊠ *East of Ellipse, near 15th St. NW. Metro: McPherson Square.*

⑧ Corcoran Gallery of Art. The Corcoran is Washington's largest nonfederal art museum, as well as its first. The beaux arts–style building, its copper roof green with age, was designed by Ernest Flagg and completed in 1897. (The museum's first home was in what is now the Renwick Gallery.) The gallery's permanent collection numbers more than 14,000 works, including paintings by the first great American portraitists John Copley, Gilbert Stuart, and Rembrandt Peale. The Hudson River School is represented by such works as *Mount Corcoran* by Albert Bierstadt and Frederic Church's *Niagara*. There are also portraits by John Singer Sargent, Thomas Eakins, and Mary Cassatt. European art is displayed in the Walker Collection (late-19th- and early 20th-century paintings, including works by Gustave Courbet, Claude Monet, Camille Pissarro, and Pierre-Auguste Renoir) and the Clark Collection (Dutch, Flemish, and French Romantic paintings, and the restored entire 18th-century Salon Doré of the Hotel de Clermont in Paris). Be sure to see Samuel Morse's *Old House of Representatives* and Hiram Powers's *Greek Slave*, which scandalized Victorian society. (The latter, a statue of a nude woman with her wrists chained, was considered so shocking by Victorian audiences that separate viewing hours were established for men and women; children under 16 weren't allowed to see it at all.) Photography and works by contemporary American artists are also among the Corcoran's strengths. The Corcoran College of Art and Design, housed in the museum, is the only four-year art college in the Washington area. The **Winder Building** (⊠ 604 17th St.), one block north, was erected in 1848 as one of the first office blocks in the capital and served as the headquarters of the Union Army during the Civil War. ⊠ *500 17th St. NW,* ☎ *202/639–1700,* WEB *www.corcoran.org.* ☞ *$5.* ☉ *Mon., Wed., and Fri.–Sun. 10–5; Thurs. 10–9; tours of permanent collection Mon., Wed., and Fri. at noon; weekends at 10:30 AM, noon, and 2:30 PM; Thurs. at 7:30 PM. Metro: Farragut West or Farragut North.*

NEED A BREAK?	In the Corcoran Gallery, **Café des Artistes** (☎ 202/639–1700) has a lunch menu that includes salads, light entrées, desserts, and a refreshing assortment of fruit and vegetable shakes. The café also serves a Continental breakfast, an English tea complete with scones and clotted cream, and light fare on Thursday, when the museum is open late. The Sunday brunch, when gospel singers and a jazz band perform live, is very popular.

⑪ DAR Museum. A beaux arts building serving as headquarters of the Daughters of the American Revolution, Memorial Continental Hall was the site each year of the DAR's congress until the larger Constitution Hall was built around the corner. An entrance on D Street leads to the DAR Museum. Its 33,000-item collection includes fine examples of Colonial and federal furniture, textiles, quilts, silver, china, porcelain, stoneware, earthenware, and glass. Thirty-three period rooms are decorated in styles representative of various U.S. states, ranging from an 1850 California adobe parlor to a New Hampshire attic filled with toys from the 18th and 19th centuries. Two galleries—one a permanent exhibition, the other a rotating one—display decorative arts. Docents are available for tours weekdays 10–2:30 and Sunday 1–5. Youngsters may especially love the "Colonial Adventure" tours, which are usually held the first and third Sundays of the month. Costumed docents lead children ages five to seven through the museum, explaining the exhibits and describing life in Colonial America. Make reservations at least 10 days in advance. ✉ *1776 D St. NW,* ☎ *202/879–3241,* WEB *www.dar.org.* 🎫 *Free.* ◷ *Weekdays 8:30–4, Sun. 1–5. Metro: Farragut West.*

❺ Decatur House. Designed by Benjamin Latrobe, Decatur House was built for naval hero Stephen Decatur and his wife, Susan, in 1819. A red-brick, federal-style building on the corner of H Street and Jackson Place, it was the first private residence on President's Park (the White House doesn't really count as *private*). Decatur had earned the affection of the nation in battles against the British and the Barbary pirates. Planning to start a political career, he used the money Congress awarded him for his exploits to build this home near the White House. Tragically, only 14 months after he moved in, Decatur was killed in a duel with James Barron, a disgruntled former navy officer who held Decatur responsible for his court-martial. Later occupants of the house included Henry Clay, Martin Van Buren, and the Beales, a prominent family from the west whose modifications of the building include a parquet floor showing the state seal of California. The house is now operated by the National Trust for Historic Preservation. The first floor is furnished as it was in Decatur's time. The second floor is furnished in the Victorian style favored by the Beale family, who owned it until 1956 (thus making Decatur House both the first and *last* private residence on Lafayette Square). The museum shop around the corner (entrance on H Street) sells a variety of books, postcards, and gifts.

Many of the row houses along Jackson Place date from the pre–Civil War or Victorian period; even the more modern additions, though—such as those at 718 and 726—are designed to blend with their more historic neighbors. Count Rochambeau, aide to General Lafayette, is honored with a statue at Lafayette Square's southwest corner. ✉ *748 Jackson Pl. NW,* ☎ *202/842–0920,* WEB *www.decaturhouse.org.* 🎫 *Free.* ◷ *Tues.–Fri. 10–3, weekends noon–4; tours on the hr and ½ hr. Metro: Farragut West.*

❿ Department of the Interior. Designed by Waddy B. Wood, the Department of the Interior was the most modern government building in the city and the first large federal building with escalators and central air-conditioning at the time of its construction in 1937. The outside of the building is somewhat plain, but much of the inside is decorated with artwork that reflects the department's work. Hallways feature heroic oil paintings of dam construction, gold panning, and cattle drives. Much of the artwork can be seen at the **Department of the Interior Museum** (☎ 202/208–4743) on the first floor. (You can enter the building at its E Street or C Street door; adults must show photo ID.) A guided tour takes you past more of the three dozen murals throughout the building. The small museum tells the story of the Department of the Interior, a huge agency dubbed "the Mother of Departments" because from it grew the Departments of Agriculture, Labor, Education, and Energy. Soon after it opened in 1938, the museum became one of the most popular attractions in Washington; evening hours were maintained even during World War II. The museum is open weekdays from 8:30 to 4:30, and the third Saturday of the month, from 1 to 4; admission is free.

Today the Department of the Interior oversees most federally owned land and natural resources, and exhibits in the museum outline the work of the Bureau of Land Management, the U.S. Geological Survey, the Bureau of Indian Affairs, the National Park Service, and other department branches. The museum retains a New Deal–era flavor—including meticulously created dioramas depicting historic events and American locales—and is, depending on your tastes, either quaint or outdated. The Indian Craft Shop across the hall from the museum sells Native

American pottery, dolls, carvings, jewelry, baskets, and books. Reservations are required at least two weeks in advance for a tour of the building's architecture and murals. ✉ *C and E Sts. between 18th and 19th Sts. NW,* WEB *www.doi.gov.* ✉ *Free. Metro: Farragut West.*

⑭ Ellipse. From the Ellipse you can see the Washington Monument and the Jefferson Memorial to the south and the red-tile roof of the Department of Commerce to the east, with the tower of the Old Post Office Building sticking up above it. To the north you have a good view of the rear of the White House (the Ellipse was once part of its backyard); the rounded portico and Harry Truman's second-story porch are clearly visible. The south lawn of the White House—also visible from here—serves as a heliport for *Marine One,* the president's helicopter. The National Christmas Tree is put up on the northern edge of the Ellipse. Each year in mid-December it's lit by the president during a festive ceremony that marks the beginning of the holiday season.

The Ellipse's rather weather-beaten **gatehouse** at the corner of Constitution Avenue and 17th Street once stood on Capitol Hill. It was designed in 1828 by Charles Bulfinch, the first native-born American to serve as architect of the Capitol, and was moved here in 1874 after the Capitol grounds were redesigned by Frederick Law Olmsted. A twin of the gatehouse stands at Constitution Avenue and 15th Street. The **Boy Scouts Memorial** is nearby. ✉ *Bounded by Constitution Ave. and E, 15th, and 17th Sts. Metro: Farragut West or McPherson Square.*

❸ Lafayette Square. With such an important resident living across the street, the National Capital Region's National Park Service gardeners lavish extra attention on this square's trees and flower beds. It's an intimate oasis amid downtown Washington.

When Pierre-Charles L'Enfant proposed the location for the Executive Mansion, the only building north of what is today Pennsylvania Avenue was the Pierce family farmhouse, which stood at the northeast corner of the present square. An apple orchard and a family burial ground were the area's two other features. During the construction of the White House, workers' huts and a brick kiln were set up, and soon residences began popping up around the square (though sheep would continue to graze on it for years). Soldiers camped in the square during the War of 1812 and the Civil War, turning it at both times into a muddy pit. Today, protesters set their placards up in Lafayette Square, jockeying for positions that face the White House. Although the National Park Service can't restrict the protesters' freedom of speech, it does try to restrict the size of their signs.

In the center of the park—and dominating the square—is a large **statue of Andrew Jackson.** Erected in 1853 and cast from bronze cannons that Jackson captured during the War of 1812, this was the first equestrian statue made in America. (There's a duplicate in front of St. Louis Cathedral in New Orleans's Jackson Square.) Jackson's is the only statue of an American in the park. The other statues are of foreign-born soldiers who helped in America's fight for independence. In the southeast corner is the park's namesake, the **Marquis de Lafayette,** the young French nobleman who came to America to fight in the Revolution. When Lafayette returned to the United States in 1824 he was given a rousing welcome: he was wined and dined in the finest homes and showered with gifts of cash and land.

The colonnaded building across Madison Place at the corner of Pennsylvania Avenue is an annex to the Treasury Department. The modern redbrick building farther on, at 717 Madison Place, houses a variety of judicial offices. Its design—with the squared-off bay windows—is echoed in the taller building that rises behind it and is mirrored in the **New Executive Office Building** on the other side of Lafayette Square. Planners in the '20s recommended that the private houses on Lafayette Square, many built in the federal period, be torn down and replaced with a collection of uniform neoclassical-style government buildings. A lack of funds providentially kept the neighborhood intact, and in the early '60s John and Jacqueline Kennedy worked to save the historic town houses.

The next house down, yellow with a second-story ironwork balcony, was built in 1828 by Benjamin Ogle Tayloe. During the McKinley administration, Ohio senator Marcus Hanna lived here, and the president's frequent visits earned it the nickname the "Little White House." Dolley Madison lived in the next-door Cutts-Madison House after her husband died. Both the Tayloe and Madison houses are now part of the Federal Judicial Center.

Continue down Madison Place. The next statue is that of **Thaddeus Kosciuszko**, the Polish general who fought alongside American colonists against the British. If you head east on H Street for half a block, you'll come to the **United States Government Bookstore** (✉ 1510 H St. NW, ☎ 202/653–5075, WEB www.gpo.gov/su_docs), the place to visit if you'd like to buy a few pounds of the millions of tons of paper the government churns out each year. Here is where you can find a copy of the latest federal budget or the *Surgeon General's Report on Nutrition and Health*. ✉ *Bounded by Pennsylvania Ave., Madison Pl., H St., and Jackson Pl. Metro: McPherson Square.*

NEED A BREAK?	Bernard Baruch, adviser to Woodrow Wilson and other presidents, used to eat his lunch in Lafayette Park; you can, too. Nearby, **Loeb's Restaurant** (✉ 15th and I Sts. NW, ☎ 202/371–1150) is a New York–style deli that serves salads and sandwiches to eat there or to go.

9 **Octagon.** Why this six-sided building is named the Octagon remains a subject of debate. Some say it's because the main room is a circle, and was built by rounding out the angles of an octagon; others say it's for the eight angles formed by the odd shape of the six walls—the true definition of an octagon. Designed by Dr. William Thornton (the Capitol's architect), it was built for John Tayloe III, a wealthy Virginia plantation owner, and was completed in 1801. Thornton chose the unusual shape to conform to the acute angle formed by L'Enfant's intersection of New York Avenue and 18th Street.

After the White House was burned in 1814 the Tayloes invited James and Dolley Madison to stay in the Octagon. It was in a second-floor study that the Treaty of Ghent, ending the War of 1812, was signed. By the late 1800s the building was used as a rooming house. In the 20th century the house served as the headquarters of the American Institute of Architects before the construction of AIA's rather unexceptional building behind it. It's now the Museum of the American Architectural Foundation.

A renovation in the 1960s revealed the intricate plaster molding and the original 1799 Coade stone mantels (named for the woman who invented a now-lost method of casting crushed stone). A far more thorough restoration, completed in 1996, returned the Octagon to its 1815 appearance, topped off by an historically accurate, cypress-shingle roof with balustrade. The galleries inside host changing exhibits on architecture, city planning, and Washington history and design. ✉ *1799 New York Ave. NW, ☎ 202/638–3105, WEB www.archfoundation.org. ✉ $5. ☉ Tues.–Sun. 10–4. Metro: Farragut West or Farragut North.*

HOW TO
USE THIS GUIDE

Great trips begin with great planning, and this guide makes planning easy. It's packed with everything you need—insider advice on hotels and restaurants, cool tools, practical tips, essential maps, and much more.

COOL TOOLS

Fodor's Choice Top picks are marked throughout with a star.

Great Itineraries These tours, planned by Fodor's experts, give you the skinny on what you can see and do in the time you have.

Smart Travel Tips A to Z This special section is packed with important contacts and advice on everything from how to get around to what to pack.

Good Walks You won't miss a thing if you follow the numbered bullets on our maps.

Need a Break? Looking for a quick bite to eat or a spot to rest? These sure bets are along the way.

Off the Beaten Path Some lesser-known sights are worth a detour. We've marked those you should make time for.

POST-IT® FLAGS
Dog-ear no more!

"Post-it" is a registered trademark of 3M.

Favorite restaurants • Essential maps • Frequently used numbers • Walking tours • Can't-miss sights • Smart Travel Tips • Web sites • Top shops • Hot nightclubs • Addresses • Smart contacts • Events • Off-the-beaten-path spots • Favorite restaurants • Essential maps • Frequently used numbers • Walking tours • Can't-miss sights • Smart Travel Tips • Web sites • Top shops • Hot nightclubs • Addresses • Smart contacts • Events • Off-the-beaten-path spots • Favorite restaurants • Essential maps • Frequently used numbers • Walking tours •

ICONS AND SYMBOLS

Watch for these symbols throughout:

★	Our special recommendations
✕	Restaurant
🏠	Lodging establishment
✕🏠	Lodging establishment whose restaurant warrants a special trip
☜	Good for kids
☞	Sends you to another section of the guide for more information
✉	Address
☎	Telephone number
FAX	Fax number
WEB	Web site
💲	Admission price
☉	Opening hours
$-$$$$	Lodging and dining price categories, keyed to strategically sited price charts. Check the index for locations.
①❶	Numbers in white and black circles on the maps, in the margins, and within tours correspond to one another.

ON THE WEB

Continue your planning with these useful tools found at **www.fodors.com**, the Web's best source for travel information.

"Rich with resources." —*New York Times*

"Navigation is a cinch." —*Forbes* "Best of the Web" list

"Put together by people bursting with know-how."
　　　　　　　　　　　　　　　—*Sunday Times* (London)

Create a Miniguide Pinpoint hotels, restaurants, and attractions that have what you want at the price you want to pay.

Rants and Raves Find out what readers say about Fodor's picks—or write your own reviews of hotels and restaurants you've just visited.

Travel Talk Post your questions and get answers from fellow travelers, or share your own experiences.

On-Line Booking Find the best prices on airline tickets, rental cars, cruises, or vacations, and book them on the spot.

About our Books Learn about other Fodor's guides to your destination and many others.

Expert Advice and Trip Ideas From what to tip to how to take great photos, from the national parks to Nepal, Fodors.com has suggestions that'll make your trip a breeze. Log on and get informed and inspired.

Smart Resources Check the weather in your destination or convert your currency. Learn the local language or link to the latest event listings. Or consult hundreds of detailed maps—all in one place.

❼ Old Executive Office Building. Once one of the most detested buildings in the city, the Old Executive Office Building (officially renamed the Dwight D. Eisenhower Executive Office Building, but still called its original name by locals) is now one of the most beloved. It was built between 1871 and 1888 as the State, War, and Navy Building, headquarters of those three executive-branch offices. Its architect, Alfred B. Mullett, patterned it after the style of the Louvre, but detractors quickly criticized the busy French Empire design—with its mansard roof, tall chimneys, and 900 freestanding columns—as an inappropriate counterpoint to the Greek Revival Treasury Building that sits on the other side of the White House. Numerous plans to alter the facade foundered because of lack of money. The granite edifice may look like a wedding cake, but its high ceilings and spacious offices make it popular with occupants, who include members of the executive branch. Several presidents, including both Roosevelts, Richard Nixon, and George Bush, Sr., have served here during their careers. The former office of the secretary of the navy, restored in the 1980s, shows the opulent style of that office at the turn of the 20th century and has been an office for every vice president (except Hubert Humphrey) since Lyndon B. Johnson. The Old Executive Office Building has hosted numerous historic events. It was here that Secretary of State Cordell Hull met with Japanese diplomats after the bombing of Pearl Harbor, and it was the site of both the first presidential press conference, given by President Truman in 1950, and the first televised press conference, given by President Eisenhower in 1955. ⊠ *East side of 17th St., west of White House,* ☏ *202/395–5895. Tours available certain Saturdays; reservations and security clearance required. Metro: Farragut West.*

⓬ Organization of American States. The headquarters of the Organization of American States, which is made up of nations from North, South, and Central America, contains a patio adorned with a pre-Columbian–style fountain and lush tropical plants. This tiny rain forest is a good place to rest when Washington's summer heat is at its most oppressive. The upstairs Hall of the Americas contains busts of generals and statesmen from the 34 OAS member nations, as well as each country's flag. The OAS runs the ☞ **Art Museum of the Americas.** ⊠ *17th St. and Constitution Ave. NW,* ☏ *202/458–3000.* WEB *www.oas.org.* ⌨ *Free.* ☉ *Weekdays 9–5:30. Metro: Farragut West.*

⓰ Pershing Park. A quiet sunken garden honors General John J. "Blackjack" Pershing, famed for failing to capture the Mexican revolutionary Pancho Villa in 1916–17 and then for commanding the American expeditionary force in World War I, among other military exploits. Engravings on the stone walls recount pivotal campaigns from that war. Ice-skaters glide on the square pool here in winter. ⊠ *15th St. and Pennsylvania Ave. Metro: McPherson Square.*

NEED A BREAK? One block to the north of Pershing Park is the venerable **Hotel Washington** (⊠ 515 15th St. NW, ☏ 202/638–5900, WEB www.hotelwashington.com), whose view from the rooftop Sky Top Terrace—open May to October—is one of the best in the city.

❻ Renwick Gallery. The Renwick Gallery of the Smithsonian American Art Museum remains at the forefront of the crafts movement, and its collection includes exquisitely designed and made utilitarian items, as well as objects created out of such traditional crafts media as fiber and glass. The words "Dedicated to Art" are engraved above the entrance to the French Second Empire–style building, designed by Smithsonian Castle architect James Renwick in 1859 to house the art collection of Washington merchant and banker William Wilson Corcoran. Corcoran was a Southern sympathizer who spent the duration of the Civil War in Europe. While he was away, his unfinished building was pressed into service by the government as a quartermaster general's post.

In 1874 the Corcoran, as it was then called, opened as the first private art museum in the city. Corcoran's collection quickly outgrew the building, and in 1897 it was moved to a new gallery a few blocks south on 17th Street to what is now the Corcoran Gallery of Art. After a stint as the U.S. Court of Claims, this building was restored, renamed after its architect, and opened in 1972 as the Smithsonian's Museum of American Crafts. Although crafts were once the poor relations of the art world—handwoven rugs and delicately carved tables were considered somehow less "artistic" than, say, oil paintings and sculptures—they have since come into their own. Not everything in the museum is Shaker furniture and enamel jewelry, though. The second-floor Grand Salon is still furnished in the opulent Victorian style Corcoran favored when his collection adorned its walls. ⊠ *Pennsylvania Ave. and 17th St. NW,* ☎ *202/357–2531; 202/357–1729 TDD,* WEB *americanart.si.edu.* 🎟 *Free.* ☉ *Daily 10–5:30. Metro: Farragut West.*

❹ **St. John's Episcopal Church.** The golden-domed so-called Church of the Presidents sits across Lafayette Park from the White House. Every president since Madison has visited the church, and many worshiped here regularly. Built in 1816, the church was the second building on the square. Benjamin Latrobe, who worked on both the Capitol and the White House, designed it in the form of a Greek cross, with a flat dome and a lantern cupola. The church has been altered somewhat since then; later additions include the Doric portico and the cupola tower. You can best sense the intent of Latrobe's design while standing inside under the saucer-shape dome of the original building. Not far from the center of the church is Pew 54, where visiting presidents are seated. The prie-dieux of many of the pews are embroidered with the presidential seal and the names of several chief executives. If you want to take a self-guided tour, brochures are available inside. ⊠ *16th and H Sts. NW,* ☎ *202/347–8766.* 🎟 *Free.* ☉ *Weekdays 9–3; guided tours by appointment. Metro: McPherson Square.*

⑰ **Treasury Building.** Once used as a repository for currency, this is the largest Greek Revival edifice in Washington. Robert Mills, the architect responsible for the Washington Monument and the Patent Office (now the Smithsonian American Art Museum), designed the grand colonnade that stretches down 15th Street. Construction of the Treasury Building started in 1836 and, after several additions, was finally completed in 1869. Its southern facade has a **statue of Alexander Hamilton,** the department's first secretary. Guided 90-minute tours, given every Saturday, take you past the Andrew Johnson Suite, used by Johnson as the executive office while Mrs. Lincoln moved out of the White House; the two-story marble Cash Room; and a 19th-century burglarproof vault lining that saw duty when the building stored currency. Register at least one week ahead for the tour; you must provide name, date of birth, and Social Security number and show a photo ID at the start of the tour. ⊠ *15th St. and Pennsylvania Ave. NW,* ☎ *202/622–0896; 202/622–0692 TDD.* 🎟 *Free.* ☉ *Guided tours Sat. at 10, 10:20, 10:40, and 11. Metro: McPherson Square or Metro Center.*

NEED A BREAK?   **Benkay** (⊠ 727 15th St. NW, lower level, ☎ 202/737–1515) has a lunchtime sushi buffet. The luxurious **Old Ebbitt Grill** (⊠ 675 15th St. NW, ☎ 202/347–4800) is a popular watering spot for journalists and TV news correspondents. About a block from the Treasury Building is a glittering urban mall, the **Shops** (⊠ National Press Bldg., F and G Sts.

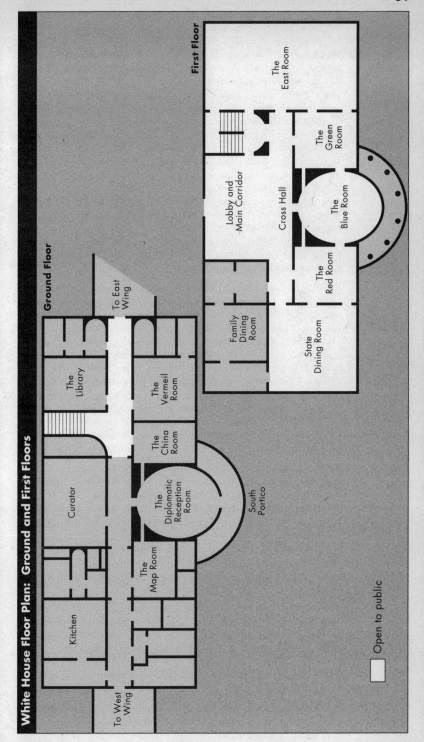

White House Floor Plan: Ground and First Floors

51

between 13th and 14th Sts. NW), which houses full-service restaurants as well as faster and cheaper fare in its top-floor food court.

★ ☾ ❷   **White House.** This "house" surely has the best-known address in the United States: 1600 Pennsylvania Avenue. Pierre-Charles L'Enfant called it the President's House; it was known formally as the Executive Mansion; and in 1902 Congress officially proclaimed it the White House after longstanding common usage of that name. Irishman James Hoban's plan, based on the Georgian design of Leinster Hall in Dublin and of other Irish country houses, was selected in a 1792 contest. The building wasn't ready for its first occupant, John Adams, the second U.S. president, until 1800, and so, in a colossal irony, George Washington, who seems to have slept everyplace else, never slept here. Completed in 1829, it has undergone many structural changes since then. Andrew Jackson installed running water. James Garfield put in the first elevator. Between 1948 and 1952, Harry Truman had the entire structure gutted and restored, adding a second-story porch to the south portico. Each family that has called the White House home has left its imprint on the 132-room mansion. The most recent update is a running track that was installed for Bill Clinton.

Tuesday through Saturday morning (except holidays), from 10 AM to noon, selected public rooms on the ground floor and first floor are open to visitors. There are two ways to visit the White House. The most popular (and easiest) way is to pick up timed tickets from the ☞ **White House Visitor Center.** Your ticket tells you where and when your tour starts. Plan to be there 5–10 minutes before your tour is scheduled to begin. The other option is to write to your representative or senator's office 8–10 weeks in advance of your trip to request special VIP passes for tours between 8 and 9 AM, but these tickets are extremely limited. (Keep in mind that the White House is occasionally closed without notice for official functions.) Baby strollers are not allowed on the tour. On selected weekends in April and October, the White House is open for garden tours. In December it's decorated for the holidays.

Enter the White House through the East Wing lobby on the ground floor, walking past the Jacqueline Kennedy Rose Garden. You can view several rooms on the ground floor, then proceed to the State Floor and enter the large white-and-gold **East Room,** the site of presidential social events. In 1814 Dolley Madison saved the room's full-length portrait of George Washington from torch-carrying British soldiers by cutting it from its frame, rolling it up, and spiriting it out of the White House. (No fool she, Dolley also rescued her own portrait.) One of Abraham Lincoln's sons once harnessed a pet goat to a chair and went for a ride through the East Room during a reception.

The federal-style **Green Room,** named for the moss-green watered silk that covers its walls, is used for informal receptions and "photo opportunities" with foreign heads of state. Notable furnishings here include a New England sofa that once belonged to Daniel Webster and portraits of Benjamin Franklin, John Quincy Adams, and Abigail Adams. The president and his guests are often shown on TV sitting in front of the Green Room's English Empire mantel, engaging in what are invariably described as "frank and cordial" discussions.

The elliptical **Blue Room,** the most formal space in the White House, is furnished with a gilded Empire-style settee and chairs that were ordered by James Monroe. (Monroe asked for plain wooden chairs, but the furniture manufacturer thought such unadorned furnishings too simple for the White House and took it upon himself to supply chairs more in keeping with their surroundings.) The White House Christmas tree is placed in this room each year. (Another well-known elliptical room, the president's **Oval Office,** is in the West Wing of the White House, along with other executive offices, and isn't part of the tour.)

The **Red Room** is decorated as an American Empire–style parlor of the early 19th century, with furniture by the New York cabinetmaker Charles-Honoré Lannuier. The marble mantel is the twin of the mantel in the Green Room.

The **State Dining Room,** second in size only to the East Room, can seat 140 guests. It's dominated by G. P. A. Healy's portrait of Abraham Lincoln, painted after the president's death. The stone mantel is inscribed with a quote from one of John Adams's letters: "I pray heaven to bestow the best of blessings on this house and all that shall hereafter inhabit it. May none but honest and wise men ever rule under this roof." In Teddy Roosevelt's day a stuffed moose head hung over the mantel. ⊠ *1600 Pennsylvania Ave. NW, ☎ 202/456–7041 or 202/208–1631,* WEB *www.whitehouse.gov. ◨ Free. ◷ Tues.–Sat. 10–noon. Metro: Federal Triangle.*

❶ **White House Visitor Center.** If you're visiting the White House, you need to stop by the visitor center for free tickets from March through August and in December. (Tickets aren't usually required September to November or January to February, typically slower seasons. But it's always a good idea to call ahead to check.) Tickets are dispensed on a first-come, first-serve basis beginning at 7:30 AM. (They're usually gone by 9 AM.) You can get up to four tickets and each person, including infants, must have a ticket and hand-stamp validation. Also at the center are exhibits pertaining to the White House's construction, its decor, and the families who've lived there. Photographs, artifacts, and videos relate the house's history to those who don't have the opportunity to tour the building; if you're taking the tour, they help you better appreciate and understand what you'll see. *Official address:* ⊠ *1450 Pennsylvania Ave. NW; entrance:* ⊠ *Department of Commerce's Baldrige Hall, E St. between 14th and 15th Sts., ☎ 202/208–1631,* WEB *www.nps.gov/whho. ◨ Free. ◷ Daily 7:30–4. Metro: Federal Triangle.*

❶❺ **William Tecumseh Sherman Monument.** Sherman, whose Atlanta Campaign in 1864 cut a bloody swath of destruction through the Confederacy, was said to be the greatest Civil War general, as the sheer size of this massive monument, set in a small park, would seem to attest. ⊠ *Bounded by E and 15th Sts., East Executive Ave., and Alexander Hamilton Pl. Metro: Federal Triangle.*

CAPITOL HILL

Revised by
Maureen
Graney

The people who live and work on "the Hill" do so in the shadow of the edifice that lends the neighborhood its name: the gleaming white Capitol. More than just the center of government, however, the Hill also includes charming residential blocks lined with Victorian row houses and a fine assortment of restaurants, bars, and shops. Capitol Hill's boundaries are disputed: it's bordered to the west, north, and south by the Capitol, H Street NE, and I Street SE, respectively. Some argue that Capitol Hill extends east to the Anacostia River, others that it ends at 14th Street near Lincoln Park. The neighborhood does in fact seem to extend its boundaries as urban pioneers and members of Capitol Hill's active historic-preservation movement restore more and more 19th-century houses.

The Capitol also serves as the point from which the city is divided into quadrants: northwest, southwest, northeast, and southeast. North

Capitol Street, which runs north from the Capitol, separates northeast from northwest; East Capitol Street separates northeast and southeast; South Capitol Street separates southwest and southeast; and the Mall (Independence Avenue on the south and Constitution Avenue on the north) separates northwest from southwest.

Numbers in the text correspond to numbers in the margin and on the Capitol Hill map.

A Good Walk

Start your exploration of the Hill at **Union Station** ①, beautifully restored in 1988. You can take a side trip to the new John Paul II Cultural Center and the National Shrine of the Immaculate Conception by taking the Metro from Union Station to Brookland–Catholic University. Otherwise, go next door to the **National Postal Museum** ②, under the arcade to the right of the main Union Station exit. Just east of the station is the **Thurgood Marshall Federal Judiciary Building** ③, with its spectacular atrium. For a detour to the Capital Children's Museum, walk alongside this building to 2nd Street NE and turn left; the museum is just across H Street NE. If you're staying on the main tour, follow Delaware Avenue from the Columbus fountain in front of Union Station. On the left you pass the Russell Senate Office Building (1st Street and Constitution Avenue NE); note the delicate treatment below the second-story windows that resembles twisted lengths of fringed cloth. To the right, a block west on Constitution Avenue, is the **Robert A. Taft Memorial** ④. Behind it, on the triangle formed by New Jersey and Louisiana avenues and D Street NW, is the National Japanese American Memorial to Patriotism; its granite walls honor the Japanese-American soldiers who fought in World War II and also list the ten internment camps where 120,000 Japanese-Americans were held from 1942 to 1945. Heading southward again, cross Constitution Avenue to the **Capitol** ⑤, where Congress decides how to spend your federal tax dollars. Walk down Capitol Hill and out the westernmost exit to the white-marble **Peace Monument** ⑥. Walking south on 1st Street NW, you pass the Capitol Reflecting Pool, the **Grant Memorial** ⑦, and the **James Garfield Memorial** ⑧. Across Maryland Avenue is the **United States Botanic Garden** ⑨, an indoor museum of orchids, cacti, and other kinds of plant life. The ornate **Bartholdi Fountain** ⑩ is in a park across Independence Avenue. Continue east on Independence Avenue, walking back up Capitol Hill past the Rayburn, Longworth, and Cannon House office buildings, to the Jefferson Building of the **Library of Congress** ⑪.

Continue on 1st Street NE to the **Supreme Court Building** ⑫, near East Capitol Street. One block north, at the corner of Constitution Avenue and 2nd Street, is the redbrick **Sewall-Belmont House** ⑬, the oldest house on Capitol Hill and the site of a museum chronicling women's suffrage. For a taste of the residential side of the Hill, follow Maryland Avenue to Stanton Park; then walk two blocks south on 4th Street NE to A Street NE. The Frederick Douglass Townhouse (316-320 A St. NE; open Monday, Wednesdays, and Fridays from 12–2) was the first Washington home of the fiery abolitionist and writer; two restored rooms contain Douglass memorabilia, and the rest of the structure houses the Hall of Fame for Caring Americans. The houses on the **south side of East Capitol Street** ⑭, one block south on 4th Street, offer a sample of the different architectural styles on the Hill. At the corner of 3rd and East Capitol streets stands the **Folger Shakespeare Library** ⑮, the world's foremost collection of works by and about Shakespeare and his times.

If you'd like to make a side trip to visit the Navy and Marine Corps sites on Capitol Hill, head east on East Capitol Street to 8th Street SE and take the bus south to I Street SE, in front of the **Marine Corps Bar-**

racks. Walk under the highway overpass to the **Washington Navy Yard** complex, enter from the gate at 9th and M streets SE, and follow signs for the Navy Art Museum, Navy Art Gallery, Marine Corps Historical Center, and the USS *Barry*.

TIMING

Touring Capitol Hill should take you about four hours, allowing for about an hour each at the Capitol, the Botanic Garden, and the Library of Congress. If you want to see Congress in action, bear in mind that the House and Senate are usually not in session during August. Supreme Court cases are usually heard October through June, Monday through Thursday of two weeks in each month. The side trip to the two sites near Catholic University—the Pope John Paul II Cultural Center and the National Shrine of the Immaculate Conception—should take half a day. The side trip to the Navy and Marine sites takes a similar amount of time, about four hours. A detour to the Capitol Children's Museum takes a full morning or afternoon.

Sights to See

⑩ Bartholdi Fountain. Frédéric-Auguste Bartholdi, sculptor of the more famous—and much larger—Statue of Liberty, created this delightful fountain, some 30 ft tall, for the Philadelphia International Exposition of 1876. With its aquatic monsters, sea nymphs, tritons, and lighted globes (once gas, now electric), the fountain represents the elements of water and light. The U.S. Government purchased the fountain after the exposition and placed it on the grounds of the old Botanic Garden on the Mall. It was moved to its present location in 1932 and was restored in 1986. The surrounding Bartholdi Park—with its park benches and dense plantings—is a brown-bagger's delight at lunchtime. ✉ *1st St. and Independence Ave. SW. Metro: Federal Center.*

☾ Capital Children's Museum. This sprawling, hands-on museum with culture, science, and crafts keeps kids ages 1 through 12 busy. Children can "drive" a Metrobus, stage a puppet show, or enclose themselves in huge soap bubbles. The museum has in-depth exhibitions on the cultures of Mexico and Japan, including a spectacular Mexican plaza re-created in the museum's three-story atrium. Kids can board a re-creation of Japan's famous bullet train, sit cross-legged in a Japanese living room, and leaf through kanji-filled schoolbooks in a Japanese-style classroom. Young scientists can watch demonstrations by "stand-up" chemists at the chemical science center; kids ages six and up may perform their own experiments in the lab. The museum is a bit frayed around the edges—but it's the comfortable sort of wear and tear achieved through the inquisitive hands of countless youngsters. The only refreshments available are from vending machines in a lunchroom. Daily activities are posted at the entrance. ✉ *800 3rd St. NE,* ☎ *202/675–4120,* WEB *www.ccm.org.* ✉ *$6.* ☾ *Daily 10–5. Metro: Union Station.*

★ ☾ ⑤ Capitol. As beautiful as the building itself are the Capitol grounds, landscaped in the late 19th century by Frederick Law Olmsted, who, along with Calvert Vaux, created New York City's Central Park. On these 68 acres are both the city's tamest squirrels and the highest concentration of TV news correspondents, jockeying for a good position in front of the Capitol for their "stand-ups." A few hundred feet northeast of the Capitol are two cast-iron car shelters, left from the days when horse-drawn trolleys served the Hill. Olmsted's six pinkish, bronze-top lamps directly east from the Capitol are worth a look, too.

The design of this monument was the result of a competition held in 1792; the winner was William Thornton, a physician and amateur architect from the West Indies. With its central rotunda and dome,

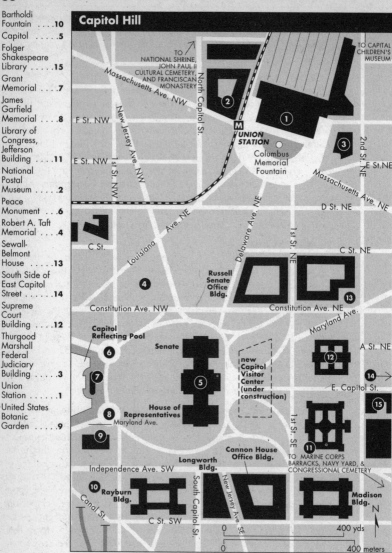

Capitol Hill

Thornton's Capitol is reminiscent of Rome's Pantheon, a similarity that must have delighted the nation's founders, who felt the American government was based on the principles of the Republic of Rome.

The cornerstone was laid by George Washington in a Masonic ceremony on September 18, 1793, and in November 1800, both the Senate and the House of Representatives moved down from Philadelphia to occupy the first completed section: the boxlike portion between the central rotunda and today's north wing. (Subsequent efforts to find the cornerstone Washington laid have been unsuccessful, though when the east front was extended in the 1950s, workers found a knee joint thought to be from a 500-pound ox that was roasted at the 1793 celebration.) By 1807 the House wing had been completed, just to the south of what's now the domed center, and a covered wooden walkway joined the two wings.

The Congress House grew slowly and suffered a grave setback on August 24, 1814, when British troops led by Sir George Cockburn marched

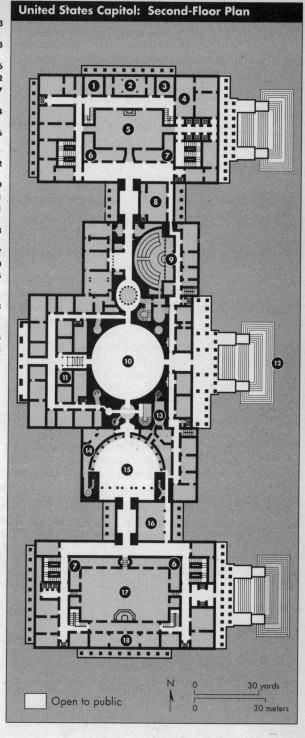

United States Capitol: Second-Floor Plan

N   0   30 yards
     0   30 meters

☐ Open to public

on Washington and set fire to the Capitol, the White House, and numerous other government buildings. (Cockburn reportedly stood on the House Speaker's chair and asked his men, "Shall this harbor of Yankee democracy be burned?" The question was rhetorical; the building was torched.) The wooden walkway was destroyed and the two wings gutted, but the walls were left standing after a violent rainstorm doused the flames. Fearful that Congress might leave Washington, residents raised money for a hastily built "Brick Capitol" that stood where the Supreme Court is today. Architect Benjamin Henry Latrobe supervised the rebuilding, adding such American touches as the corncob-and-tobacco-leaf capitals to columns in the east entrance of the Senate wing. He was followed by Boston-born Charles Bulfinch, and in 1826 the Capitol, its low wooden dome sheathed in copper, was finished.

North and south wings were added in the 1850s and '60s to accommodate a growing government trying to keep pace with a growing country. The elongated edifice extended farther north and south than Thornton had planned, and in 1855, to keep the scale correct, work began on a tall cast-iron dome. President Lincoln was criticized for continuing this expensive project while the country was in the throes of the Civil War, but he called the construction "a sign we intend the Union shall go on." This twin-shell dome, a marvel of 19th-century engineering, rises 285 ft above the ground and weighs 9 million pounds. It expands and contracts up to 4 inches a day, depending on the outside temperature. The figure atop the dome, often mistaken for Pocahontas, is called *Freedom.* Sculptor Thomas Crawford had first planned for the 19½-ft-tall bronze statue to wear the cloth liberty cap of a freed Roman slave, but Southern lawmakers, led by Jefferson Davis, objected. An "American" headdress composed of a star-encircled helmet surmounted with an eagle's head and feathers was substituted. A light just below the statue burns whenever Congress is in session.

The Capitol has continued to grow. In 1962 the east front was extended 33½ ft, creating 100 additional offices. Preservationists have fought to keep the west front from being extended, since it's the last remaining section of the Capitol's original facade. A compromise was reached in 1983, when it was agreed that the facade's crumbling sandstone blocks would simply be replaced with stronger limestone.

Guided tours of the Capitol usually start beneath the **Rotunda's** dome, but during the busy season, lines form outside along the east-front drive. If you want to forgo the tour, which is brief but informative, you may look around on your own. If you'd like to arrange a tour through your local representative, the Capitol switchboard can connect you to your member of Congress. Enter through one of the lower doors to the right or left of the main steps. Start your exploration under Constantino Brumidi's 1865 fresco, *Apotheosis of Washington,* in the center of the dome. The figures in the inner circle represent the 13 original states; those in the outer ring symbolize arts, sciences, and industry. The flat, sculpture-style frieze around the Rotunda's rim depicts 400 years of American history and was started by Brumidi in 1877. While painting Penn's treaty with the Indians, the 74-year-old artist slipped on the 58-ft-high scaffold and almost fell off. Brumidi managed to hang on until help arrived, but he died a few months later from the shock of the incident. The work was continued by another Italian, Filippo Costaggini, but the frieze wasn't finished until American Allyn Cox added the final touches in 1953.

Notice the Rotunda's eight immense oil paintings of scenes from American history. The four scenes from the Revolutionary War are by John Trumbull, who served alongside George Washington and painted the first president from life. Twenty-nine people have lain in state or in honor in the Rotunda, including nine presidents, from Abraham Lincoln to Lyndon Baines Johnson. The most recently honored were the two U.S. Capitol policemen killed in the line of duty in 1998.

South of the Rotunda is **Statuary Hall,** once the legislative chamber of the House of Representatives. The room has an interesting architectural feature that maddened early legislators: a slight whisper uttered on one side of the hall can be heard on the other. (Don't be disappointed if this parlor trick doesn't work when you're visiting the Capitol; sometimes the hall is just too noisy.) When the House moved out, Congress invited each state to send statues of two great deceased citizens for placement in the former chamber. Because the weight of the accumulated statues threatened to cave the floor in, some of the sculptures were dispersed to other spots in the Capitol.

To the north, on the Senate side, you can look into the chamber once used by the Supreme Court and into the splendid Old Senate Chamber above it, both of which have been restored. Also be sure to see the Brumidi Corridor on the ground floor of the Senate wing. Frescoes and oil paintings of birds, plants, and American inventions adorn the walls and ceilings, and intricate, Brumidi-designed bronze stairways lead to the second floor. The Italian artist also memorialized several American heroes, painting them inside trompe l'oeil frames. Some frames were left blank. The most recent one to be filled, in 1987, honors the crew of the space shuttle *Challenger.*

If you want to watch some of the legislative action in the **House or Senate Chambers** while you're on the Hill, you'll have to get a gallery pass from the office of your representative or senator. To find out where those offices are, ask any Capitol police officer, or call the Capitol Switchboard. In the chambers, notice that Democrats sit to the right of the presiding officer, Republicans to the left—the opposite, it's often noted, of their political leanings. You may be disappointed by watching from the gallery. Most of the day-to-day business is conducted in the legislative committees, many of which meet in the congressional office buildings. The *Washington Post*'s daily "Today in Congress" lists when and where the committees are meeting. To get to a House or Senate office building, go to the Capitol's basement and ride the miniature subway used by legislators.

When you're finished exploring the inside of the Capitol, make your way to the **west side.** In 1981, Congress broke with tradition and moved the presidential swearing-in ceremony to this side of the Capitol, which offers a dramatic view of the Mall and monuments below and can accommodate more guests than the east side, where most previous presidents took the oath of office.

Construction of the new **Capitol Visitor Center,** a three-story subterranean education and information area beneath the east side of the building that is scheduled to open in 2005, may affect your visit to the Capitol. The Capitol will remain open, but visitors should expect a changing series of detours as sidewalks and roads are periodically closed. ⊠ *East end of Mall,* ☎ *202/224–3121 Capitol switchboard; 202/225–6827 guide service,* ᴡᴇʙ *www.aoc.gov, www.senate.gov, www.house.gov.* ⊡ *Free.* ☉ *Sept.–Feb., daily 9–4:30; Mar.–Aug., daily 9–8. Metro: Capitol South or Union Station.*

NEED A
BREAK?
A meal at a **Capitol cafeteria** may give you a glimpse of a well-known politician or two. A public dining room on the first floor, Senate side (north side), is open weekdays 11:30 AM–2:30 PM. A favorite with legis-

lators is the Senate bean soup, served every day since 1901 (no one is sure exactly why, though the menu, which you can take with you, outlines a few popular theories).

Congressional Cemetery. Established in 1807 "for all denomination of people," the Congressional Cemetery was the first national cemetery created by the government. Notables buried here include U.S. Capitol architect William Thornton, Marine Corps march composer John Philip Sousa, Civil War photographer Mathew Brady, and FBI director J. Edgar Hoover. There are also 76 members of Congress, many of them beneath ponderous markers. A brochure for a self-guided walking tour is available at the office. ⊠ *1801 E St. SE,* ☎ *202/543–0539,* WEB *www.geocities.com/Heartland/Meadows/4633.* ☉ *Daily dawn–dusk; office Mon.–Wed. and Fri.–Sat. 9:30–2:30. Metro: Stadium Armory or Potomac Avenue.*

⑮ Folger Shakespeare Library. The Folger Library's collection of works by and about Shakespeare and his times is second to none. The white-marble art deco building, designed by architect Paul Philippe Cret, is decorated with scenes from the Bard's plays. Inside is a reproduction of an inn-yard theater—the setting for performances of chamber music, baroque opera, and other events appropriate to the surroundings—and a gallery, designed in the manner of an Elizabethan Great Hall, which hosts rotating exhibits from the library's collection. ⊠ *201 E. Capitol St. SE,* ☎ *202/544–4600,* WEB *www.folger.edu.* ⊠ *Free.* ☉ *Mon.–Sat. 10–4. Metro: Capitol South.*

OFF THE
BEATEN PATH

FRANCISCAN MONASTERY AND GARDENS – Not far from the National Shrine of the Immaculate Conception, the Byzantine-style Franciscan monastery contains facsimiles of such Holy Land shrines as the Grotto of Bethlehem and the Holy Sepulchre. Underground are reproductions of the catacombs of Rome. The rose gardens are especially beautiful. Take the Metro here from Union Station. The monastery and shrine are about the same distance from the metro, but in opposite directions. ⊠ *14th and Quincy Sts. NE,* ☎ *202/526–6800,* WEB *www.pressroom.com/ ~Franciscan.* ⊠ *Free.* ☉ *Daily 9–5; catacombs tour on the hr (except noon) Mon.–Sat. 9–4, Sun. 1–4. Metro: Brookland/Catholic University.*

Glenwood Cemetery. Not far from Catholic University, Glenwood has its share of notable residents, including the artists Constantino Brumidi, responsible for much of the Capitol building's beauty (among other things, he painted the frescoes adorning the inside of the great dome), and Emanuel Leutze, painter of *Washington Crossing the Delaware,* one of the most famous paintings in American history. More striking are the tombstones of two more-obscure citizens: Benjamin Greenup was the first firefighter killed on duty in Washington, and he's honored with an obelisk carved with his death scene. Teresina Vasco, a child who died at age two after playing with matches, is immortalized sitting in her favorite rocking chair. ⊠ *2219 Lincoln Rd. NE,* ☎ *202/667–1016.* ☉ *Daily dawn–dusk; office weekdays 9:30– 3:30. Metro: Brookland/Catholic University.*

❼ Grant Memorial. The 252-ft-long memorial to the 18th American president and commander in chief of the Union forces during the Civil War is one of the largest sculpture groups in the city. The pedestal statue of Ulysses S. Grant on horseback displays his composure in the face of chaos. The soldiers and horses are notable for their realism; sculptor Henry Shrady spent 20 years researching and completing the memorial. ⊠ *Near 1st St. and Maryland Ave. SW. Metro: Federal Center.*

⑧ James Garfield Memorial. Near the Grant Memorial and the United States Botanic Garden is a memorial to the 20th president of the United States. James Garfield was assassinated in 1881 after only a few months in office. His bronze statue stands on a pedestal with three other bronze figures seated around it; one bears a tablet inscribed with the words "Law," "Justice," and "Prosperity," which the figures presumably represent. Garfield's two primary claims to fame were that he was the last log-cabin president and that his was the second presidential assassination (Lincoln's was first), ending the second-shortest presidency (the shortest was William Henry Harrison's, who died less than a month into his term in office from a cold that developed into pneumonia). ⊠ *1st St. and Maryland Ave. SW. Metro: Federal Center.*

OFF THE
BEATEN PATH

KENILWORTH AQUATIC GARDENS – Exotic water lilies, lotuses, hyacinths, and other water-loving plants thrive in this 14-acre sanctuary of quiet ponds and marshy flats. The gardens are home to a variety of wetland animals, including turtles, frogs, beavers, spring azure butterflies, and some 40 species of birds. In July nearly everything blossoms; early morning is the best time to visit, when day-bloomers are just opening and night-bloomers have yet to close. ⊠ *Anacostia Ave. and Douglas St. SE,* ☎ *202/426–6905,* WEB *www.nps.gov/nace/keaq.* ☜ *Free.* ☉ *Gardens daily 6:30–4; visitor center daily 8–4.*

⑪ Library of Congress, Jefferson Building. One of the world's largest libraries, the Library of Congress contains some 115 million items, of which only a quarter are books. The remainder includes manuscripts, prints, films, photographs, sheet music, and the largest collection of maps in the world. Also part of the library is the Congressional Research Service, which, as the name implies, works on special projects for senators and representatives.

The copper-domed Thomas Jefferson Building is the oldest of the three buildings that make up the library. Like many other structures in Washington that seem a bit overwrought, the library was criticized when it was completed, in 1897. Detractors felt its design, based on the Paris Opera House, was too florid. Congressmen were even heard to grumble that its dome—topped with the gilt "Flame of Knowledge"—competed with that of their Capitol. It's certainly decorative, with busts of Dante, Johann Wolfgang von Goethe, Nathaniel Hawthorne, and other great writers perched above its entryway. The *Court of Neptune,* Roland Hinton Perry's fountain at the base of the front steps, rivals some of Rome's best fountains.

Provisions for a library to serve members of Congress were originally made in 1800, when the government set aside $5,000 to purchase and house books that legislators might need to consult. This small collection was housed in the Capitol but was destroyed in 1814, when the British burned the city. Thomas Jefferson, then in retirement at Monticello, offered his personal library as a replacement, noting that "there is, in fact, no subject to which a Member of Congress may not have occasion to refer." Jefferson's collection of 6,487 books, for which Congress eventually paid him $23,950, laid the foundation for the great national library. (Sadly, another fire in 1851 destroyed two-thirds of Jefferson's books.) By the late 1800s it was clear the Capitol could no longer contain the growing library, and the Jefferson Building was constructed. The **Adams Building,** on 2nd Street behind the Jefferson, was added in 1939. A third structure, the **James Madison Building,** opened in 1980; it's just south of the Jefferson Building, between Independence Avenue and C Street. Though not as interesting architecturally as the Jefferson building, evening literary readings, small exhibitions, and an interesting gift shop draw visitors here. The U.S. Copyright Office, in Room 401, is where all copyright registrations are issued.

The recently renovated Jefferson Building opens into the Great Hall, richly adorned with mosaics, paintings, and curving marble stairways. The grand, octagonal Main Reading Room, its central desk surrounded by mahogany readers' tables under a 160-ft-high domed ceiling, is either inspiring or overwhelming to researchers. Computer terminals have replaced the wood card catalogs, but books are still retrieved and dispersed the same way: readers (18 years or older) hand request slips to librarians and wait patiently for their materials to be delivered. Researchers aren't allowed in the stacks, and only members of Congress and other special borrowers can check books out.

But books are only part of the story. Family trees are explored in the Local History and Genealogy Reading Room. In the Folklife Reading Room, researchers can listen to LP recordings of American Indian music or hear the story of B'rer Rabbit read in the Gullah dialect of coastal Georgia and South Carolina. Items from the library's collection—which includes one of only three perfect Gutenberg Bibles in the world—are on display in the Jefferson Building's second-floor Southwest Gallery and Pavilion. ⊠ *Jefferson Bldg., 1st St. and Independence Ave. SE,* ☎ *202/707–4604 taped exhibit information; 202/707–5000 Library of Congress operator; 202/707–6400 taped schedule of general and Reading Room hrs,* WEB *www.loc.gov.* ⊠ *Free.* ☉ *Mon.–Sat. 10–5:30. Tours Mon.–Sat. at 11:30, 1, 2:30, and 4 leave from the Great Hall. Metro: Capitol South.*

NEED A BREAK? It's easy to grab a bite near the Library of Congress. The sixth-floor dining halls of the library's **Madison Building** offer great views and inexpensive fare. Or head for the south side of Pennsylvania Avenue SE, between 2nd and 4th streets, which is lined with restaurants and bars frequented by those who live and work on the Hill. **Le Bon Café** (⊠ 210 2nd St. SE, ☎ 202/547-7200), is a cozy French bistro that serves excellent coffees, pastries, and light lunches.

Marine Corps Barracks and Commandant's House. The Marine Corps Barracks is the nation's oldest continuously active Marine installation and home of the Marine Band. The Commandant's House has status—to Marines—equivalent to that of the White House. On Friday nights from May to August, visitors are allowed on the Marine Barracks' parade deck for an hour-long concert by the U.S. Marine Band (the "President's Own") and the Drum and Bugle Corps (the "Commandant's Own"). For entry to the grounds at other times, make an advance reservation for a tour. ⊠ *8th and I streets SE,* ☎ *202/433–4172,* WEB *www.mbw.usmc.mil.* ⊠ *Free.* ☉ *Public concerts May–Aug., 8 PM. Tours Mon.–Thurs. 10 AM and 1 PM by advance telephone reservation only. Metro: Eastern Market.*

National Postal Museum. This museum is home to, among other things, the Smithsonian's priceless stamp collection, consisting of a whopping 11 million stamps. Exhibits underscore the important part the mail has played in the development of America and include horse-drawn mail coaches, railway mail cars, airmail planes, and a collection of philatelic rarities. The National Museum of Natural History may have the Hope Diamond, but the National Postal Museum has the container used to mail the priceless gem to the Smithsonian. The family-oriented museum has more than 40 interactive and touch-screen exhibits. The museum takes up only a portion of what is the old Washington City Post Office, designed by Daniel Burnham and completed in 1914. Nostalgic odes to the noble mail carrier are inscribed on the exterior of the marble building; one of them eulogizes the "Messenger of sympathy and love, servant of parted friends, consoler of the lonely, bond of the scattered family, enlarger of the common life." ✉ *2 Massachusetts Ave. NE,* ☎ *202/357–2700; 202/357–1729 TDD,* WEB *www.si.edu/postal.* 🎟 *Free.* ☉ *Daily 10–5:30. Metro: Union Station.*

OFF THE BEATEN PATH

NATIONAL SHRINE OF THE IMMACULATE CONCEPTION – The largest Catholic church in the United States, the National Shrine of the Immaculate Conception was begun in 1920 and built with funds contributed by every parish in the country. Dedicated in 1959, the shrine is a blend of Romanesque and Byzantine styles, with a bell tower that reminds many of St. Mark's in Venice. Take the Metro here from Union Station; the shrine is about a half mile from the station, half-way to the Pope John Paul II Cultural Center. ✉ *Michigan Ave. and 4th St. NE,* ☎ *202/526–8300,* WEB *www.nationalshrine.com.* ☉ *Apr.–Oct., daily 7–7; Nov.–Mar., daily 7–6; Sat. vigil mass at 5:15; Sun. mass at 7:30, 9, 10:30, noon, 1:30 (in Latin), and 4:30. Metro: Brookland/Catholic University.*

6 **Peace Monument.** A white-marble memorial depicts America in the form of a woman grief-stricken over sailors lost at sea during the Civil War; she is weeping on the shoulder of a second female figure representing History. The plaque inscription refers movingly to Navy personnel who "fell in defence of the union and liberty of their country 1861–1865." ✉ *Traffic circle at 1st St. NW and Pennsylvania Ave. Metro: Union Station.*

Pope John Paul II Cultural Center. Part museum, part shrine, part place of pilgrimage, the Pope John Paul II Cultural Center is a spectacular architectural embodiment of the Roman Catholic church's desire to celebrate its charismatic leader and its rich artistic tradition. Themes covered include church and papal history, representations of the Blessed Virgin Mary, Polish heritage, and the Catholic tradition of community activism. These are explored through traditional displays of art and artifacts as well as with audio-visual presentations and interactive computer stations. The center is about a mile from the Metro and can easily be combined with a visit to the National Shrine of the Immaculate Conception. ✉ *3900 Harewood Rd., NE,* ☎ *202/635–5400,* WEB *www.jp2culturalcenter.org.* 🎟 *$8.* ☉ *Tues.–Sat 10–5, Sun. 12–5. Metro: Brookland/Catholic University.*

4 **Robert A. Taft Memorial.** Rising above the trees in the triangle formed by Louisiana, New Jersey, and Constitution avenues, a monolithic carillon pays tribute to the longtime Republican senator and son of the 27th president. ✉ *Constitution and New Jersey Aves. NW. Metro: Union Station.*

Rock Creek Cemetery. Rock Creek, the city's oldest cemetery, is administered by the city's oldest church, St. Paul's Episcopal, which erected its first building in 1775. (What remains of the original structure is a single brick wall.) Many beautiful and imposing monuments are in the cemetery. The best known and most moving honors Marion Hooper "Clover" Adams, wife of historian Henry Adams; she committed suicide in 1885. Sculptor Augustus Saint-Gaudens created the enigmatic figure of a seated, shroud-draped woman, calling it *The Peace of God that Passeth Understanding,* though it's best known by the nickname "Grief." It's thought by many to be the most moving sculpture in the city. ✉ *Rock Creek Church Rd. and Webster St. NW,* ☎ *202/829–0585.* ☉ *Daily 7:30–dusk.*

⑬ Sewall-Belmont House. Built in 1800 by Robert Sewall, this is one of the oldest homes on Capitol Hill. Today it's the headquarters of the National Woman's Party and contains a museum that chronicles the early days of the women's movement and the history of the house as well as a library that's open to researchers by appointment. The house is filled with period furniture and portraits and busts of such suffrage-movement leaders as Lucretia Mott, Elizabeth Cady Stanton, and Alice Paul, who wrote the Equal Rights Amendment in 1923. From 1801 to 1813 Secretary of the Treasury Albert Gallatin, who finalized the details of the Louisiana Purchase in his front-parlor office, lived here. This building was the only private house the British set fire to in Washington during their invasion of 1814, after a citizen fired on advancing British troops from an upper-story window (a fact later documented by the offending British general's sworn testimony, 30 years later, on behalf of Sewalls in their attempt to secure war reparations from the U.S. government). This was, in fact, the only armed resistance the British met that day. ⊠ *144 Constitution Ave. NE,* ☎ *202/546–3989,* WEB *www.natwomanparty.org.* ⌑ *Free.* ☉ *Jan.–Feb. and Apr.–Oct., Tues.–Fri. 10–3, Sat. noon–4; Mar. and Nov.–Dec., Tues.–Fri. 10–3, Sat. noon–4, Sun. 1–4. Metro: Union Station.*

⑭ South Side of East Capitol Street. Walk along East Capitol Street, the border between the northeast and southeast quadrants of the city, for a sample of the residential area of the Hill. The house on the corner of East Capitol Street, No. 329, has a striking tower with a bay window and stained glass. Next door are two Victorian houses with iron trim below the second floor. A pre–Civil War Greek Revival frame house sits behind a tidy garden at No. 317. ⊠ *Between 3rd and 4th Sts. SE. Metro: Capitol South or Union Station.*

⑫ Supreme Court Building. It wasn't until 1935 that the Supreme Court got its own building: a white-marble temple with twin rows of Corinthian columns designed by Cass Gilbert. In 1800, the justices arrived in Washington along with the rest of the government but were for years shunted around various rooms in the Capitol; for a while they even met in a tavern. William Howard Taft, the only man to serve as both president and chief justice, was instrumental in getting the court a home of its own, though he died before it was completed.

The Supreme Court convenes on the first Monday in October and remains in session until it has heard all of its cases and handed down all of its decisions (usually the end of June). On Monday through Wednesday of two weeks in each month, the justices hear oral arguments in the velvet-swathed court chamber. Visitors who want to listen can choose to wait in either of two lines. One, the "three-to-five-minute" line, shuttles visitors through, giving them a quick impression of the court at work. If you choose the other, and you'd like to stay for the whole show, it's best to be in line by 8:30 AM. The main hall of the Supreme Court is lined with busts of former chief justices; the courtroom itself is decorated with allegorical friezes. Perhaps the most interesting appurtenance in the imposing building, however, is a basketball court on one of the upper floors (it's been called the highest court in the land). ⊠ *1st and E. Capitol Sts. NE,* ☎ *202/479–3000,* WEB *www.supremecourtus.gov.* ⌑ *Free.* ☉ *Weekdays 9–4:30. Metro: Capitol South.*

❸ Thurgood Marshall Federal Judiciary Building. If you're in the Union Station neighborhood, it's worth taking a moment to pop inside the signature work of architect Edward Larabee Barnes for a look at its spectacular atrium with a garden of bamboo five stories tall. ⊠ *Massachusetts Ave. opposite Union Station. Metro: Union Station.*

❶ Union Station. With its 96-ft-high coffered ceiling gilded with 8 pounds of gold leaf, the city's train station is one of the capital's great spaces and is used for inaugural balls and other festive events. In 1902 the McMillan Commission—charged with suggesting ways to improve the appearance of the city—recommended that the many train lines that sliced through the capital share one main depot. Union Station was opened in 1908 and was the first building completed under the commission's plan. Chicago architect and commission member Daniel H. Burnham patterned the station after the Roman Baths of Diocletian.

For many visitors to Washington, the capital city is first seen framed through the grand station's arched doorways. In its heyday, during World War II, more than 200,000 people swarmed through the building daily. By the '60s, however, the decline in train travel had turned the station into an expensive white-marble elephant. It was briefly, and unsuccessfully, transformed into a visitor center for the Bicentennial; but by 1981 rain was pouring in through its neglected roof, and passengers boarded trains at a ramshackle depot behind the station.

The Union Station you see today is the result of a restoration, completed in 1988, intended to begin a revival of Washington's east end. Between train travelers and visitors to the shops, restaurants, and a nine-screen movie theater, 70,000 people a day pass through the beaux arts building. The jewel of the structure is its main waiting room. Forty-six statues of Roman legionnaires, one for each state in the Union when the station was completed, ring the grand room. The statues were the subject of controversy when the building was first opened. Pennsylvania Railroad president Alexander Cassatt (brother of artist Mary) ordered sculptor Louis Saint-Gaudens (brother of sculptor Augustus) to alter the statues, convinced that the legionnaires' skimpy outfits would upset female passengers. The sculptor obligingly added a shield to each figure, obscuring any offending body parts.

The east hall, now filled with vendors, is decorated with Pompeiian-style tracery and plaster walls and columns painted to look like marble. At one time the station also had a secure presidential waiting room, now restored. This room was by no means frivolous: 20 years before Union Station was built, President Garfield was assassinated in the public waiting room of the old Baltimore and Potomac terminal on 6th Street.

The **Columbus Memorial Fountain,** designed by Lorado Taft, sits in the plaza in front of Union Station. A caped, steely-eyed Christopher Columbus stares into the distance, flanked by a hoary, bearded figure (the Old World) and an Indian brave (the New). ✉ *Massachusetts Ave., north of Capitol,* ☎ *202/289–1908,* WEB *www.unionstationdc.com.* Metro: *Union Station.*

NEED A
BREAK?
On Union Station's lower level are more than 20 food stalls offering everything from pizza to sushi. There are several restaurants throughout the station, the largest of which is **America** (☎ 202/682–9555), with a menu of regional foods that lives up to its expansive name. The two-level **Center Cafe,** in the main hall of Union Station, is a perfect spot for people-watching.

❾ United States Botanic Garden. This peaceful, plant-filled oasis, established by Congress in 1820, is the oldest botanic garden in North America. The conservatory, in the process of a complete renovation, is scheduled to reopen in Fall 2001 with replantings including the Palm House—which has the look of an abandoned plantation being reclaimed by nature—and the Garden Primeval, which re-creates the landscape of nonflowering plants that prevailed when dinosaurs walked the earth. With equal attention paid to science and aesthetics, the Botanic Garden contains plants from all around the world with an emphasis on tropical and economically useful plants, desert plants, and orchids. On a three-acre plot immediately to the west, the new **National Garden** is being constructed and is scheduled to open in 2005. ✉ *1st St. and Maryland Ave. SW,* ☎ *202/225–8333,* WEB *www.aoc.gov.* 🎫 *Free.* ⏲ *Daily 9–5. Metro: Federal Center SW.*

OFF THE BEATEN PATH

UNITED STATES NATIONAL ARBORETUM – During azalea season (mid-April through May), this 444-acre oasis is a blaze of color. In early summer, clematis, peonies, rhododendrons, and roses bloom. At any time of year, the 22 original Corinthian columns from the U.S. Capitol reerected here in 1990 are striking. The arboretum is ideal for a relaxing stroll or scenic drive. The **National Herb Garden** and the **National Bonsai Collection** are also here. ✉ *3501 New York Ave. NE,* ☎ *202/245–2726,* WEB *www.usna.usda.gov.* 🎫 *Free.* ⏲ *Arboretum and herb garden daily 8–5; bonsai collection daily 10–3:30.*

Washington Navy Yard. A 115-acre historic district with its own street system, the Washington Navy Yard is the Navy's oldest outpost on shore. Established in 1799 as a shipbuilding facility and converted to weapons production by the mid 19th century, it gradually fell into disuse over the next hundred years. In the early '60s the Navy Yard was revived as an administrative center. The **Navy Art Museum** (☎ 202/433–4882 Navy Museum; 202/433–3377 USS *Barry*, WEB www.history.navy.mil) in Building 76 chronicles the history of the U.S. Navy from the Revolution to the present. Exhibits range from the fully rigged foremast of the USS *Constitution* (better known as "Old Ironsides") to a U.S. Navy Corsair fighter plane dangling from the ceiling. All around are models of fighting ships, displays on battles, and portraits of the sailors who fought them. Children especially enjoy peering through the operating periscopes and pretending to launch torpedoes at the decommissioned U.S. Navy destroyer *Barry*, floating a few hundred yards away in the Anacostia River. In front of the museum is a collection of guns, cannons, and missiles. Call ahead to schedule a free weekday highlights tour. Hours for the Navy Museum are September through April, weekdays 9–4 and weekends 10–5; from May through August, weekdays 9–5 and weekends 10–5. The USS *Barry* is open daily from 10–4.The **Navy Art Gallery** (☎ 202/433–3815, WEB www.history.navy.mil), in Building 67, exhibits navy-related paintings, sketches, and drawings, many created during combat by navy artists, in a two-room gallery. The bulk of the collection illustrates World War II. Hours for the Navy Art Gallery are Wednesday through Friday from 9–4 and weekends 10–4. The **Marine Corps Museum** (☎ 202/433–3840, WEB www.hqmc.usmc.mil), within the Marine Corps Historical Center in Building 58, tells the story of the corps from its inception in 1775 to its role in Desert Storm. A variety of artifacts—uniforms, weapons, documents, photographs—outlines the growth of the corps, including its embrace of amphibious assault and the strategy of "vertical envelopment" (helicopters, to you and me). The Marine Corps Museum is open from September through April, Monday and Wednesday–Saturday 10–4, Sunday noon–5; from May through August, hours are Monday, Wednesday–Thursday, and Saturday 10–4, Friday 10–8, and Sunday noon–5. ✉ *Main Gate, 9th and M Sts. SE.* 🎫 *Free. Metro: Eastern Market.*

OLD DOWNTOWN AND FEDERAL TRIANGLE

Revised by
Maureen
Graney

Just because Washington is a planned city doesn't mean the plan was executed flawlessly. Pierre-Charles L'Enfant's design has been alternately shelved and rediscovered several times in the past 200 years. Nowhere have the city's imperfections been more visible than on L'Enfant's grand thoroughfare, Pennsylvania Avenue. By the early '60s it had become a national disgrace; the dilapidated buildings that lined it were home to pawn shops and cheap souvenir stores. While riding up Pennsylvania Avenue in his inaugural parade, a disgusted John F. Kennedy is said to have turned to an aide and said, "Fix it!" Washington's downtown—once within the diamond formed by Massachusetts, Louisiana, Pennsylvania, and New York avenues—had its problems, too, many the result of riots that rocked the capital in 1968 after the assassination of Martin Luther King, Jr. In their wake, many businesses left the area and moved north of the White House.

In recent years developers have rediscovered "old downtown," and buildings are now being torn down or remodeled at an amazing pace. After several false starts, Pennsylvania Avenue is shining once again. This walk explores the old downtown section of the city, then swings around to check the progress on the monumental street that links the Congress House—the Capitol—with the President's House. (Note: where E Street meets Pennsylvania Avenue, the intersection creates an odd one-block stretch that looks like Pennsylvania Avenue but is technically E Street. Buildings usually choose to associate themselves with the more prestigious-sounding "Pennsylvania Avenue" rather than "E Street.")

Numbers in the text correspond to numbers in the margin and on the Old Downtown and Federal Triangle map.

A Good Walk

Start at the redbrick **National Building Museum** ①, formerly known as the Pension Building, at 4th and F streets, one of the city's great spaces and the site of inaugural balls for more than 100 years. Across F Street from the National Building Museum is Judiciary Square, where city and federal courthouses, as well as the **National Law Enforcement Officers Memorial** ②—dedicated to police officers killed in the line of duty—are located. Walk over to 6th Street and up to H Street to Washington's tiny Chinatown, home to the **Surratt Boarding House** ③, a meeting place for the assassins of Abraham Lincoln. The **Friendship Arch** ④ spans H Street at 7th Street and marks the entrance to Chinatown. To the west, at 9th and H streets, is the Washington Convention Center.

Continue west on H Street and right on 13th Street to the **National Museum of Women in the Arts** ⑤, with exhibits dating from the Renaissance to the present. Across the street is the InterAmerican Development Bank Cultural Center, with changing exhibits by artists from member countries in Latin America and the Caribbean. Walking south to 12th and G streets, you pass Hecht's, the downtown area's remaining major department store. The city's largest public library, the **Martin Luther King Memorial Library** ⑥, is at 9th and G streets. Two of the Smithsonian's non-Mall museums, the National Portrait Gallery on the south and the Smithsonian American Art Museum on the north, are catercorner to the library in the **Old Patent Office Building** ⑦; due to major renovation of the building, both museums are closed through 2004. Just across the F Street pedestrian mall and to the left is the Tariff Commission Building. The stretch of F Street west of here, once a

Old Downtown and Federal Triangle

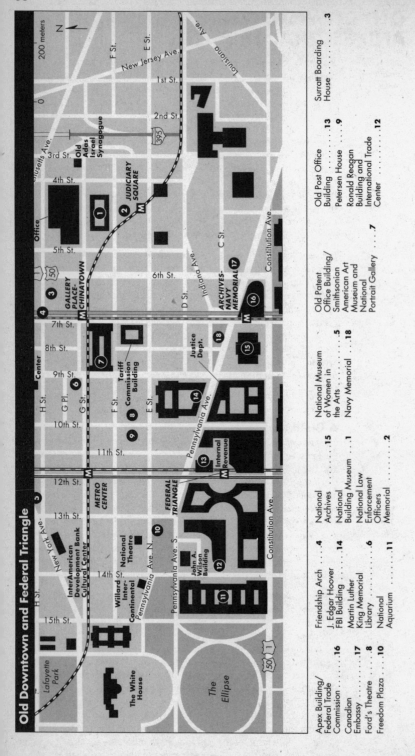

Apex Building/
Federal Trade
Commission **16**
Canadian
Embassy **17**
Ford's Theatre **8**
Freedom Plaza **10**

Friendship Arch **4**
J. Edgar Hoover
FBI Building **14**
Martin Luther
King Memorial
Library **6**
National
Aquarium **11**

National
Archives **15**
National
Building Museum . . .**1**
National Law
Enforcement
Officers
Memorial **2**

National Museum
of Women in
the Arts **5**
Navy Memorial . . .**18**

Old Patent
Office Building/
Smithsonian
American Art
Museum and
National
Portrait Gallery **7**

Old Post Office
Building **13**
Petersen House **9**
Ronald Reagan
Building and
International Trade
Center **12**

Surratt Boarding
House **3**

main shopping area, is now dotted with discount electronics stores, vacant shops and offices, and street vendors.

Turn left off F Street onto 10th Street to **Ford's Theatre** ⑧, where Abraham Lincoln was shot. The place where he died, the **Petersen House** ⑨, is across the street. Follow Pennsylvania Avenue three blocks west to **Freedom Plaza** ⑩, with its statue of Revolutionary War hero General Casimir Pulaski. Across E Street from the plaza is Washington's oldest stage, the National Theatre.

The cluster of limestone government buildings south of Freedom Plaza between 15th Street, Pennsylvania Avenue, and Constitution Avenue is Federal Triangle. The triangle includes, from west to east, the Department of Commerce Building, home of the **National Aquarium** ⑪; the John A. Wilson Building; the **Ronald Reagan Building and International Trade Center** ⑫; the **Old Post Office Building** ⑬; the Internal Revenue Service Building; the Department of Justice (the **J. Edgar Hoover Federal Bureau of Investigation Building** ⑭ is across Pennsylvania Avenue and not actually part of the Federal Triangle); the **National Archives** ⑮; and the **Apex Building** ⑯, home of the Federal Trade Commission. The white-stone-and-glass building across Pennsylvania Avenue is the **Canadian Embassy** ⑰. The intersection of 7th Street and Pennsylvania and Indiana avenues has numerous statues and memorials and a fountain. Across 7th Street, near the General Winfield Scott memorial, is the **Navy Memorial** ⑱, consisting of a huge map carved into the plaza and a statue of a lone sailor.

TIMING

Although many of the attractions on this walk are places you look at rather than enter, it's still an all-day affair, especially if you plan to tour the FBI headquarters, where there's usually a three- to four-hour wait. If the popularity of the FBI tour is any indication, most people are glad they stuck it out. You may or may not think the best time to visit the National Aquarium is for the shark feedings (Monday, Wednesday, and Saturday at 2), piranha feedings (Tuesday, Thursday, and Sunday at 2), or alligator feedings (Friday at 2) when the frenzy inside the tanks often seems well matched by that of the crowds jockeying to see the action.

Sights to See

OFF THE
BEATEN PATH

ANACOSTIA MUSEUM AND CENTER FOR AFRICAN AMERICAN HISTORY AND CULTURE – The richness of African-American culture is on display in this Smithsonian museum in southeast Washington's historic Anacostia neighborhood. After a year-long renovation and expansion (the museum was scheduled to reopen late in 2001), exhibitions for the year 2002 will feature highlights of prominent private collections in the Washington, D.C. area—art, artifacts, and historical items. Past exhibits have covered black inventors and aviators, the influential role of black churches, the history of the civil rights movement, African-American life in the antebellum South, and the beauty of African-American quilts. ⊠ *1901 Fort Pl. SE*, ☏ *202/287–3369*, WEB *www.si.edu/anacostia*. ⊡ *Free.* ☉ *Daily 10–5. Metro: Navy Yard.*

⑯ **Apex Building.** The triangular Apex Building, completed in 1938, is the home of the Federal Trade Commission. Adorning the building is a carving that depicts aspects of trade. The relief decorations over the doorways on the Constitution Avenue side depict agriculture (the harvesting of grain, by Concetta Scaravaglione) and trade (two men bartering over an ivory tusk, by Carl Schmitz). Two heroic statues by Michael Lantz on either side of the rounded eastern portico, each depicting a muscular, shirtless workman wrestling with a wild horse, represent man controlling trade. Just across 6th Street is a three-tier fountain decorated with the signs of the zodiac; it's a memorial to Andrew Mellon, who, as secretary of the treasury, oversaw construction of the $125 million Federal Triangle (and who, as a deep-pocketed philanthropist, was the driving force behind the National Gallery of Art, just across Constitution Avenue). ⊠ *7th St. and Pennsylvania Ave. NW. Metro: Archives/Navy Memorial.*

⓱ Canadian Embassy. A spectacular edifice constructed of stone and glass, the Canadian Embassy was designed by Arthur Erickson and completed in 1988. The columns of the rotunda represent Canada's 12 provinces and territories. Inside, a gallery periodically displays exhibits on Canadian culture and history. ⊠ *501 Pennsylvania Ave. NW,* ☎ *202/682–1740,* WEB *www.canadianembassy.org.* ☒ *Free.* ☉ *Weekdays 10–5 during exhibitions only. Metro: Archives/Navy Memorial.*

Chinatown. If you don't notice you're entering Washington's compact Chinatown by the Chinese characters on the street signs, the ornate, **❹** 75-ft-wide **Friendship Arch** spanning H Street might clue you in. Although this neighborhood shows some early signs of revitalization, it's still somewhat down-at-the-heels—you'll find boarded-up buildings and graffiti-covered walls—but this is the place to go for Chinese food in the District. Cantonese, Szechuan, Hunan, and Mongolian are among the delectable culinary styles you'll find here. Nearly every restaurant has a roast duck hanging in the window, and the shops here sell a wide variety of Chinese goods. Most interesting are traditional pharmacies purveying folk medicines such as dried eels, powdered bones, and a variety of unusual herbs for teas and broths believed to promote health, longevity, and sexual potency. ⊠ *Bounded by G, H, 5th, and 8th Sts. Metro: Gallery Place/Chinatown.*

NEED A BREAK?

If the smells of Chinese cooking have activated your taste buds, try the highly rated **Mr. Yung's** (⊠ 740 6th St. NW), which specializes in Cantonese cuisine. If you're lucky enough to be in the neighborhood between 11 and 3, be sure to sample the addictively delicious bite-size appetizers known as dim sum, a traditional Chinese breakfast or lunch.

At **Planet Hollywood** (⊠ 1101 Pennsylvania Ave. NW, ☎ 202/783–7827) you can eat and drink surrounded by such Hollywood set pieces and costumes as Darth Vader's shiny black mask and a Klingon battle cruiser from the *Star Trek* movies. Meanwhile, film clips run on drop-down movie screens; the works of chain co-owners Bruce Willis and Arnold Schwarzenegger are, naturally, well represented.

Federal Triangle. To the south of Freedom Plaza, Federal Triangle consists of a mass of government buildings constructed between 1929 and 1938. Notable are the Department of Commerce (with the National Aquarium inside), the District Building, the Old Post Office Building, the Internal Revenue Service Building, the Department of Justice, the National Archives, and the Apex Building, which houses the Federal Trade Commission.

Before Federal Triangle was developed, government workers were scattered throughout the city, largely in rented offices. Looking for a place to consolidate this workforce, city planners hit on the area south of Pennsylvania Avenue known, at the time, as "Murder Bay," a notorious collection of rooming houses, taverns, tattoo parlors, and brothels. A uniform classical architectural style, with Italianate red-tile roofs and interior plazas reminiscent of the Louvre, was chosen for the building project. Federal Triangle's planners envisioned interior courts filled with plazas and parks, but the needs of the motorcar foiled any such grand plans. ⊠ *15th St. and Pennsylvania and Constitution Aves. Metro: Federal Triangle.*

☝ ❽ **Ford's Theatre.** In 1859, Baltimore theater impresario John T. Ford leased the First Baptist Church building that stood on this site and turned it into a successful music hall. The building burned down late in 1863, and Ford built a new structure on the same spot. The events of April 14, 1865, would shock the nation and close the theater. On that night, during a performance of *Our American Cousin,* John Wilkes Booth entered the state box and assassinated Abraham Lincoln. The stricken president was carried across the street to the house of tailor William Petersen. Charles Augustus Leale, a 23-year-old surgeon, was the first man to attend to the president. To let Lincoln know that someone was nearby, Leale held his hand throughout the night. Lincoln died the next morning.

The federal government bought Ford's Theatre in 1866 for $100,000 and converted it into office space. It was remodeled as a Lincoln museum in 1932 and was restored to its 1865 appearance in 1968. The basement museum—with artifacts such as Booth's pistol and the clothes Lincoln was wearing when he was shot—reopened in 1990. The theater itself continues to present a complete schedule of plays. *A Christmas Carol* is an annual holiday favorite. ⊠ *511 10th St. NW,* ☎ *202/ 426–6924,* WEB *www.nps.gov/foth.* ⊠ *Free.* ☉ *Daily 9–5; theater closed when rehearsals or matinees are in progress (generally Thurs. and weekends); Lincoln museum in basement remains open at these times. Metro: Metro Center or Gallery Place.*

OFF THE BEATEN PATH	**FREDERICK DOUGLASS NATIONAL HISTORIC SITE –** Cedar Hill, the Anacostia home of abolitionist Frederick Douglass, was the first place designated by Congress as a Black National Historic Site. Douglass, a former slave who delivered rousing abolitionist speeches at home and abroad, resided here from 1877 until his death in 1895. The house has a wonderful view of the Federal City across the Anacostia River and contains many of Douglass's personal belongings. A short film on his life is shown at a nearby visitor center. Reservations are required for tours. ⊠ *1411 W St. SE,* ☎ *202/426–5961 or 800/967–2283 for tour reservations,* WEB *www.nps.gov/fdro.* ⊠ *$3.* ☉ *Mid-Oct.–mid-Apr., daily 9–4 (last tour at 3); mid-Apr.–mid-Oct., daily 9–5 (last tour at 4); films on the hr; tours on the ½ hr (except noon). Metro: Anacostia, then take Bus B2 or U2.*

❿ **Freedom Plaza.** In 1988, Western Plaza was renamed Freedom Plaza in honor of Martin Luther King, Jr. Its east end is dominated by a statue of General Casimir Pulaski, the Polish nobleman who led an American cavalry corps during the Revolutionary War and was mortally wounded in 1779 at the Siege of Savannah. He gazes over a plaza inlaid in bronze with a detail from L'Enfant's original 1791 plan for the Federal City. Bronze outlines the President's Palace and the Congress House; the Mall is represented by a green lawn. Cut into the edges are quotations about the capital city, not all of them complimentary. To compare L'Enfant's vision with today's reality, stand in the middle of the map's Pennsylvania Avenue and look west. L'Enfant had planned an unbroken vista from the Capitol to the White House, but the Treasury Building, begun in 1836, ruined the view. Turning to the east, you'll see the U.S. Capitol sitting on Jenkins Hill like an American Taj Mahal.

There's a lot to see and explore in the blocks near Freedom Plaza. The beaux arts ☞ **Willard Inter-Continental** is on the corner of 14th Street and Pennsylvania Avenue NW. Just north of Freedom Plaza, on F Street between 13th and 14th streets, are The Shops, a collection of stores in the **National Press Building**, itself home to dozens of media organizations. The Shops' upstairs Food Hall has sit-down restaurants and fast-food places. Washington's oldest stage, the National Theatre, also overlooks the plaza. ⊠ *Bounded by 13th, 14th, and E Sts. and Pennsylvania Ave. Metro: Federal Triangle.*

InterAmerican Development Bank Cultural Center. Founded in 1959, the IADB is an international bank that finances economic and social development in Latin America and the Caribbean. Its small cultural center hosts changing exhibits of paintings, sculptures, and artifacts from member countries. It's across the street from the National Museum of Women in the Arts. ⊠ *1300 New York Ave. NW,* ☎ *202/623–3774,* WEB *www.iadb.org.* 🎟 *Free.* ⊙ *Weekdays 11–6. Metro: Metro Center.*

☜ ⑭ **J. Edgar Hoover Federal Bureau of Investigation Building.** The one-hour tour of the FBI building is one of the most popular activities in the city. A brief film outlines the bureau's work, and exhibits describe famous past cases and illustrate the FBI's fight against organized crime, terrorism, bank robbery, espionage, extortion, and other criminal activities. There's everything from gangster John Dillinger's death mask to a poster display of the 10 Most Wanted criminals. (Look carefully: two bad guys were apprehended as a result of tips from tour takers!) You'll also see the laboratories where the FBI painstakingly studies evidence. The high point of the tour comes at the end: an agent gives a live-ammo firearms demonstration in the indoor shooting range.

Although it overlooks Federal Triangle, the FBI building is on the wrong side of Pennsylvania Avenue to be part of it. (The main Department of Justice Building, however, *is* part of it; like the rest of Federal Triangle, this building is sprinkled with art deco details, including cylindrical aluminum torches outside the doorways and bas-relief figures of bison, dolphins, and birds.) A hulking presence on the avenue, the FBI building was decried from birth as hideous. Even Hoover himself is said to have called it the "ugliest building I've ever seen." Opened in 1974, it hangs over 9th Street like a poured-concrete Big Brother. One thing is certain—it's secure. At peak times there may be a three- to four-hour wait for a tour, so be prepared. ⊠ *10th St. and Pennsylvania Ave. NW (tour entrance on E St. NW),* ☎ *202/324–3447.* 🎟 *Free.* ⊙ *Weekdays 8:45–4:15; tours every 20 mins (line for tours can be closed on short notice when it gets crowded). Metro: Federal Triangle or Gallery Place/Chinatown.*

John A. Wilson Building. Renamed in honor of the late city council chairman, the beaux arts structure, formerly known as the District Building, was built in 1908 and listed on the National Register of Historic Places in 1972. ⊠ *Federal Triangle, 14th St. and Pennsylvania Ave. S,* WEB *www.fbi.gov. Metro: Federal Triangle.*

❻ **Martin Luther King Memorial Library.** The only D.C. building designed by Ludwig Mies van der Rohe, one of the founders of modern architecture, this squat black building at 9th and G streets is the largest public library in the city. A mural on the first floor depicts events in the life of the Nobel Prize–winning civil rights activist. Used books are almost always on sale at bargain prices in the library's gift shop. ⊠ *901 G St. NW,* ☎ *202/727–1111.* 🎟 *Free.* ⊙ *Mon.–Thurs. 10–9, Fri.–Sat. 10–5:30, Sun. 1–5. Metro: Gallery Place/Chinatown.*

☜ **MCI Center.** The Washington Wizards, Washington Mystics, and Georgetown Hoyas play basketball here, and the Washington Capitals call it home during hockey season. This is also the site of concerts and shows—including ice-skating extravaganzas and the circus. ⊠ *601 F*

St. NW (between 6th and 7th Sts.), ☎ *202/628–3200 MCI Center; 202/ 432–7328 Ticketmaster. Metro: Gallery Place/Chinatown.*

☞ ⑪ **National Aquarium.** The western base of Federal Triangle between 14th and 15th streets is the home of the Department of Commerce, charged with promoting U.S. economic development and technological advancement. When it opened in 1932 it was the world's largest government office building. It's a good thing there's plenty of space; incongruously, the National Aquarium is housed inside. Established in 1873, it's the country's oldest public aquarium, with more than 1,200 fish and other creatures—such as eels, sharks, and alligators—representing 270 species of fresh- and saltwater life. The exhibits have a somewhat dated look; but the easy-to-view tanks, accessible touching pool (with crabs and sea urchins), low admission fee, and general lack of crowds make this a good outing with children. ✉ *14th St. and Pennsylvania Ave. NW,* ☎ *202/482–2825.* ⊠ *$3 adults, 75¢ children.* ☉ *Daily 9–5 (last admission 4:30); sharks fed Mon., Wed., and Sat. at 2; piranhas fed Tues., Thurs., and Sun. at 2; alligators fed Fri. at 2. Metro: Federal Triangle.*

⑮ **National Archives.** If the Smithsonian Institution is the nation's attic, the Archives is the nation's basement, and it bears responsibility for important government documents and other items. The Declaration of Independence, the Constitution, and the Bill of Rights are on display in the building's rotunda, in a case made of bulletproof glass, equipped with green filters and filled with helium gas (to protect the irreplaceable documents). At night and on Christmas—the only day the Archives is closed—the cases and documents are lowered into a vault. Other objects in the Archives' vast collection include bureaucratic correspondence, veterans and immigration records, treaties, Richard Nixon's resignation letter, and the rifle Lee Harvey Oswald used to assassinate John F. Kennedy.

The Archives fills the area between 7th and 9th streets and Pennsylvania and Constitution avenues on Federal Triangle. Beside it is a small park with a modest memorial to Franklin Roosevelt. The desk-size piece of marble on the sliver of grass is exactly what the president asked for (though this hasn't stopped fans of the 32nd president from building a grand memorial at the Tidal Basin). Designed by John Russell Pope, the Archives was erected in 1935 on the site of the old Center Market. This large block had been a center of commerce since the early 1800s, when barges plying the City Canal (which flowed where Constitution Avenue is now) were loaded and unloaded here. A vestige of this mercantile past lives on in the name given to the two semicircular developments across Pennsylvania Avenue from the Archives—Market Square. Residential development is enlivening this stretch of Pennsylvania Avenue.

Turn right onto 9th Street and head to the Constitution Avenue side of the Archives. All the sculpture that adorns the building was carved on the site, including the two statues that flank the flight of steps facing the Mall, *Heritage* and *Guardianship,* by James Earle Fraser. Fraser also carved the scene on the pediment, which represents the transfer of historic documents to the recorder of the Archives. (Like nearly all pediment decorations in Washington, this one is bristling with electric wires designed to thwart the advances of destructive starlings.) Call at least three weeks in advance to arrange a behind-the-scenes tour. ✉ *Constitution Ave. between 7th and 9th Sts. NW,* ☎ *202/501–5000; 202/501–5205 tours,* 🄦🄴🄱 *www.nara.gov.* ⊠ *Free.* ☉ *Apr.–Labor Day, daily 10–9; Labor Day–Mar., daily 10–5:30; tours weekdays at 10:15 and 1:15. Metro: Archives/Navy Memorial.*

🖤 ❶ **National Building Museum.** The open interior of this mammoth red-brick edifice is one of the city's great spaces and has been the site of inaugural balls for more than 100 years. (The first ball was for Grover Cleveland in 1885; because the building wasn't finished at the time, a temporary wooden roof and floor were erected.) The eight central Corinthian columns are among the largest in the world, rising to a height of 75 ft. Although they look like marble, each is made of 70,000 bricks, covered with plaster and painted to resemble Siena marble. For years, this breathtaking hall has been the setting for the annual *Christmas in Washington* TV special.

Formerly known as the Pension Building, it was erected between 1882 and 1887 to house workers who processed the pension claims of veterans and their survivors, an activity that intensified after the Civil War. The architect was U.S. Army Corps of Engineers general Montgomery C. Meigs, who took as his inspiration the Italian Renaissance–style Palazzo Farnese in Rome. The museum is devoted to architecture and the building arts, with recent exhibits on office design, the many uses of wood, and designing Disney theme parks. There are also some hands-on displays here that are great for kids.

Before entering the building, walk down its F Street side. The terra-cotta frieze by Caspar Buberl between the first and second floors depicts soldiers marching and sailing in an endless procession around the building. Architect Meigs lost his oldest son in the Civil War, and, though the frieze depicts Union troops, he intended it as a memorial to all who were killed in the bloody war. Meigs designed the Pension Building with workers' comfort in mind long before anyone knew that cramped, stuffy offices could cause "sick building syndrome." Note the three "missing" bricks under each window that helped keep the building cool by allowing air to circulate. ✉ *401 F St. NW (between 4th and 5th Sts.),* ☎ *202/272–2448,* 🕸 *www.nbm.org.* 🎫 *Free.* ☉ *Mon.–Sat. 10–5, Sun. noon–5; tours Mon.–Weds. at 12:30, Thurs.–Sat. at 11:30, 12:30, and 1:30, Sun 12:30 and 1:30. Metro: Judiciary Square.*

❷ **National Law Enforcement Officers Memorial.** The National Law Enforcement Officers Memorial is a 3-ft-high wall that bears the names of more than 15,000 American police officers killed in the line of duty since 1792. On the third line of panel 13W are the names of six officers killed by William Bonney, better known as Billy the Kid. J. D. Tippit, the Dallas policeman killed by Lee Harvey Oswald, is honored on the ninth line of panel 63E. Given the dangerous nature of police work, it is one of the few memorials to which names will continue to be added. Two blocks away is a visitor center with exhibits on the history of the memorial and computers that allow you to look up officers by name, date of death, state, and department. A small shop sells souvenirs. Call to arrange for a free tour. ✉ *E St. between 4th and 5th Sts.; visitor center, 605 E St. NW,* ☎ *202/737–3400,* 🕸 *www.nleomf.com.* 🎫 *Free.* ☉ *Weekdays 9–5, Sat. 10–5, Sun. noon–5. Metro: Chinatown/Gallery Place.*

❺ **National Museum of Women in the Arts.** Works by female artists from the Renaissance to the present are showcased at this museum, which opened its permanent collection in 1987. The beautifully restored 1907 Renaissance Revival building was designed by Waddy Wood; ironically, it was once a men-only Masonic temple. In addition to displaying traveling shows, the museum has a permanent collection that includes paintings, drawings, sculpture, prints, and photographs by such artists as Georgia O'Keeffe, Mary Cassatt, Élisabeth Vigée-Lebrun, Frida Kahlo, and Camille Claudel. ✉ *1250 New York Ave. NW,* ☎ *202/783–5000,* 🕸 *www.nmwa.org.* 🎫 *Suggested donation $3.* ☉ *Mon.–Sat. 10–5, Sun. noon–5. Metro: Metro Center.*

National Portrait Gallery. This museum is in the ☞ Old Patent Office Building along with the Smithsonian American Art Museum. Unfortunately, a major renovation of the Old Patent Office Building, begun in January 2000, is set to last through 2004, and the gallery is closed. ✉ *8th and F Sts. NW,* ☎ *202/357–2700; 202/357–1729 TDD,* WEB *www. npg.si.edu.* ☼ *Closed during renovation. Metro: Gallery Place/ Chinatown.*

National Theatre. The National Theatre has been here since 1922, but it is the sixth theater on this spot since 1835—each of the other buildings burned down. After seeing her first play here at the age of six, Helen Hayes vowed to become an actress. If you plan ahead, you can take a free tour that includes the house, stage, backstage, wardrobe room, dressing rooms, the area under the stage, the Helen Hayes Lounge, and the memorabilia-filled archives. Tours are given for a minimum of 10 people, and only when there is no show; make reservations at least two weeks in advance. ✉ *1321 Pennsylvania Ave. NW (13th and E Sts.),* ☎ *202/783–3370,* WEB *www.nationaltheatre.org.* ✎ *Free. Metro: Metro Center.*

⑱ Navy Memorial. A huge outdoor plaza, this memorial includes a granite map of the world and a 7-ft statue, *The Lone Sailor.* In summer, its concert stage is the site of military band performances. Next to the memorial, in the Market Square East Building, is the Naval Heritage Center, which has a gift shop and the Navy Log Room, where you can use computers to look up the service records of navy veterans entered into the log. There's also the 242-seat, wide-screen Arleigh & Roberta Burke Theater, which shows a rotating series of historical sea service movies at noon. A memorial to General Winfield Scott is in the park adjacent to the Navy Memorial. ✉ *701 Pennsylvania Ave. NW,* ☎ *202/ 737–2300,* WEB *www.lonesailor.org.* ✎ *Films free.* ☼ *Naval Heritage Center Mar.–Nov., Mon.–Sat. 9:30–5:30; Dec.–Feb., Tues.–Sat. 9:30– 5:30. Metro: Archives/Navy Memorial.*

Old Adas Israel Synagogue. This is the oldest synagogue in Washington. Built in 1876 at 6th and G streets NW, the redbrick federal Revival–style building was moved to its present location in 1969 to make way for an office building. Exhibits in the Lillian and Albert Small Jewish Museum inside explore Jewish life in Washington. ✉ *701 3rd St. NW,* ☎ *202/789–0900.* ✎ *Suggested donation $2.* ☼ *Museum Sun.– Thurs. noon–4. Metro: Judiciary Square.*

❼ Old Patent Office Building. Two Smithsonian museums now share the Old Patent Office Building, which is closed for renovation through 2004. The ☞ National Portrait Gallery, with its presidential portraits, *Time* magazine covers, and Civil War photographs, paintings, and prints, is on the south side. The ☞ Smithsonian American Art Museum, with displays on Early American and western art, is on the north. Construction on the south wing, which was designed by Washington Monument architect Robert Mills, started in 1836. When the huge Greek Revival quadrangle was completed in 1867 it was the largest building in the country. Many of its rooms housed glass display cabinets filled with the models that inventors were required to submit with their patent applications.

During the Civil War, the Patent Office, like many other buildings in the city, was turned into a hospital. Among those caring for the wounded here were Clara Barton and Walt Whitman. In the 1950s the building was threatened with demolition to make way for a parking lot, but the efforts of preservationists saved it. ✉ *G St. between 7th and 9th Sts.,* WEB *www.nps.gov.opot. Metro: Gallery Place/Chinatown.*

🖐 ⑬ **Old Post Office Building.** When it was completed in 1899, this Romanesque structure on Federal Triangle was the largest government building in the District, the first with a clock tower, and the first with an electric power plant. Despite these innovations, it earned the sobriquet "old" after only 15 years, when a new District post office was constructed near Union Station. When urban planners in the '20s decided to impose a uniform design on Federal Triangle, the Old Post Office was slated for demolition. The fanciful granite building was saved first because of a lack of money during the Depression, then thanks to the intercession of preservationists. Major renovation was begun in 1978, and in 1983 the public areas in the Old Post Office Pavilion—an assortment of shops and restaurants inside the airy central courtyard—were opened.

Park service rangers who work at the Old Post Office consider the observation deck in the clock tower one of Washington's best-kept secrets. Although not as tall as the Washington Monument, it offers nearly as impressive a view. Even better, it's usually not as crowded, the windows are bigger, and—unlike the monument's windows—they're open, allowing cool breezes to waft through. (The tour is about 15 minutes long.) On the way down be sure to look at the Congress Bells, cast at the same British foundry that made the bells in London's Westminster Abbey. The bells are rung to honor the opening and closing of Congress and on other important occasions, such as when the Redskins win the Super Bowl.

Cross 10th Street from the Old Post Office Pavilion. Look to your left at the delightful trompe l'oeil mural on the side of the **Lincoln Building** two blocks up. It appears as if there's a hole in the building. There's also a portrait of the building's namesake. ✉ *Pennsylvania Ave. and 12th St. NW,* ☎ *202/606–8691 tower; 202/289–4224 pavilion.* 🎟 *Free.* 🕐 *Tower April–Labor Day, daily 9 AM–9 PM (last tour at 8:45); Labor Day–Mar., daily 10–5 (last tour at 4:45). Metro: Federal Triangle.*

Pennsylvania Avenue. The capital's most historically important thoroughfare repeatedly threads through sightseeing walks. Newly inaugurated presidents travel west on Pennsylvania Avenue en route to the White House. Thomas Jefferson started the parade tradition in 1805 after taking the oath of office for his second term. He was accompanied by a few friends and a handful of congressmen. Four years later James Madison made things official by instituting a proper inaugural celebration. The flag holders on the lampposts are clues that Pennsylvania Avenue remains the city's foremost parade route. With the Capitol at one end and the White House at the other, the avenue symbolizes both the distance and the connection between these two branches of government.

When Pennsylvania Avenue first opened in 1796, it was an ugly and dangerous bog. Attempts by Jefferson to beautify the road by planting poplar trees were only partially successful: many were chopped down for firewood. In the mid-19th century, crossing the rutted thoroughfare was treacherous, and rainstorms often turned the street into a river. The avenue was finally paved with wooden blocks in 1871.

At the convergence of 7th Street and Pennsylvania and Indiana avenues is a multitude of statues and monuments. The **Grand Army of the Republic** memorial pays tribute to the soldiers who won the Civil War. Less conventional is the nearby stork-surmounted **Temperance Fountain.** It was erected in the 19th century by a teetotaling physician named Cogswell who hoped the fountain, which once dispensed ice-cold water, would lure people from the evils of drink.

Redevelopment has rejuvenated Pennsylvania Avenue and the neighboring **Pennsylvania Quarter,** the name given to the mix of condominiums, apartments, retail spaces, and restaurants in the blocks bounded by Pennsylvania Avenue and 6th, 9th, and G streets. The area includes the Lansburgh complex, at the corner of 8th and E streets. Built around three existing buildings (including the defunct Lansburgh department store), the complex includes the Shakespeare Theatre, a state-of-the-art, 447-seat space. *Metro: Archives/Navy Memorial.*

❾ Petersen House. Lincoln died in the house of William Petersen, a tailor, on the morning of April 15, 1865, after being shot at Ford's Theatre the night before. You can see the restored front and back parlors of the house, as well as the bedroom where the president died. ✉ *516 10th St. NW,* ☎ *202/426–6830,* WEB *www.nps/gov/foth.* ☜ *Free.* ☾ *Daily 9–5. Metro: Metro Center or Gallery Place/Chinatown.*

NEED A
BREAK?

Around the corner and across the street from Petersen House is the **Hard Rock Cafe** (✉ 999 E St. NW, ☎ 202/737–7625), serving hearty American food and a modest selection of beers, and selling lots of those famous T-shirts. (The Hard Rock's gift shop opened a full year before the restaurant did.) This is a popular spot, so if you're not up to waiting in line, try to arrive early.

⓬ Ronald Reagan Building and International Trade Center. This $818-million, 3.1-million-square-ft colossus is the largest federal building to be constructed in the Washington area since the Pentagon, and the first to be designed for use by both the government and the private sector. A blend of classical and modern architecture, the Indiana limestone structure replaced what for 50 years had been an enormous parking lot, an eyesore that interrupted the flow of the buildings of Federal Triangle. At present, the Reagan Building is home to the Environmental Protection Agency, an irony considering the building's namesake's dislike for this agency. The building is also home to the U.S. Customs Service and U.S. AID. The **D.C. Visitor Information Center** (☎ 202/328–4748), located here, is a convenient place to pick up brochures, see a free historical video, and get tickets for tours or evening performances. There's also a multi-lingual touch-screen computer kiosk with information about the city, and the same machine lets you send a free email postcard with your photo to anyone in the world. Each Wednesday morning at 8:30, speakers from a fascinating variety of Washington's cultural organizations shed light on topics such as Civil War sites in the District. Hours for the visitor center are Monday through Saturday from 8 to 6. The building has a food court on the lower level, and a theatrical group, the Capitol Steps, performs works of political satire here on Friday and Saturday nights. ✉ *1300 Pennsylvania Ave. NW.* ☜ *Free. Metro: Federal Triangle.*

Smithsonian American Art Museum. This museum (formerly the National Museum of American Art), is housed in the ☞ **Old Patent Office Building,** which is under major renovation through 2004. The museum and the National Portrait Gallery, which share the building, are closed during the renovation, but the Smithsonian American Art Museum continues its public presence through its Web site and a full program at its ☞ **Renwick Gallery.** ✉ *8th and G Sts. NW,* ☎ *202/ 357–2700; 202/357–1729 TDD,* WEB *americanart.si.edu. Metro: Gallery Place/Chinatown.*

❸ Surratt Boarding House. A plaque by the front door attests that it was here that John Wilkes Booth and his coconspirators plotted the assassination of Abraham Lincoln. The current occupant of the building is a Chinese restaurant. ☒ *604 H St. NW. Metro: Gallery Place/Chinatown.*

Tariff Commission Building. The Tariff Commission Building, designed by Robert Mills and finished in 1866, is one of three historic structures to occupy the same site. When the Capitol was burned by the British in 1814, Congress met temporarily in a hotel that stood here. Another earlier building housed the nation's first public telegraph office, operated by Samuel F. B. Morse. ☒ *Diagonally opposite F St. mall. Metro: Gallery Place/Chinatown.*

Willard Inter-Continental. There was a Willard Hotel on this spot long before this ornate structure was built in 1901. The original Willard was *the* place to stay in Washington if you were rich or influential (or wanted to give that impression). Abraham Lincoln stayed there while waiting to move into the nearby White House. Julia Ward Howe stayed there during the Civil War and wrote "The Battle Hymn of the Republic" after gazing down from her window to see Union troops drilling on Pennsylvania Avenue. It's said the term "lobbyist" was coined to describe the favor seekers who would buttonhole President Ulysses S. Grant in the hotel's public rooms. The second Willard, its mansard roof dotted with circular windows, was designed by Henry Hardenbergh, architect of New York's Plaza hotel. Although it was just as opulent as the hotel it replaced, it fell on hard times after World War II. In 1968 it closed, standing empty until 1986, when it reopened, amid much fanfare, after an ambitious restoration. The Willard's rebirth is one of the most visible successes of the Pennsylvania Avenue Development Corporation, the organization charged with reversing the decay of America's Main Street. ☒ *1401 Pennsylvania Ave. NW,* ☎ *202/628–9100,* WEB *www.washington.interconti.com.*

GEORGETOWN

Updated by
Robin
Dougherty

Long before the District of Columbia was formed, Georgetown, Washington's oldest neighborhood, was a separate city with a harbor full of ships and warehouses filled with tobacco. Washington has filled in around Georgetown over the years, but the former tobacco port retains an air of aloofness. Its narrow streets, which don't conform to Pierre-Charles L'Enfant's plan for the Federal City, make up the capital's wealthiest neighborhood and are the nucleus of its nightlife.

The area that would come to be known as George (after George II), then George Towne and, finally, Georgetown, was part of Maryland when it was settled in the early 1700s by Scottish immigrants, many of whom were attracted to the region's tolerant religious climate. Georgetown's position at the farthest point up the Potomac accessible by boat made it an ideal transit and inspection point for farmers who grew tobacco in Maryland's interior. In 1789 the state granted the town a charter, but two years later Georgetown—along with Alexandria, its counterpart in Virginia—was included by George Washington in the Territory of Columbia, site of the new capital.

While Washington struggled, Georgetown thrived. Wealthy traders built their mansions on the hills overlooking the river; merchants and the working class lived in modest homes closer to the water's edge. In 1810 a third of Georgetown's population was black—both free people and slaves. The Mt. Zion United Methodist Church on 29th Street is the oldest organized black congregation in the city and was a stop on the Underground Railroad when it stood at 27th and P streets (the original burned down in the mid-1800s). Georgetown's rich history and success instilled in all its citizens a feeling of pride that still lingers today. (When Georgetowners thought the dismal capital was dragging them down, they asked to be given back to Maryland, the way Alexandria was given back to Virginia in 1845.) Tobacco eventually became a less important commodity, and Georgetown became a milling center, using water power from the Potomac. When the Chesapeake & Ohio (C&O) Canal was completed in 1850, the city intensified its milling operations and became the eastern end of a waterway that stretched 184 mi to the west. The canal took up some of the slack when Georgetown's harbor began to fill with silt and the port lost business to Alexandria and Baltimore, but the canal never became the success it was meant to be.

In the years that followed, Georgetown was a far cry from the fashionable spot it is today. Clustered near the water were a foundry, a fish market, paper and cotton mills, and a power station for the city's streetcar system, all of which made Georgetown a smelly industrial district. It still had its Georgian, federal, and Victorian homes, though, and when the New Deal and World War II brought a flood of newcomers to Washington, Georgetown's tree-shaded streets and handsome brick houses were rediscovered. Pushed out in the process were many of Georgetown's black residents who rented the houses in which they lived.

Today some of Washington's most famous citizens call Georgetown home, including former *Washington Post* editor Ben Bradlee and celebrity biographer Kitty Kelley. Georgetown's historic preservationists are among the most vocal in the city. Part of what the activists want protection from is the crush of people who descend on their community every night. This is Washington's center for restaurants, bars, nightclubs, and trendy boutiques. On M Street and Wisconsin Avenue, you can indulge just about any taste and take home almost any upscale souvenir. Harder to find is a parking place.

Georgetown owes some of its charm and separate growth to geography. This town-unto-itself is separated from Washington to the east by Rock Creek. On the south it's bordered by the Potomac, on the west by Georgetown University. How far north does Georgetown reach? Probably not much farther than the large estates and parks above R Street, though developers and real estate agents would be happy to take Georgetown right up to the Canadian border if it increased the value of property along the way.

The lack of a Metro station in Georgetown means you have to take a bus or taxi or walk to this part of Washington. It's about a 15-minute walk from the Dupont Circle or Foggy Bottom Metro station. (If you'd rather take a bus, the G2 Georgetown University bus goes from Dupont Circle west along P Street. The 34 and 36 Friendship Heights buses leave from 22nd and Pennsylvania and deposit you at 31st and M.)

Numbers in the text correspond to numbers in the margin and on the Georgetown map.

A Good Walk

Georgetown's largest and grandest estates occupy the northern part of the neighborhood, commanding fine views of Rock Creek to the east and of the Potomac River below. If you're in the mood for a stroll, the best way to get to the estates is to walk north either on Wisconsin Avenue (the bustling commercial route) or a block east, on 31st Street (a quieter residential street). Otherwise, start your exploration of Georgetown at 31st and M streets, in front of the **Old Stone House** ①, possibly Washington's only pre-Revolutionary building. From the Old Stone House, cross over M Street to Thomas Jefferson Street (between 30th and 31st streets). The 200-year-old, two-story brick structure at No.

1058 was built as a **Masonic Lodge** ②. Follow Thomas Jefferson Street as it passes over the **C&O Canal** ③, now used by runners, bikers, and canoeists. In spring and summer, you can take a mule-drawn canal boat ride. Cross K Street to **Washington Harbour** ④, a development that includes restaurants, offices, apartments, and pricey shops. Across the street at 31st and K streets is the site, no longer recognizable, that's thought to be the location of Suter's Tavern, where George Washington made the land deal that became the District of Columbia. The original building was torn down during the late 19th century. Nearby, the three Francis Dodge warehouses along Wisconsin Avenue, built around 1830, make a good backdrop for a photo. Up Wisconsin Avenue, across the street, stands the Gothic Revival Grace Episcopal Church.

Cross the canal again at Wisconsin Avenue. At 1066 Wisconsin Avenue, Papa Razzi restaurant inhabits the building that was once the Vigilant Firehouse, built in 1840. Near the door of the restaurant, a plaque reads BUSH, THE OLD FIRE DOG, DIED OF POISON, JULY 5TH, 1869, R.I.P. Nearby is a simple granite obelisk honoring the men who built the C&O Canal. At the intersection of Wisconsin Avenue and M Street—the heart of Georgetown—turn left to the upscale Victorian-style Georgetown Park (✉ 3222 M Street NW), that rarest of rarities: an architecturally attractive shopping mall. Both M Street and Wisconsin Avenue are lined with restaurants and boutiques selling just about anything you could want, from the latest fashions to antique furniture and jewelry—but don't expect any bargains. Continue along M Street to the Markethouse, an 1865 brick building currently occupied by Dean & Deluca, the trendy gourmet food store. M Street west leads to the Key Bridge into Rosslyn, Virginia. A house owned by Francis Scott Key, author of the national anthem, was demolished in 1947 to make way for the bridge that would bear his name. The **Francis Scott Key Memorial Park** ⑤ lies at the foot of the D.C. side of Key Bridge.

To head to the residential area, continue on M Street past the old brick streetcar barn at No. 3600 (now a block of offices), turn right, and climb the 75 **Exorcist steps** ⑥ from the film *The Exorcist.* You can see that it is indeed a truly terrifying fall, especially when being hurled by a demon. If you're not up to the climb, walk up 34th Street instead. **Halcyon House** ⑦, built by the first secretary of the navy, is a hodge-podge of architectural styles. The beautiful campus of **Georgetown University** ⑧, the oldest Jesuit school in the country, is a few blocks to the west. **Cox's Row** ⑨, a group of five federal houses between 3339 and 3327 N Street, was built in 1817 by a former mayor of Georgetown. The redbrick house at 3307 N Street was the home of then-Senator John F. Kennedy and his family before they moved downtown to 1600 Pennsylvania Avenue.

Turn left onto Potomac Street and walk a block up to O Street, several blocks of which still have cobblestones and trolley tracks. **St. John's Church** ⑩ was built in 1809. Cross Wisconsin Avenue and go up 31st Street to Q Street, where through the trees you can see **Tudor Place** ⑪, a neoclassical mansion with a dramatic domed portico. Walk up 32nd Street to **Dumbarton Oaks** ⑫, which contains two world-class art collections and 10 acres of formal gardens. If you're interested in visiting the Washington National Cathedral, St. Sophia Cathedral, or the Washington Dolls' House and Toy Museum, walk back west to Wisconsin Avenue and catch a Friendship Heights bus, which travels north. Otherwise stay on the tour to see the three other sylvan retreats that lie north of Dumbarton Oaks. Dumbarton Oaks Park sprawls to the north and west of the estate, Montrose Park lies to the east, and farther east is **Oak Hill Cemetery** ⑬, overlooking Rock Creek, where many historical figures are interred. Walk south on 28th Street past the 200-year-old Georgian manor house **Evermay** ⑭, now a private home with lovely grounds. Around the corner on Q Street is **Dumbarton House** ⑮, headquarters of the National Society of the Colonial Dames of America. It's filled with magnificent period antiques.

TIMING

You can easily spend a pleasant day in Georgetown, partly because some sights (Tudor Place, Dumbarton Oaks, Oak Hill Cemetery, Evermay, and Dumbarton House) are somewhat removed from the others and partly because the street scene, with its intriguing shops and people-watching, invites you to linger. Georgetown is almost always crowded and, especially at night, not very automobile-friendly; driving and parking are usually difficult. The wise take the Metro (although the nearest station is a 15-minute walk away), the bus, or a taxi.

Sights to See

C&O Canal. This waterway kept Georgetown open to shipping after its harbor had filled with silt. George Washington was one of the first to advance the idea of a canal linking the Potomac with the Ohio River across the Appalachians. Work started on the C&O Canal in 1828, and when it opened in 1850, its 74 locks linked Georgetown with Cumberland, Maryland, 184 mi to the northwest (still short of its intended destination). Lumber, coal, iron, wheat, and flour moved up and down the canal, but it was never as successful as its planners had hoped it would be. Many of the bridges spanning the canal in Georgetown were too low to allow anything other than fully loaded barges to pass underneath, and competition from the Baltimore & Ohio Railroad eventually spelled an end to profitability. Today the canal is a part of the National Park System, and walkers follow the towpath once used by mules while canoeists paddle the canal's calm waters. Between April and November you can go on a leisurely (about an hour) mule-drawn trip aboard the *Georgetown* canal boat. Tickets are available across the canal, next to the Foundry. Barge rides are also available at Great Falls, at the end of MacArthur Boulevard, in nearby Potomac, Maryland. Barge rides are given late March through mid-June and September 9 through November 1, Wednesday to Friday at 11 and 2:30, and on weekends at 11, 1, 2:30, and 4. From June 17 through September 7, barge rides are Wednesday to Friday at 11, 1, and 2:30, and on weekends at 11, 1, 2:30, and 4; the cost is $8. ⊠ *Canal Visitor Center, 1057 Thomas Jefferson St. NW,* ☎ *202/653–5190.*

Canal Square. This 1850s warehouse was converted into a retail and office complex in the 1970s, retaining much of the original brickwork. Its interior courtyard is home to retail shops and several art galleries, notably the small but innovative **Museum of Contemporary Art** (☎ 202/342–6230). ⊠ *1054 31st St. NW.*

⑨ Cox's Row. Architecture buffs, especially those interested in federal and Victorian houses, enjoy wandering along the redbrick sidewalks of upper Georgetown. The average house here has two signs on it: a brass plaque notifying passersby of the building's historic interest and a window decal that warns burglars of its state-of-the-art alarm system. To get a representative taste of the houses in the area, walk along the 3300 block of N Street. The group of five federal houses between 3339 and 3327 N Street is known collectively as Cox's Row, after Colonel John Cox, a former mayor of Georgetown, who built them in 1817 and resided at 3339 N Street. The flat-front, redbrick federal house at 3307 N Street was the home of then-Senator John F. Kennedy and his family before the White House beckoned.

82

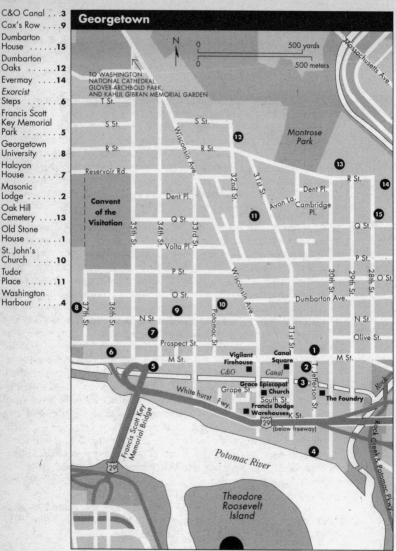

⓯ **Dumbarton House.** Its symmetry and the two curved wings on its north side make Dumbarton, built around 1800, a distinctive example of Georgian architecture. The first occupant of the house, Joseph Nourse, was registrar of the U.S. Treasury. Other well-known Americans have spent time here, including Dolley Madison, who stopped here when fleeing Washington in 1814. One hundred years later, the house was saved from demolition by being moved 100 ft up the hill, when Q Street was cut through to the Dumbarton Bridge. Since 1928, it has served as the headquarters of the National Society of the Colonial Dames of America.

Eight rooms inside Dumbarton House have been restored to federal-period splendor, with period furnishings such as mahogany American Chippendale chairs, hallmark silver, Persian rugs, and a breakfront cabinet filled with rare books. Other notable items include a 1789 Charles Willson Peale portrait of Benjamin Stoddert's children (with an early view of Georgetown harbor in the background), Martha Washington's traveling cloak, and a British redcoat's red coat. In order to see the house's interior, visitors must take the guided 45-minute tour. ⊠ *2715 Q St.NW,*

☎ *202/337–2288.* ✉ *Suggested donation $3.* ☉ *Labor Day–July, Tues.– Sat. 10–1 (last tour at 12:15). Tours begin at 10:15, 11:15, and 12:15.*

🔢 **Dumbarton Oaks.** Don't confuse Dumbarton Oaks with the nearby Dumbarton House. In 1944 one of the most important events of the 20th century took place in Dumbarton Oaks, when representatives of the United States, Great Britain, China, and the Soviet Union met in the music room here to lay the groundwork for the United Nations.

Career diplomat Robert Woods Bliss and his wife, Mildred, bought the property in 1920 and set about taming the sprawling grounds and removing later 19th-century additions that had marred the federal lines of the 1801 mansion. In 1940 the Blisses conveyed the estate to Harvard University, which maintains world-renowned collections of Byzantine and pre-Columbian art here. Both collections are small but choice, reflecting the enormous skill and creativity going on at roughly the same time on two sides of the Atlantic. The Byzantine collection includes beautiful examples of both religious and secular items executed in mosaic, metal, enamel, and ivory. Pre-Columbian works—artifacts and textiles from Mexico and Central and South America by such peoples as the Aztec, Maya, and Olmec—are arranged in an enclosed glass pavilion designed by Philip Johnson. Also on view to the public are the lavishly decorated music room and selections from Mrs. Bliss's collection of rare illustrated garden books.

If you have even a mild interest in flowers, shrubs, trees, and magnificent natural beauty, visit Dumbarton Oaks's 10 acres of formal gardens, one of the loveliest spots in Washington (enter via R Street). Designed by noted landscape architect Beatrix Farrand, the gardens incorporate elements of traditional English, Italian, and French styles such as a formal rose garden, an English country garden, and an Orangery (circa 1810). A full-time crew of a dozen gardeners toils to maintain the stunning collection of terraces, geometric gardens, tree-shaded brick walks, fountains, arbors, and pools. Plenty of well-positioned benches make this a good place for resting weary feet, too. ✉ *Art collections: 1703 32nd St. NW,* ☎ *202/339–6401 or 202/339–6400;* ✉ *gardens: 31st and R Sts. NW.* ✉ *Art collections suggested donation $1; gardens Apr.–Oct. $5, Nov.–Mar. free.* ☉ *Art collections Tues.– Sun. 2–5; gardens Apr.–Oct., daily 2–6; Nov.–Mar., daily 2–5.*

🔢 **Evermay.** A Georgian manor house built around 1800 by real estate speculator Samuel Davidson, Evermay is almost hidden by its black-and-gold gates and high brick wall. Davidson wanted it that way. He sometimes took out advertisements in newspapers warning sightseers to avoid his estate "as they would a den of devils or rattlesnakes." The mansion is in private hands, but its grounds are occasionally opened for garden tours. ✉ *1623 28th St. NW.*

🔢 ***Exorcist* Steps.** The heights of Georgetown to the north above N Street contrast with the busy jumble of the old waterfront. To reach the higher ground you can walk up M Street, past the old brick streetcar barn at No. 3600 (now a block of offices), turn right, and climb the 75 steps that figured prominently in the eerie movie *The Exorcist*. If you prefer a less-demanding climb, walk up 34th Street instead. ✉ *M and 36th Sts.*

The Foundry. This building gets its name from the machine shop that was here from 1856 to 1866. It housed several businesses after that, and around the turn of the 19th century it was a veterinary hospital for mules that worked on the canal. In 1976, the Foundry was reborn as a mall, with restaurants, art galleries, and a movie theater. ✉ *1055 Thomas Jefferson St. NW.*

NEED A
BREAK? If the crowds of Georgetown become overwhelming, step into **ching
ching CHA** (⊠ 1063 Wisconsin Ave. NW, ☎ 202/333–8288), a Chinese tea house where tranquility reigns supreme. In addition to tea,
lunch and dinner may be ordered from a simple menu with light, healthy
meals presented in lacquer boxes.

Francis Dodge Warehouses. The last three buildings at the foot of the
west side of Wisconsin Avenue are reminders of Georgetown's mercantile past. They were built around 1830 by trader and merchant Francis Dodge. Note the heavy stone foundation of the southernmost
warehouse, its star-end braces, and the broken hoist in the gable end.
According to an 1838 newspaper ad, Georgetown shoppers could visit
Dodge's grocery to buy such items as "Porto Rico Sugar, Marseilles
soft-shelled Almonds and Havanna Segars." Although the traders of
yesteryear have been replaced by small nonprofit organizations, the buildings don't look as if they house modern offices, and their facades make
an interesting snapshot. ⊠ *1000–1002 Wisconsin Ave. NW.*

❺ Francis Scott Key Memorial Park. A small, noisy park near the Key Bridge
honors the Washington attorney who "by the dawn's early light"
penned the national anthem, upon seeing that the flag had survived
the night's British bombardment of Ft. McHenry in Baltimore harbor
during the War of 1812. A replica of the 15-star, 15-stripe flag that inspired Key flies over the park 24 hours a day (the original is on display at the National Museum of American History). Here Georgetown's
quaint demeanor contrasts with the silvery skyscrapers of Rosslyn, Virginia, across the Potomac. ⊠ *M St. between 34th St. and Key Bridge.*

★ ❽ Georgetown University. Founded in 1789 by John Carroll, first American bishop and first archbishop of Baltimore, Georgetown is the oldest Jesuit school in the country. About 12,000 students attend
Georgetown, known now as much for its perennially successful basketball team as for its fine programs in law, medicine, foreign service,
and the liberal arts. When seen from the Potomac or from Washington's high ground, the Gothic spires of Georgetown's older buildings
give the university an almost medieval look. ⊠ *37th and O Sts.,* ☎
202/687–5055, WEB *www.georgetown.edu.*

OFF THE
BEATEN PATH **GLOVER-ARCHBOLD PARK –** Groves of beeches, elms, and oaks flourish
at this 183-acre park, which is part of the Rock Creek system. A 3½-mi
nature trail runs the length of Glover-Archbold, a gift to the city in 1924.
⊠ *Garfield St. and New Mexico Ave. NW.*

Grace Episcopal Church. In the mid- to late-19th century the Gothic
Revival Grace Episcopal Church served the boatmen and workers
from the nearby C&O Canal. At the time the area was one of the poor-
est in Georgetown. ⊠ *Wisconsin Ave. near C&O Canal,* ☎ *202/333–
7100.* ☉ *Services Sun. 8:30 and 10:30.*

❼ Halcyon House. Built in 1783 by Benjamin Stoddert, the first secretary
of the navy, Halcyon House has been the object of many subsequent
additions and renovations. It's now a motley assortment of architectural styles. Prospect Street, where the house is set, gets its name from
the fine views it affords of the waterfront and the river below. The house
is not open to the public. ⊠ *34th and Prospect Sts.*

OFF THE
BEATEN PATH **KAHLIL GIBRAN MEMORIAL GARDEN –** Dedicated in 1991, this tiny urban
park combining Western and Arabian symbols is perfect for quiet contemplation. Entering from Massachusetts Avenue, a stone walk bridges a
grassy swale, leading to limestone benches engraved with sayings from

Gibran curving around a fountain and a bust of the Lebanese-born poet. ⊠ *3100 block of Massachusetts Ave. NW.*

② **Masonic Lodge.** A two-story brick structure, Georgetown's Masonic Lodge, which isn't open to visitors, was built around 1810. Freemasonry, the world's largest secret society, was started by British stonemasons and cathedral builders as early as the 14th century; the fraternal order now has a much broader international membership that has included U.S. presidents—among them George Washington—as well as members of Congress. It's no accident that the Freemasons chose Georgetown to be the site of a lodge. Although Georgetown today is synonymous with affluence, for most of its history it was a working-class city, and the original names of its streets—Water Street, Canal Road, Fishing Lane—attest to the past importance of traditional trades to the region's economy. The area south of M Street (originally called Bridge Street because of the bridge that spanned Rock Creek to the east) was inhabited by tradesmen, laborers, and merchants who were good candidates for expanding the Masons' ranks. Among the lodge's interesting details are a pointed facade and recessed central arch, features that suggest the society's traditional attachment to the building arts. ⊠ *1058 Thomas Jefferson St.*

Montrose Park. Originally owned by 19th-century rope-making magnate Richard Parrot, this tract of land was purchased by Congress in the early part of this century "for the recreation and pleasure of the people." A popular spot for locals out with their toddlers and dogs, the park is a great spot for an outdoor outing or short break, with tennis courts, a swing set, and picnic tables. ⊠ *3001 R St. NW.*

⑬ **Oak Hill Cemetery.** Oak Hill Cemetery's funerary obelisks, crosses, and gravestones spread out over four landscaped terraces on a hill overlooking Rock Creek. Near the brick and sandstone gatehouse entrance is an 1850 Gothic-style chapel designed by Smithsonian Castle architect James Renwick. Across from the chapel is the resting place of actor, playwright, and diplomat John H. Payne, who is remembered today primarily for his song "Home Sweet Home." A few hundred feet to the north is the circular tomb of William Corcoran, founder of the Corcoran Gallery of Art, who donated the land for the cemetery. Cameras and backpacks are not allowed in the cemetery. ⊠ *30th and R Sts. NW,* ☎ *202/337–2835.* ◨ *Free.* ☉ *Weekdays 10–4.*

❶ **Old Stone House.** What was early American life like? Here's the capital's oldest window into the past. Work on this fieldstone house, thought to be Washington's only surviving pre-Revolutionary building, was begun in 1764 by a cabinetmaker named Christopher Layman. The house, now a museum, was used as both a residence and a place of business by a succession of occupants. Five of the house's rooms are furnished with the simple, sturdy artifacts—plain tables, spinning wheels, and so forth—of 18th-century middle-class life. The National Park Service maintains the house and its lovely gardens in the rear, which are planted with fruit trees and perennials. ⊠ *3051 M St. NW,* ☎ *202/ 426–6851.* ◨ *Free.* ☉ *Wed.–Sun. 10–4.*

⑩ **St. John's Church.** West of Wisconsin Avenue, a several-blocks-long stretch of O Street has remnants from an earlier age: cobblestones and streetcar tracks. Residents are so proud of the cobblestones that newer concrete patches have been scored to resemble them. Prominent in this section of Georgetown is St. John's Church, built in 1809 and attributed to Dr. William Thornton, architect of the Capitol. However, later alterations have left it looking more Victorian than federal. St. John's is also noted for its stained-glass windows, including a small

Tiffany. ⊠ *3240 O St. NW,* ☎ *202/338–1796.* ⊙ *Services Sun. 9 and 11, Thurs. 11:30.*

OFF THE
BEATEN PATH

ST. SOPHIA CATHEDRAL – The Greek Orthodox St. Sophia Cathedral is noted for the handsome mosaic work on the interior of its dome. The cathedral holds a festival of Greek food and crafts each spring and fall. ⊠ *Massachusetts Ave. and 36th St. NW,* ☎ *202/333–4730.* ⊙ *Service Sun. 9:30.*

⑪ **Tudor Place.** Stop at Q Street between 31st and 32nd streets; look through the trees to the north, at the top of a sloping lawn; and you'll see the neoclassical Tudor Place, designed by Capitol architect Dr. William Thornton and completed in 1816. On a house tour you'll see items that belonged to George Washington, Francis Scott Key's desk, and spurs belonging to members of the Peter family who were killed in the Civil War. The grounds contain many specimens planted in the early 19th century. The house was built for Thomas Peter, son of Georgetown's first mayor, and his wife, Martha Custis, Martha Washington's granddaughter. It was because of this connection to the president's family that Tudor Place came to house many items from Mount Vernon. The yellow stucco house is interesting for its architecture—especially the dramatic, two-story domed portico on the south side—but its familial heritage is even more remarkable: Tudor Place stayed in the same family for 178 years, until 1983, when Armistead Peter III died. Before his death, Peter established a foundation to restore the house and open it to the public. Tour reservations are advised. ⊠ *1644 31st St. NW,* ☎ *202/965–0400,* WEB *www.tudorplace.org.* ☞ *House and garden tour suggested donation $6, self-guided garden tour $2.* ⊙ *House tours Tues.– Fri. at 10, 11:30, 1, and 2:30; Sat. hourly 10–4 (last tour at 3); garden Mon.–Sat. 10–4 (also Apr.–May and Sept.–Oct., Sun. noon–4).*

OFF THE
BEATEN PATH

WASHINGTON DOLLS' HOUSE AND TOY MUSEUM – A collection of American and imported dolls, dollhouses, toys, and games—most from the Victorian period—fills a compact museum founded in 1975 by a dollhouse historian. Miniature accessories, dollhouse kits, and antique toys and games are on sale in the museum's shops. ⊠ *5236 44th St. NW,* ☎ *202/244–0024.* ☞ *$4.* ⊙ *Tues.–Sat. 10–5, Sun. noon–5. Metro: Friendship Heights.*

④ **Washington Harbour.** Stately columns and the liberal use of glass as a construction material are hallmarks of Washington Harbour, a six-acre glittering postmodern riverfront development designed by Arthur Cotton Moore. Included are such restaurants as the two-story Sequoia, Tony & Joe's Seafood Place, and the Riverside Grille, as well as offices, apartments, and upscale shops. Highlights of the central plaza are a large fountain and a futuristic, lighthouselike structure made up of four towering white columns. Several restaurants offer outdoor dining. From the edge of Washington Harbour you can see the Watergate complex and Kennedy Center to the east while the waters of the Potomac gently lap at the edge of the dock. Those who prefer the water to the streets often arrive by boat, docking just yards from outdoor diners. At night, the area sparkles like a Christmas scene with hundreds of twinkling white lights. ⊠ *3000 K St. NW.*

OFF THE
BEATEN PATH

WASHINGTON NATIONAL CATHEDRAL – Construction of Washington National Cathedral, a stunning Gothic church—the sixth-largest cathedral in the world—started in 1907 and was finished on September 30, 1990, when the building was consecrated. Like its 14th-century counterparts, the National Cathedral (officially the Cathedral Church of St. Peter and St. Paul) has a nave, flying buttresses, transepts, and vaults that were built stone by stone. It's adorned with fanciful gargoyles created by skilled stone carvers. The tomb of Woodrow Wilson, the only president buried in Washington, is on the south side of the nave. The expansive view of the city from the Pilgrim Gallery is exceptional. The cathedral is under the governance of the Episcopal Church but has hosted services of many denominations.

On the grounds of the cathedral is the compact, English-style **Bishop's Garden.** Boxwoods, ivy, tea roses, yew trees, and an assortment of arches, bas-reliefs, and stonework from European ruins provide a restful counterpoint to the cathedral's Gothic towers. ⊠ *Wisconsin and Massachusetts Aves. NW,* ☎ *202/537–6200; 202/537–6207 tour information,* WEB *www.cathedral.org.* ⊠ *Suggested tour donation $3.* ⊙ *Labor Day–Memorial Day, 10–4:30; Memorial Day–Labor Day, weekdays 10–9, weekends 10–4:30. Sun. services at 8, 9, 10, 11, and 6:30; evensong daily at 4; tours every 15 mins Mon.–Sat. 10–11:30 and 12:45–3:15, Sun. 12:30–2:45.*

DUPONT CIRCLE

Updated by
Robin
Dougherty

Three of Washington's main thoroughfares intersect at Dupont Circle: Connecticut, New Hampshire, and Massachusetts avenues. With a small, handsome park and a splashing fountain in the center, Dupont Circle is more than an island around which traffic flows, making it an exception among Washington circles. The activity spills over into the surrounding streets, one of the liveliest, most vibrant neighborhoods in D.C.

Development near Dupont Circle started during the post–Civil War boom of the 1870s. As the city increased in stature, the nation's wealthy and influential citizens began building their mansions near the circle. The area underwent a different kind of transformation in the middle of the 20th century, when the middle and upper classes deserted Washington for the suburbs, and in the 1960s the circle became the starting point for rowdy, litter-strewn marches sponsored by countercultural groups. Today the neighborhood is once again fashionable, and its many restaurants, offbeat shops, coffeehouses, art galleries and specialty bookstores lend it a distinctive, cosmopolitan air. Stores and clubs catering to the neighborhood's large gay community are abundant.

Numbers in the text correspond to numbers in the margin and on the Dupont Circle map.

A Good Walk

Start your exploration in **Dupont Circle** ① itself, with its large central fountain. Carefully cross the circle traffic and head down New Hampshire Avenue to the **Heurich House Museum** ②, a Romanesque Revival mansion full of Victoriana. Cross New Hampshire Avenue and go left on O Street. Not all the homes here are mansions, but the typical brick Victorian row houses on this block tend to be large. Turn right on 21st Street to admire the opulent **Walsh-McLean House** ③, which isn't open to tours. Head west on Massachusetts Avenue to No. 2118, **Anderson House** ④, where you can see the art and treasures a former diplomat collected during his travels.

Head west on Q Street to the **Bison Bridge** ⑤, so called because of its four bronze statues of the shaggy horned beasts. Walk north on 23rd Street and pass between two embassies, those of Turkey and Romania, both on Sheridan Circle. This area of Massachusetts Avenue, going either direction from the circle, is known as Embassy Row, with the various nations' flags flying in front of their respective embassies. Turn left on Massachusetts Avenue and walk north one block, where the **Cameroon Embassy** ⑥ is housed in a fanciful mansion. Turn right on S Street and go past the statue of Irish patriot Robert Emmet, dedicated in 1966 to celebrate the 50th anniversary of Irish independence. The former home of the 28th president, the **Woodrow Wilson House** ⑦, is a few hundred feet down S Street. Right next door is the **Textile Museum** ⑧, founded by Bristol-Myers heir George Hewitt Myers to house and show some of his 12,000 textiles and 1,500 carpets. If you're interested in visiting the Islamic Mosque and Cultural Center, take a detour and walk in the opposite direction, continuing to Massachusetts Avenue, and turning right in two blocks.

From the Textile Museum, walk north on 23rd Street until it dead-ends at the Tudor mansion at **2221 Kalorama Road** ⑨, currently the residence of the French ambassador. As you walk down Kalorama toward Connecticut Avenue, the large beige building on the left near Connecticut Avenue is the Chinese Embassy. Turn right down Connecticut Avenue. On the left at 1919 Connecticut is the Washington Hilton & Towers, the site of John Hinckley's 1981 failed assassination attempt on Ronald Reagan (at the entrance on T Street NW). Go left on R Street for two blocks to the **National Museum of American Jewish Military History** ⑩, which chronicles Jews' military service in every war this country has fought. Follow R Street back across Connecticut Avenue to the **Fondo Del Sol Visual Arts Center**, a nonprofit center featuring art, poetry, and music of the Americas. Walk south on 21st Street and discover some of the many private art galleries in the area.

One of Washington's great art museums is the **Phillips Collection** ⑪ at 21st and Q streets, filled with modern art masterpieces. The neighborhood surrounding the Phillips has a large concentration of art galleries that hold evening receptions the first Friday of the month. Continue east on Q Street, and then turn right at Connecticut to the circle. Follow Massachusetts Avenue east to the National Trust for Historic Preservation (✉ 18th Street and Massachusetts Avenue), which isn't open to the public; however, a quick peek at the circular lobby gives you an idea of the lavish world its onetime residents inhabited. At the corner of 16th Street is the **Australian Embassy**, which has occasional art exhibits. And now you've arrived at yet another circle— **Scott Circle** ⑫, with its equestrian statue of General Winfield Scott.

Take a slight detour along N Street to Vermont Avenue to visit **Mary McLeod Bethune Council House** ⑬, the museum honoring the achievements of African-American women. Follow Vermont Avenue south to Thomas Circle and turn right on M Street. After a block, the **Metropolitan African Methodist Episcopal Church** ⑭ is on your left. Continue on M Street to 17th Street, to the headquarters of the **National Geographic Society** ⑮, where you can explore the interactive video touch screens in Explorers Hall. The **Charles E. Sumner School Museum and Archives** ⑯, across M Street from the National Geographic offices, was built in 1872 as a school for black children. It's now used mainly for conferences, but it also has a permanent exhibit on the history of the city's public school system and hosts occasional art exhibits. Head up 17th Street to Rhode Island Avenue, where you can visit the **B'nai B'rith Klutznick National Jewish Museum** ⑰, which follows the history of the Jewish people for the past 20 centuries. A half block west on Rhode Island Avenue is **St. Matthew's Cathedral** ⑱, the seat of Washington's Catholic archbishop. John F. Kennedy frequently attended the church, which also was the site of his funeral mass.

Visiting the Dupont Circle area takes at least half a day, although you can find things to keep you busy all day. The most time-consuming sites are probably the National Geographic Society's Explorers Hall, the Phillips Collection, and Anderson House, although the treasures inside the Textile, B'nai B'rith Klutznik, and American Jewish Military History museums are captivating as well.

Sights to See

④ Anderson House. A palatial home that's a mystery even to many longtime Washingtonians, Anderson House isn't an embassy, though it does have a link to the diplomatic world. Larz Anderson was a diplomat whose career included postings to Japan and Belgium. Anderson and his heiress wife, Isabel, toured the world, picking up objects that struck their fancy. They filled their residence, which was constructed in 1905, with the booty of their travels, including choir stalls from an Italian Renaissance church, Flemish tapestries, and a large—if spotty—collection of Asian art. All this remains in the house for you to see.

In accordance with the Andersons' wishes, the building also serves as the headquarters of a group to which Larz belonged: the Society of the Cincinnati. The oldest patriotic organization in the country, the society was formed in 1783 by a group of officers who had served with George Washington during the Revolutionary War. The group took the name Cincinnati from Cincinnatus, a distinguished Roman who, circa 500 BC, led an army against Rome's enemies and later quelled civil disturbances in the city. After each success, rather than seek political power that could have easily been his, he returned to the simple life on his farm. The story impressed the American officers, who saw in it a mirror of their own situation: they, too, would leave the battlefields to get on with the business of forging a new nation. (One such member went on to name the city in Ohio.) Today's members are direct descendants of those American revolutionaries.

Many of the displays in the society's museum focus on the Colonial period and the Revolutionary War. One room—painted in a marvelous trompe l'oeil style that deceives you into thinking the walls are covered with sculpture—is filled with military miniatures from the United States and France. (Because of the important role France played in defeating the British, French officers were invited to join the society. Pierre-Charles L'Enfant, "Artist of the Revolution" and planner of Washington, designed the society's eagle medallion.)

The house is often used by the federal government to entertain visiting dignitaries. Amid the glitz, glamour, beauty, and patriotic spectacle of the mansion are two delightful painted panels in the solarium that depict the Andersons' favorite motorcar sightseeing routes around Washington. ⊠ *2118 Massachusetts Ave. NW,* ☎ *202/785–2040.* ☒ *Free.* ☉ *Tues.–Sat. 1–4. Metro: Dupont Circle.*

Australian Embassy. Many foreign embassies in Washington host art exhibits or cultural programs open to the public. One of the best galleries is at the Australian Embassy, which periodically displays masterpieces from Down Under. If you're lucky, you might see aboriginal artifacts and dot paintings of striking originality and beauty, as well as contemporary landscapes and portraits with a uniquely Australian character. ⊠ *1601 Massachusetts Ave. NW,* ☎ *202/797–3000,* WEB *www.austemb.org.* ☒ *Free.* ☉ *Weekdays 9–5. Metro: Dupont Circle.*

⑤ Bison Bridge. Tour guides at the Smithsonian's National Museum of Natural History are quick to remind you that America never had buffalo; the big, shaggy animals that roamed the plains were bison. (True

Dupont Circle

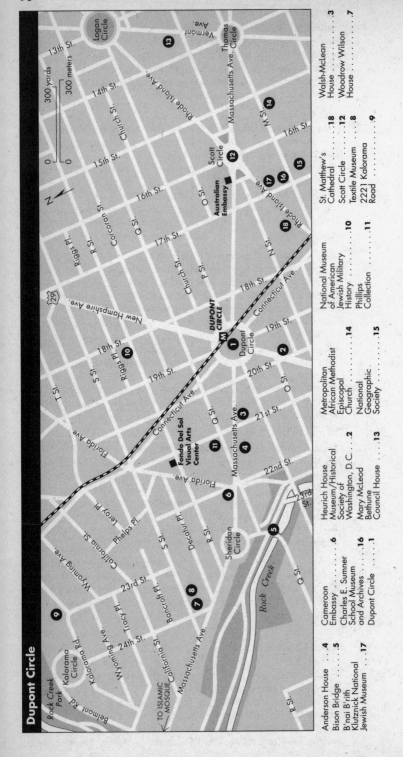

Rock Creek Park

Kalorama Circle

13th St.

Logan Circle

Vermont Ave.

Thomas Circle

Massachusetts Ave.

Scott Circle

14th St.

Church St.

15th St.

16th St.

Rhode Island Ave.

16th St.

Corcoran St.

Q St.

Q St.

Australian Embassy

17th St.

Church St.

P St.

Rhode Island Ave.

N St.

M St.

Riggs Pl.

R St.

18th St.

Connecticut Ave.

New Hampshire Ave.

19th St.

DUPONT CIRCLE

Dupont Circle

20th St.

O St.

18th St.

Riggs Pl.

S St.

T St.

19th St.

Connecticut Ave.

Florida Ave.

21st St.

Massachusetts Ave.

Q St.

Fondo Del Sol Visual Arts Center

Florida Ave.

22nd St.

Leroy Pl.

Phelps Pl.

Decatur Pl.

R St.

S St.

Sheridan Circle

23rd St.

California St.

Bancroft Pl.

Tracy Pl.

23rd St.

24th St.

Wyoming Ave.

Massachusetts Ave.

Kalorama Rd.

Belmont Rd.

California St.

Wyoming Ave.

TO ISLAMIC MOSQUE

Rock Creek

Q St.

R St.

300 yards

300 meters

N

29

Anderson House 4
Bison Bridge 5
B'nai B'rith Klutznick National Jewish Museum ...17

Cameroon Embassy 6
Charles E. Sumner School Museum and Archives 16
Dupont Circle 1

Heurich House Museum/Historical Society of Washington, D.C. ...2
Mary McLeod Bethune Council House ...13

Metropolitan African Methodist Episcopal Church 14
National Geographic Society 15

National Museum of American Jewish Military History 10
Phillips Collection 11

St. Matthew's Cathedral 18
Scott Circle 12
Textile Museum 8
2221 Kalorama Road 9

Walsh-McLean House 3
Woodrow Wilson House 7

buffalo are African and Asian animals of the same family.) Officially called the Dumbarton Bridge—though locals call it the Bison Bridge, thanks to the four bronze statues designed by A. Phimister Proctor—the structure stretches across Rock Creek Park into Georgetown. Its sides are decorated with busts of Native Americans, the work of architect Glenn Brown, who, along with his son Bedford, designed the bridge in 1914. The best way to see the busts is to walk the footpath along Rock Creek. ⊠ *23rd and Q Sts. NW. Metro: Dupont Circle.*

⑰ B'nai B'rith Klutznick National Jewish Museum. Devoted to the history of Jewish people, this museum's permanent exhibits span 20 centuries and highlight Jewish festivals and the rituals employed to mark the stages of life. A wide variety of Jewish decorative art, adorning such items as spice boxes and Torah covers, is on display. Changing exhibits highlight the work of contemporary Jewish artists. ⊠ *1640 Rhode Island Ave. NW,* ☎ *202/857–6583.* ⊞ *Suggested donation $2.* ☉ *Sun.–Fri. 10–5 most of the year. The museum closes at 3:30 on Fri. during the winter. Metro: Dupont Circle or Farragut North.*

❻ Cameroon Embassy. The westernmost of the beaux arts–style mansions built along Massachusetts Avenue in the late 19th and early 20th centuries today houses the Cameroon Embassy. The building is a fanciful castle with a conical tower, bronze weather vane, and intricate detailing around the windows and balconies. ⊠ *2349 Massachusetts Ave. NW. Metro: Dupont Circle.*

⑯ Charles E. Sumner School Museum and Archives. Built in 1872 for the education of black children, the Charles Sumner School takes its name from the Massachusetts senator who delivered a blistering attack against slavery in 1856 and was savagely caned as a result by a congressman from South Carolina. The building was designed by Adolph Cluss, who created the Arts and Industries Building on the Washington Mall. It's typical of the District's Victorian-era public schools. Beautifully restored in 1986, the school serves mainly as a conference center, though it hosts changing art exhibits and houses a permanent collection of memorabilia relating to the city's public school system. ⊠ *1201 17th St. NW,* ☎ *202/442–6060.* ⊞ *Free.* ☉ *Mon.–Sat. 10–5; often closed for conferences. Metro: Farragut North.*

❶ Dupont Circle. Originally known as Pacific Circle, this hub was the westernmost circle in Pierre-Charles L'Enfant's original design for the Federal City. The name was changed in 1884, when Congress authorized construction of a bronze statue honoring Civil War hero Admiral Samuel F. Dupont. The statue fell into disrepair, and Dupont's family—who had never liked it anyway—replaced it in 1921. The marble fountain that stands in its place, with allegorical figures Sea, Stars, and Wind, was created by Daniel Chester French, the sculptor of Lincoln's statue in the Lincoln Memorial.

As you look around the circumference of the circle, you can see the special constraints within which architects in Washington must work. Since a half dozen streets converge on Dupont Circle, the buildings around it are, for the most part, wedge-shaped and set on plots of land formed like massive slices of pie. Only two of the great houses that stood on the circle in the early 20th century remain today. The Renaissance-style house at **15 Dupont Circle**, next to P Street, was built in 1903 for Robert W. Patterson, publisher of the *Washington Times-Herald.* Patterson's daughter, Cissy, who succeeded him as publisher, was known for hosting parties that attracted such notables as William Randolph Hearst, Douglas MacArthur, and J. Edgar Hoover. In 1927, while Cissy was living in New York City and the White House was being refurbished, Calvin Coolidge and his family stayed here. While they did, they received American aviator Charles Lindbergh; some of the most famous photographs of Lindy were taken as he stood on the house's balcony and smiled down at the crowds below. In 1948 Cissy willed the house to the American Red Cross, and the Washington Club, a private club, bought it from the organization in 1951. The **Sulgrave Club,** at the corner of Massachusetts Avenue, with its rounded apex facing the circle, was also once a private home and is now likewise a private club. *Metro: Dupont Circle.*

NEED A
BREAK?

Connecticut Avenue near Dupont Circle is chockablock with restaurants. At **Kramerbooks and Afterwords** (⊠ 1517 Connecticut Ave. NW, ☎ 202/387–1400), relax over dinner or a drink after browsing through the volumes on display. **Starbucks** (⊠ three locations along Connecticut Ave. NW, at N St., P St., and R St.) is a big part of the invasion of specialty coffee shops that also serve sweets and snacks. For lunch or a light dinner (or just a cup of tea and an oatmeal cookie), visit **Teaism** (⊠ 2009 R St. NW, ☎ 202/667–3827). This tea bar/restaurant features several dozen varieties of tea, plus a menu with seafood and vegetarian entrées, many available in bento boxes and all seasoned with tea.

Fondo Del Sol Visual Arts Center. A nonprofit museum devoted to the cultural heritage of Latin America and the Caribbean, the Fondo Del Sol Visual Arts Center has changing exhibitions covering contemporary, pre-Columbian, and folk art. The museum also offers a program of lectures, concerts, poetry readings, exhibit tours, and an annual summer festival featuring salsa and reggae music. ⊠ *2112 R St. NW,* ☎ *202/483–2777.* ▣ *$3.* ☽ *Wed.–Sat. 12:30–5. Metro: Dupont Circle.*

❷ **Heurich House Museum.** Currently housing the **Historical Society of Washington, D.C.,** this opulent Romanesque Revival was the home of Christian Heurich, a German orphan who made his fortune in this country in the beer business. Heurich's brewery was in Foggy Bottom, where the Kennedy Center stands today. Brewing was a dangerous business in the 19th century, and fires more than once reduced Heurich's brewery to ashes. Perhaps because of this he insisted that his home, completed in 1894, be fireproof; in fact, it was the first building in Washington with residential fireproofing. Although 17 fireplaces were installed—some with onyx facings, one with the bronze image of a lion staring out from the back—not a single one ever held a fire.

After Heurich's widow died in 1955, the house was turned over to the historical society and today houses a research library and museum. Most of the furnishings in the house were owned and used by the Heurichs. The interior is an eclectic Victorian treasure trove of plaster detailing, carved wooden doors, and painted ceilings. The downstairs breakfast room, in which Heurich, his wife, and their three children ate most of their meals, is decorated like a rathskeller and is adorned with such German sayings as "A good drink makes old people young."

Heurich must have taken the German proverbs seriously. He drank his beer every day, had three wives (not all at once), and lived to be 102. (In 1986 Heurich's grandson Gary started brewing the family beer again. Though it's made in Utica, New York, he vows someday to build another Heurich brewery near Washington.) Tours are self-guided, or you can make an advance request for a guided tour. The docents who give the tours are also adept at answering questions about other Washington landmarks. ⊠ *1307 New Hampshire Ave. NW,* ☎ *202/785–2068,* WEB *www.hswdc.org.* ▣ *$3.* ☽ *Mon.–Sat. 10–4. Metro: Dupont Circle.*

<table>
<tr><td>NEED A
BREAK?</td><td>The Dupont Circle branch of **Pan Asian Noodles & Grill** (⊠ 2020 P St. NW, ☎ 202/872–8889) is one of two locations in Washington. Both offer reasonably priced Asian noodle dishes.</td></tr>
</table>

<table>
<tr><td>OFF THE
BEATEN PATH</td><td>**ISLAMIC MOSQUE AND CULTURAL CENTER –** The Muslim faithful are called to prayer five times a day from atop the 162-ft-high minaret of the Islamic Mosque and Cultural Center. The ornate interior is filled with deep-pile Persian rugs and covered with Arabic art. Each May the Muslim Women's Association sponsors a bazaar, with crafts, clothing, and food for sale. Visitors wearing shorts will not be admitted to the mosque; women must wear scarves to cover their heads. ⊠ *2551 Massachusetts Ave. NW,* ☎ *202/332–8343.* ☉ *Center daily 10–5; mosque open for all 5 prayers, dawn–after sunset.*</td></tr>
</table>

⓭ **Mary McLeod Bethune Council House.** Exhibits in this museum focus on the achievements of African-American women, including Mary McLeod Bethune, who founded Florida's Bethune-Cookman College, established the National Council of Negro Women, and served as an adviser to President Franklin D. Roosevelt. ⊠ *1318 Vermont Ave. NW,* ☎ *202/673–2402.* 🎫 *Free.* ☉ *Mon.–Sat. 10–4. Metro: McPherson Square.*

⓮ **Metropolitan African Methodist Episcopal Church.** Completed in 1886, the Gothic-style Metropolitan African Methodist Episcopal Church has become one of the most influential African-American churches in the city. Abolitionist orator Frederick Douglass worshiped here, and Bill Clinton chose the church as the setting for both of his inaugural prayer services. ⊠ *1518 M St. NW,* ☎ *202/331–1426. Metro: Farragut North.*

⓯ **National Geographic Society.** Founded in 1888, the society is best known for its yellow-border magazine, found in doctor's offices, family rooms, and attics across the country. The society has sponsored numerous expeditions throughout its 100-year history, including those of Admirals Peary and Byrd and underwater explorer Jacques Cousteau. Explorers Hall, entered from 17th Street, is the magazine come to life. It invites you to learn about the world in a decidedly interactive way: you can experience everything from a mini tornado to video touch screens that explain geographic concepts and then quiz you on what you've learned. The most dramatic events take place in Earth Station One Interactive Theatre, a 72-seat amphitheater that sends the audience on a journey around the world. The centerpiece is a hand-painted globe, 11 ft in diameter, that floats and spins on a cushion of air, showing off different features of the planet. ⊠ *17th and M Sts. NW,* ☎ *202/857–7588; 202/857–7689 group tours.* 🎫 *Free.* ☉ *Mon.–Sat. 9–5, Sun. 10–5. Metro: Farragut North.*

⓾ **National Museum of American Jewish Military History.** The museum's focus is on American Jews who have served in every war the nation has fought. On display are their weapons, uniforms, medals, recruitment posters, and other military memorabilia. The few specifically religious items—a camouflage yarmulke, rabbinical supplies fashioned from shell casings and parachute silk—underscore the strange demands placed on religion during war. ⊠ *1811 R St. NW,* ☎ *202/265–6280.* 🎫 *Free.* ☉ *Weekdays 9–5, Sun. 1–5. Metro: Dupont Circle.*

★ ⑪ **Phillips Collection.** The first permanent museum of modern art in the country, the masterpiece-filled Phillips Collection is unique both in origin and content. In 1918 Duncan Phillips, grandson of a founder of the Jones and Laughlin Steel Company, started to collect art for a museum that would stand as a memorial to his father and brother, who had died within 13 months of each other. Three years later what was first called the Phillips Memorial Art Gallery opened in two rooms of this Georgian Revival home near Dupont Circle.

Not interested in a painting's market value or its faddishness, Phillips searched for works that impressed him as outstanding products of a particular artist's unique vision. Holdings include works by Georges Braque, Paul Cézanne, Paul Klee, Henri Matisse, John Henry Twacht-man, and the largest museum collection in the country of the work of Pierre Bonnard. The exhibits change regularly. The collection's best-known paintings include Renoir's *Luncheon of the Boating Party, Repentant Peter* by both Goya and El Greco, *A Bowl of Plums* by 18th-century artist Jean-Baptiste Siméon Chardin, Degas's *Dancers at the Bar,* Vincent van Gogh's *Entrance to the Public Garden at Arles,* and Cézanne's self-portrait, the painting Phillips said he would save first if his gallery caught fire. During the '20s, Phillips and his wife, Marjorie, started to support American Modernists such as John Marin, Georgia O'Keeffe, and Arthur Dove.

The Phillips is a comfortable museum. Works of an artist are often grouped together in "exhibition units," and, unlike most other galleries (where uniformed guards appear uninterested in the masterpieces around them), the Phillips employs students of art, many of whom are artists themselves, to sit by the paintings and answer questions.

The Phillips family moved out of the house in 1930. On Thursday the museum stays open late, enticing people with live jazz, gallery talks, and a cash bar. From September to May, the museum hosts a Sunday afternoon concert series at 5 in the music room, free with museum admission. ⊠ *1600 21st St. NW,* ☎ *202/387–2151.* ⌑ *$6.50; Thurs. night $7.50; some exhibitions may require an additional charge.* ⊘ *Tues.– Wed. and Fri.–Sat. 10–5; Thurs. 10–8:30; Sun. noon–7 (June–Aug., noon–5); tour Wed. and Sat. at 2; gallery talks 1st and 3rd Thurs. of month at 12:30. Metro: Dupont Circle.*

⓲ St. Matthew's Cathedral. St. Matthew's is the seat of Washington's Catholic archbishop. John F. Kennedy frequently worshiped in this Renaissance-style church, and in 1963 his funeral mass was held within its richly decorated walls. Set in the floor, directly in front of the main altar, is a memorial to the slain president: "Here rested the remains of President Kennedy at the requiem mass November 25, 1963, before their removal to Arlington where they lie in expectation of a heavenly resurrection." A memorial to nuns who served as nurses during the Civil War is across Rhode Island Avenue. ⊠ *1725 Rhode Island Ave. NW,* ☎ *202/347–3215.* ⌑ *Free.* ⊘ *Weekdays and Sun. 7–6:30, Sat. 8–6:30; tour usually Sun. at 2:30. Metro: Farragut North.*

⓬ Scott Circle. The equestrian statue of General Winfield Scott here was cast from cannons captured in the Mexican War. On the west side of the traffic circle is a statue of fiery orator Daniel Webster. If you walk to the south side of the circle and look down 16th Street, you'll get a familiar view of the columns of the White House, six blocks away. Across the circle is a memorial to S. C. F. Hahnemann, his statue sitting in a recessed wall, his head surrounded by a mosaic of colorful tiles. Who, you ask, was S. C. F. Hahnemann? He was the founder of the homeopathic system of medicine and the namesake of Hahnemann Medical School in Philadelphia. ⊠ *Massachusetts and Rhode Island Aves. and 16th St. Metro: Archives/Navy Memorial.*

❽ Textile Museum. In the 1890s, founder George Hewitt Myers purchased his first Oriental rug for his dorm room at Yale. An heir to the Bristol-Myers fortune, Myers and his wife lived two houses down from Woodrow Wilson, at 2310 S Street, in a home designed by John Russell Pope, architect of the National Archives and the Jefferson Memorial. Myers bought the Waddy B. Wood–designed house next door, at No. 2320, and opened his museum to the public in 1925. Today the collection includes more than 15,500 rugs and textiles. Rotating exhibits are taken from a permanent collection of historic and ethnographic items that include Coptic and pre-Columbian textiles, Kashmir embroidery, and Turkman tribal rugs. At least one show of modern textiles—such as quilts or fiber art—is mounted each year. The Activity Gallery in the new Textile Learning Center has hands-on exhibits and activities. You can look at several textile techniques, then try your hand at doing them yourself. ⊠ *2320 S St. NW,* ☎ *202/667–0441.* ⊡ *Suggested donation $5.* ☉ *Mon.–Sat. 10–5, Sun. 1–5; highlight tour Sept.– May, Wed. and weekends at 1:30. Metro: Dupont Circle.*

❾ 2221 Kalorama Road. S Street is an informal dividing line between the Dupont Circle area to the south and the Kalorama neighborhood to the north. The name for this peaceful, tree-filled enclave—Greek for "beautiful view"—was contributed by politician and writer Joel Barlow, who bought the large tract in 1807. Kalorama is filled with embassies and luxurious homes. The Tudor mansion at 2221 Kalorama Road, where 23rd Street runs into Kalorama Road, was built in 1911 for mining millionaire W. W. Lawrence, but since 1936 it has been the residence of the French ambassador. For a taste of the beautiful view that so captivated Barlow, walk west on Kalorama Road, and then turn right on Kalorama Circle. At the bottom of the circle you can look down over Rock Creek Park, the finger of green that pokes into northwest Washington.

❸ Walsh-McLean House. Tom McLean was an Irishman who made a fortune with a Colorado gold mine and came to Washington to show his wealth. The city on the Potomac was the perfect place to establish a presence for America's late-19th-century nouveau riche. It was easier to enter "society" in the nation's planned capital than in New York or Philadelphia, and wealthy industrialists and entrepreneurs flocked here. Walsh announced his arrival with this 60-room mansion. His daughter, Evalyn Walsh-McLean, the last private owner of the Hope Diamond (now in the National Museum of Natural History), was one of the city's leading hostesses. Today the house is used as an embassy by the Indonesian government and isn't open for tours. ⊠ *2020 Massachusetts Ave. NW. Metro: Dupont Circle.*

OFF THE BEATEN PATH
THE WASHINGTON POST BUILDING – Although the newspaper is no longer printed here, the claim to fame of the main *Washington Post* building when it opened in 1951 was that the printing plant and editorial offices were stacked so compactly in one small downtown location. You can see the newsroom that broke the Watergate story on a 45-minute guided tour of the building, which is otherwise not open to the public. In addition to the newsroom, there's a small museum dedicated to the history of the newspaper and old and new printing processes. For the guided tour, you must reserve a spot by phone two to six weeks in advance. ⊠ *1150 15th St. NW,* ☎ *202/334–7969,* WEB *washpost. com/community/you/.* ⊡ *Free.* ☉ *Tours Mon. on the hr 10 am–3 pm.*

❼ Woodrow Wilson House. Until the Clintons bought a house here, Wilson was the only president who stayed in D.C. after leaving the White House. (He's also the only president buried in the city, inside the National Cathedral.) He and his second wife, Edith Bolling Wilson, retired in 1920 to this Georgian Revival designed by Washington architect Waddy B. Wood. (Wood also designed the Department of the Interior and the National Museum of Women in the Arts.) The house was built in 1915 for a carpet magnate.

President Wilson suffered a stroke toward the end of his second term, in 1919, and he lived out the last few years of his life on this quiet street. Edith made sure he was comfortable; she had a bed constructed that was the same dimensions as the large Lincoln bed Wilson had slept in while in the White House. She also had the house's trunk lift electrified so the partially paralyzed president could move from floor to floor. When the streetcars stopped running in 1962 the elevator stopped working; it had received its electricity directly from the streetcar line.

Wilson died in 1924. Edith survived him by 37 years. After she died in 1961, the house and its contents were bequeathed to the National Trust for Historic Preservation. On view inside are such items as a Gobelins tapestry, a baseball signed by King George V, and the shell casing from the first shot fired by U.S. forces in World War I. The house also contains memorabilia related to the history of the short-lived League of Nations, including the colorful flag Wilson hoped would be adopted by that organization. ⊠ *2340 S St. NW,* ☎ *202/387–4062.* ▨ *$5.* ☉ *Tues.–Sun. 10–4. Metro: Dupont Circle.*

FOGGY BOTTOM

Updated by
Robin
Dougherty

The Foggy Bottom area of Washington—bordered roughly by the Potomac and Rock Creek to the west, 20th Street to the east, Pennsylvania Avenue to the north, and Constitution Avenue to the south—has three main claims to fame: the State Department, the Kennedy Center, and George Washington University. In 1763 a German immigrant named Jacob Funk purchased this land, and a community called Funkstown sprang up on the Potomac. This nickname is only slightly less amusing than the present one, an appellation derived from the wharves, breweries, lime kilns, and glassworks that were near the water. Smoke from these factories combined with the swampy air of the low-lying ground to produce a permanent fog along the waterfront.

The smoke-belching factories ensured work for the hundreds of German and Irish immigrants who settled in Foggy Bottom in the 19th century. By the 1930s, however, industry was on the way out, and Foggy Bottom had become a poor part of Washington. The opening of the State Department headquarters in 1947 reawakened middle-class interest in the neighborhood's modest row houses. Many of them are now gone, and Foggy Bottom today suffers from a split personality as tiny, one-room-wide row houses sit next to large, mixed-use developments.

Although the Foggy Bottom neighborhood has its own Metro stop, many attractions are a considerable distance away. If you don't relish long walks or time is limited, check the Foggy Bottom map to see if you need to make alternate travel arrangements to visit specific sights.

Numbers in the text correspond to numbers in the margin and on the Foggy Bottom map.

A Good Walk

Start your exploration near the Foggy Bottom Metro station at 23rd and I streets. The sprawling campus of **George Washington University** ① covers much of Foggy Bottom south of Pennsylvania Avenue between 19th and 24th streets. Walk west from the Metro station on the I Street pedestrian mall, and then turn left on New Hampshire Avenue. At Virginia Avenue you run into the **Watergate** ②, possibly the world's most notorious apartment-office complex, forever a part of our language for the role it played in the downfall of a president. Walk south on New Hampshire Avenue, past the Saudi Arabian Embassy, to the **John F. Kennedy Center for the Performing Arts** ③, Washington's premier cultural center. Walk back up New Hampshire Avenue; then turn right on G Street, right on Virginia Avenue (follow the outstretched arm of the statue of Benito Juárez, the 19th-century Mexican statesman), and right on 23rd Street. The Pan American Health Organization, American headquarters of the World Health Organization, is at 23rd Street and Virginia Avenue, in the circular building that looks like a huge car air filter. Two blocks down 23rd Street is the massive **Department of State** ④, with its opulent Diplomatic Reception Rooms, filled with museum-quality furnishings.

Follow 23rd Street to Constitution Avenue and turn left. On the south side of Constitution are the Lincoln and Vietnam Veterans memorials. The John Russell Pope–designed **American Pharmaceutical Association** ⑤ building sits at the corner of Constitution Avenue and 23rd Street. One block east is the **National Academy of Sciences** ⑥, where there are often free art exhibits. You can tour the white-marble **Federal Reserve Building** ⑦, which has an art collection, to find out exactly what it is "the Fed" does. Turn left on 20th Street. Crossing Virginia Avenue and continuing north on 20th Street takes you back onto the campus of George Washington University. Foggy Bottom's immigrant past is apparent in the United Church, which still conducts services in German. Walk north to Pennsylvania Avenue. To the right—near No. 1901—are the only two survivors of a string of 18th-century row houses known as the **Seven Buildings** ⑧, both now dwarfed by the taller office block behind them. The modern glass office building at **2000 Pennsylvania Avenue** ⑨ incorporates a row of hollowed-out and refurbished Victorian houses as part of its facade. Across Pennsylvania Avenue, on the small triangle where I Street intersects it, is the federal-style **Arts Club of Washington** ⑩, once the home of James Monroe.

TIMING

Foggy Bottom is a half-day walk. Touring the State Department and the Federal Reserve Building should take about two hours. A good chunk of time can be spent walking between sites, because this area isn't as densely packed with points of interest as are most others.

Sights to See

❺ **American Pharmaceutical Association.** You might think the American Pharmaceutical Association is a rather odd sightseeing recommendation, even just for a casual glance as you're passing. But aside from the fact that the white-marble building was designed in 1934 by noted architect John Russell Pope, who also designed the Lincoln Memorial and the National Gallery of Art, the American Pharmaceutical Association is as much a symbol of modern Washington as any government edifice. It's the home of one of more than 3,000 trade and professional associations (as obscure as the Cast Iron Soil Pipe Institute and as well-known as the National Association of Broadcasters) that have chosen the capital for their headquarters, eager to represent their members' interests before the government. ⊠ *Constitution Ave. and 23rd St. Metro: Foggy Bottom.*

❿ **Arts Club of Washington.** Built in 1806 by Timothy Caldwell, this federal-style house was once the residence of James Monroe and has been home to the Arts Club, a nonprofit organization dedicated to the promotion of the arts in the nation's capital, since 1916. Exhibits in the Monroe House and adjoining MacFeely House galleries represent a wide range of styles, with the work of local artists well represented. ⊠ *2017 I St. NW,* ☎ *202/331–7282.* ▨ *Free.* ☉ *Tues.–Fri. 10–5, Sat. 10–2. Metro: Farragut West.*

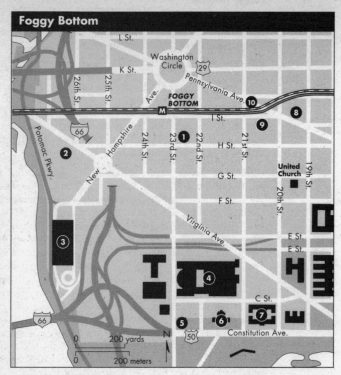

Foggy Bottom

❹ Department of State. The foreign policy of the United States is formulated and administered by battalions of brainy analysts in the huge Department of State Building (often referred to as the State Department), which also serves as the headquarters of the United States Diplomatic Corps. All is presided over by the secretary of state, who is fourth in line for the presidency (after the vice president, speaker of the House, and president *pro tempore* of the Senate, respectively) should the president be unable to serve. On the top floor are the opulent Diplomatic Reception Rooms, decorated in the manner of great halls of Europe, and the rooms of Colonial American plantations. The museum-quality furnishings include a Philadelphia highboy, a Paul Revere bowl, and the desk on which the Treaty of Paris was signed. The largest room has a specially loomed carpet so heavy and large it had to be airlifted in by helicopter. The rooms are used 15–20 times a week to entertain foreign diplomats and heads of state; you can see them, too, but you need to register for a tour well ahead of your visit. Summer tours must be booked up to three months in advance. ⊠ *23rd and C Sts. NW,* ☎ *202/647–3241; 202/736–4474 TDD.* ☛ *Free.* ☉ *Tours weekdays at 9:30, 10:30, and 2:45; book well in advance. Metro: Foggy Bottom.*

❼ Federal Reserve Building. Whether interest rates are raised or lowered in attempts to control the economy is decided in this imposing marble edifice, its bronze entryway topped by a massive eagle. Designed by Folger Library architect Paul Cret, "the Fed" is on Constitution Avenue between 20th and 21st streets. It seems to say, "Your money's safe with us." Even so, there isn't any money here. Ft. Knox holds most of the government's gold. The Fed's stately facade belies a friendlier interior, with a varied collection of art and four special art exhibitions every year. A 45-minute tour includes a film that explains exactly what it is that the Fed does. ⊠ *Enter on C St. between 20th and 21st Sts.,* ☎ *202/452–3000; 202/452–3149 building tours; 202/452–3686 art tours.* ☛ *Free.* ☉ *Weekdays 11–2 during art exhibitions (tours of per-*

manent art collection by appointment only); building tour Thurs. at 2:30. Metro: Foggy Bottom.

❶ George Washington University. George Washington had always hoped the capital would be home to a world-class university. He even left 50 shares of stock in the Patowmack Canal Co. to endow it. Congress never acted upon his wishes, however, and it wasn't until 1822 that the university that would eventually be named after the first president began to take shape. The private Columbian College in the District of Columbia opened that year with the aim of training students for the Baptist ministry. In 1904 the university shed its Baptist connections and changed its name to George Washington University. In 1912 it moved to its present location and since that time has become the second largest landholder in the District (after the federal government). Students have ranged from J. Edgar Hoover to Jacqueline Bouvier. In addition to residing in modern university buildings, GWU occupies many 19th-century houses. ✉ *Downtown campus covers much of Foggy Bottom south of Pennsylvania Ave. between 19th and 24th Sts.,* ☎ *202/994–1000,* WEB *www.gwu.edu. Metro: Foggy Bottom.*

❸ John F. Kennedy Center for the Performing Arts. Thanks to the Kennedy Center, Washington regularly hosts world-class performers. Prior to 1971, Washington after dark was primarily known for cocktail parties, not culture. The opening of the Kennedy Center in that year instantly established the capital as a cultural mecca on an international scale. Concerts, ballets, opera, musicals, and drama are presented in the center's five theaters, and movies are screened periodically in the theater of the American Film Institute, which resides here through the September of 2002, when it's scheduled to move into its new home in Silver Spring, Maryland.

The idea for a national cultural center had been proposed by President Eisenhower in 1955. John F. Kennedy had also strongly supported the idea, and after his assassination it was decided to dedicate the center to him. Some critics have called the center's square design unimaginative—it has been dubbed the cake box that the more decorative Watergate came in—but no one has denied that the building is immense. The Grand Foyer, lighted by 18 1-ton Orrefors crystal chandeliers, is 630 ft long. (Even at this size it's mobbed at intermission.) Many of the center's furnishings were donated by foreign countries: the chandeliers came from Sweden; the tapestries on the walls came from Brazil, France, and Mexico; and the 3,700 tons of white Carrara marble for the interior and exterior of the building were a gift from Italy. Flags fly in the Hall of Nations and the Hall of States, and in the center of the foyer is a 7-ft-high, bronze, oddly textured bust of Kennedy by sculptor Robert Berks.

In addition to the regular performances in the five theaters, each year the Kennedy Center also produces a variety of festivals that highlight different musical traditions and cultures. The hugely popular annual open house is a free, daylong extravaganza of theater, dance, and music, with nonstop entertainment both indoors and outdoors. There also are free performances every evening at 6 on the Millennium Stage.

Two restaurants on the Roof Terrace Level range from casual fare to more formal dining. It can get noisy as jets fly overhead to nearby Ronald Reagan National Airport, but you can get one of the city's better views from the terrace: to the north are Georgetown and the National Cathedral; to the west, Theodore Roosevelt Island and Rosslyn, Virginia; and to the south, the Lincoln and Jefferson memorials. ✉ *New Hampshire Ave. and Rock Creek Pkwy. NW,* ☎ *202/467–4600.* ☑ *Free.* ☉ *Daily*

10–9 (or until last show lets out); box office Mon.–Sat. 10–9, Sun. noon–9; tours weekdays 10–5, weekends 10–1. Metro: Foggy Bottom, with free shuttle bus service every 15 minutes to and from the Kennedy Center on performance days.

⑥ National Academy of Sciences. Inscribed in Greek under the cornice is a quotation from Aristotle on the value of science—appropriate for a building that houses the offices of the National Academy of Sciences, the National Academy of Engineering, the Institute of Medicine, and the National Research Council. There are often free art exhibits—not all of them relating to science—and weekend concerts. In front of the academy is Robert Berks's sculpture of Albert Einstein, done in the same lumpy, mashed-potato style as the artist's bust of JFK in the Kennedy Center. ✉ *2101 Constitution Ave. NW,* ☎ *202/334–2000.* 🎫 *Free.* ☉ *Weekdays 8–5. Metro: Foggy Bottom.*

⑧ Seven Buildings. Only two structures remain of the string of 18th-century row houses known as the Seven Buildings. One of the five that have been demolished served as President Madison's executive mansion after the British burned the White House in 1814. The two survivors are now dwarfed by the taller office block behind them and have been integrated into the Mexican Embassy, which is at 1911 Pennsylvania Avenue NW. ✉ *Near 1901 Pennsylvania Ave. Metro: Foggy Bottom.*

⑨ 2000 Pennsylvania Avenue. It's a shame that so many important historical buildings fail to survive as a city matures. The row of residences on Pennsylvania Avenue between 20th and 21st streets escaped the fate of the **Seven Buildings** by being incorporated—literally—into the present. The Victorian houses have been hollowed out and refurbished to serve as the entryway for a modern glass office structure at 2000 Pennsylvania Avenue. The backs of the buildings are under the sloping roof of the new development, preserved as if in an urban terrarium. *Metro: Foggy Bottom.*

United Church. Foggy Bottom's immigrant past is apparent in the United Church. Built in 1891 for blue-collar Germans in the neighborhood, the church still conducts services in German the first and third Sunday of every month at 9:30, September through May. ✉ *20th and G Sts.,* ☎ *202/331–1495. Metro: Foggy Bottom.*

② Watergate. Thanks to the events that took place on the night of June 17, 1972, the Watergate is possibly the world's most notorious apartment-office complex. As President Richard Nixon's aides E. Howard Hunt Jr. and G. Gordon Liddy sat in the Howard Johnson Motor Lodge across the street, five of their men were caught trying to bug the Democratic National Committee, headquartered on the building's sixth floor, in an attempt to subvert the democratic process on behalf of the then-president of the United States. A marketing company occupies the space today.

The suffix "-gate" is attached to any political scandal nowadays, but the Watergate itself was named after a monumental flight of steps that led down to the Potomac behind the Lincoln Memorial. The original Watergate was the site of band concerts until plane noise from nearby Ronald Reagan National Airport made the locale impractical.

Even before the break-in, the Watergate—which opened in 1965—was well known in the capital. Within its curving lines and behind its "toothpick" balusters have lived some of Washington's most famous—and infamous—citizens, including attorney general John Mitchell and presidential secretary Rose Mary Woods of Nixon White House fame as well as such power brokers as Jacob Javits, Alan Cranston, and Bob and Elizabeth Dole, and, more recently, Monica Lewinsky, the world's most famous intern. The embassies of Brunei and Yemen are also in the Watergate. ⊠ *2600 Virginia Ave. Metro: Foggy Bottom.*

CLEVELAND PARK
AND THE NATIONAL ZOO

Updated by
Robin
Dougherty

Cleveland Park, a tree-shaded neighborhood in northwest Washington, owes its name to onetime summer resident Grover Cleveland and its development to the streetcar line that was laid along Connecticut Avenue in the 1890s. President Cleveland and his wife, Frances Folson, escaped the heat of downtown Washington in 1886 by establishing a summer White House on Newark Street between 35th and 36th streets. Many prominent Washingtonians followed suit. When the streetcar came through in 1892, construction in the area snowballed. Developer John Sherman hired local architects to design houses and provided amenities such as a fire station and a streetcar-waiting lodge to entice home buyers out of the city and into "rural" Cleveland Park. Today the neighborhood's attractive houses and suburban character are popular with Washington professionals. (The Cleveland's retreat no longer stands, but on the same block is Rosedale, an 18th-century estate that was the home of another famous summer visitor, young Cuban refugee Elian Gonzalez, in 2000.)

Numbers in the text correspond to numbers in the margin and on the Cleveland Park and the National Zoo map.

A Good Walk

Start your exploration at the Cleveland Park Metro station at Connecticut Avenue and Ordway Street NW. The Colonial-style Park and Shop on the east side of Connecticut Avenue was Washington's first shopping center with off-street parking. The art deco style is well represented by many of the buildings and apartments along some of the main thoroughfares in northwest Washington, including Connecticut Avenue. The **Cineplex Odeon Uptown** ①, a marvelous vintage-1936 art deco movie house, is a reminder of the days when movie theaters were something other than boring little boxes. Continue south on Connecticut Avenue, where you cross a sliver of Rock Creek Park, via a bridge decorated with eight art deco lights. Off to your left is the city's finest art deco apartment house, the **Kennedy-Warren** ②, with stylized carved eagles flanking the driveways. Follow Connecticut Avenue two more blocks to the **National Zoological Park** ③, another member of the Smithsonian family, Tian Tian and Mei Xiang, the zoo's most famous residents, are among a small handful of giant pandas in the United States.

Stately old apartment buildings line Connecticut Avenue south of the zoo. Cross Cathedral Avenue and enter the Woodley Park section of the city. The cross-shape **Wardman Tower** ④, at the corner of Connecticut Avenue and Woodley Road, was built in 1928 as a luxury apartment building. Once known for its famous residents, it's now part of the Marriott Wardman Park. Get back on the Metro and ride two stops to Van Ness to visit **Hillwood Museum and Gardens**, a mansion with beautiful gardens.

TIMING

The amount of time you spend at the zoo depends on how much you like zoos. Popular visiting times are when the giant pandas are fed at 11 and 3, and during the sea-lion training demonstration at 11:30.

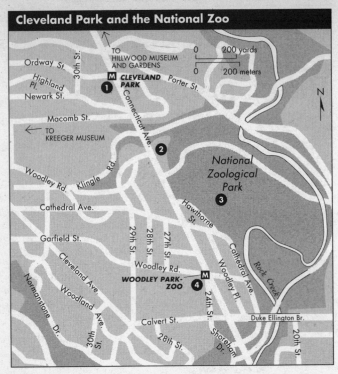

Sights to See

1 Cineplex Odeon Uptown. If you're in the mood for a movie during your stay and want to see it in a grand entertainment palace of yesteryear, the Cineplex Odeon Uptown is the place to go. Unlike most of the nation's other old theaters, which have been chopped up and transformed into multiplexes, this marvelous vintage-1936 art deco movie house, the only one of its kind left in Washington, has remained true to its origins, with a single huge screen and an inviting balcony. ⊠ 3426 Connecticut Ave. NW, ☎ 202/966–5400. Metro: Cleveland Park.

OFF THE BEATEN PATH

HILLWOOD MUSEUM AND GARDENS – Hillwood House, cereal heiress Marjorie Merriweather Post's 40-room Georgian mansion, contains a large collection of 18th- and 19th-century French and Russian decorative art that includes gold and silver work, icons, lace, tapestries, china, and Fabergé eggs. Also on the estate are a dacha filled with Russian objects and an Adirondacks-style cabin that houses an assortment of Native American artifacts. The 25-acre estate grounds are composed of lawns, formal French and Japanese gardens, greenhouses, and paths that wind through plantings of azaleas, laurels, and rhododendrons. Make reservations for the house tour well in advance. Hillwood is one or two Metro stops from the zoo, depending on which station you use. ⊠ 4155 Linnean Ave. NW, ☎ 202/686–5807 or 202/686–8500. ☞ House and grounds $10; grounds only $2. ⊙ House tours Mar.–Jan., Tues.–Sat. 9:30–3; grounds Mar.–Jan., Tues.–Sat. 9–5. Metro: Van Ness/UDC.

2 Kennedy-Warren. Lovers of the art deco–style won't want to miss the Kennedy-Warren. The apartment house is a superb example, with such period detailing as decorative aluminum panels and a streamlined entryway, stone griffins under the pyramidal copper roof, and stylized carved eagles flanking the driveways. Perhaps in keeping with its elegant architecture, this is one of the last apartment buildings in town still to have a doorman. ✉ *3133 Connecticut Ave. NW. Metro: Cleveland Park.*

OFF THE
BEATEN PATH

KREEGER MUSEUM – You need to travel by car or taxi to the Kreeger Museum. Its cool white domes and elegant lines stand in stark contrast to the traditional feel of the rest of the Foxhall Road neighborhood. One of Washington's newer museums, and originally the home of GEICO insurance executive David Lloyd Kreeger and his wife Carmen, the building was designed by Philip Johnson. The collection includes works by Renoir, Degas, Cezanne, Munch and other as well as traditional African artifacts. Entrance is by reservation only. ✉ *2401 Foxhall Rd. NW,* ☎ *202/338–3553.* 🎟 *$5.* ⊙ *Tours Tues.–Sat. 10:30 and 1:30.*

🖑 ❸ **National Zoological Park.** Part of the Smithsonian Institution, the National Zoo is one of the foremost zoos in the world. Created by an Act of Congress in 1889, the 163-acre park was designed by landscape architect Frederick Law Olmsted, the man who designed the U.S. Capitol grounds. (Before the zoo opened in 1890, live animals used as taxidermists' models had been kept on the Mall.) For years the zoo's most famous residents were the giant pandas Hsing-Hsing and Ling-Ling, gifts from China in 1972. Both are gone now, but panda fans can welcome Tian Tian and Mei Xiang, who arrived from China in 2001. They receive visitors from 9 to 4:30 each day, but you should expect a half hour's wait.

Throughout the zoo, innovative compounds show many animals in naturalistic settings, including the Great Flight Cage—a walk-in aviary in which birds fly unrestricted from May to October (they're moved indoors during the colder months). Zoolab, the Reptile Discovery Center, and the Bird Resource Center all offer activities that teach young visitors about biology. The most ambitious addition to the zoo is Amazonia, a reproduction of a South American rain-forest ecosystem. Fish swim behind glass walls, while overhead, monkeys and birds flit from tree to tree. The temperature is a constant 85°F, with 85% humidity. The Cheetah Conservation Area is a grassy compound that's home to a family of the world's fastest cats. Amazonia and the Cheetah Conservation Area, as well as the Gorilla Outdoor Yard and the Sea Lion Exhibit, are the most visible attempts by the zoo to show animals in more naturalistic settings and heighten your appreciation of those environments. The American Prairie exhibit celebrates grasses that truly are as high as an elephant's eye, and explores the resurgence of the bison, nearly killed off in the 19th century. ✉ *3001 Connecticut Ave. NW,* ☎ *202/673–4800 or 202/673–4717,* 🖵 *www.si.edu/natzoo.* 🎟 *Free.* ⊙ *May–mid-Sept., grounds daily 6 AM–8 PM, animal buildings daily 10–6 (may be open later in summer); mid-Sept.–Apr., grounds daily 6–6, animal buildings daily 10–4:30. Metro: Cleveland Park or Woodley Park/Zoo.*

❹ **Wardman Tower.** At the corner of Connecticut Avenue and Woodley Road is the cross-shape, Georgian-style tower built by developer Harry Wardman in 1928 as a luxury apartment building. Washingtonians called the project "Wardman's Folly," convinced no one would want to stay in a hotel so far from the city—some 25 blocks from the White House; most upscale residential buildings, especially older ones, are within a few blocks. Contrary to early predictions, however, Wardman Tower was famous for its well-known residents, who included Dwight D. Eisenhower, Herbert Hoover, Clare Booth Luce, Dean Rusk, Earl Warren, and Caspar Weinberger. It's now part of the Marriott Wardman Park. ✉ *2660 Woodley Rd. NW. Metro: Woodley Park/Zoo.*

Woodley Park. The stretch of Connecticut Avenue south of the National Zoo is bordered by venerable apartment buildings. Passing Cathedral Avenue (the first cross street south of the zoo), you enter a part of town known as Woodley Park. Like Cleveland Park to the north, Woodley Park grew as the streetcar advanced into this part of Washington. In 1800 Philip Barton Key, uncle of Francis Scott Key, built Woodley, a Georgian mansion on Cathedral Avenue between 29th and 31st streets. The white stucco mansion was the summer home of four presidents: Van Buren, Tyler, Buchanan, and Cleveland. It's now owned by the private Maret School. *Metro: Woodley Park/Zoo.*

ADAMS-MORGAN

Updated by
Robin
Dougherty

To the young, the hip, the cool, and the postmodern, Washington has the reputation of being a rather staid town, more interested in bureaucracy than boogie, with all the vitality of a seersucker suit. It may have the Hope Diamond, these detractors say, but that's about the only thing that really sparkles. What they mean, of course, is that Washington isn't New York City. And thank goodness, say Washingtonians, who wouldn't want to give up their clean subway, comfortable standard of living, or place in the political spotlight, even if it did mean being able to get a decent corned beef sandwich or a double espresso at three in the morning. Besides, Washington does have Adams-Morgan. It may not be Greenwich Village, but it's close enough in spirit to satisfy all but the most hardened black-clad, shade-sporting cynics.

Adams-Morgan (roughly, the blocks north of Florida Avenue, between Connecticut Avenue and 16th Street NW) is Washington's most ethnically diverse neighborhood. And as is so often the case, that means it's one of Washington's most interesting areas—home to a veritable United Nations of cuisines, offbeat shops, and funky bars and clubs. The name itself, fashioned in the 1950s by neighborhood civic groups, serves as a symbol of the area's melting pot character: it's a conjunction of the names of two local schools, the predominantly Caucasian Adams School and the largely African-American Morgan School. Today Adams-Morgan is home to every shade in between, with large Latin American and West African populations.

The neighborhood's grand 19th-century apartment buildings and row houses along with its bohemian atmosphere have attracted young professionals, the businesses that cater to them, the attendant parking and crowd problems, and the rise in real estate values. All this has caused some longtime Adams-Morganites to wonder if their neighborhood is in danger of becoming another Georgetown.

Adams-Morgan already has one thing in common with Georgetown: there's no Metro stop. It's a pleasant 15-minute walk from the Woodley Park/Zoo Metro station: walk south on Connecticut, then turn left on Calvert Street, and cross over Rock Creek Park on the Duke Ellington Bridge. Or you can get off at the Dupont Circle Metro stop and walk east to (and turn left onto) 18th Street. The heart of Adams-Morgan is at the crossroads of Adams Mill Road, Columbia Road, and 18th Street.

Numbers in the text correspond to numbers in the margin and on the Adams-Morgan map.

A Good Walk

Some walks are most enjoyable if followed in the suggested sequence though here we suggest wandering from the path described to make your own discoveries in the serendipitous spirit of this area. Begin by walking east on Calvert Street from the Woodley Park/Zoo Metro stop and turning left on Columbia Road. At tables stretched along the street, vendors hawk watches, leather goods, knockoff perfumes, cassette tapes (blank and prerecorded), sneakers, clothes, and handmade jewelry. The store signs—Casa Lebrato, Urgente Express (the latter the name of a business that specializes in shipping to and from Central America)—are a testament to the area's Latin flavor; on these blocks you hear as much Spanish as you do English.

Cross Columbia at Ontario Road and backtrack west. On Saturday morning a market springs up on the plaza in front of the Suntrust bank, at the southwest corner of 18th and Columbia, with vendors selling fruits, vegetables, flowers, and fresh bread.

If Columbia Road east of 18th is Adams-Morgan's Latin Quarter, 18th Street south of Columbia is its restaurant corridor. In the next few blocks are restaurants serving the cuisines of China, Mexico, India, El Salvador, Ethiopia, France, the Caribbean, Thailand, Argentina, Italy, Vietnam, and, believe it or not, the United States. If you can't make up your mind, there's even a palm reader who can help decide what your future has in store.

You can also feed your hunger for the outré or offbeat with the funky shops on 18th Street. Here you find the Mission-style furniture, Russell Wright crockery and Fiesta ware, aerodynamic art deco armchairs, Bakelite telephones, massive chromium toasters, kidney-shape Formica-top coffee tables, skinny neckties, and tacky salt-and-pepper shakers that—through time and TV reruns—have been transformed from kitsch into collectibles. The west side of 18th Street is home to a gamut of antiques shops as well as secondhand shops set up in alleys or warehouses. Nearby is the **District of Columbia Arts Center** ①, a combination art gallery and performance space.

On 16th Street there are several points of interest, including the **All Souls' Unitarian Church** ②, the **Mexican Cultural Institute** ③, the **Meridian House and the White-Meyer House** ④, and the **House of the Temple** ⑤. Hop on an S2 or S4 bus toward Silver Spring to visit the National Museum of Health and Medicine.

Of course, the measure of any neighborhood is the tone it takes when the sun goes down. In the spring and summer, restaurants open their windows or set out tables on the sidewalks. Those lucky enough to have rooftop seating find diners lining up to eat under the stars. Washington can be notoriously hot in the summer, but one of Adams-Morgan's charms has always been that its slight elevation wraps it in cooling breezes. Although the neighborhood's bar and club scene isn't as varied as its restaurant scene, there are some standouts. Remember that the last trains leave the Woodley Park Metro station at around midnight. If you can't tear yourself away, be prepared to take a cab.

TIMING
If you're in a shopping mood, a wander around Adams-Morgan can occupy the better part of an afternoon. And if you take advantage of the restaurants and nightlife here, there's no telling when your head will hit the pillow.

Sights to See
② **All Souls' Unitarian Church.** The design of All Souls', erected in 1924, is based on that of St. Martin-in-the-Fields in London. ✉ *16th and Harvard Sts. NW,* ☎ *202/332–5266.* ☉ *Sun. services at 10:50 AM.*

① **District of Columbia Arts Center.** A combination art gallery and performance space, the DCAC exhibits the cutting-edge work of local artists

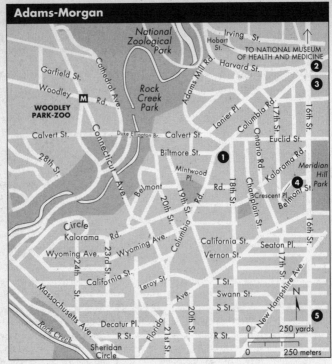

Adams-Morgan

and is the host of offbeat plays, and that uncategorizable category known as performance art. ✉ 2438 18th St. NW, ☎ 202/462–7833. 🗺 *Gallery free, performance costs vary.* ⊘ *Wed.–Sun. 2–7, Fri.–Sat. 2–10, and during performances (generally Thurs.–Sun. 7 PM–midnight).*

❺ House of the Temple. A dramatic Masonic shrine, the House of the Temple was patterned after the Mausoleum of Halicarnassus. Tours are available on a drop-in basis. ✉ 1733 16th St. NW, ☎ 202/232–3579. 🗺 *Free.* ⊘ *Tours weekdays 8–2.*

❹ Meridian House and the White-Meyer House. Meridian International Center, a nonprofit institution promoting international understanding, owns two handsome mansions designed by John Russell Pope. The 30-room Meridian House was built in 1920 by Irwin Boyle Laughlin, scion of a Pittsburgh steel family and former ambassador to Spain. The Louis XVI–style home features parquet floors, ornamental iron grillwork, handsome moldings, period furniture, tapestries, and a garden planted with European linden trees. Next door is the Georgian-style house built for Henry White (former ambassador to France) that was later the home of the Meyer family, publishers of the *Washington Post*. The first floors of both houses are open to the public and are the scene of periodic art exhibits with an international flavor. ✉ 1630 and 1624 Crescent Pl. NW, ☎ 202/667–6800. 🗺 *Free.* ⊘ *Wed.–Sun. 2–5.*

❸ Mexican Cultural Institute. This glorious Italianate house, designed by Nathan Wyeth and George A. Fuller, architects of the West Wing of the White House, housed the Embassy of Mexico until 1989. In 1990, the Mexican Cultural Institute opened to promote Mexican art, culture, and science. Exhibits have included works by 19th- and 20th-century Mexican artists such as Diego Rivera, José Clemente Orozco, David Alfaro, and Juan O'Gorman. ✉ 2829 16th St. NW, ☎ 202/728–1628. 🗺 *Free.* ⊘ *Tues.–Sat. 11–5:30.*

NATIONAL MUSEUM OF HEALTH AND MEDICINE – Opened more than 125 years ago, the medical museum has exhibits that illustrate medicine's fight against injury and disease. Included are displays on the Lincoln and Garfield assassinations and one of the world's largest collections of microscopes. Because some exhibits are fairly graphic (the wax surgical models and organs floating in alcohol, for example), the museum may not be suitable for young children or the squeamish. To get here from Adams-Morgan, catch Bus S2 or S4 to Silver Spring on 16th Street. ⊠ *Walter Reed Army Medical Center, 6825 16th St. NW,* ☎ *202/ 782–2200.* ⊠ *Free.* ⊙ *Daily 10–5:30.*

☞ **Rock Creek Park.** The 1,800 acres of park on either side of Rock Creek have provided a cool oasis for D.C. residents ever since Congress set them aside in 1890. Bicycle routes and hiking and equestrian trails wind through the groves of dogwoods, beeches, oaks, and cedar, and 30 picnic areas are scattered about. Rangers at the **Nature Center and Planetarium** (⊠ South of Military Rd. at 5200 Glover Rd. NW, ☎ 202/ 426–6829) introduce the park and list daily events; guided nature walks leave from the center weekends at 2. The center and planetarium is open Wednesday to Sunday from 9 to 5. The **Peirce Mill** (⊠ Rock Creek Park at Tilden St. and Beach Dr., ☎ 202/426–6908) is where park service employees grind grain into flour at this 19th-century gristmill—powered by the falling water of Rock Creek—and sell it to visitors. Mill hours are Wednesday through Sunday from noon to 4. Other park features include Ft. Reno, Ft. Bayard, Ft. Stevens, and Ft. DeRussy, remnants of the original ring of forts that guarded Washington during the Civil War, and the Rock Creek Park Golf Course, an 18-hole public course. Landscape architect Horace Peaslee created oft-overlooked **Meridian Hill Park** (⊠ 16th and Euclid Sts.), which is part of Rock Creek Park, after a 1917 study of the parks of Europe. As a result, it contains elements of parks in France (a long, straight mall bordered with plants), Italy (terraces and wall fountains), and Switzerland (a lower-level reflecting pool based on one in Zurich). It's also unofficially known as Malcolm X Park, renamed by the D.C. Council in the 1970s in honor of Malcolm X, who once spoke here. Drug activity once made it unwise to visit this park alone. It's somewhat safer now, but avoid it after dark. ☎ *Park information, 202/282–1063.*

ARLINGTON

Updated by
John A. Kelly

The Virginia suburb of Arlington County was once part of the District of Columbia. Carved out of the Old Dominion when Washington was created, it was returned to Virginia along with the rest of the land west of the Potomac in 1845. Washington hasn't held a grudge, though, and there are two attractions in Arlington—both linked to the military—that should be a part of any complete visit to the nation's capital: Arlington National Cemetery and the U.S. Marine Corps War Memorial. Both are accessible by Metro, and a trip across the Potomac to Arlington is a very worthwhile half day of sightseeing. The news business pays homage to itself at the Newseum, which chronicles the history of news gathering and gives a behind-the-scenes look at the industry.

Numbers in the text correspond to numbers in the margin and on the Arlington, Virginia, map.

A Good Walk

To begin your exploration, take the Metro to the Arlington Cemetery station (about a 10-minute ride from downtown) or walk across Memorial Bridge from the District (southwest of the Lincoln Memorial) to **Arlington National Cemetery** ①. The visitor center has detailed maps of the cemetery, and the staff can help you find specific graves. Next to the visitor center is the Women in Military Service for America Memorial. West of the visitor center are the **Kennedy graves** ②, where John F. Kennedy, two of his children who died in infancy, and his wife, Jacqueline Bouvier Kennedy Onassis, are buried. Long before it was a cemetery, this land was part of the 1,100-acre estate of George Washington Parke Custis, a descendant of Martha and (by marriage) George Washington whose daughter married Robert E. Lee. The Lees lived in **Arlington House** ③, a fine example of Greek Revival architecture. Walk south on Crook Walk past row upon row of simple white headstones, following the signs to the **Tomb of the Unknowns** ④, where the remains of unknown servicemen from both world wars and Korea are buried. Steps from the Tomb of the Unknowns is **Section 7A** ⑤, where many distinguished veterans are buried. To reach the sites at the northern end of the cemetery and to make your way into the city of Arlington, first walk north along Roosevelt Drive to Schley Drive (past the Memorial Gate); then turn right on Custis Walk to the Ord and Weitzel Gate. On your way you pass **Section 27** ⑥, where 3,800 former slaves are buried. Leave the cemetery through the Ord and Weitzel Gate, cross Marshall Drive carefully, and walk to the 49-bell **Netherlands Carillon** ⑦, where, even if your visit doesn't coincide with a performance, you can enjoy a good vista of Washington. To the north is the **United States Marine Corps War Memorial** ⑧, perhaps better known as the Iwo Jima Memorial, honoring all Marines who lost their lives while serving their country. The **Newseum,** the only museum dedicated to the news business, is north of the Marine Corps War Memorial; it can also be reached by taking the Metro to Rosslyn.

TIMING

Visiting all the sites at Arlington National Cemetery could take a half day or longer, depending on your stamina and interest. Factor in an hour and a half or so for the Newseum.

Sights to See

❸ **Arlington House.** The somber plot of land composing Arlington Cemetery hasn't always been a cemetery. It was in Arlington that the two most famous names in Virginia history—Washington and Lee—became intertwined. George Washington Parke Custis—raised by Martha and George Washington, his grandmother and step-grandfather—built Arlington House (also known as the Custis-Lee Mansion) between 1802 and 1817 on his 1,100-acre estate overlooking the Potomac. After his death, the property went to his daughter, Mary Anna Randolph Custis. In 1831, Mary married Robert E. Lee, a graduate of West Point. For the next 30 years the Custis-Lee family lived at Arlington House.

In 1861, Lee was offered command of the Union forces. He declined, insisting that he could never take up arms against his native Virginia. The Lees left Arlington House that spring, never to return. Federal troops crossed the Potomac not long after that, fortified the estate's ridges, and turned the home into the Army of the Potomac's headquarters. Arlington House and the estate were confiscated in May 1864 and sold to the federal government when the Lees failed to pay $92.07 in property taxes in person. (Survivors of General Lee were eventually compensated for the land.) Union forces built three fortifications on the

THE REBEL GENERAL

ROBERT E. LEE (1807–70) is a truly tragic figure in American history. Lee felt forced by principle and his family connections to lead a rebellion that resulted in more than half a million deaths and left the South in ruins. The only greater tragedy might have been if the Confederate States of America had won independence, which very probably would have led to even further political fractures and endless fighting among half a dozen nations across North America.

The youngest of the seven children of Revolutionary War hero Colonel Henry ("Light-Horse Harry") Lee, Robert Edward Lee was born to Ann Hill Carter at Stratford Plantation on Virginia's genteel Northern Neck. His family tree is a chart of the Old Dominion's leading families, crowned by his marriage to Martha Washington's great-granddaughter, Mary Anna Randolph Custis. Light-Horse Harry's improvidence left the boy unable to afford a private education. Lee sought and won appointment to West Point, and there began the legend of his prowess: he rose to corps adjutant, the highest cadet rank; stood second in the Class of 1829; and never received a single demerit over the course of the four years. Advancement in the peacetime army was slow, even after he transferred from the elite engineer corps to the casualty-prone cavalry, and Lee still was but a captain when the Mexican War began in 1846. There his skill at military engineering, his strength and powers of endurance, and his great personal bravery caused his commander, General Winfield Scott, to describe Lee as "the very best soldier I ever saw in the field."

When the Civil War broke out in the spring of 1861, Scott advised President Abraham Lincoln to offer Colonel Lee command of the Union Army. Lee agonized but finally concluded that "I cannot raise my hand against my native state" and resigned his federal commission. Then, although he despised slavery, the root cause of the conflict, he offered his sword to the South. Union troops quickly overtook his house, and the plantation was converted into a refuge for fleeing slaves and a graveyard that eventually became Arlington National Cemetery. Lee was appointed military advisor to President Jefferson Davis, receiving a field command only after Confederate general Joseph E. Johnston was wounded in 1862. Lee so harried Union general George McClellan in the bloody Seven Days Battles that McClellan went into camp and abandoned any attempt to further menace the Confederate capital of Richmond.

LEE RENAMED HIS FORCE the Army of Northern Virginia and launched a series of campaigns in which, by vigorous movement and audacious tactics, he repeatedly defeated superior Union forces. His troops so revered their gentle, soft-spoken leader that for his sake they would attempt, and often accomplish, the impossible. Lincoln was forced to fire one commanding general after another until he found the fierce bulldog he needed, Ulysses S. Grant. Finally, in the spring of 1865, Grant smashed his way into Richmond and defeated Lee.

At the age of 58, ailing and penniless, Lee began a new career as president of Washington College (now Washington and Lee University), in Lexington, Virginia. There his powerful personality, prestige, and progressive ideas, and his deep loyalty to the United States, produced southern leaders whose influence was sorely needed during Reconstruction. Lee died in 1870 and was entombed in a crypt beneath the college chapel.

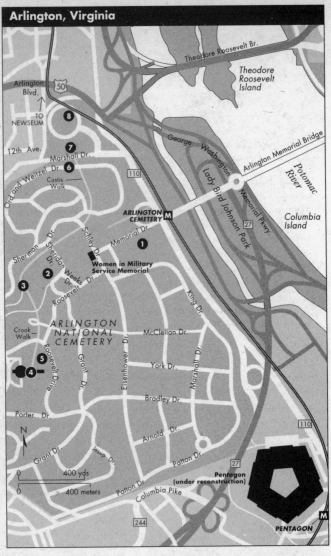

Arlington, Virginia

land, and 200 nearby acres were set aside as a national cemetery. Sixty-five soldiers were buried there on June 15, 1864, and by the end of the Civil War more than 16,000 headstones dotted Arlington plantation's rolling hills. Soldiers from the Revolutionary War and the War of 1812 were reinterred at Arlington as their bodies were discovered in other resting places.

The building's heavy Doric columns and severe pediment make Arlington House one of the area's best examples of Greek Revival architecture. The plantation home was designed by George Hadfield, a young English architect who, for a while, supervised construction of the Capitol. The view of Washington from the front of the house is superb. In 1955 Arlington House was designated a memorial to Robert E. Lee. It looks much as it did in the 19th century, and a quick tour takes you past objects once owned by the Custises and the Lees.

In front of Arlington House, next to a flag that flies at half staff whenever there's a funeral in the cemetery, is the flat-top **grave of Pierre-**

Charles L'Enfant, designer of the Federal City. ⊠ *Between Lee and Sherman Drs.*, ☎ *703/557–0613.* ▣ *Free.* ☉ *Daily 9:30–4:30.*

★ ❶ **Arlington National Cemetery.** More than 250,000 American war dead, as well as many notable Americans (among them Presidents William Howard Taft and John F. Kennedy, General John Pershing, and Admiral Robert E. Peary), are interred in these 612 acres across the Potomac River from Washington, established as the nation's cemetery in 1864. While you're at Arlington there's a good chance you might hear the clear, doleful sound of a trumpet playing taps or the sharp reports of a gun salute. Approximately 20 funerals are held daily (it's projected that the cemetery will be filled in 2020). Although not the largest cemetery in the country, Arlington is certainly the best known, a place where you can trace America's history through the aftermath of its battles.

To get here, you can take the Metro, travel on a Tourmobile bus, or walk across Arlington Memorial Bridge from the District (southwest of the Lincoln Memorial). If you're driving, there's a large paid parking lot at the skylighted visitor center on Memorial Drive. Stop at the center for a free brochure with a detailed map of the cemetery. If you're looking for a specific grave, the staff can consult microfilm records and give you directions to it. You should know the deceased's full name and, if possible, his or her branch of service and year of death.

Tourmobile tour buses leave from just outside the visitor center April–September, daily 8:30–6:30, and October–March, daily 8:30–4:30. You can buy tickets here for the 40-minute tour of the cemetery, which includes stops at the Kennedy grave sites, the Tomb of the Unknowns, and Arlington House. Touring the cemetery on foot means a fair bit of hiking, but it can give you a closer look at some of the thousands of graves spread over these rolling Virginia hills. If you decide to walk, head west from the visitor center on Roosevelt Drive and then turn right on Weeks Drive. ⊠ *West end of Memorial Bridge, Arlington, VA,* ☎ *703/607–8052,* 𝕎𝔼𝔹 *www.arlingtoncemetery.org/default.html.* ▣ *Cemetery free; Tourmobile $4.75.* ☉ *Apr.–Sept., daily 8–7; Oct.–Mar., daily 8–5 (Tourmobile 8:30–4:30).*

❷ **Kennedy graves.** An important part of any visit to Arlington National Cemetery is a visit to the graves of John F. Kennedy and other members of his family. JFK is buried under an eternal flame near two of his children, who died in infancy, and his wife, Jacqueline Bouvier Kennedy Onassis. The graves are a short walk west of the visitor center. Across from them is a low wall engraved with quotations from Kennedy's inaugural address. JFK's grave was opened to the public in 1967 and since that time has become the most-visited grave site in the country. Nearby, marked by a simple white cross, is the grave of his brother Robert Kennedy. ⊠ *Sheridan and Weeks Drs.*

❼ **Netherlands Carillon.** A visit to Arlington National Cemetery affords the opportunity for a lovely and unusual musical experience, thanks to a 49-bell carillon presented to the United States by the Dutch people in 1960 in gratitude for aid received during World War II. Guest carillonneurs perform on Saturday afternoon May through September and on July 4. Times vary; call for details. For one of the most inclusive views of Washington, look to the east across the Potomac. From this vantage point, the Lincoln Memorial, the Washington Monument, and the Capitol appear in a side-by-side formation. ⊠ *Meade and Marshall Drs.*, ☎ *703/289–2500.*

....
OFF THE   **NEWSEUM –** At the first and only museum dedicated to news, you can try
BEATEN PATH your hand at being a reporter, TV news anchor, or weathercaster; relive
  ☾   history's defining moments through news artifacts, vintage radio and TV

news broadcasts, and historic newspaper front pages dating from the 1600s; and see breaking news as it happens on a block-long video news wall. News surrounds you, from up-to-the-minute headlines that scroll continuously on a news "zipper" to a display of that day's front page from 70 newspapers. The Newseum can be reached on foot from the Key Bridge; it's two blocks from the Rosslyn Metro Station. ✉ *1101 Wilson Blvd.*, ☎ *703/284–3544 or 888/639–7386*, WEB *www.arlingtoncemetery.org/default.html.* ✆ *Free.* ◔ *Tues.–Sun. 10– 5. Metro: Rosslyn.*

Pentagon. This office building housing the headquarters of the United States Department of Defense is, quite simply, the largest in the world. It's twice the size of the Merchandise Mart in Chicago, and has three times the floor space of the Empire State Building in New York. The National Capitol could fit into any one of its five wedge-shape sections. Approximately 23,000 military and civilian workers arrive daily. Astonishingly, this mammoth office building was completed in 1943 after just two years of construction.

At this writing, the structure is being reconstructed following the September 2001 crash of a hijacked Boeing 757 into the northwest side of the building. The section that was hit and destroyed contained the offices of Army and Navy operations personnel; fire and water damage had spread far enough to render more than a third of the structure useless. The reconstruction is expected to take at least a couple of years.

Tours of the building, which were available to the public prior to the attack, have been suspended indefinitely. ✉ *I–395 at Columbia Pike and Route 27, Arlington, VA,* ☎ *703/695–1776,* WEB *www.military-info.com/bases/pentagon.htm.*

❺ **Section 7A.** Many distinguished veterans are buried in this area of Arlington National Cemetery below the **Tomb of the Unknowns** including boxing champ Joe Louis, ABC newsman Frank Reynolds, actor Lee Marvin, and World War II fighter pilot Colonel "Pappy" Boyington. ✉ *Crook Walk near Roosevelt Dr.*

❻ **Section 27.** More than 3,800 former slaves are buried in this part of Arlington National Cemetery, all former residents of Freedman's Village. The Village operated at the Custis-Lee estate for more than 30 years beginning in 1863 to provide housing, education, and employment training for ex-slaves who had traveled to the capital. In the cemetery, the headstones are marked with their names and the word "Civilian" or "Citizen." Buried at Grave 19 in the first row of Section 27 is William Christman, a Union private who died of peritonitis in Washington on May 13, 1864. He was the first soldier interred at Arlington National Cemetery during the Civil War. ✉ *Ord and Weitzel Dr. near Custis Walk.*

❹ **Tomb of the Unknowns.** Many countries established a memorial to their war dead after World War I. In the United States, the first burial at the Tomb of the Unknowns took place at Arlington National Cemetery on November 11, 1921, when the Unknown Soldier from the "Great War" was interred under the large white-marble sarcophagus. Unknown servicemen killed in World War II and Korea were buried in

1958. The unknown serviceman killed in Vietnam was laid to rest on the plaza on Memorial Day 1984 but was disinterred and identified in 1998. It was decided to leave the Vietnam War unknown crypt vacant. Soldiers from the Army's U.S. 3rd Infantry ("The Old Guard") keep watch over the tomb 24 hours a day, regardless of weather conditions. Each sentinel marches exactly 21 steps, then faces the tomb for 21 seconds, symbolizing the 21-gun salute, America's highest military honor. The guard is changed with a precise ceremony during the day—every half hour from April 1 to September 30 and every hour the rest of the year. At night the guard is changed every hour.

The Memorial Amphitheater west of the tomb is the scene of special ceremonies on Veterans' Day, Memorial Day, and Easter. Decorations awarded to the unknowns by foreign governments and U.S. and foreign organizations are displayed in an indoor trophy room. Across from the amphitheater are memorials to the astronauts killed in the *Challenger* shuttle explosion and to the servicemen killed in 1980 while trying to rescue American hostages in Iran. Rising beyond that is the mainmast of the USS *Maine*, the American ship that was sunk in Havana Harbor in 1898, killing 299 men and sparking the Spanish-American War. ⊠ *End of Crook Walk.*

8 **United States Marine Corps War Memorial.** Better known simply as "the Iwo Jima," this memorial, despite its familiarity, has lost none of its power to stir the emotions. Honoring Marines who've given their lives since the Corps was formed in 1775, the statue, sculpted by Felix W. de Weldon, is based on Joe Rosenthal's Pulitzer Prize–winning photograph of five Marines and a Navy corpsman raising a flag atop Mt. Suribachi on the Japanese island of Iwo Jima on February 19, 1945. By executive order, a real flag flies 24 hours a day from the 78-ft-high memorial. On Tuesday evening at 7 from late May to late August there's a Marine Corps sunset parade on the grounds of the memorial. On parade nights a free shuttle bus runs from the Arlington Cemetery visitors' parking lot.

North of the memorial is the Arlington neighborhood of Rosslyn. Like parts of downtown Washington and Crystal City farther to the south, Rosslyn is almost empty at night, once the thousands of people who work there have gone home. Its tall buildings provide a bit of a skyline, but this has come about with some controversy: some say the silvery, wing-shape Gannett Buildings are too close to the flight path followed by jets landing at Ronald Reagan National Airport.

Women in Military Service for America Memorial. What is now this memorial (opened in 1997) next to the visitor center was once the Hemicycle, a huge carved retaining wall faced with granite at the entrance to Arlington National Cemetery. Built in 1932, the wall was restored, with stairways added leading to a rooftop terrace. Inside are 16 exhibit alcoves, which show the contributions that women have made to the military—from the Revolutionary War to the present—as well as the history of the memorial itself. A 196-seat theater shows films and is used for lectures and conferences. A computer database has pictures, military histories, and stories of thousands of women veterans. A fountain and reflecting pool front the classical-style Hemicycle and entry gates.

OFF THE
BEATEN PATH
THEODORE ROOSEVELT ISLAND – An island wilderness preserve in the Potomac River—including 2½ mi of nature trails through marshland, swampland, and upland forest—is an 88-acre tribute to the conservation-minded 26th president. Cattails, arrowarum, pickerelweed, willow, ash, maple, and oak all grow on the island, which is also a habitat for frogs, raccoons, birds, squirrels, and the occasional red or gray fox. The 17-ft bronze statue of Roosevelt was done by Paul Manship. A pedestrian bridge connects the island to a parking lot on the Virginia shore, accessible from the northbound lanes of the George Washington Memorial Parkway. ⊠ *From downtown, take Constitution Ave. west across the Theodore Roosevelt Bridge to George Washington Memorial Pkwy. north and follow signs or walk or bike across the Bridge beginning at the Kennedy Center,* ☎ *703/289–2500 for park info.* 🎫 *Free.* 🕐 *Island daily dawn–dusk.*

ALEXANDRIA

Updated by
John A. Kelly

Just a Metro ride (or bike ride) from Washington, Alexandria attracts those who seek a break from the monuments and hustle-and-bustle of the District and who are interested in an encounter with America's Colonial heritage. Founded in 1749 by Scottish merchants eager to capitalize on the booming tobacco trade, Alexandria emerged as one of the most important Colonial ports and predates Washington. Alexandria's history is linked to the most significant events and personages of the Colonial, Revolutionary, and Civil War periods. In the part of Alexandria called Old Town, this colorful past is still alive in restored 18th- and 19th-century homes, churches, and taverns; on the cobbled streets; and on the revitalized waterfront, where clipper ships dock and artisans display their wares.

One way to reach Alexandria is to take the Metro to the King Street stop (about 25 minutes from Metro Center) and walk about 10 blocks on King Street going away from the Masonic memorial. If you're driving, you can take either the George Washington Memorial Parkway or Jefferson Davis Highway (Route 1) south from Arlington.

Numbers in the text correspond to numbers in the margin and on the Old Town Alexandria, Virginia, map.

A Good Walk

Start your walk through Old Town at the Alexandria Convention & Visitors Association, in **Ramsay House** ①, the oldest house in Alexandria. Across the street, near the corner of Fairfax and King streets, is the **Stabler-Leadbeater Apothecary** ②, the country's second-oldest apothecary. It was the equivalent of a corner drugstore to Alexandrians, including George Washington and the Lee family. Two blocks south on Fairfax Street, just beyond Duke Street, stands the **Old Presbyterian Meetinghouse** ③, where Scottish patriots met during the Revolutionary War. Walk back up Fairfax Street one block and turn right on Prince Street to Gentry Row, the block between Fairfax and Lee streets. The striking edifice at the corner of Prince and Lee streets is the **Athenaeum** ④. Many of the city's sea captains built their homes on the block of Prince Street between Lee and Union, which became known as **Captain's Row** ⑤. Walk a block north on Union to King Street, where there are many shops and restaurants. One of Alexandria's most popular attractions is the **Torpedo Factory Arts Center** ⑥, a collection of art studios and galleries in a former munitions plant (on Union at the foot of King Street). Also here is the Alexandria Archaeology Museum, with exhibits of artifacts found during excavations in Alexandria. Take Cameron Street away from the river. **Carlyle House** ⑦, which was patterned after a Scottish country manor house, is at the corner of Cameron and North Fairfax streets.

One block west along Cameron, at Royal Street, is **Gadsby's Tavern Museum** ⑧, a political and social center during the late 18th century. Continue west on Cameron Street for two blocks, turn right on St. Asaph Street and walk up to Oronoco Street. Two historic Lee homes are on the short stretch of Oronoco between North Washington and St. Asaph streets. On the near side of Oronoco is the **Lee-Fendall House** ⑨; the **boyhood home of Robert E. Lee** ⑩ is across Oronoco on the St. Asaph Street corner.

Although they were a tiny minority, there were in fact 52 free blacks living in Alexandria in 1790. This population grew to become a significant factor in Alexandria's successful development. The **Alexandria Black History Resource Center** ⑪, two blocks north and two blocks west of Lee's boyhood home, tells the history of African-Americans in Alexandria and Virginia. Head back to North Washington Street and go south to the corner of Queen Street. The **Lloyd House** ⑫, a fine example of Georgian architecture, is owned by the City of Alexandria. At the corner of Cameron and North Washington streets, one block south, stands the English Georgian country-style **Christ Church** ⑬. Walk south two blocks to the **Lyceum** ⑭ at the corner of South Washington and Prince streets; it now houses two art galleries and a museum focusing on local history. The Confederate Statue is in the middle of South Washington and Prince streets, and two blocks to the west on South Alfred Street is the **Friendship Fire House** ⑮, restored and outfitted like a typical 19th-century firehouse. It's a long walk (or a quick ride on Bus 2 or 5 west on King Street) but worth the trouble to visit the **George Washington Masonic National Memorial** ⑯ on Callahan Drive at the King Street Metro station 1 mi west of the center of the city. In good weather, the open ninth-floor observation deck affords spectacular views of Alexandria and Washington.

TIMING

The Alexandria tour should take about four hours, not counting a trip to the George Washington Masonic National Memorial. A visit to the memorial adds about another hour and a half if you walk there and take the guided tour. If you're traveling by Metro, plan to finish your visit at the memorial and then get on the Metro at the King Street station.

Sights to See

⑪ **Alexandria Black History Resource Center.** The history of African-Americans in Alexandria and Virginia from 1749 to the present is recounted here. Alexandria's history is hardly limited to the families of George Washington and Robert E. Lee. The federal census of 1790 recorded 52 free blacks living in the city, and the port town was one of the largest slave exportation points in the South, with at least two bustling slave markets. ✉ *638 N. Alfred St.,* ☎ *703/838–4356.* ✇ *Free.* ☉ *Tues.–Sat. 9–4.*

④ **Athenaeum.** One of the most noteworthy structures in Alexandria, the Athenaeum is a striking, reddish-brown Greek Revival edifice at the corner of Prince and Lee streets. It was built as a bank in the 1850s. ✉ *201 Prince St.*

⑩ **Boyhood Home of Robert E. Lee.** The childhood home in Alexandria of the commander in chief of the Confederate forces, Robert E. Lee, is a fine example of a 19th-century town house with federal architecture. The house was sold in 2000 to private owners who have made it their home, over the objections of many Virginians, including the

Alexandria
Black History
Resource
Center 11

Athenaeum . .4

Boyhood
Home
of Robert
E. Lee 10

Captain's Row . .5

Carlyle
House 7

Christ
Church 13

Friendship
Fire
House 15

Gadsby's
Tavern
Museum 8

G. W. Masonic
Nat. Mem. . .16

Lee-Fendall
House 9

Lloyd House . .12

Lyceum 14

Old
Presbyterian
Meetinghouse .3

Ramsay
House 1

Stabler-
Leadbeater
Apothecary . .2

Torpedo
Factory Arts
Center 6

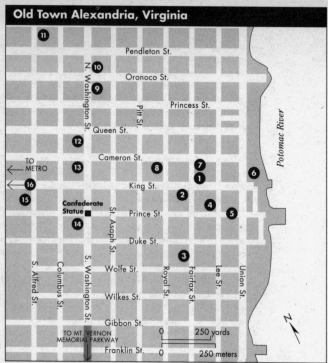

governor; it's no longer open to visitors, but some of the home's furnishings are displayed at the Lyceum. ⊠ *607 Oronoco St.*

⑤ Captain's Row. Many of Alexandria's sea captains once lived on this block. The cobblestones in the street were allegedly laid by Hessian mercenaries who had fought for the British during the Revolution and were held in Alexandria as prisoners of war. ⊠ *Prince St. between Lee and Union Sts.*

⑦ Carlyle House. The grandest of Alexandria's older houses, Carlyle House was patterned after a Scottish country manor house. The structure was completed in 1753 by Scottish merchant John Carlyle. This was General Braddock's headquarters and the place where he met with five royal governors in 1755 to plan the strategy and funding of the early campaigns of the French and Indian War. ⊠ *121 N. Fairfax St.*, ☎ *703/549–2997.* ⊡ *$4.* ☉ *Tues.–Sat. 10–4, Sun. noon–4; guided tour every ½ hr.*

⑬ Christ Church. Both Washington and Lee were pewholders in this Alexandria, Virginia, Episcopal church. (Washington paid £36 and 10 shillings—a lot of money in those days—for Pew 60.) Built in 1773, Christ Church is a good example of an English Georgian country-style church. It has a fine Palladian window, an interior balcony, and a wrought-brass-and-crystal chandelier brought from England at Washington's expense. Docents give tours during visiting hours. ⊠ *118 N. Washington St.*, ☎ *703/549–1450.* ⊡ *Free.* ☉ *Mon.–Sat. 9–4, Sun. 2–4; occasionally closed weekends for private events.*

Confederate Statue. In 1861, when Alexandria was occupied by Union forces, the 800 soldiers of the city's garrison marched out of town to join the Confederate Army. In the middle of Washington and Prince streets stands a statue marking the point at which they assembled. In

1885 Confederate veterans proposed a memorial to honor their fallen comrades. This statue, based on John A. Elder's painting *Appomattox*, is of a lone soldier glumly surveying the battlefields after General Robert E. Lee's surrender. The names of 100 Alexandria Confederate dead are carved on the base.

⑮ Friendship Fire House. Alexandria's showcase firehouse is outfitted in typical 19th-century firefighting fashion. ⊠ *107 S. Alfred St.,* ☎ *703/ 838–3891.* 🎟 *Free.* ☉ *Fri.–Sat. 10–4, Sun. 1–4.*

❽ Gadsby's Tavern Museum. This museum is housed in the old City Tavern and Hotel, which was a center of political and social life in the late 18th century. George Washington attended birthday celebrations in the ballroom here. A tour takes you through the taproom, dining room, assembly room, ballroom, and communal bedrooms. Lantern tours, held on Friday evenings only, visit the same rooms and are led by a costumed guide using a candlelit lantern. ⊠ *134 N. Royal St.,* ☎ *703/838–4242.* 🎟 *$4, $5 for lantern tour.* ☉ *Oct.–Mar., Tues.–Sat. 11–4, Sun. 1–4 (last tour at 3:15); Apr.–Sept., Tues.–Sat. 10–5, Sun. 1–5 (last tour at 4:15); tours 15 mins before and 15 mins after the hr. Lantern tours Mar.–Nov., Fri. 7–9:30.*

⑯ George Washington Masonic National Memorial. Because Alexandria, like Washington, has no really tall buildings, the spire of this memorial dominates the surroundings. The building fronts King Street, one of Alexandria's major east–west arteries; from the ninth-floor observation deck you get a spectacular view of Alexandria, with Washington in the distance. The building contains furnishings from the first Masonic lodge in Alexandria, in which George Washington was a member; he became a Mason in 1752 and was a Worshipful Master, a high rank, at the same time he served as president. ⊠ *101 Callahan Dr.,* ☎ *703/683–2007.* 🎟 *Free.* ☉ *Daily 9–5; 50-min guided tour of building and deck daily at 9:30, 10:30, 11:30, 1, 2, 3, and 4.*

❾ Lee-Fendall House. The short block of Alexandria's Oronoco Street between Washington and St. Asaph streets is the site of two Lee-owned houses. One is the Lee-Fendall House, the home of several illustrious members of the Lee family, and the other is the boyhood home of Robert E. Lee. The Lee-Fendall House is decorated with Victorian furnishings and some Lee pieces. ⊠ *614 Oronoco St.* 🎟 *$4.* ☉ *Feb.–Dec. 15, Tues.– Sat. 10–4, Sun. 1–4; sometimes closed on weekends for private events.*

⑫ Lloyd House. A fine example of Georgian architecture, Lloyd House was built in 1797 and is owned by the City of Alexandria. Up until recently it housed the genealogical library; now the interior is no longer open to visitors, so it can only be admired from outside. ⊠ *220 N. Washington St.*

⑭ Lyceum. Built in 1839, the Lyceum served as a library, a Civil War hospital, a residence, and an office building. It was restored in the 1970s and now houses two galleries with exhibits on the history of Alexandria, a third gallery with changing exhibits, and a gift shop. Some travel information for the entire state is also available here. ⊠ *201 S. Washington St.,* ☎ *703/838–4994,* 🕸 *www.ci.alexandria.va.us/.* 🎟 *Free.* ☉ *Mon.–Sat. 10–5, Sun. 1–5.*

❸ Old Presbyterian Meetinghouse. Built in 1774, the Old Presbyterian Meetinghouse was, as its name suggests, more than a church. It was a gathering place in Alexandria vital to Scottish patriots during the Revolution. Eulogies for George Washington were delivered here on December 29, 1799. In a corner of the churchyard is the Tomb of the Unknown Soldier of the American Revolution. ⊠ *321 S. Fairfax St.,* ☎ *703/549–*

6670, WEB *www.opmh.org.* 🔲 *Free.* ☉ *Sanctuary weekdays 9–3 (if it's locked, get the key from church office at 316 S. Royal St.).*

❶ Ramsay House. The best place to start a tour of Alexandria's Old Town is at the **Alexandria Convention & Visitors Association,** in Ramsay House, the home of the town's first postmaster and lord mayor, William Ramsay. The structure is believed to be the oldest house in Alexandria. Ramsay was a Scotsman, as a swatch of his tartan on the door proclaims. Travel counselors here provide brochures and maps for self-guided walking tours. You're given a 24-hour permit that allows you to park free at any two-hour metered spot. ✉ *221 King St.,* ☎ *703/ 838–4200; 800/388–9119; 703/838–6494 TDD.* ☉ *Daily 9–5.*

❷ Stabler-Leadbeater Apothecary. Once patronized by George Washington and the Lee family, Alexandria's Stabler-Leadbeater Apothecary is the second-oldest apothecary in the country (the oldest is reputedly in Bethlehem, PA). Some believe that it was here, on October 17, 1859, that Lt. Col. Robert E. Lee received orders to lead Marines sent from the Washington Barracks to help suppress John Brown's insurrection at Harper's Ferry (then part of Virginia). The shop now houses a small museum of 18th- and 19th-century apothecary memorabilia, including one of the finest collections of apothecary bottles in the country (some 800 bottles in all). ✉ *105–107 S. Fairfax St.,* ☎ *703/ 836–3713.* 🔲 *$2.50.* ☉ *Mon.–Sat. 10–4, Sun. 1–5.*

❻ Torpedo Factory Art Center. Torpedoes were manufactured here by the U.S. Navy during World War I and World War II. Now known as the Torpedo Factory Arts Center, the building houses the studios and workshops of about 160 artists and artisans and has become one of Alexandria's most popular attractions. You can view the workshops of printmakers, jewelry makers, sculptors, painters, and potters, and most of the art and crafts are for sale. The Torpedo Factory also houses the **Alexandria Archaeology Program** (☎ 703/838–4399), a city-operated research facility devoted to urban archaeology and conservation. Artifacts from excavations in Alexandria are on display here. Admission is free; hours are Tuesday through Saturday from 10–3 and Sunday 1–5. ✉ *105 N. Union St.,* ☎ *703/838–4565.* 🔲 *Free.* ☉ *Daily 10–5.*

AROUND WASHINGTON

Updated by
John A. Kelly

The city and environs of Washington (including parts of Maryland and Virginia) are dotted with worthwhile attractions that are outside the range of the walks in this chapter. You may find some intriguing enough to go a little out of your way to visit. The nearest Metro stop is noted only if it's within reasonable walking distance of a given sight.

Bethesda, Maryland

Bethesda was named in 1871 after the Bethesda Meeting House, which was built by the Presbyterians, who named their house of worship after the biblical pool of Bethesda, which had great healing power. Today, people seek healing in Bethesda at the U.S. Naval Regional Medical Center and the National Institutes of Health, and meet here to enjoy the burgeoning restaurant scene. While Bethesda has changed from a small community into an urban destination, time has stood still east of Bethesda in much of Chevy Chase, home to exclusive country clubs, stately houses, and huge trees.

McCrillis Gardens and Gallery. McCrillis Gardens is a premier shade garden with choice ornamental trees and shrubs. Bulbs, ground cover, and shade-loving perennials add ongoing color and texture. The gallery features artists from the Washington area. ⊠ *6910 Greentree Rd.,* ☎ *301/365–1657,* WEB *www.mc-mncppc.org/parks/brookside/mccrilli.htm.* ⊠ *Free.* ☉ *Gardens daily 10–sunset; phone for gallery hours.*

Montgomery County Farm Woman's Cooperative Market. This market is one of the remaining vestiges of Montgomery County's agricultural society. In the midst of the Great Depression, women gathered goods from their gardens to sell in Bethesda to residents of the District of Columbia and its growing suburbs. Today the tradition continues. Baked goods, fresh fruits and vegetables, crafts, and even flea-market goods are still sold in a low, white building in the midst of high-rise office buildings. (A view of the market in the 1930s is depicted in a mural on the wall of the Bethesda Post Office at 7400 Wisconsin Avenue.) ⊠ *7155 Wisconsin Ave.,* ☎ *301/652–2291,* WEB *montgomerycountymd.com/events/montgomery_market.htm.* ☉ *Wed. and Sat. 7–3, flea market Wed., Sat.–Sun. 7–5. Metro: Bethesda.*

National Institutes of Health (NIH). One of the world's foremost biomedical research centers, the NIH offers two one-hour tours for the public. Both the orientation tour at the NIH Visitor Information Center and the one at the National Library of Medicine include a video presentation, lecture, and question-and-answer session. Many people take both tours; walk 10 minutes from one building to the other or take the free NIH shuttle bus. At the orientation tour, learn how the NIH works to help prevent, detect, and diagnose diseases and disabilities; then go up to the 14th floor for a panoramic view of this sprawling 300-acre campus. Although best known for its books and journals— there are more than 5 million—the library also houses historical medical references dating from the 11th century. The library tour includes a look at historical documents, the library's databases, and their "visible human," which provides a view of everything from how the kneecap works to how physicians use surgical simulators. Most people enjoy the tips from the guides on how to start medical searches (to do any research, you must arrive at least an hour and a half before closing time). ⊠ *Visitor Information Center, 9000 Rockville Pike, Bldg. 10,* ☎ *301/496–1776, www.nih.gov/about/#visitor,library;* ⊠ *National Library of Medicine, 8600 Rockville Pike, Bldg. 38A,* ☎ *301/ 496–6308,* WEB *www.nlm.nih.gov.* ⊠ *Free.* ☉ *Orientation tours Mon., Wed., and Fri. at 11 AM. Library weekdays 8:30–5 (Thurs. 8:30 AM– 9 PM in winter), Sat. 8:30–12:30. Library tours weekdays at 1:30. Metro: Medical Center.*

Strathmore Hall Arts Center. Local and national artists exhibit in the galleries and musicians perform year-round at this mansion built at the turn of the 20th century. A free series that includes poetry, music, art talks, and demonstrations takes place on Wednesday evening (call ahead for specific hours). On Tuesday and Thursday during the summer, concert goers spread out on the expansive lawn to listen to a variety of free concerts—everything from classical to Cajun and even world beat. Strathmore's Tea is served in a well-lit wood-panel salon, Tuesday and Wednesday at 1. During July and August, "Backyard Theater" performers entertain children. ⊠ *10701 Rockville Pike,* ☎ *301/530– 0540,* WEB *www.strathmore.org/.* ⊠ *Free; Backyard Theater $6. Tea $12 (reservations required).* ☉ *Mon.–Tues. and Thurs.–Fri. 10–4, Wed. 10–9, Sat. 10–3. Metro: Grosvenor/Strathmore.*

Elsewhere in Maryland

Brookside Gardens. A 50-acre garden within Wheaton Regional Park, Brookside includes several distinct gardens: azalea, rose, yew, formal, fragrance, Japanese-style, and trial. Brookside also has two conservatories for year-round floral enjoyment. A horticultural reference library is in the airy visitor center. ⊠ *1500 Glenallan Ave., Wheaton,* ☎ *301/949–8230,* WEB *www.mc-mncppc.org/prks/brookside/about.htm.* ⊠ *Free.* ☉ *Conservatory daily 10–5; gardens daily sunrise–sunset.*

⏱ **College Park Aviation Museum.** One of College Park, Maryland's claims to fame is the world's oldest operating airport. Opened in 1909, it has been the site of numerous aviation firsts. Orville and Wilbur Wright tested military planes here, and their presence is evident in the museum's early aviation memorabilia. The 27,000-square-ft museum has interactive exhibits and an Animatronic Wilbur Wright. A full-scale reproduction of the 1911 Wright Model B Aeroplane is also here. The airport's Air Fair every September features antique airplanes, hot-air balloons, and a Wright Brothers look-alike contest. ⊠ *1985 Corporal Frank Scott Dr., College Park,* ☎ *301/864–6029.* ⊠ *$4.* ☉ *Daily 10–5.*

⏱ **Goddard Space Flight Center.** Goddard Space Flight Center was established in 1959 as NASA's first center devoted to the exploration of space. Since then, it has continued to take a leading role in Earth science, space science, and the development of cutting-edge technologies. The visitor center highlights Goddard's contributions to America's space program through exhibits, tours, and special programs for adults and children. The Main Gallery reflects the space program's legendary past and exciting future, and the Earth Science Gallery has earth science themes in a high-tech, 2,600-ft gallery. The Educator Resource Center, on the 2nd floor, offers a variety of free teaching materials to educators. Walking tours (about 2 ½ hours) visit the Spacecraft Operations Facility and cover NASA communications, the Operations Control Center, and Hubble Space Telescope operations. Children under 10 aren't allowed on the walking tour. Van tours take about one hour and demonstrate how spacecraft are tested prior to launch. ⊠ *Soil Conservation Rd. and Greenbelt Rd., Greenbelt,* ☎ *301/286–8981,* WEB *www.pao.gsfc.nasa.gov/vc/public_tours.htm.* ⊠ *Free.* ☉ *Daily 9–4; Walking tours Oct.–Mar., Mon., Wed., and Fri. at 1:30, 1st and 3rd Sat.–Sun. at 11; Apr.–Sept., daily at 11:30 and 1:30. Van tours Oct.–Mar., 2nd and 4th Sun. at 11; Apr.–Sept., Sun. 10:30, plus 2nd and 4th Sun. at 1:30. Metro: Greenbelt, then Bus T15, T16, or T17.*

⏱ **National Capital Trolley Museum.** A selection of the capital's historic trolleys have been rescued and restored and are now on display at a museum in suburban Maryland, along with streetcars from Europe and elsewhere in America. For a nominal fare you can go on a 2-mi ride through the countryside. ⊠ *313 Bonifant Rd., between Layhill Rd. and New Hampshire Ave., Silver Spring,* ☎ *301/384–6088,* WEB *www.dc-trolley.org/.* ⊠ *Trolley ride $2.50.* ☉ *Jan.–Nov., weekends noon–5; plus Mar. 15–May 15, Thur. and Fri. 10–2, June 15–Aug. 15, Thur. and Fri. 11–3; Oct.–Nov. 15 Thur. and Fri. 1–2; Dec., weekends 5–9.*

National Cryptologic Museum. A 30-minute drive from Washington, Maryland's National Cryptologic Museum is a surprise, telling in a public way the anything but public story of "signals intelligence," the government's gleaning of intelligence from radio signals, messages, radar, and the cracking of other governments' secret codes. Connected to the supersecret National Security Agency, the museum recounts the history of intelligence from 1526 to the present. Displays include rare cryptographic books from the 16th century, items used in the Civil War, World War II cipher machines, and a Cray supercomputer of the sort that does the code work today. ⊠ *Colony Seven Rd., near Fort Meade, (Baltimore–Washington Pkwy. north to Rte. 32E),* ☎ *301/688–5849,* WEB *www.nsa.gov/museum/index.html.* ⊠ *Free.* ☉ *Weekdays 9–4, Sat. 10–2.*

Paul E. Garber Facility. A collection of Smithsonian warehouses in suburban Maryland, the Paul E. Garber Facility is where flight-related artifacts are stored and restored prior to their display at the National Air and Space Museum on the Mall. Among the approximately 140 aircraft you may see are such historic craft as a Soviet MiG-15 from the Korean War and a Battle of Britain–era Hawker Hurricane IIC, as well as model satellites and assorted engines and propellers. The list changes as aircraft exit the restoration process and go on display. A behind-the-scenes look at how the artifacts are preserved is included on the three-hour walking tour. Note: the tour is for ages 14 and up, and there's no heating or air-conditioning at the facility (and no rest-room stops once the three-hour tour begins), so plan accordingly. Reservations for a tour should be requested through the phone number below or by writing to the National Air and Space Museum Reservation Office (✉ Theater, Planetarium Operations Unit, Washington, D.C. 20560) at least two weeks in advance. Next-day reservations are sometimes available by telephone. ✉ *3904 Old Silver Hill Rd., at St. Barnabas Rd., Suitland,* ☎ *202/357–1400,* WEB *www.nasm.edu/nasm/garber.* ✆ *Free.* ☉ *Tours weekdays at 10, weekends at 10 and 1.*

Temple of the Church of Jesus Christ of Latter-Day Saints. A striking Mormon temple in suburban Maryland—one of its white towers is topped with a golden statue of the Mormon angel and prophet Moroni—the Temple of the Church of Jesus Christ of the Latter-Day Saints has become a Washington landmark for the way it seems to rise up from the distance, appearing like a modern-day Oz. The temple is closed to non-Mormons, but the grounds and visitor center offer a lovely view of the white-marble temple and surroundings. Tulips, dogwoods, and azaleas bloom in the 57-acre grounds each spring. In December, Washingtonians enjoy the Festival of Lights—300,000 of them—and a live nativity scene. ✉ *9900 Stoneybrook Dr., Kensington,* ☎ *301/ 587–0144,* WEB *www.washingtonlds.org.* ☉ *Grounds and visitor center daily 10–9.*

Elsewhere in Virginia

Flying Circus Airshow. Stunt flying and wing walking are among the attractions at the Flying Circus Airshow. Billing itself as the only remaining barnstorming show in the country, the Flying Circus operates out of a Virginia aerodrome about 90 minutes by car from Washington. Biplane rides are available before and after the show. In addition to the the the airshow, special events—like model rocket day, antique car day, motorcycle day, and hot rod day—are held most Sundays. Call ahead for attraction information. ✉ *Rte. 17, Bealeton (between Fredericksburg and Warrenton),* ☎ *540/439–8661,* WEB *www.flyingcircusairshow.com.* ✆ *$10.* ☉ *May–Oct., Sun.; gates open at 11, show starts at 2:30.*

2 DINING

You won't find obvious ethnic neighborhoods
in Washington, but you will find a world of
tempting tastes befitting the capital city of a
melting-pot country. In addition to the cuisines
of France, Italy, and China, D.C. has food
from places as far-flung as Senegal, Brazil,
India, and the Caribbean—not to mention
stateside specialties like California cuisine,
Maryland crab cakes, and New Orleans
Creole cooking.

Reviewed by
Thomas Head

ENJOY SUNNY AFRICAN pop music while you sample such delicacies as *moi-moi* (black-eyed peas, tomatoes, and corned beef) and *nklakla* (tomato soup with goat). Feast on *feijoada,* a rich Brazilian stew of black beans, pork, and smoked meats. Sample French specialties such as the delicious fish stew called bouillabaisse, Italian favorites such as fusilli with broccoli and whole cloves of roasted garlic, Middle Eastern delicacies like succulent lamb kabobs and crisp vegetable fritters known as *falafel,* crunchily addictive Vietnamese spring rolls, spicy Carolina shrimp (peel 'em and eat with steaming white grits), and some of the finest marbled steaks and butter-soft roast beef this side of the Mississippi.

As the nation's capital, Washington hosts an international array of visitors and new residents. This infusion of cultures means that despite the dearth of ethnic neighborhoods and the kinds of restaurant districts found in many other cities, you *can* find almost any type of food here, from Burmese to Ethiopian. Even the city's French-trained chefs, who have traditionally set the standard in fine dining, have been turning to health-conscious contemporary cuisine, spicy southwestern recipes, or appetizer-size Spanish tapas for inspiration.

In the city's one officially recognized ethnic enclave, Chinatown (centered on G and H streets NW between 6th and 8th), Burmese, Thai, and other Asian cuisines add variety to the many traditional Chinese restaurants. The latter entice you with huge, brightly lit signs and offer such staples as beef with broccoli or *kung pao* chicken in a spicy sauce with roasted peanuts. But discriminating diners will find far better food at the smaller, less obvious restaurants. Look for recent reviews in *Washingtonian* magazine, the *Washington Post,* and the *Washington Times*; proud restaurant owners display good reviews on doors or in windows.

The opening of the nearby MCI Arena has been a mixed blessing for Chinatown. The fans who throng the arena for professional hockey and basketball have to eat somewhere, and Chinatown is handy and cheap. This has made Chinatown and the area around the Gallery Place Metro station a hot area for restaurant development, but the resulting competition for space has forced many smaller restaurants out of business.

For fine dining, don't overlook restaurants in the city's luxury hotels. The formal dining room at the Willard Inter-Continental, Seasons at the Four Seasons, Citronelle at the Latham, and the dining room at the Morrison-Clark Inn are noteworthy. The cuisine is often artful and fresh. Of course, such attention to detail comes at a price. One less expensive way to experience these nationally recognized restaurants is a weekday lunch.

Note that although most restaurants are easily accessible by Metro, some are not. Details on Metro stops are provided when this form of public transportation is realistic for the average traveler. For details on price categories, *see* Dining *in* Smart Travel Tips A to Z.

What to Wear
Gentlemen may be more comfortable wearing jackets and/or ties in $$$ and $$$$ restaurants, even when there is no formal dress code.

Adams-Morgan/Woodley Park

Eighteenth Street NW extending south from Columbia Road is wall-to-wall restaurants. Small ethnic spots open and close frequently, and it's worth taking a walk down the street to see what looks new and

124

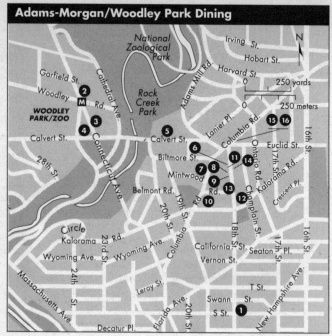

interesting. Although the area has retained some of its Latin American identity, the new eating establishments tend to be Asian, contemporary, Italian, and Ethiopian. Parking can be impossible on weekends. The nearest Metro stop—Woodley Park/Zoo—is a 10- to 15-minute walk; although it's a safe stroll at night, it may be more convenient to take a cab. Woodley Park has culinary temptations of its own, with a lineup of popular ethnic restaurants right by the Metro.

African

$–$$ ✕ **Bukom Café.** Sunny African pop music, a palm-frond and *kente*-cloth decor, and a spicy West African menu brighten this narrow, two-story dining room. Appetizers include moi-moi and nklakla. Entrées range from *egussi* (goat with melon seeds) to *kumasi* (chicken in a peanut sauce) to vegetarian dishes such as *jollof* rice and fried plantains. Live music nightly (Sunday through Thursday until 1:30 AM, Friday through Saturday until 2:30 AM) keeps this place hopping. ✉ *2442 18th St. NW,* ☎ *202/265–4600. AE, D, MC, V. No lunch. Metro: Woodley Park/Zoo.*

$–$$ ✕ **Meskerem.** Ethiopian restaurants abound in Adams-Morgan, but
★ Meskerem is distinctive for its bright, appealingly decorated dining room and the balcony, where you can eat Ethiopian-style—seated on the floor on leather cushions, with large woven baskets for tables. Entrées are served on a large piece of *injera*, a sourdough flat bread; you eat family-style, and you scoop up mouthful-size portions of the hearty dishes with extra injera. Specialties include stews made with spicy *berbere* chili sauce; *kitfo*, buttery beef served raw like steak tartare or very rare; and a tangy, green-chili–vinaigrette potato salad. ✉ *2434 18th St. NW,* ☎ *202/462–4100. AE, DC, MC, V. Metro: Woodley Park/Zoo.*

Asian

$–$$ ✕ **Saigon Gourmet.** Service is brisk and friendly at this popular, French-influenced Vietnamese restaurant. The upscale neighborhood patrons return for the ultracrisp *cha-gio* (spring rolls), the savory *pho* (beef broth), seafood soups, and the delicately seasoned and richly sauced entrées.

Shrimp Saigon mixes prawns and pork in a peppery marinade, and another Saigon dish—grilled pork with rice crepes—is a Vietnamese variation on Chinese moo shu. ⊠ *2635 Connecticut Ave. NW,* ☎ *202/265–1360. AE, D, DC, MC, V. Metro: Woodley Park/Zoo.*

Cajun/Creole

$–$$ ✕ **Bardia's New Orleans Café.** This café quickly created a loyal clientele with its cozy atmosphere, small staff, and great food accompanied by jazz tunes. Seafood, whether batter-fried, blackened, or sautéed, is always a winner. Po'boy sandwiches (hefty French-bread subs) are also a good bet. Some may find the smoky gumbos disappointing, but the rest of the menu more than makes up for them. Breakfast—served all day—includes traditional eggs Benedict or New Orleans style, with fried oysters, crabmeat, and hollandaise, prepared to perfection. Don't leave without trying the outstanding beignets (fried dough puffs sprinkled with powdered sugar). ⊠ *2412 18th St. NW,* ☎ *202/234–0420. Reservations not accepted. AE, MC, V. Metro: Woodley Park/Zoo.*

Contemporary

$$$–$$$$ ✕ **New Heights.** This inviting restaurant has 11 large windows that overlook nearby Rock Creek Park. The sophisticated contemporary cooking blends the bold flavors of Asia and the Southwest into the traditional dishes of the American repertoire. Oysters may be fried in a buttermilk batter and then served with a sage aioli. Quail might be grilled and served with roasted beets and ginger–lime vinaigrette. Sunday brunch in this lovely room is a particular treat. ⊠ *2317 Calvert St. NW,* ☎ *202/234–4110. AE, D, DC, MC, V. No lunch Mon.–Sat. Metro: Woodley Park/Zoo.*

$$–$$$ ✕ **Cashion's Eat Place.** In Ann Cashion's very personal restaurant, the walls are hung with family photos and the tables are usually jammed with regulars feasting on her up-to-date, home-style cooking. The menu changes daily, but roast chicken, a steak entrée, and several seafood dishes are frequent choices. Duck, lamb, and pork are featured in seasonal preparations and are always skillfully cooked. Side dishes such as garlicky mashed potatoes or buttery potatoes Anna sometimes upstage the main course. Desserts, made by pastry chef Beth Christianson, range from the homey to the sophisticated. If it's offered, don't miss the chocolate cake, one of the best anywhere. ⊠ *1819 Columbia Rd. NW,* ☎ *202/797–1819. MC, V. Closed Mon. No lunch Tues.–Sat. Metro: Woodley Park/Zoo.*

$$–$$$ ✕ **Felix.** With neon on the exterior and a stylized cityscape in the dining room, Felix may look more like a nightclub than a restaurant, but tasting chef David Scribner's contemporary cooking should allay any fears. Start with spring rolls made from duck confit and leeks, then choose pork chops or seared loin of tuna served with wasabi cream. If you come on a Friday, you'll find an unsuspected treat—challah, matzo-ball soup, and brisket, just like Scribner's mother used to make. At 11 PM nightly Felix becomes a nightclub, with live music and a separate lounge offering an upscale bar menu. ⊠ *2406 18th St. NW,* ☎ *202/ 483–3549. AE, DC, MC, V. No lunch. Metro: Woodley Park/Zoo.*

French

$$–$$$ ✕ **La Fourchette.** On a block in Adams-Morgan where new restaurants seem to open and close weekly, La Fourchette has stayed in business for nearly a quarter of a century by offering good bistro food at reasonable prices. Most of the menu consists of daily specials, but you can pretty much count on finding bouillabaisse and rabbit on the list; other entrées might include chicken in beurre blanc or sweetbreads in a mushroom-cream sauce. La Fourchette looks the way a bistro should, with an exposed-brick wall, a tin ceiling, bentwood chairs, and quasi-

Postimpressionist murals. ✉ *2429 18th St. NW,* ☎ *202/332–3077. AE, DC, MC, V. No lunch weekends. Metro: Woodley Park/Zoo.*

Italian

$$ ✕ **I Matti.** A less formal trattoria from Roberta Donna, local Italian restaurant entrepreneur and owner of the much more expensive Galileo restaurant downtown, I Matti serves a varied menu of sophisticated dishes to a largely neighborhood clientele. If you stop by for lunch or a light snack, try one of the thin, crisp-crust pizzas or a pasta dish. Meat and fish dishes—which might include rabbit, veal, or *bollito misto* (meat and capon cooked in a flavorful broth)—are pricier but well worth it. Service is often perfunctory, particularly on busy weekend evenings. ✉ *2436 18th St. NW,* ☎ *202/462–8844. AE, DC, MC, V. No lunch in Summer. Metro: Woodley Park/Zoo.*

$–$$ ✕ **Pasta Mia.** Pasta Mia's southern Italian appetizers and entrées all cost a palatable $7–$10. Large bowls of steaming pasta are served with a generous layer of fresh-grated Parmesan. Best-sellers include fusilli with broccoli and whole cloves of roasted garlic, rich spinach fettuc-cine *verde,* and penne *arrabiata* (in spicy marinara sauce with olives). Tiramisu, served in a teacup, is an elegant way to finish your meal. ✉ *1790 Columbia Rd. NW,* ☎ *202/328–9114. Reservations not ac-cepted. MC, V. Closed Sun. No lunch. Metro: Woodley Park/Zoo.*

Latin American

$$–$$$ ✕ **Grill from Ipanema.** The Grill focuses on Brazilian cuisine, from spicy seafood stews to grilled steak and other hearty meat dishes. Appetiz-ers include fried yuca with spicy sausages and—for adventurous eaters—fried alligator. Former Second Lady Tipper Gore adores the *mexilhão á carioca,* garlicky mussels cooked in a clay pot. Traditional feijoada, the national dish of Brazil, is served every day. ✉ *1858 Columbia Rd. NW,* ☎ *202/986–0757. AE, D, DC, MC, V. No lunch Mon.–Tues. Metro: Woodley Park/Zoo.*

$–$$ ✕ **Lauriol Plaza.** This longtime favorite on the border of Adams-Mor-gan and Dupont Circle continues to serve Latin American, Cuban, and Spanish dishes—ceviche, paella, fajitas, and so on—to enthusiastic crowds. Rustic entrées such as Cuban-style pork and *lomo saltado* (Pe-ruvian-style strip steak with onions, tomatoes, and fiery jalapeño pep-pers) are specialties. The dining room can get noisy, but the roof terrace of the modern, custom-design building offers an airy alternative in good weather. ✉ *1835 18th St. NW,* ☎ *202/387–0035. AE, D, DC, MC, V. Metro: Dupont Circle.*

Mexican

$$ ✕ **Mixtec.** Don't expect tortilla chips as a starter at this truly Mexican restaurant—it simply doesn't serve them. It does, however, offer a trio of delicious salsas to season the array of authentic dishes. Unlike their fast-food counterparts topped with lettuce and cheese, the tacos *al car-bón* here consist only of grilled beef or pork and fresh corn tortillas; grilled spring onions are a nice accompaniment. Fajitas, enchiladas, and seafood are cooked in the regional styles of Veracruz, Mazatlán, and Acapulco, which the menu does a good job of explaining. The *licua-dos* (fruit drinks) are refreshing complements to the sometimes spicy dishes. ✉ *1792 Columbia Rd. NW,* ☎ *202/332–1011. Reservations not accepted. MC, V. Metro: Woodley Park/Zoo.*

Middle Eastern

$$ ✕ **Lebanese Taverna.** Arched ceilings, cedar panels etched with leaf pat-terns, woven rugs, and brass lighting fixtures give the Taverna a feel-ing of warm elegance. Start your meal with an order of Arabic bread that's baked in a wood-burning oven. Small fried pies filled with spinach, cheese, or meat are buttery and surprisingly light. Lamb, beef, chicken, and seafood are either grilled on kabobs, slow-roasted, or smothered with a garlicky yogurt sauce. Pomegranate seeds are sprinkled atop many dishes for a colorful accent. A group can make a meal of the *mezza* platters—a mix of appetizers and sliced *shawarma* (spit-roasted lamb). The atmosphere is not as lively at the more casual Virginia branch, and even though the owners are the same, the food has never quite reached the high standard set at the Connecticut Avenue location. ⊠ *2641 Connecticut Ave. NW,* ☎ *202/265–8681. Metro: Woodley Park/Zoo;* ⊠ *5900 Washington Blvd., Arlington, VA,* ☎ *703/ 241–8681. AE, D, DC, MC, V. No lunch Sun.*

\$–\$\$ ✕ **Mama Ayesha's Restaurant.** Journalists and politicians are known to frequent this family-run eatery for its reasonably priced fare. Staples such as chicken and lamb kabobs can be had for less than \$10, baskets of complimentary pita bread are served hot, and the crisp falafel is among the best in town. Weekends sometimes bring Arabic bands and belly dancing. ⊠ *1967 Calvert St. NW,* ☎ *202/232–5431. AE, DC, MC, V. Metro: Woodley Park/Zoo.*

Southwestern

\$\$–\$\$\$\$ ✕ **Peyote Café/Roxanne Restaurant/On the Rooftop.** Mexican influences on traditional southern food define the southwestern menus at these connected restaurants. All offer great food, and you can order from any menu no matter where you sit. Twinkling lights, tables with bar stools, and a rockin' jukebox attract a young crowd of primarily students and singles to the cozy Peyote Café. Roxanne, on the middle floor, is decorated in a Mexican theme and offers passable Mexican food and margaritas. On the Rooftop has outdoor dining in warm weather. *Carne asada* (grilled rib-eye steak) is popular among carnivores. Not in the mood for meat? Choose from grilled salmon, rotisserie-style "thunder" chicken, and "sweat hot fire" shrimp. Finish with Calvados-brandy cherry cobbler or the white-and-dark-chocolate bread pudding. ⊠ *2319 18th St. NW,* ☎ *202/462–8330. AE, DC, MC, V. No lunch weekdays. Metro: Woodley Park/Zoo.*

Capitol Hill

The Hill has a number of bar–eateries that cater to Congressional types in need of fortification after a day spent running the country. Dining options are augmented by Union Station, which contains some decent—if pricey—restaurants. It also has a large food court offering quick bites that range from barbecue to sushi.

American

\$\$–\$\$\$\$ ✕ **Monocle.** This, the nearest restaurant to the Senate side of the Capitol, is a great place to spot members of Congress at lunch and dinner. The regional American cuisine is rarely adventurous but is thoroughly reliable. The crab cakes, either as a platter or a sandwich, are a specialty, and, depending on the day of the week, you might encounter pot roast or a first-rate fish dish as a special. Still, the draw here is the old-style Capitol Hill atmosphere. ⊠ *107 D St. NE,* ☎ *202/546– 4488. AE, DC, MC, V. Closed weekends. Metro: Union Station.*

\$\$–\$\$\$ ✕ **Two Quail.** A welcome respite from the men's-club atmosphere of traditional Capitol Hill eateries, this quaint, floral-pattern tearoom allows for power dining in an almost-romantic setting. The seasonal menu has both hearty fare—Muscovy duck, pork loin, chicken stuffed with corn bread and pecans, game meats, filet mignon—and lighter seafood pastas and meal-size salads. Service can be leisurely. ⊠ *320 Massachusetts Ave. NE,* ☎ *202/543–8030. AE, DC, MC, V. No lunch weekends. Metro: Union Station.*

French

$$$–$$$$ ✕ **La Colline.** Chef Robert Gréault has worked to make La Colline one
★   of the city's best French restaurants. The seasonal menu emphasizes
fresh vegetables and seafood, with offerings that range from simple grilled
preparations to fricassees and gratins with imaginative sauces. Other
choices include duck with orange or cassis sauce and veal with chanterelle
mushrooms. ✉ *400 N. Capitol St. NW,* ☎ *202/737–0400. AE, DC,
MC, V. Closed Sun. No lunch Sat. Metro: Union Station.*

$$–$$$$ ✕ **La Brasserie.** One of the Hill's most pleasant and satisfying restaurants for breakfast, lunch, or dinner, La Brasserie occupies two floors
of adjoining town houses and has outdoor dining in the warmer
months. The basically French menu changes seasonally, with poached
salmon and breast of duck featured daily. Likewise, the small, selective wine list changes often. The crème brûlée, served cold or hot with
fruit, is superb. ✉ *239 Massachusetts Ave. NE,* ☎ *202/546–9154. AE,
DC, MC, V. No breakfast or lunch Sat. Metro: Union Station.*

$$$ ✕ **Bistro Bis.** A zinc bar, spacious brown leather booths, and a glass-
front display kitchen create delicious expectations at Bistro Bis, the sec-
ond restaurant from chef Jeffrey Buben, owner of the much-acclaimed
Vidalia restaurant downtown. Buben calls his restaurant a modern bistro
serving French food with an American sensibility. His menu seamlessly
merges standards of the modern American repertory with French bistro
classics. For a first course, don't miss the ragout of snails with arti-
chokes and potatoes. Main-course hits include *goujonettes* (fried fil-
lets) of sole; seared sea scallops Provençale served in a sauce of garlic,
tomato, and olives and accompanied by a custardy timbale of roasted
eggplant; roast chicken; and veal stew. ✉ *Hotel George, 15 E St. NW,*
☎ *202/661–2700. AE, D, DC, MC, V. Metro: Union Station.*

Indian

$–$$ ✕ **Aatish.** *Aatish* means volcano, an appropriate name for a restaurant specializing in tandoori cooking—meats, seafood, vegetables, and
breads cooked in the intense heat of a clay oven. What distinguishes
this restaurant is not so much the variety of its menu as the quality of
its cooking. The appetizer samosa is a model version, with flaky pastry enclosing a delicious spiced mixture of potatoes and peas. The tandoori chicken is moist and delicious. Lamb dishes, especially the lamb
karahi, sautéed in a wok with ginger, garlic, tomatoes, vegetables, and
spices, are very well prepared. ✉ *609 Pennsylvania Ave. SE,* ☎ *202/
544–0931. AE, D, MC, V. Metro: Eastern Market.*

Italian

$$–$$$$ ✕ **Barolo.** Chef Roberto Donna of the downtown standout Galileo seems
to have his hand in many of the best Italian restaurants in town. This
one is a collaboration with Enzo Fargione, a cooking-school friend of
Donna's and a former sous-chef at Galileo. Barolo specializes in the
food of their native Piedmont region. Fargione has a sure hand with
pastas (fettuccine with asparagus and black-truffle sauce), fish (baked
salmon on a bed of asparagus), and game (quail with truffle–shallot
sauce and a red pepper timbale). To end your meal, try the *panna cotta,*
a creamy, gelatin-thickened dessert. ✉ *223 Pennsylvania Ave. SE,* ☎
*202/547–5011. AE, DC, MC, V. Closed Sun. No lunch weekends. Metro:
Capitol South.*

Seafood

$$$–$$$$ ✕ **Phillip's Flagship.** The best of the enormous seafood restaurants that
overlook the Capital Yacht Club's marina, Phillip's has cavernous
rooms and capacious decks that are fully capable of accommodating
the crowds from the tour buses that fill the parking lot. There's a sushi
bar and seafood buffet Monday through Saturday, a party room with

its own deck, and space for 1,400. Despite its size, the restaurant is distinguished by the quality of its raw materials, such as local fish and crab, which it acquires from a network of dealers built up over the years. ⊠ *900 Water St. SW,* ☎ *202/488–8515. AE, D, DC, MC, V. Metro: L'Enfant Plaza.*

Southern

$$–$$$$ ✕ **B. Smith's.** The D.C. location of southern-influenced B. Smith's bears the distinctive mark of chef James Oakley. For appetizers, try the grilled cheddar cheese grits or the jambalaya—but skip the overly breaded fried green tomatoes and the too-sweet sweet potatoes. Signature entrée Swamp Thing may not sound pretty, but this mix of mustard-seasoned shrimp and crawfish with collard greens is delicious. Seafood and anything with barbecue sauce are highly recommended. Desserts are comforting classics, slightly dressed up: bananas Foster, warm bread pudding, and sweet-potato pecan pie. ⊠ *50 Massachusetts Ave. NE (in Union Station),* ☎ *202/289–6188. AE, D, DC, MC, V. Metro: Union Station.*

$$ ✕ **Heart & Soul.** Paintings by African-American artists adorn the walls here, and the extensive menu gives southern favorites a Caribbean-Creole flair. You can order your catfish blackened or corn-fried and enjoy chicken wings cooked with Jamaican spices or barbecue sauce. It's easy to make a meal out of the delicious sides: mashed potatoes, red beans and rice, candied sweet potatoes, collard greens. The corn bread is a house specialty. The service, though friendly, can be slow; plan accordingly. Live entertainment Sunday night helps ease you into the workweek. ⊠ *801 Pennsylvania Ave. SE,* ☎ *202/546–8801. AE, MC, V. Closed Mon. Metro: Eastern Market.*

Turkish

$$ ✕ **Anatolia.** Soft contemporary Turkish music plays and copper pails serving as lamp shades cast a warm light in this intimate restaurant run by a husband-and-wife team. Scoop up the appetizer spreads—such as sweet roasted eggplant or peppery hummus—with wedges of warm, grilled pita. In addition to a standard array of kabobs, the *adana* kabob, a grilled homemade lamb sausage specific to Turkey, is delicious. For dessert, try baklava and a cup of strong espresso-like Turkish coffee. ⊠ *633 Pennsylvania Ave. SE,* ☎ *202/544–4753. AE, D, MC, V. Closed Sun. No lunch Sat. Metro: Eastern Market.*

Downtown

"Downtown" covers everything between Georgetown and Capitol Hill. The "new downtown," centered at Connecticut Avenue and K Street, has many of the city's blue-chip law firms and deluxe eateries—places that feed off expense-account diners and provide the most elegant atmospheres, most attentive service, and often the best food. But the "old downtown," farther east, is where the action is these days. Restaurants of all stripes (usually casual and moderately priced) have sprung up to serve the crowds that attend games at the MCI Arena. The entire downtown area, however, has been in a state of flux gastronomically, with famed restaurants closing their doors and new ones blossoming. Trendy microbrewery-restaurants and cigar lounges are part of the new wave, and Chinatown has been suffering as rents go up and long-standing favorite restaurants are forced to go out of business or relocate.

African

$$$ ✕ **Marrakesh.** A happy surprise is Marrakesh, a bit of Morocco in a
★ part of the city better known for auto-supply shops. The menu is a fixed-price ($25) feast shared by everyone at your table and eaten without

silverware; flat bread, served with the meal, is used as a scoop. Appetizers consist of a platter of three salads followed by *b'stella*, a chicken version of Morocco's traditional pie made with crisp layers of phyllo dough and seasoned with cinnamon. The first main course is chicken with lemon and olive. A beef or lamb dish is served next, followed by vegetable couscous, fresh fruit, mint tea, and pastries. Belly dancers put on a nightly show. Alcoholic drinks can really drive up the tab. ⊠ *617 New York Ave. NW,* ☎ *202/393–9393. Reservations essential. No credit cards. Lunch only for groups of 10 or more by reservation. Metro: Mt. Vernon/UDC.*

American

$$$–$$$$ ✕ **Butterfield 9.** Light-color wood paneling, gleaming white linen, and stunning black-and-white photographs make Butterfield 9, carved out of a corner of the old Garfinckels department store, one of the most elegant restaurants in town. Chef Martin Saylor's style of contemporary cooking glories in complexity. Imaginative appetizers, such as a foie gras pancake—foie gras atop an egg-inflated pancake rather like a Yorkshire pudding—have been hits, as have main courses like barbecued salmon on couscous, and cod with truffled brandade on a pool of clam chowder. Others, like chorizo-stuffed squid on a pile of mashed avocado, need to be rethought. Pastry chef Rita Garruba's desserts are seasonal and delicious; the peach shortcake is superb. ⊠ *600 14th St. NW,* ☎ *202/289–8810. Reservations essential. AE, D, MC, V. No lunch weekends. Metro: Metro Center.*

$$$–$$$$ ✕ **Sam and Harry's.** Cigar-friendly Sam and Harry's is understated, genteel, and packed at lunch and dinner. Although the miniature crab cakes are a good way to begin, the real draws are such prime meats as porterhouse and New York strip steak served on the bone. For those who've sworn off beef, daily seafood specials include Maine lobster. End the meal with warm pecan pie laced with melted chocolate or a "turtle cake," full of caramel and chocolate and big enough for two. ⊠ *1200 19th St. NW,* ☎ *202/296–4333. AE, D, DC, MC, V. Closed Sun. No lunch Sat. Metro: Dupont Circle.*

$$–$$$ ✕ **Old Ebbitt Grill.** People flock here to drink at the several bars, which seem to go on for miles, and to enjoy carefully prepared bar food that includes buffalo chicken wings, hamburgers, and Reuben sandwiches. The Old Ebbitt also has Washington's most popular oyster bar (called "raw bar" locally), which serves a rotating selection of farm-raised oysters from certified waters. Serious diners will appreciate the homemade pasta and the daily fresh fish or steak specials (served until 1 AM). Despite the crowds, the restaurant never feels cramped, thanks to its well-spaced, comfortable booths. Service can be slow at lunch; if you're in a hurry, try the quick, café-style Ebbitt Express next door. ⊠ *675 15th St. NW,* ☎ *202/347–4800. AE, D, DC, MC, V. Metro: Metro Center.*

$ ✕ **Sholl's Colonial Cafeteria.** Here the slogan is "Where good foods are prepared right, served right, and priced right"—and truer words were never spoken. Suited federal workers line up next to pensioners and students to grab a bite at this D.C. institution, which is open for breakfast, lunch, and an early dinner. Favorites include chopped steak, roast beef, liver and onions, and baked chicken and fish for less than $5. Sholl's is famous for its fruit pies: all the desserts are scrumptious and cost around $1. ⊠ *1990 K St. NW,* ☎ *202/296–3065. Reservations not accepted. MC, V. No dinner Sun. Metro: Farragut West.*

Asian

$$–$$$$ ✕ **TenPenh.** It didn't take long for this offering from chef Jeff Tunks and the team that owns DC Coast to become hot. The menu draws from many Asian cuisines—Chinese, Japanese, Thai, Vietnamese, even Filipino—but even the pickiest of eaters is likely to find something ap-

pealing here. An appetizer of spiced fried quail with green-papaya salad combines two favorite Vietnamese dishes. Main courses range from Tunks's signature Chinese smoked lobster to lamb chops with an Asian pesto crust. Pastry chef David Guas's treats include banana spring rolls with ginger ice cream and mango salsa. The contemporary Asian furnishings and tableware were purchased by the owners on a buying trip through Asia. ✉ *1001 Pennsylvania Ave. NW,* ☎ *202/393–4500. Reservations essential. AE, D, DC, MC, V. Closed Sun. Metro: Navy Archives.*

$–$$$$ ✗ **Full Kee.** Many locals swear by Full Kee, which has a competitive assortment of Cantonese-style roasted meats. Order from the house specialties, not the tourist menu; the meal-size soups garnished with roast meats are the best in Chinatown. ✉ *509 H St. NW,* ☎ *202/371–2233. No credit cards. Metro: Gallery Place/Chinatown.*

$–$$$$ ✗ **Hunan Chinatown.** One of Chinatown's most attractive and most attentive restaurants, Hunan serves very good versions of familiar dishes. Try the fried dumplings, the tea-smoked duck, the Szechuan eggplant, and the crispy whole fish Hunan-style. ✉ *624 H St. NW,* ☎ *202/783–5858. AE, D, DC, MC, V. Metro: Gallery Place/Chinatown.*

$$–$$$ ✗ **Kaz Sushi Bistro.** In serene downtown surroundings, chef–owner Kaz Okochi combines traditional Japanese cookery with often inspired improvisations. For a first-rate experience, sit at the sushi bar and ask the chef to give you whatever is freshest and best. You might be surprised with buttery, fatty tuna; raw, fresh shrimp; monkfish liver; or maybe, if you're lucky, fugu—that legendarily dangerous Japanese blowfish only recently available in the United States. The chef's years of experience preparing fugu mean you're in good hands. But it's not all sushi here: Kaz's innovations might include sake-poached scallops with lemon-cilantro dressing or an eggplant "carpaccio." Sake sorbet is a light and unusual dessert. ✉ *1915 I St NW,* ☎ *202/530–5500. AE, D, DC, MC, V. Closed Sun. No lunch weekends. Metro: Farragut West.*

$–$$$ ✗ **Miss Saigon.** Shades of mauve and green, black art-deco accents, and potted palms decorate this Vietnamese restaurant, where careful attention is paid to presentation as well as to seasoning. Begin with crisp egg rolls or chilled spring rolls, then proceed to exquisite salads of shredded green papaya topped with shrimp or beef. The daily specials feature the freshest seafood prepared in exciting ways. "Caramel"-cooked meats are standouts, as are the grilled meats. Prices are moderate, especially for lunch, but you may have to order several dishes to have your fill. ✉ *3057 M St. NW,* ☎ *202/333–5545. AE, DC, MC, V. Metro: Foggy Bottom.*

$–$$ ✗ **Li Ho.** Head for unassuming Li Ho if you're seeking good Chinese food in satisfying portions. Kitchen specialties—including duck soup with mustard greens, and Singapore noodles, a rice-noodle dish seasoned with curry and bits of meat—are favorites among the lunchtime crowd. ✉ *501 H St. NW,* ☎ *202/289–2059. No credit cards. Metro: Gallery Place/Chinatown.*

$–$$ ✗ **Oodles Noodles.** Packed from the day they opened and with long lines waiting for tables and takeout, these attractive Pan-Asian noodle houses offer terrific Asian cooking. You'll find Chinese, Japanese, Thai, Indonesian, Malaysian, and Vietnamese dishes. The quality of each is remarkably high, and all are served on plates appropriate to the cuisine. Try the Thai drunken noodles, the Chinese clay-pot noodles, or the Vietnamese rice noodles with grilled chicken. ✉ *1120 19th St. NW,* ☎ *202/293–3138. AE, DC, MC, V. Closed Sun. Metro: Farragut North.* ✉ *4907 Cordell Ave., Bethesda, MD,* ☎ *301/986–8833. AE, DC, MC, V. Metro: Bethesda.*

$ ✗ **Burma.** The country of Burma (now called Myanmar) is bordered by India, Thailand, and China, which gives a good indication of the cuisine at this Chinatown restaurant. Curry and tamarind share pride of place with lemon, cilantro, and soy seasonings. Batter-fried eggplant and squash are paired with complex, peppery sauces. Green-tea-leaf and other salads, despite their odd-sounding names and ingredients, leave the tongue with a pleasant tingle. Such entrées as mango pork and tamarind fish are equally satisfying. ⊠ *740 6th St. NW, 2nd floor,* ☎ *202/638–1280. AE, D, DC, MC, V. No lunch weekends. Metro: Gallery Place/Chinatown.*

Contemporary

$$$–$$$$ ✕ **DC Coast.** Chef Jeff Tunks's menu at this sophisticated downtown spot brings the foods of three coasts—Atlantic, Gulf, and Pacific—to Washington. Try his version of the mid-Atlantic's best-known seafood delicacy, crab cakes. They're among the best in town. If you're homesick for New Orleans, try the gumbo, and for Pacific Rim cooking you can't beat the tea-smoked lobster. The bar scene is one of the liveliest in the downtown area. ⊠ *1401 K St. NW,* ☎ *202/216–5988. Reservations essential. AE, D, DC, MC, V. Closed Sun. No lunch Sat. Metro: McPherson Square.*

$$$–$$$$ ✕ **Equinox.** Chef Todd Gray headed the kitchen at Galileo, Washington's best Italian restaurant, for seven years, but when he started his own place, the Virginia-born chef knew it had to be American. Both the decor and the style of cooking are simple and elegant. Gray takes good local ingredients and lets them speak for themselves: grilled quail with a truffle reduction, rare duck breast served on a cabbage slaw, crab cakes given interest with a dice of mango, and barbecued salmon with a sauce of roasted peppers and corn. The five-course prix fixe ($65) dinner menu is a cost-effective introduction to his cooking. ⊠ *818 Connecticut Ave. NW,* ☎ *202/331–8118. Reservations essential. AE, DC, MC, V. Closed Sun. No lunch Sat. Metro: Farragut West.*

$$$–$$$$ ✕ **Occidental Grill.** In the Willard Inter-Continental, the popular Occidental Grill is one of the most venerable restaurants in the city. The setting is clubby, the walls are covered with photos of politicians and other notables who have dined here, and the service is attentive. This is a place that's best for the tried and true—chopped salad, grilled tuna, veal meat loaf. ⊠ *1475 Pennsylvania Ave. NW,* ☎ *202/783–1475. AE, DC, MC, V. Metro: Metro Center.*

$$$–$$$$ ✕ **Vidalia.** There's a lot more to chef Jeffrey Buben's distinguished restau-
  ★   rant than the Vidalia onion, which is a specialty in season. Inspired by the cooking and the ingredients of the South and the Chesapeake Bay region, Buben's version of New American cuisine revolves around the best seasonal fruits, vegetables, and seafood he can find. Don't miss the roasted onion soup with spoon bread, the shrimp on yellow grits, or the sensational lemon chess pie. ⊠ *1990 M St. NW,* ☎ *202/659–1990. AE, D, DC, MC, V. Closed Sun. July–Aug. No lunch weekends. Metro: Dupont Circle.*

$$–$$$$ ✕ **Red Sage.** This upscale rancher's delight near the White House has a multimillion-dollar southwestern decor with a barbed-wire-and-lizard theme and a pseudo-adobe warren of dining rooms. Upstairs is the Border Café, where thrifty trendsetters can enjoy a comparatively inexpensive Tex-Mex menu. Downstairs, owner Mark Miller's Berkeley–Santa Fe background surfaces in elaborate, artful presentations of such tony chow as smoky pecan-crusted chicken with a chili-honey glaze. But other influences are also at work here, including those of Africa and Asia. ⊠ *605 14th St. NW,* ☎ *202/638–4444. AE, D, DC, MC, V. Sat. lunch in café only. No lunch Sun. Metro: Metro Center.*

$$$ ✕ **Rupperts.** Set at the edge of the wasteland that eventually is to be Washington's new convention center is this very hip spot. Chef John Cochran makes a point of finding the freshest regional ingredients for

his menu, which changes daily. Look for vegetable soups (made entirely without cream), game birds, the mushrooms of the season, and such southern regional delicacies as greens and grits. ✉ *1017 7th St. NW,* ☎ *202/783–0699. AE, MC, V. Closed Sun.–Mon. No lunch Fri.– Wed. Metro: Mt. Vernon Sq./UDC.*

$ ✕ **Bread Line.** This crowded, quirky, sometimes chaotic restaurant specializes in breads and bread-based foods and not only makes the city's best baguette but also some of the best sandwiches in town. Owner Mark Furstenburg makes everything on the premises, from the breakfast bagels and muffins to the ciabatta loaves for the tuna salad sandwich with preserved lemons. It's best to arrive early or late to avoid the noontime rush. Outdoor seating is available in warmer months. ✉ *1751 Pennsylvania Ave. NW,* ☎ *202/822–8900. Reservations not accepted. MC, V. Closed weekends. No dinner. Metro: Farragut West.*

Eclectic

$$$–$$$$ ✕ **Kinkead's.** This multichambered restaurant includes a downstairs pub and raw bar and more-formal dining rooms upstairs. The open kitchen upstairs allows you to watch chef Robert Kinkead and company turn out an eclectic menu of mostly seafood dishes, inspired by Kinkead's New England roots and by the cooking of Asia and Latin America. Main-course soups and seafood stews, such as Scandinavian salmon stew, are specialties. The menu also has a selection of grilled fish made simply, without sauces. Save room for dessert—the chocolate *dacquoise* (layer cake) is a knockout. ✉ *2000 Pennsylvania Ave. NW,* ☎ *202/296–7700. AE, DC, MC, V. Metro: Foggy Bottom.*

$$–$$$$ ✕ **701 Pennsylvania Avenue.** Cuisine drawn from Italy, France, Asia, and the Americas graces the menu of this sleek restaurant, where an elegant meal might begin with tuna tartare topped with caviar or salmon ceviche, progress to chicken on a bed of mashed potatoes or blue marlin on a black bean puree, and finish with chocolate-raspberry marquis. The Caviar Lounge offers caviar and tapas menus and more than 30 types of vodka. The three-course fixed-price ($24.50) pretheater dinner is popular; if you're attending a performance at the Shakespeare Theatre, this is a convenient, upper-crust choice. Live jazz plays nightly. ✉ *701 Pennsylvania Ave. NW,* ☎ *202/393–0701. Reservations essential. AE, DC, MC, V. No lunch weekends. Metro: Archives/Navy Memorial.*

French

$$$$ ✕ **Gerard's Place.** Don't let the simplicity of the name cause you to
★ underestimate the cooking at this sophisticated spot owned by acclaimed French chef Gerard Pangaud. In the striking gray and burntumber dining room you'll be served dishes with intriguing combinations of ingredients. The menu, which changes daily, might include Gerard's signature poached lobster with a ginger, lime, and Sauternes sauce; venison served with dried fruits and pumpkin and beetroot purees; or seared tuna with black olives and roasted red peppers. Memorable desserts have included the Chocolate Tear, a teardrop-shape flourless chocolate cake veined with raspberry. If your appetite is willing, the five-course fixed-price ($72) dinner is a relative bargain. ✉ *915 15th St. NW,* ☎ *202/737–4445. Reservations essential. AE, DC, MC, V. Closed Sun. No lunch Sat. Metro: McPherson Square.*

$$–$$$$ ✕ **Les Halles.** This is about as close as you can come to a Parisian bistro without going to France. The cooking is plain and hearty, and the portions are large. The best first course is a sensational salad of *frisée* (a bitter salad green), bacon, and Roquefort cheese. Order steak for a main course, either the *onglet* (hanger steak) with the best pommes frîtes in town or, for two, the gargantuan grilled rib. If you're lucky enough to visit in February, don't miss the Choûcroute Festival, when four different versions of this hearty meat-and-sauerkraut treat are offered. ⊠ *1201 Pennsylvania Ave. NW, ☎ 202/347–6848. AE, D, DC, MC, V. Metro: Metro Center.*

Indian

$$ ✕ **Bombay Club.** Just one block from the White House, the beautiful
★   Bombay Club tries to re-create the kind of solace the Beltway elite might
have found in a private club had they been 19th-century British colonials in India rather than modern-day Washingtonians. The bar, which serves hot hors d'oeuvres at cocktail hour, is furnished with rattan chairs and paneled with dark wood. The dining room, with potted palms and a bright blue ceiling above white plaster moldings, is elegant and decorous. The menu includes unusual seafood specialties and a large number of vegetarian dishes, but the real standouts are the breads and the seafood appetizers. ⊠ *815 Connecticut Ave. NW, ☎ 202/659–3727. AE, DC, MC, V. No lunch Sat. Metro: Farragut West.*

Italian

$$$–$$$$ ✕ **Galileo.** This flagship restaurant of Washington entrepreneur–chef
★   Roberto Donna serves sophisticated Piedmontese-style cooking. The specials vary daily, but to get the full Galileo experience, order an antipasto, a pasta (perhaps split between two), and a main course of grilled fish, game, or veal. Preparations are generally simple: the veal chop might be served with mushroom-and-rosemary sauce, the beef with black-olive sauce and polenta. Both the four-course ($60) and six-course ($75) fixed-price menus are good values. In a move unusual for downtown restaurants, Galileo is open for breakfast weekdays. Several nights a week (call for a schedule), Donna cooks in his restaurant within a restaurant, Laboratorio da Galileo. This intimate space, with about 25 seats, allows for an up-close view of the kitchen and the master at work. The price for twelve courses is around $100. ⊠ *1110 21st St. NW, ☎ 202/293–7191. AE, D, DC, MC, V. No lunch weekends. Metro: Foggy Bottom.*

$$$–$$$$ ✕ **i Ricchi.** An airy dining room decorated with terra-cotta tiles, cream-
★   color archways, and floral frescoes, i Ricchi remains a favorite of critics and upscale crowds for its earthy Tuscan cuisine, often prepared on its wood-burning grill or oven. The spring–summer menu includes such offerings as rolled pork roasted in wine and fresh herbs and skewered shrimp; the fall–winter bill of fare brings grilled lamb chops, thick soups, and sautéed beef filet. ⊠ *1220 19th St. NW, ☎ 202/835–0459. AE, DC, MC, V. Closed Sun. No lunch Sat. Metro: Dupont Circle.*

$$$–$$$$ ✕ **Olives.** A D.C. outpost of Boston celebrity chef Todd English, Olives plays to a crowded dining room at lunch and dinner. The upstairs room, which overlooks the open kitchen, is where the action is, but the spacious downstairs dining room is more comfortable, albeit formal. Hearty beginnings include a goat-cheese-and-onion tart topped with a boned quail and English's signature butternut-squash–stuffed tortelli. Most plates have so much going on that there are bound to be some hits and some misses, but the spit-roasted chicken is done well, as is the salmon atop a bowl of clam chowder. ⊠ *1600 K St. NW, ☎ 202/452–1866. AE, D, MC, V. Closed Sun. No lunch Sat. Metro: Farragut North.*

$$–$$$$ ✕ **Osteria Goldoni.** Chef Fabrizio Aielli, a veteran of Roberto Donna's kitchen at Galileo, specializes in Venetian cooking that draws a celeb clientele. Osteria Goldoni has a lively downstairs café and a more sedate upstairs dining room, both with the same menu. Pastas, even familiar ones, achieve a new dimension of excellence under Aielli's skilled hand. Tiny veal ravioli are beautifully sauced with tomato, pesto, and mushrooms. Seafood is a specialty; try the whole fish baked in a parchment bag and garnished with artichokes and polenta. The house-made ice creams and sorbets are wonderful. ⊠ *1120 20th St. NW, ☎ 202/293–1511. AE, D, DC, MC, V. No lunch weekends. Metro: Farragut North.*

$$–$$$$ ✕ **Teatro Goldoni.** Named for an 18th-century playwright, this elegant Italian restaurant with a mostly seafood menu has a colorful Venetian-inspired decor. Teatro Goldoni is as much a showcase for chef Fabrizio Aielli's modern Italian cooking as it is for traditional Venetian cuisine. For a first course, try one of the unusual pasta dishes, such as squid-ink noodles or cannelloni stuffed with shiitake mushroom puree. At the center of the menu is a selection of fresh fish, which may be grilled, roasted, or cooked in parchment paper Venetian style. There's also a good selection of vegetarian entrées and a selection of more than 30 frozen vodkas at the bar. Live jazz plays Wednesday, Friday, and Saturday. ✉ 1909 K St. NW, ☎ 202/955–9494. AE, D, MC, V. Closed Sun. No lunch Sat. Metro: Farragut North.

$$–$$$ ✕ **Tosca.** Chef Cesare Lanfranconi spent several years in the kitchen at Washington's best Italian restaurant, Galileo, before leaving to start his own place. The room, on the ground floor of a downtown office building, is sleek and sophisticated, dressed in muted tones. Lanfranconi's cooking draws heavily on the food of his native region of Italy, the Lake Como area, but isn't limited by it. His combinations of American ingredients and Italian technique are sometimes dazzling. Polenta, made from freshly ground cornmeal and topped with wild mushrooms, is a good example: the taste of sweet corn is intense but tempered by the mushrooms' earthiness. Pasta dishes include an unusual and delicious ravioli stuffed with ricotta and crushed amaretto cookies. Desserts, particularly a deconstructed tiramisu served in a martini glass, are worth saving room for. ✉ 1112 F St. NW, ☎ 202/367–1990. AE, DC, MC, V. No lunch weekends. Metro: Metro Center.

Latin American

$$–$$$ ✕ **Café Atlántico.** Offering the essence of *nuevo Latino* cooking, Café Atlántico always has exciting, and often adventurous, new dishes. Guacamole made table-side by your waiter is unmistakably fresh. The menu changes often, but if they're offered, try duck confit, baby chicken with mole sauce, Puerto Rican shrimp *asopao* (a traditional thin stew made with rice), or feijoada, which also comes as a salad—minus the meat. Service is friendly and helpful, and the bar makes a mean pisco sour cocktail. ✉ 8th and E Sts. NW, ☎ 202/393–0812. AE, DC, MC, V. No lunch Sun. Metro: Archives/Navy Memorial.

Seafood

$$$–$$$$ ✕ **Oceanaire Seafood Room.** This outpost of a Minneapolis-based chain is beautiful, a throwback to another era, with dark wood paneling, semicircular red booths, white tablecloths, and a pink glow that makes everybody look their best. Oceanaire primarily distinguishes itself with first-rate ingredients; you'll see it at its best if you order simply, picking from the list of fresh fish that heads the menu—perhaps lovely walleye pike or local rockfish. The portions are often big enough to feed a family of four. Oceanaire is a good time, and even better if you go with a group. ✉ 1201 F St. NW, ☎ 202/347–2277. AE, D, DC, MC, V. No lunch weekends. Metro: Metro Center.

Southern

$$–$$$ ✕ **Georgia Brown's.** An elegant "new South" eatery and a favorite hangout of local politicians, Georgia Brown's serves shrimp Carolina-style (with the head on and steaming grits on the side); beef tenderloin medallions with a bourbon–pecan sauce; thick, rich crab soup; and such specials as grilled salmon and smoked-bacon green beans. Fried green tomatoes are given the gourmet treatment, as is the sweet-potato cheesecake. The airy, curving dining room has white honeycomb windows and an unusual ceiling ornamentation of bronze ribbons. ✉ 950 15th St. NW, ☎ 202/393–4499. AE, D, DC, MC, V. No lunch Sat. Metro: McPherson Square.

Spanish

$$$–$$$$ ✕ **Taberna del Alabardero.** A lovely formal dining room, skillful ser-
★ vice, and sophisticated Spanish cooking make this restaurant one of
Washington's best. Start with such tapas as piquillo peppers stuffed
with *bacalao* (salted cod) or roasted leg of duck wrapped in a phyllo
pastry pouch. Proceed to a hefty bowl of gazpacho or white garlic soup
and venture on to authentic paella and elegant Spanish country dishes.
Ask the sommelier to pick a good Spanish wine to accompany your
meal. Pineapple tart is a light ending to rich fare. The plush old-world
decor and handsome bar create a romantic atmosphere that attracts a
well-heeled, cosmopolitan clientele. ⊠ *1776 I St. NW (entrance on 18th
St.),* ☎ *202/429–2200. Reservations essential. AE, D, DC, MC, V. Closed
Sun. No lunch Sat. Metro: Farragut West.*

$$–$$$ ✕ **Jaleo.** These lively Spanish bistros encourage you to make meals out
★ of their long lists of tapas, although such entrées as grilled fish and
paella—which comes in four versions—are just as tasty. Tapas high-
lights are *gambas al ajillo* (sautéed garlic shrimp), fried potatoes with
spicy tomato sauce, and *pinchitos* (a skewer of grilled chorizo) with
garlic mashed potatoes. At the Bethesda location, try *la plancha*
(seafood seared on a flat-top grill with garlic, olive oil, and parsley).
For dessert, don't miss the crisp apple Charlotte and the chocolate hazel-
nut tart. Live flamenco dancing heats up the downtown branch Wednes-
days, the Bethesda branch Mondays and Tuesdays. ⊠ *480 7th St.
NW,* ☎ *202/628–7949. Metro: Gallery Place/Chinatown.* ⊠ *7271
Woodmont Ave., Bethesda, MD,* ☎ *301/913–0003. Metro: Bethesda.
AE, D, DC, MC, V.*

Steak

$$–$$$$ ✕ **Palm.** A favorite lunchtime hangout of power brokers, the walls of
Palm are papered with caricatures of the famous patrons who have dined
here. Main attractions include gargantuan steaks and Nova Scotia
lobsters, several kinds of potatoes, and New York cheesecake. But one
of Palm's best-kept secrets is that it's also a terrific, old-fashioned Italian restaurant. Try the veal marsala for lunch or, on Thursday, the terrific shrimp in marinara sauce. ⊠ *1225 19th St. NW,* ☎ *202/293–9091.
AE, DC, MC, V. No lunch weekends. Metro: Dupont Circle.*

Dupont Circle

South from U Street and north from K Street is Dupont Circle, around
which a number of restaurants are clustered. You can also find a variety of cafés, most with outdoor seating. The District's better gay-friendly
establishments are here as well, especially along 17th Street. Chains
such as Starbucks have put fancy coffee on every corner, but long-es-
tablished espresso bars, like the 24-hour Afterwords, are a better
source for breakfast and light or late fare.

American

$$$–$$$$ ✕ **Caucus Room.** Here is the apotheosis of the Washington political
restaurant. The limited partnership that owns it includes a Demo-
cratic super-lobbyist and a former Republican National Committee chair-
man. The updated clubby decor is perfect for business lunches or
dinners, and the many private dining rooms are popular locations for
political fundraising events. The menu is a combination of steakhouse
classics and "Continental cuisine" resurrected from an earlier era of
American cooking. You're safer with the steakhouse favorites: crab cakes,
Caesar salad, Dover sole, swordfish chops, and great steaks. ⊠ *401
9th St. NW,* ☎ *202/393–1300. AE, D, DC, MC, V. No lunch week-
ends. Closed Sun. Metro: Navy Archives.*

American/Casual

$–$$ ✕ **Kramer Books & Afterwords: A Cafe.** This popular bookstore-cum-café is a favorite neighborhood breakfast spot and a late-night haunt on weekends, when it's open around the clock. There's a simple menu with soups, salads, and sandwiches, but many people drop in just for cappuccino and dessert. Live music, from rock to blues, is on Wednesday through Sunday from 9 PM to midnight. ✉ *1517 Connecticut Ave. NW,* ☎ *202/387–1462. Reservations not accepted. AE, D, MC, V. Metro: Dupont Circle.*

Asian

$–$$$$ ✕ **City Lights of China.** The Chinese fare and art-deco decor at City Lights have made it a consistent pick on critics' lists. The traditional fare is excellent, as are less common specialties such as lamb in a tangy peppery sauce and shark's-fin soup. Seafood items tend to be costly, but there are plenty of reasonably priced alternatives. For satisfying and inexpensive one-dish meals try the pickled-mustard-green soup with noodles and pork, or the *cha chang mein,* the Chinese counterpart to spaghetti with meat sauce. The mint-green booths and elegant silk-flower arrangements conjure up breezy spring days, even in the midst of a frenzied dinner rush. ✉ *1731 Connecticut Ave. NW,* ☎ *202/265–6688. AE, D, DC, MC, V. Metro: Dupont Circle.*

$–$$$ ✕ **Sala Thai.** Who says Thai food has to be scalp-sweating hot? Sala Thai makes the food as spicy as you wish, but the chef is interested in flavor, not fire. Among the subtly seasoned offerings are *panang goong* (shrimp in curry–peanut sauce), chicken sautéed with ginger and pineapple, and flounder with a choice of four sauces. Mirrored walls and warm lights soften the ambience of this small downstairs dining room, as do the friendly service and largely neighborhood clientele. ✉ *2016 P St. NW,* ☎ *202/ 872–1144. AE, D, DC, MC, V. Metro: Dupont Circle.*

$ ✕ **Teaism.** A novel counterpoint to all the area's coffee bars, Teaism offers not only an impressive selection of more than 50 teas but also delicious Japanese, Indian, and Thai foods. Diners mix small dishes—tandoori kabobs, tea-cured salmon, Indian flat breads, salads, and various chutneys—to create meals or snacks. Japanese *bento* boxes—which contain a salad, entrée, rice, and cookies—are full meals. Another unique favorite is the *ochazuke,* green tea poured over seasoned rice. Teaism is also a good place to enjoy a hot drink with ginger scones or other sweet treats. ✉ *2009 R St. NW,* ☎ *202/667–3827. Reservations not accepted. AE, MC, V. Metro: Dupont Circle.*

Contemporary

$$$–$$$$ ✕ **Nora.** Although it bills itself as an "organic restaurant," Nora is no collective-run juice bar. The food, like the quilt-decorated dining room, is sophisticated and attractive. Peppered beef carpaccio with Manchego cheese is a good starter. Entrées—such as seared rockfish with artichoke broth, grilled lamb chops with white-bean *ragù* (sauce), and risotto with winter vegetables—exemplify the chef's emphasis on well-balanced, complex ingredients. Warm chocolate cake with cappuccino ice cream and pear-and-blueberry crisp with praline ice cream are among the sublime desserts. You may also want to try chef Nora Pouillon's West End restaurant, Asia Nora (✉ 2213 M St. NW, ☎ 202/797–4860), where organic ingredients are put to good use in Pan-Asian dishes. ✉ *2132 Florida Ave. NW,* ☎ *202/462–5143. AE, D, MC, V. Closed Sun. No lunch. Metro: Dupont Circle.*

$$$–$$$$ ✕ **Tabard Inn.** The lobby lounge of the Hotel Tabard Inn—stuffed with fading portraits and overstuffed furniture—may look like an antiques store, but the restaurant's culinary sensibility is thoroughly modern. Chef David Craig made his reputation as a seafood chef, so fish is always a good bet here. First courses have included a confit of duck leg with a compote of figs and cherries, various composed salads, and gumbo. The strongest entrées are such slightly dressed-up classics as grilled New York strip steak and, in season, sautéed soft-shell crabs over wilted greens. Desserts—strawberry–rhubarb crisp or white-chocolate cheesecake—get raves. In good weather, courtyard dining is available. ⊠ *1739 N St. NW,* ☎ *202/833–2668. AE, DC, MC, V. Metro: Dupont Circle.*

French

$–$$$ ✕ **Bistrot du Coin.** An instant hit in its Dupont Circle neighborhood, this moderately priced French steakhouse is noisy, crowded, and great fun. The brainchild of Michel Verdon (formerly of Les Halles) and chef Yannis Felix has a monumental zinc bar and serves comforting traditional bistro fare. Mussels in any of several preparations are good starters. Steaks, garnished with a wonderful pile of crisp fries, are the main attraction, but there are good options, including a duck-leg confit and tripe *à la niçoise,* a delicious stew of tripe and fresh tomatoes. You can wash it all down with a carafe of Beaujolais or Côtes du Rhone, or with a pitcher of Alsatian white. ⊠ *1738 Connecticut Ave. NW,* ☎ *202/234–6969. AE, D, MC, V. Metro: Dupont Circle.*

Italian

$$$$ ✕ **Obelisk.** The attractions here are eclectic Italian cuisine and a five-course fixed-price ($55) menu that changes every day and includes both traditional dishes and chef Peter Pastan's imaginative innovations. For the main course, you might try the lamb with garlic and sage or the braised grouper with artichoke and thyme. The minimally decorated dining room is tiny, with tables closely spaced. ⊠ *2029 P St. NW,* ☎ *202/872–1180. Reservations essential. DC, MC, V. Closed Sun. No lunch. Metro: Dupont Circle.*

$$–$$$ ✕ **La Tomate.** The owners of this popular neighborhood Italian restaurant have transformed a previously neglected corner near Dupont Circle into an attractive garden-dining space. La Tomate is notable for its dependable pastas, traditional veal preparations, and friendly, if occasionally harried, service. ⊠ *1701 Connecticut Ave. NW,* ☎ *202/667–5505. AE, DC, MC, V. Metro: Dupont Circle.*

$ ✕ **Pizzeria Paradiso.** A sister restaurant to the pricier Obelisk next door, the petite Pizzeria Paradiso sticks to crowd-pleasing basics: pizzas, *panini* (sandwiches such as Italian cured ham and sun-dried tomatoes and basil), salads, and desserts. Although the standard pizza is satisfying, you can enliven things by ordering it with fresh buffalo mozzarella or unusual toppings such as potatoes, capers, and mussels. The intensely flavored gelato is a house specialty. A trompe l'oeil ceiling adds space and light to a simple interior. ⊠ *2029 P St. NW,* ☎ *202/223–1245. DC, MC, V. Metro: Dupont Circle.*

Latin American

$$–$$$$ ✕ **Gabriel.** Chef Gregory Hill brings a nouvelle approach to Gabriel's traditional Latin American and Spanish dishes. *Pupusas,* Salvadoran meat patties, are filled with chorizo; appetizer sea scallops are grilled and served with lime, cilantro, and garlic cream. The bar is a popular after-work hangout because of the extensive tapas buffet, but the restaurant really comes into its own on Sunday with its outstanding brunch buffet. In addition to traditional breakfast items, whole suckling pig and made-to-order quesadillas from the carving table and Mediterranean specialties like paella, cassoulet, and salads are available. The dessert table offers tiny fruit tarts, bread and rice pudding, mini crème brûlée, and cheesecake. ⊠ *Radisson Barceló Hotel, 2121 P St. NW,* ☎ *202/956–6690. Reservations essential. AE, D, DC, MC, V. No lunch Sat. Metro: Dupont Circle.*

Middle Eastern

$–$$$ ✕ **Skewers/Café Luna.** As the name implies, the focus at Skewers is on kabobs, here served with almond-flaked rice or pasta. Lamb with eggplant and chicken with roasted pepper are the most popular variations, but vegetable kabobs and skewers of filet mignon and seasonal seafood are equally tasty. With nearly 20 choices, the appetizer selection is huge. If the restaurant is too crowded, you can enjoy the cheap eats (chicken and avocado salad, mozzarella and tomato sandwiches, vegetable lasagna, pizza, and salads) downstairs at Café Luna or the reading room–coffeehouse upstairs at Luna Books. ✉ *1633 P St. NW,* ☎ *202/387–7400 Skewers; 202/387–4005 Café Luna; 202/332–2543 Luna Books. AE, D, DC, MC, V. Metro: Dupont Circle.*

Seafood

$$–$$$$ ✕ **Johnny's Half Shell.** It doesn't take reservations and it's almost always crowded, but Johnny's Half Shell is worth the wait. Owners John Fulchino and Ann Cashion (both of Cashion's Eat Place in Woodley Park) have created a modern version of the traditional mid-Atlantic seafood house, where you can be comfortable ordering oysters on the half shell and a beer at the bar or settling into one of the roomy booths for a first course of the best fried oysters in town followed by local rockfish or broiled lobster. Don't miss the spectacular chocolate angel food cake with caramel sauce for dessert. ✉ *2002 P St. NW,* ☎ *202/ 296–2021. Reservations not accepted. AE, MC, V. Closed Sun. Metro: Dupont Circle.*

Georgetown/West End/Glover Park

In Georgetown, whose central intersection is Wisconsin Avenue and M Street, white-tablecloth establishments sit next door to hole-in-the-wall joints. The closest Metro stop is Foggy Bottom, a 15- to 20-minute walk away; consult the Georgetown map before you set out, and consider taking a cab. Restaurants in the adjacent West End—bounded roughly by Rock Creek Park to the west, N Street to the north, 20th Street to the east, and K Street to the south—are worth checking out as well. North from Georgetown on Wisconsin Avenue, there's a cluster of good restaurants in the Glover Park area, including the city's best sushi bar, Sushi-Ko.

American

$$$$ ✕ **Morton's of Chicago.** A national steak-house chain that claims to serve the country's best beef, Morton's is always jumping. In classic steak-house tradition, the emphasis is on quantity as well as quality; the New York strip and porterhouse steaks are well over a pound each. If you have an even larger appetite (or you plan to share with someone else), there's a 48-ounce porterhouse. The menu also includes prime rib, lamb, veal, chicken, lobster, and grilled fish. ✉ *3251 Prospect St.,* ☎ *202/342–6258;* ✉ *1050 Connecticut Ave.,* ☎ *202/955–5997;* ✉ *8075 Leesburg Pike, Vienna, VA,* ☎ *703/883–0800. AE, D, DC, MC, V. No lunch weekends.*

$$$–$$$$ ✕ **Palena.** Chef Frank Ruta and pastry chef Ann Amernick met when they were both working in the White House kitchens in 1980; now they've teamed up to open this contemporary American restaurant named for the Italian village where Ruta's grandmother's mother lived. The menu combines French, Italian, and American influences, reflecting Ruta's experience in each, and changes seasonally. Sometimes Amernick and Ruta team up, as for an appetizer of crisp puff pastry with fresh sardines and greens. In other instances—a veal chop with a barley-stuffed pepper or a pork chop with flavorful baked beans—Ruta goes it alone. The desserts—a spritely lemon–caramel tart or a choco-

late torte—are homey and comforting, a perfect match for Ruta's earthy cooking. ⊠ *3529 Connecticut Ave. NW,* ☎ *202/537–9250. AE, DC, MC, V. Closed Sun. No lunch. Metro: Cleveland Park.*

$ ✕ **Georgetown Café.** With its unpretentious decor, cheap prices, and eclectic, lowbrow menu, this café is a bit of a neighborhood oddball. Students and other locals are known to frequent it for the pasta, pizzas, kabobs, gyros, and such home-style American favorites as roast beef, baked chicken, and mashed potatoes. Closed only from 6 to 9 AM weekdays and open 24 hours on weekends, Georgetown Café is also good for a late-night snack. ⊠ *1623 Wisconsin Ave. NW,* ☎ *202/ 333–0215. D, MC, V.*

Asian

$$ ✕ **Sushi-Ko.** At the city's best Japanese restaurant, daily specials are
★   always innovative: sesame oil–seasoned trout is layered with crisp wonton crackers, and a sushi special might be salmon topped with a touch of mango sauce and a tiny sprig of dill. And you won't find the whimsical desserts—green-tea ice cream or sake sorbet—at the local Baskin-Robbins. ⊠ *2309 Wisconsin Ave. NW,* ☎ *202/333–4187. AE, MC, V. No lunch Sat.–Mon.*

Belgian

$$$–$$$$ ✕ **Marcel's.** Chef Robert Wiedmaier trained in Michelin-starred restaurants in the Netherlands and Belgium, and in this, his first solo venture, his French-inspired Belgian cooking focuses on robust seafood and poultry preparations. Start with mussels, if they're available, and move on to perfectly seared diver scallops in saffron broth or tender roasted monkfish on a ragout of potatoes, olives, and onions. The roast chicken is a marvel, white and dark cooked separately to perfect tenderness and moistness. If figs are in season, be sure to order the fig tart with citrus crème anglaise and honey-cinnamon ice cream. ⊠ *2401 Pennsylvania Ave. NW,* ☎ *202/296–1166. AE, DC, MC, V. Closed Sun. No lunch Sat. Metro: Foggy Bottom.*

Contemporary

$$$$ ✕ **Citronelle.** California–French chef Michel Richard's flagship restau-
★   rant in the Latham Hotel has a glass-front kitchen, which allows you to see all the action. Richard's witty appetizer specials might include an impressive "tart" of thinly sliced grilled scallops or "beignets" of foie gras coated with *kataife* (a grain product that resembles shredded wheat) and deep-fried. Main courses might include loin of venison with chestnuts, mushrooms, and wine sauce; breast of squab with an ethereal truffle sauce; or rabbit with a small rabbit torte. Desserts are equally luscious: the crunchy napoleon—layers of caramelized phyllo dough and creamy vanilla custard—is drizzled with butterscotch and dark chocolate. A special chef's table in the kitchen gives lucky diners a ringside seat. Service is attentive and knowledgeable and the wine list is exceptional. ⊠ *3000 M St. NW,* ☎ *202/625–2150. Reservations essential. AE, DC, MC, V. No lunch.*

$$$–$$$$ ✕ **1789.** This elegant dining room, with Early American paintings and
★   a fireplace, could easily be a room in the White House. But although the decor is proper and genteel, the food is down-to-earth and delicious. Soups, such as the rich black bean soup with unsweetened chocolate and the seafood stew, are flavorful. Rack of lamb and filet of beef are specialties, and seared tuna stands out among the excellent seafood dishes. Service is fluid and attentive. Hazelnut chocolate bars with espresso sauce will pep you up for a night on the town, or opt for the homier nectarine cobbler. ⊠ *1226 36th St. NW,* ☎ *202/965– 1789. AE, D, DC, MC, V. No lunch.*

$$$–$$$$ ✕ **Tahoga.** The stark white dining room of this popular spot is a perfect setting for its beautifully prepared, elegantly presented New American cooking. Start with duck lasagna, savory confit of duck layered between crisp potato slices and mashed potatoes. Main courses are modernized versions of American and French classics and might include roast chicken, braised lamb shank, bourbon-glazed pork chops, and chicken-fried beef tenderloin. The pretty garden is a lovely place for lunch. Take advantage of the lunchtime special: any wine on the wine list for half price. ✉ *2815 M St. NW,* ☎ *202/338–5380. AE, DC, MC, V. No lunch weekends.*

French

$$–$$$$ ✕ **La Chaumière.** A favorite of Washingtonians seeking an escape from the hurly-burly of Georgetown, La Chaumière (which means "the thatched cottage") has the rustic charm of a French country inn, particularly in winter, when its central stone fireplace warms the room. Fish stew, mussels, and scallops are on the regular menu, and there are always several grilled fish specials. Meat dishes include such hard-to-find entrées as venison. Many local diners plan their meals around La Chaumière's specials, particularly the couscous on Wednesday and the tasty cassoulet on Thursday. ✉ *2813 M St. NW,* ☎ *202/338–1784. AE, DC, MC, V. Closed Sun. No lunch Sat.*

$$–$$$ ✕ **Bistro Français.** Washington's chefs head to Bistro Français for its minute steak maître d'hôtel or the sirloin with black pepper or red wine sauce. For many, the big draw is the rotisserie chicken. Daily specials may include *suprême* of salmon with broccoli mousse and beurre blanc. The restaurant is divided into two parts—the café side and the more formal dining room; the café menu includes sandwiches and omelets in addition to entrées. The Bistro also offers fixed-price ($13.95) lunches, $18.95 early and late-night dinner specials, and $15.95 all-you-can-eat brunches on weekends. It stays open until 3 AM Sunday through Thursday, 4 AM Friday and Saturday. ✉ *3128 M St. NW,* ☎ *202/338–3830. AE, DC, MC, V.*

Indian

$–$$ ✕ **Aditi.** The two-story dining room—with its burgundy carpets and chairs and pastel-color walls with brass sconces—seems too elegant for a moderately priced Indian restaurant. The first floor is small, with a dramatic staircase leading to a larger room with windows that overlook the busy street. Tandoori and curry dishes are expertly prepared and not aggressively spiced; if you want your food spicy, request it. Rice *biryani* entrées are good for lighter appetites. ✉ *3299 M St. NW,* ☎ *202/625–6825. AE, D, DC, MC, V.*

Italian

$$$–$$$$ ✕ **Cafe Milano.** You're likely to rub shoulders with local socialites, sports figures, and visiting celebrities at Cafe Milano's crowded bar. The authentic, sophisticated Italian cooking is very good, and specialties include pasta dishes like the elegant lobster with linguine, composed salads, and light-crust pizzas. ✉ *3251 Prospect St. NW,* ☎ *202/333–6183. AE, D, DC, MC, V.*

U Street

In the 1930s and 1940s, the U Street corridor, which begins just down the hill from 18th Street, was the place to enjoy a late-night drink and hear jazz greats such as Duke Ellington, Billie Holliday, and Charlie Parker. After decades of neglect and devastation from riots in the 1960s, the area saw a burst of revitalization. With some of the hippest bars in the District, quirky vintage stores, small but lively nightclubs, and numerous cafés, the neighborhood draws a young crowd day and night. The area is still rough around the edges, however, so use caution. Restaurants stay open late on weekend nights and offer good food—everything from burgers to gourmet pizza to Ethiopian dishes—at low prices. The U Street vicinity is known for excellent fried-fish spots, including **Webb's Southern Food** (⊠ 1361 U St. NW, ☎ 202/462–3474), which unfortunately doesn't offer seating.

American

$–$$ ✕ **Polly's Café.** Tables can be hard to come by on weekend nights at Polly's Café, a cozy U Street oasis with a fireplace. That's when locals come to swill beer, eat better-than-average bar food (burgers, catfish tacos, chicken wings), and enjoy jukebox favorites from every era. A savory Portobello mushroom "steak," crisp calamari, and Polly's own ample house salad are popular. With entrées priced from $7 to $9, the hearty brunch is one of Washington's best values. ⊠ 1342 U St. NW, ☎ 202/265–8385. MC, V. No lunch weekdays. Metro: U St./Cardozo.

$ ✕ **Ben's Chili Bowl.** Long before U Street became hip, Ben's was offering chili on hot dogs, chili on half-smoke sausages, chili on burgers, and just plain chili. Add cheese fries for $2 more and you're in cholesterol heaven. With its faux-marble bar and shiny red vinyl stools, it doesn't look like much has changed since the '50s. One nod at modern times is that it now offers turkey and vegetarian burgers and meatless chili. It's open until 2 AM Monday through Thursday and until 4 AM on Friday and Saturday, and serves a delicious southern-style breakfast starting at 6 AM Monday through Saturday. ⊠ 1213 U St. NW, ☎ 202/667–0909. No credit cards. Metro: U St./Cardozo.

Eclectic

$–$$$ ✕ **Utopia.** Here New Orleans meets Italy and the Mediterranean. Lamb couscous, seafood bisque, and pasta dishes such as the Chef's Advice (which combines shrimp, chicken, andouille sausage, and sweet peppers) are hits. Utopia has live music Thursday through Sunday with excellent jazz and Brazilian bands and a very reasonable $15 per person minimum. ⊠ 1418 U St. NW, ☎ 202/483–7669. AE, MC, V. Metro: U St./Cardozo.

$–$$ ✕ **Café Nema.** The menu at combines Somali, North African, and Middle Eastern cuisines. Entrées are simple but flavorful. Grilled chicken, lamb, and beef kabobs and salmon steak are paired with fresh vegetables and an outstanding curried basmati rice pilaf that has bits of caramelized onion, whole cloves, and raisins. The chef gives such appetizers as *sambousa* (flaky fried triangles of dough filled with curried vegetables or meat), hummus, and *baba ganoush* (eggplant purée) a distinct touch. There's also a good selection of pastas, salads, and sandwiches. Live jazz plays Thursday nights. ⊠ 1334 U St. NW, ☎ 202/667–3215. AE, D, DC, MC, V. Metro: U St./Cardozo.

Italian

$–$$ ✕ **Coppi's Restaurant.** An Italian bicycling motif permeates popular Coppi's, from the posters and gear hanging on the walls to the monogrammed racing shirts worn by the staff. The wood oven–baked pizzas are delicious and adventurous. When it appears as a special, the pizza *ai funghi di bosco* (with white-oyster, shiitake, and cremini mushrooms) is a must. ⊠ 1414 U St. NW, ☎ 202/319–7773. AE, D, DC, MC, V. No lunch. Metro: U St./Cardozo.

Maryland/Virginia Suburbs

Intriguing restaurant districts also thrive outside the city limits. Happily, all are accessible by the Metro. Eateries in downtown Bethesda, Maryland, offer spicy southwestern dishes, classic Spanish cuisine, and good old American diner food and are said to be luring the

When you pack your MCI Calling Card, it's like packing your loved ones along too.

Your MCI Calling Card is the easy way to stay in touch when you travel. Use it to call to and from over 125 countries. Plus, every time you call, you can earn frequent flier miles. So wherever your travels take you, call home with your MCI Calling Card. It's even easy to get one. Just visit **www.mci.com/worldphone.**

EASY TO CALL WORLDWIDE

1. Just enter the WorldPhone® access number of the country you're calling from.
2. Enter or give the operator your MCI Calling Card number.
3. Enter or give the number you're calling.

Aruba ⁛	800-888-8
Bahamas ⁛	1-800-888-8000

Barbados ⁛	1-800-888-8000
Bermuda ⁛	1-800-888-8000
British Virgin Islands ⁛	1-800-888-8000
Canada	1-800-888-8000
Mexico	01-800-021-8000
Puerto Rico	1-800-888-8000
United States	1-800-888-8000
U.S. Virgin Islands	1-800-888-8000

⁛ Limited availability.

EARN FREQUENT FLIER MILES

FLIGHTFUND
America West Airlines

American Airlines
AAdvantage

Delta
SkyMiles

HAWAIIAN MILES

MIDWEST EXPRESS AIRLINES
PROGRAM PARTNER

SOUTHWEST AIRLINES
RAPIDREWARDS
A Symbol of Freedom

UNITED
Mileage Plus.

US AIRWAYS
DIVIDEND MILES

SEE THE WORLD
IN FULL COLOR

Fodor's Exploring Guides bring all the great sights vividly to life with hundreds of photographs, fascinating historical background, and colorful anecdotes. Detailed maps and practical information keep you headed in the right direction.

Pair a **Fodor's** Exploring Guide with your trusted Gold Guide for a complete planning package.

cognoscenti from Georgetown. Bethesda is just a 20-minute drive from Georgetown up Wisconsin Avenue; by Metro it is a 15- to 20-minute ride from Metro Center to the Bethesda Metro stop and a 5-minute ride from the Foggy Bottom Metro stop.

Virginia has its ritzy Georgetown equivalent in quaint, historic Old Town Alexandria. And bragging rights to some of the greater D.C. area's best Asian restaurants go to Arlington, where Wilson Boulevard is lined with popular Vietnamese establishments and branches of D.C. restaurants. The Clarendon Metro station makes these Asian restaurants readily accessible, but the King Street Metro station is, unfortunately, a 15-minute walk from most Old Town Alexandria eateries.

Afghan

$$ ✕ **Panjshir.** This restaurant's Falls Church location favors a plush red and dark-wood decor while the Vienna branch is more into pinks—but both serve succulent kabobs of beef, lamb, and chicken, as well as fragrant stews (with or without meat) over impeccably cooked rice. Entrées come with Afghan salad and hearty bread. ✉ 924 W. Broad St., Falls Church, VA, ☎ 703/536–4566. AE, DC, MC, V. Closed Sun. ✉ 224 Maple Ave. W, Vienna, VA, ☎ 703/281–4183. AE, DC, MC, V. No lunch Sun.

American

$$–$$$$ ✕ **Carlyle Grand Cafe.** The bustling downstairs bar and the sleek art deco upstairs dining room serve almost the same menu but feel like two different restaurants. Both offer chef Bill Jackson's imaginative, generous interpretation of modern American cooking. Start with lobster pot stickers, then progress to such entrées as braised lamb shank served with a savory bread pudding or sea scallops served with a rock-shrimp-and-asparagus risotto. The chocolate hurricane cake is extremely popular. And if you like the bread, you can buy more to take home at the restaurant's own bakery—the Best Buns Bread Company—next door. ✉ 4000 S. 28th St., Arlington, VA, ☎ 703/931–0777. AE, D, MC, V.

$$–$$$ ✕ **Majestic Café.** Chef Susan McCreight Lindeborg, who made her reputation at the Morrison Clark Inn, has moved across the river to Old Town Alexandria to reopen the Majestic Café, a 1930s-era landmark that had been closed since 1978. She preserved the art deco facade and the general '30s appearance of the place, but updated it with skylights, maple paneling, and bentwood chairs. Lindeborg's cooking style (she calls it "modern American by way of the South") moves between trendy American dishes and traditional southern fare, from five-spice salmon in preserved-lemon broth to pork chops in onion gravy. Some of her best work is done on side dishes: hush puppies with remoulade, fluffy spoonbread, and great stewed tomatoes. Homey buttermilk pie is a great dessert. ✉ 911 King St., Alexandria, ☎ 703/837–9117. AE, MC, V. Closed Mon. Metro: King Street (and then a walk of about 8 blocks).

American/Casual

$ ✕ **Tastee Diner.** As 24-hour diners go, the Tastees are classics—sentimental favorites that each invoke a sense of old-fashioned community appropriate to its location. Students and others on low budgets (or little sleep) ignore the dust and relish the coffee, which flows endlessly. ✉ 7731 Woodmont Ave., Bethesda, MD, ☎ 301/652–3970. MC, V. Metro: Bethesda. ✉ 8516 Georgia Ave., Silver Spring, MD, ☎ 301/589–8171. MC, V. Metro: Silver Spring. ✉ 118 Washington Blvd., Laurel, MD, ☎ 301/725–1503. MC, V.

Asian

$–$$ ✕ **Café Dalat.** In the heart of Arlington's "Little Saigon," Café Dalat offers low-priced Vietnamese fare in a far-from-fancy but clean and pleasant setting, and with service that nears the speed of light. The sugarcane shrimp could inspire a trip to Southeast Asia, and *da ram gung* is a sinus-clearing dish of simmered chicken and ginger. All the appetizers are winners, in particular the crispy spring rolls and the tangy Vietnamese shrimp salad in lemon vinaigrette. ⊠ *3143 Wilson Blvd., Arlington, VA,* ☎ *703/276–0935. MC, V. Metro: Clarendon.*

$–$$ ✕ **Little Viet Garden.** Little Viet Garden's patrons swear by its spring rolls; tasty beef-broth-and-glass-noodle soups; crispy crepes stuffed with chicken, shrimp, bean sprouts, and green onion; and beef tips and potato stir-fried with onion in a smoky sauce. In warm months reserve a table on the outdoor terrace bordered by a flower box–lined white fence. ⊠ *3012 Wilson Blvd., Arlington, VA,* ☎ *703/522–9686. AE, D, DC, MC, V. Metro: Clarendon.*

$ ✕ **Pho 75.** To refer to Pho 75's product as mere soup would be a disservice to the delightful procession of flavors that comes with every mouthful—but that is essentially what *pho* is: a Hanoi-style beef soup packed with noodles and thinly sliced pieces of meat that are cooked in seconds by the steaming broth. A plate of fresh bean sprouts, mint leaves, lemon, and green chilies comes with every order so you may spice your feast-in-a-bowl as you wish. Pho comes in either a large ($5.45) or small ($4.75) bowl, a remarkable bargain either way. ⊠ *3103 Graham Rd., Suite B, Falls Church, VA,* ☎ *703/204–1490;* ⊠ *1510 University Blvd., East Langley Park, MD,* ☎ *301/434–7844. No credit cards.*

Barbecue

$–$$ ✕ **Red, Hot and Blue.** This Memphis-style barbecue joint is known for its ribs. They come "wet"—with sauce—or, when simply smoked, "dry." The delicious pulled-meat sandwiches and low prices lure hungry crowds. This chain has additional locations in Annapolis, Fairfax, Gaithersburg, and Laurel. ⊠ *1600 Wilson Blvd., Arlington, VA,* ☎ *703/276–7427. Reservations not accepted. AE, D, DC. MC, V. Metro: Court House.*

Contemporary

$$$$ ✕ **Elysium.** There's no sign on the street, but the dining room of the elegant Morrison House hotel in Old Town Alexandria is worth seeking out. Each evening chef Christopher Brooks offers his guests a three-course menu ($42.50), as well as a four-course menu ($52.75) that changes weekly. The offerings mix down-home American, traditional French, and southwestern influences, combining first-rate ingredients and good culinary imagination. ⊠ *116 S. Alfred St., Alexandria, VA,* ☎ *703/838–8000. AE, DC, MC, V. No dinner Sun.–Mon.*

$$$$ ✕ **Inn at Little Washington.** A 90-minute drive takes you past rolling
★ hills and small farms in the Virginia countryside. Entering the inn, which is decorated like a luxurious English country manor, is like being swept into a Merchant-Ivory film. Dinner without wine costs $98 Monday and Tuesday; $108 Wednesday, Thursday, and Sunday; $118 Friday; and $138 Saturday. After a first course of tiny canapés, an excellent soup follows—perhaps chilled fruit or creamy leek. Trout smoked over apple wood might come next, or medallions of veal with Virginia country ham and wild mushrooms, or roast venison with black currants and tart greens. Beautifully choreographed service makes the evening flow seamlessly. Desserts, which on warm evenings can be enjoyed in the garden, are fanciful and elegant. ⊠ *Middle and Main Sts., Washington, VA,* ☎ *540/675–3800. Reservations essential. MC, V. Closed Tues. except in May and Oct.*

$$$–$$$$ ✕ **Old Angler's Inn.** A summer dinner or Sunday brunch at the Old Angler's Inn is one of the most pleasant outdoor-dining experiences in Washington. The C&O Canal is just across the road, the woods begin at the edge of the deck, and the stars are bright overhead. The large fireplace in the lounge is the draw in winter, a great place for sipping an aperitif before heading to one of the two upstairs dining rooms. The modern American menu changes seasonally. Recent hits from the appetizer menu have included seared jumbo sea scallops with yuca and beet jus, deep-fried goat cheese with a potato crust, and sautéed foie gras deglazed with port wine and garnished with a bosc pear. Main courses often feature game: seared loin of venison with savoy cabbage and onions, or seared muscovy duck breast with shallot jus. Leave room for the lemon tart with blueberries. ✉ *10801 MacArthur Blvd., Potomac, MD,* ☎ *301/299–9097. AE, D, V. Closed Mon.*

Egyptian

$–$$ ✕ **Pasha Cafe.** If you like Middle Eastern food but haven't yet ventured outside the hummus-falafel-gyro safety zone, this quaint restaurant is a great place to start exploring. The list of appetizers, or mezes, goes on for pages. Kabobs and lamb dishes are all excellent, but for something more uniquely Egyptian try the *kosa bel zabadi,* a puréed zucchini dip, or the *moulkia,* a spinachlike vegetable stewed in broth, mixed with coriander and garlic, and served with broiled lamb or grilled chicken. Pasha was once an Italian restaurant, and the space still suggests a homespun spaghetti joint. In the rear, a take-out window still offers pizza, along with simpler, less-expensive renditions of what's on the Egyptian menu. ✉ *2109 N. Pollard St., Arlington, VA,* ☎ *703/528–2126. AE, D, DC, MC, V. No lunch Sun.*

French

$$$$ ✕ **L'Auberge Chez François.** The Haeringer family runs this sprawling
★ restaurant tucked into the Virginia countryside, serving the delicious, German-influenced cuisine of Alsace. The decor is both romantic and kitschy—a fireplace dominates the main dining room, German knick-knacks line the walls, and red-jacketed waiters courteously guide you through the meal. Sausage and foie gras served atop sauerkraut, red snapper in a pastry crust for two, and medallions of beef and veal are a few of the generously portioned, outstanding entrées. You'll be asked in advance if you'd like a soufflé—perhaps Grand Marnier or raspberry. Say yes. ✉ *332 Springvale Rd., Great Falls, VA,* ☎ *703/759–3800. Reservations essential. AE, D, DC, MC, V. Closed Mon. No lunch.*

$$–$$$$ ✕ **La Bergerie.** One brother does the cooking and the other runs the dining room of this elegant Old Town restaurant, which specializes in the food of the Basque region of southern France. Try such robust dishes as duck confit and *pipérade* (scrambled eggs with ham and green peppers), but don't neglect the specials, where some of brother Jean's most imaginative cooking shows up. Main-course selections usually include duck, venison, and lamb. Dessert soufflés and the apple tart must be ordered in advance—go for it. ✉ *218 N. Lee St., Alexandria, VA,* ☎ *703/683–1007. AE, D, DC, MC, V. No lunch Sun.*

Italian

$$$$ ✕ **Maestro.** Hotel dining has long had a bad name, but this restaurant at the Tysons Corner Ritz-Carlton is trying hard to change that. The former Dining Room now has a state-of-the-art open kitchen. Chef Fabio Trabocchi has cooked in Michelin-starred restaurants in Europe, and his style emphasizes both the tradition of Italian cooking and what he calls *l'evolutione,* his creative takes on the classics. The menu changes often, but you might find potato ravioli in black-truffle sauce, oxtail

tortellini, or caramelized sweetbreads. Desserts are no less wonderful: bonbons filled with rose, lavender, and peach ice cream, or a chocolate delice, chocolate custard wrapped in a chocolate turban. Two courses (any combination) start at $38; the seven-course tasting menu is $85. Master sommelier Vincent Feraud, well known to Washington wine lovers from his stints in other top-flight restaurants, presides over the good Italian wine list. ⊠ *Ritz-Carlton Tysons Corner, 1700 Tysons Blvd., Tysons Corner, VA,* ☎ *703/821–1515 or 703/917–5498. AE, D, DC, MC, V. No lunch Sun.*

$–$$$$ ✕ **Paolo's.** Homemade bread sticks get meals off to a good, crunchy start at Paolo's. Wise choices to follow might be the "beggar's purse" (filled with wild mushrooms, spinach, and Taleggio cheese) or grilled sea scallops. Then two of you can split a pizza from the wood-burning oven; toppings range from roasted vegetables to grilled chicken to Portobello mushrooms. Grilled meat entrées and a variety of pasta dishes are also available. The Georgetown location (Wisconsin Avenue) is noisy. ⊠ *11898 Market St., Reston, VA,* ☎ *703/318–8920. Reservations not accepted Fri.–Sat. AE, DC, MC, V.* ⊠ *1303 Wisconsin Ave. NW, Washington, DC,* ☎ *202/333–7353. AE, DC, MC, V.*

$$ ✕ **Tempo.** In a renovated gas station, Tempo is an unlikely spot for upscale suburbanites to dine out. But high ceilings and massive windows help cultivate a bright, ornate dining room, and a fawning staff fits the tony setting. The food is northern Italian—the carpaccio is excellent—with hints of French, southwestern, and Californian cuisine providing eclectic undercurrents. Seafood, the kitchen's specialty, dominates the menu. Both the sea scallops, decorated with fresh ginger and spring onions, and the garlic-and-rosemary–seasoned swordfish are invigorating; the mahimahi is tangy with cilantro and lime juice. For starters, try the smooth and peppery crab soup. ⊠ *4231 Duke St., Alexandria, VA,* ☎ *703/370–7900. AE, D, DC, MC, V. No lunch Sat.*

$–$$ ✕ **Pines of Rome.** Large, child-friendly, and inexpensive, Pines of Rome is the kind of neighborhood restaurant where you don't expect innovative cooking, but dependable and comfortable food. Pastas, which are ordinary at best, are not the reason to eat here. Regulars always start with an order of white pizza to share and then choose from the list of specials—roast meats, including pork and veal, are good, and the portions are enormous. The kitchen fries well; try the soft-shell crabs if they're in season or the calamari. Wines are inexpensive and adequate. ⊠ *4709 Hampton Lane, Bethesda, MD,* ☎ *301/657–8775. AE, D, MC, V. Metro: Bethesda.*

Seafood

$$–$$$$ ✕ **Crisfield.** Given an ambience about as elegant as a neighborhood barbershop, Crisfield's relatively high prices might seem absurd. But you get your money's worth: an eyeful of old Maryland arrested in time and some of the best no-nonsense seafood in the area. Crab cakes don't get any more authentic; they're presented with just enough structural imperfection to guarantee they're made by hand. The creamy, chunky clam chowder is rendered with similar, down-home care. The place retains an old-school charm; for maximum effect, sit at the bar, where the waiters shuck clams. ⊠ *8012 Georgia Ave., Silver Spring, MD,* ☎ *301/589–1306. AE, MC, V. Closed Mon. Metro: Silver Spring.*

$–$$$$ ✕ **Bethesda Crab House.** This modest restaurant is the best place in the Washington area to enjoy one of the Chesapeake Bay area's great delicacies—blue crabs, steamed with Old Bay seasoning. Order as many crabs as you want; when they're ready they'll be dumped on your paper-covered table. That's your clue to pick up a mallet and knife and attack the spiced hard-shells. (The waiters gladly give instructions.) Settle back with a beer and some good crab pickin'. The price varies with the time of year. It's a good idea to call in advance to reserve your crabs—the restaurant sometimes runs out. ⊠ *4958 Bethesda Ave., Bethesda, MD,* ☎ *301/ 652–3382. MC, V. Metro: Bethesda.*

$$–$$$ ✗ **Black's Bar & Kitchen.** The bar and kitchen of this warehouse-like restaurant are separated by a glass wall, and the walls are hung with a clutter of barn doors, mounted fish, and old photos. Black's specializes in seafood as served on the Gulf Coast from Florida to Mexico. Oysters are a good place to start—on the half shell, wrapped in bacon and served in lemon butter, or baked with Parmesan cheese and garlic butter. Pistachio-crusted salmon is a hit, as is the spicy Vermillion Bay seafood stew. ⊠ *7750 Woodmont Ave., Bethesda, MD,* ☎ *301/652–6278. AE, DC, MC, V. Metro: Bethesda.*

Southwestern

$–$$$$ ✗ **Rio Grande Café.** Quail, goat, and other upscale Tex-Mex fare make it worth braving Rio Grande's crowds. Crates of Mexican beer stacked against the walls add atmosphere, as does a perpetual-motion tortilla machine. Big portions make this a good spot for families. A young bar crowd likes to knock back the potent combination of frozen sangria and frozen margarita swirled in a frosted soda glass. ⊠ *4919 Fairmont Ave., Bethesda, MD,* ☎ *301/656–2981. AE, D, DC, MC, V. Metro: Bethesda.* ⊠ *4301 N. Fairfax Dr., Arlington, VA,* ☎ *703/528–3131. AE, D, DC, MC, V. Metro: Ballston.* ⊠ *1827 Library St., Reston, VA,* ☎ *703/904–0703. AE, D, DC, MC, V.*

$$–$$$ ✗ **Cottonwood Café.** The stylish Cottonwood Café offers a blend of Santa Fe, Texan, and New American dishes. The blue-cornmeal calamari appetizer is a must. Entrées are generous: try "fire and spice" linguine with andouille sausage and shrimp, "barbacoa" (grilled chicken and shrimp marinated in barbecue sauce with baked banana), or a classic mixed grill like fajitas. ⊠ *4844 Cordell Ave., Bethesda, MD,* ☎ *301/656–4844. AE, MC, V. No lunch Sun. Metro: Bethesda.*

Spanish

$$–$$$ ✗ **Andalucia.** The spartan Rockville location (hidden in an office-and-shopping strip) was popular enough to spawn the more formally furnished Bethesda branch, which has a tapas bar and a tempting dessert cart. Zarzuela, a seafood stew, is one of Andalucia's traditional specialties and is served at both locations. Classical Spanish guitarists can be heard on weeknights. ⊠ *12300 Wilkins Ave., Rockville, MD,* ☎ *301/770–1880. AE, D, DC, MC, V. Closed Mon. No lunch weekends.* ⊠ *4931 Elm St., Bethesda, MD,* ☎ *301/907–0052. AE, D, DC, MC, V. No lunch weekends. Metro: Bethesda.*

3 LODGING

Hostelries in D.C. include grand properties
with glorious histories; Victorian inns; hotel
and motel chains found in every American
city; and small, independently operated
hotels. Some are first class, and others that
offer little more than a good location, a smile,
and a comfortable place to lay your head.

Updated by
Robin
Dougherty

WITH MORE THAN 340 LOCATIONS offering upward of 63,000 guest rooms in the D.C. area, you can almost always find a place to stay—though it's prudent to make reservations. Hotels are often full of conventioneers, politicians in transit, or families, and, in spring, school groups. Rates are especially high around the Cherry Blossom Festival in April. Graduation and other big college weekends at Georgetown and George Washington University also strain the system. If you're interested in visiting Washington at a calm time—and if you can stand tropical weather—come in August, during the congressional recess. Rates drop in late December and January, except around an inauguration. Throughout the year, most hotels have weekend rates that are substantially lower than weekday rates. Discounted group and weekend package rates that include some meals and parking are also available, though not at every hotel.

The properties below were chosen because of their beauty, historical significance, location, or value. All hotels in the $$$ and $$$$ categories have concierges; some in the $$ group do, too (for details on price categories, *see* Lodging *in* Smart Travel Tips A to Z). Because Washington is an international city with a diverse population and variety of visitors, many hotel staffs are multilingual. Every hotel has no-smoking rooms, and many have no-smoking floors. Washington hotels equip their rooms to please their guests. Every place listed is air-conditioned, and many offer facilities and features—from state-of-the-art exercise equipment to modest conference rooms—for business travelers. Virtually every room in the $$ and $$$ categories has an iron and ironing board, telephone with an additional line for a computer modem connection, and hair dryer.

Some of the finer hotels have restaurants with superb food and prices to match. Several hotels have great views of Washington, but the best views of the city are from Virginia, just across Key Bridge. Hotels and motels that provide breakfast (from coffee and almost nothing to breakfast buffet or breakfast to order) are indicated by CP, which stands for Continental Plan. Most major chains have hotels or motels in desirable locations both downtown and in the nearby suburbs.

The hotel reviews here are grouped within neighborhoods in descending order of price. Hotels' parking fees range from free (usually, but not always in the suburbs) to $24 (plus tax) per night. This sometimes involves valet parking, with its implied additional gratuities. Street parking is free on Sunday and usually after 6:30 PM. But there are often far more cars searching than there are spaces available, particularly downtown, in Georgetown, and in the upper Connecticut Avenue area. During weekday rush hours many streets are unavailable for parking; illegally parked cars are towed, and reclaiming a car is expensive and very inconvenient. *Read signs carefully*; some are confusing, and the ticket writers are quick.

For a list of its member hotels, contact the **Washington, D.C., Convention and Visitors Association** (⊠ 1212 New York Ave. NW, 20005, ☎ 202/789–7000). To find reasonably priced accommodations in small guest houses and private homes, try **Bed 'n' Breakfast Accommodations Ltd. of Washington, D.C.** (⊠ Box 12011, 20005, ☎ 202/328–3510, WEB www.bedandbreakfastdc.com), which is staffed weekdays 10–5. It handles about 85 different properties in the area. The **Bed and Breakfast League, Ltd.** (⊠ Box 9490, 20016) can send you a list of its properties with accommodations priced to please.

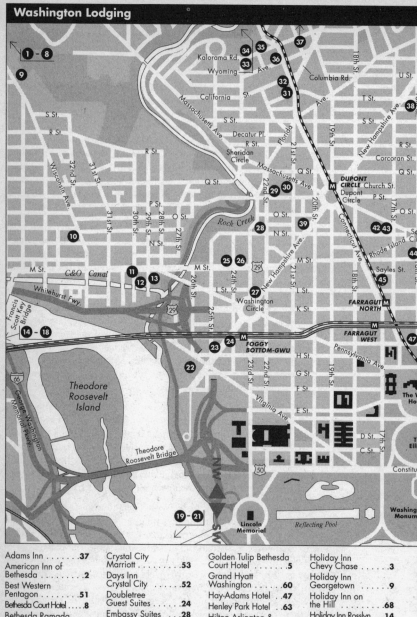

Capitol Hill

$$$ 🏨 **Washington Court Hotel.** The terraced marble stairs leading to an atrium lobby with a skylight, indoor waterfall, and glass elevators are part of a recent updating, but the discerning eye may appreciate the inlaid wood and stained glass that are part of the hotel's original art deco elements. Guest accommodations are roomy, well appointed, and equipped with modern, luxurious furnishings and high-speed modem access. Conveniently located near Union Station, the hotel offers a wonderful view of the Capitol building. ✉ *525 New Jersey Ave. NW, 20001,* ☎ *202/628–2100,* ℻ *202/879–7918. 252 rooms, 12 suites. Restaurant, bar, in-room data ports, refrigerators, room service, health club, laundry service, business services, parking (fee). AE, D, DC, MC, V. Metro: Union Station.*

$$–$$$ 🏨 **Capitol Hill Suites.** On a quiet residential street beside the Library of Congress, this all-suite hotel's proximity to the U.S. House of Representatives office buildings means that it's often filled with visiting lobbyists when Congress is in session. Guest rooms, which are actually renovated apartments, are large and cozy; the sun-filled lobby has a fireplace. ✉ *200 C St. SE, 20003,* ☎ *202/543–6000 or 800/424–9165,* ℻ *202/547–2608. 152 suites. Kitchenettes, lobby lounge, in-room data ports, health club, dry cleaning, laundry service, meeting room, parking (fee). AE, DC, MC, V. Metro: Capitol South.*

$$–$$$ 🏨 **Hotel George.** A hip stand out amid Washington's more sedate lodgings, this contemporary hotel on Capitol Hill is near Union Station and the National Mall. Guest rooms are bright and airy, with granite-topped work desks and marble bathrooms. Portraits of America's first president and the hotel's namesake, created by Andy Warhol protégé Steve Kaufman, adorn the walls in rooms and public areas. The boutique-style hotel has ample work space for business travelers, high-speed modem access, twice-daily maid service, a billiards room, and a 24-hour fitness center with separate steam rooms for men and women. The advantage of a small hotel is that the staff not only recognizes you, they give you personal attention. Bistro Bis, named one of the top hotel restaurants by Washingtonian magazine in 2001, features updated classic French dishes. ✉ *15 E St. NW, 20001,* ☎ *202/347–4200 or 800/576–8331,* ℻ *202/347–4213,* 🌐 *www.hotel-george.com. 139 rooms. Restaurant, bar, lobby lounge, in-room data ports, in-room VCRs, minibars, steam room, gym, meeting room, parking (fee). AE, D, DC, MC, V. Metro: Union Station.*

$$ 🏨 **Holiday Inn on the Hill.** You can expect clean, comfortable rooms and a friendly staff in this hotel, which is convenient to Union Station and the Capitol building. Hotel amenities include high-speed modem access and a Discovery Zone site for younger guests, with supervised educational games, snacks, and contests. The Senators Sports Grille has a fine collection of D.C. baseball memorabilia, including photographs of various Senators players. ✉ *415 New Jersey Ave. NW, 20001,* ☎ *202/638–1616 or 800/638–1116,* ℻ *202/638–0707,* 🌐 *www.holiday-inn.com. 343 rooms. Restaurant, bar, in-room data ports, room service, pool, gym, business services, laundry service, meeting room, parking (fee). AE, D, DC, MC, V. Metro: Union Station.*

$$ 🏨 **Phoenix Park Hotel.** Named for an historic park in Dublin, the Phoenix Park is an Irish-style hotel and home to the Dubliner Pub, where Irish entertainers perform nightly. In the lobby, a case of Waterford crystal advertises one of Ireland's treasures. The hotel is across the street from Union Station and only four blocks from the Capitol. Three penthouse suites have balconies that overlook Union Station; three duplex suites have spiral staircases and fireplaces. Regular rooms, which vary in size, have a Celtic theme, with Irish linen and original artwork. ✉ *520 N. Capitol St. NW, 20001,* ☎ *202/638–6900 or 800/824–5419,* FAX *202/393–3236,* WEB *www.phoenixparkhotel.com. 150 rooms, 6 suites. Pub, in-room data ports, minibars, gym, laundry service, parking (fee). AE, D, DC, MC, V. Metro: Union Station.*

Downtown

$$$$ 🏨 **Grand Hyatt Washington.** A pianist plays Cole Porter tunes on a small island surrounded by a waterfall-fed blue lagoon in the atrium of this fanciful high-rise hotel. The location can't be beat—it's across from the Washington Convention Center, two blocks from the MCI Center, and just steps from downtown shops and theaters. You can enter Metro Center—the hub of D.C.'s subway system—directly from the lobby. Rooms that face the atrium have windows that open indoors; if you don't want to be bothered by restaurant noise, ask for a room above the first few floors. Weekend brunch here is very popular. ✉ *1000 H St. NW, 20001,* ☎ *202/582–1234 or 800/233–1234,* FAX *202/637–4781,* WEB *www.washington.hyatt.com. 900 rooms, 60 suites. 4 restaurants, 2 bars, minibars, room service, in-room data ports, indoor lap pool, health club, business services, meeting room, parking (fee). AE, DC, MC, V. Metro: Metro Center.*

$$$$ 🏨 **Hay-Adams Hotel.** Two famous Americans—statesman and author
   ★   John Jay and diplomat and historian Henry Adams—once owned homes on the site where this Italian Renaissance-style landmark structure now stands, near Lafayette Park and the White House. The ghost of Henry Adams' wife is said to haunt the fourth floor. The hotel's interior—with European and Asian antiques, carved walnut wainscoting, intricate ornamental ceilings, and Doric, Ionic, and Corinthian touches—is one of eclectic grandeur. Many rooms have fireplaces and a view of the White House. An attentive staff assures warm, congenial service, including free morning car service (until 11:30 AM) to D.C. locations and airports. Limousine service is available during the day for a fee. The Lafayette restaurant, which serves elegant contemporary American cuisine, is a favorite spot for English-style high tea. ✉ *1 Lafayette Sq. NW, 20006,* ☎ *202/638–6600 or 800/853–6807,* FAX *202/638–3803,* WEB *www.hayadams.com. 125 rooms, 18 suites. Restaurant, bar, in-room data ports, room service, laundry service, parking (fee). AE, DC, MC, V. Metro: McPherson Square or Farragut North.*

$$$$ 🏨 **J. W. Marriott.** This modern flagship hotel of the Marriott chain has a prime location near the White House and next to the National Theatre. The capacious, columned lobby includes a four-story atrium, marble and mahogany accents, and Asian rugs. Rooms have dark wood furnishings and burgundy and cream interior accents. Guests have indoor access to National Place, which has 80 shops and 18 restaurants and cafés. ✉ *1331 Pennsylvania Ave. NW, 20004,* ☎ *202/393–2000 or 800/228–9290,* FAX *202/626–6991,* WEB *www.marriotthotels.com/wasjw. 772 rooms, 42 suites. 2 restaurants, 2 bars, room service, in-room data ports, in-room safes, indoor pool, hair salon, sauna, health club, laundry service, parking (fee). AE, DC, MC, V. Metro: Metro Center.*

$$$$ 🏨 **Willard Inter-Continental.** Popular with travelers who expect nothing
   ★   less than perfection, the Willard has long been a favorite of American presidents and other news-makers. Martin Luther King, Jr. drafted his famous "I Have a Dream" speech here. Superb service and a wealth of amenities are a hallmark of the hotel, which is just two blocks from the White House. The spectacular beaux arts main lobby has great columns, sparkling chandeliers, mosaic floors, and elaborate ceilings. Period detail is reflected in the rooms, which have elegant yet comfortable turn-of-the-20th-century reproduction furniture, as well as sleek mar-

ble bathrooms. Some rooms afford views of the Capitol building or the Washington Monument. The hotel's formal dining room, the Willard Room, has won nationwide acclaim. ⊠ *1401 Pennsylvania Ave., NW, 20004* ☎ *202/628–9100 or 800/327–0200,* FAX *202/637–7326,* WEB *www.washington.interconti.com. 308 rooms, 33 suites. Restaurant, 2 bars, café, in-room safes, minibars, room service, business services, in-room data ports, health club, laundry service, meeting room, parking (fee). AE, DC, MC, V. Metro: Metro Center.*

$$$–$$$$ 🖫 **Jefferson Hotel.** Federal-style elegance abounds at this small luxury
★   hotel, a Loews property. American antiques and original art fill each room, which all have VCRs and CD players (you may borrow from the hotel's video and CD libraries). A high staff-to-guest ratio ensures outstanding service—employees greet you by name, and laundry is hand-ironed and delivered in wicker baskets. The Dining Room restaurant, which serves American cuisine, is a favorite of high-ranking politicos and visiting film stars. The National Geographic Society's Explorer's Hall is next door. ⊠ *1200 16th St. NW, 20036,* ☎ *202/347–2200 or 800/368–5966,* FAX *202/331–8474,* WEB *www.thejeffersonhotel.com. 68 rooms, 32 suites. Restaurant, bar, room service, in-room VCRs, laundry service, parking (fee). AE, DC, MC, V. Metro: Farragut North.*

$$$–$$$$ 🖫 **Madison Hotel.** Old-world luxury and meticulous service prevail in the Madison (named for the fourth U.S. president), which is why the signatures of presidents, prime ministers, sultans, and kings fill the guest register. Deceivingly contemporary on the outside, the 15-story building, four blocks from the White House, has a world-class collection of European and Asian antiques. The European-style guest rooms are average size, and each of the suites is decorated individually. The Retreat restaurant serves three meals a day, as well as high tea. ⊠ *15th and M Sts. NW, 20005,* ☎ *202/862–1600 or 800/424–8577,* FAX *202/785–1255,* WEB *www.themadisonhotel.net. 301 rooms, 52 suites. 2 restaurants, bar, room service, massage, sauna, steam room, gym, business services, parking (fee). AE, DC, MC, V. Metro: McPherson Square.*

$$$–$$$$ 🖫 **Renaissance Mayflower Hotel.** A National Historic Landmark, this 10-story hotel four blocks from the White House opened in 1925 for Calvin Coolidge's inauguration. Franklin Delano Roosevelt wrote "We have nothing to fear but fear itself" in Suite 776, and J. Edgar Hoover ate here at the same table every day for 20 years. Sunlight spills through a skylight into the majestic lobby, causing the gilded trim to gleam, and Asian rugs add a splash of color. Guest rooms are filled with antiques and have marble bathrooms. Contemporary Mediterranean cuisine is served at the Café Promenade restaurant amid silver, crystal, and artful flower arrangements. ⊠ *1127 Connecticut Ave. NW, 20036,* ☎ *202/347–3000 or 800/468–3571,* FAX *202/466–9082,* WEB *www.renaissancehotels.com. 660 rooms, 80 suites. Restaurant, bar, kitchenettes, room service, sauna, gym, business services, in-room data ports, laundry service, parking (fee). AE, DC, MC, V. Metro: Farragut North.*

$$$–$$$$ 🖫 **St. Regis.** With gilded ornamental ceilings and Louis XVI furnish-
★   ings, the luxurious St. Regis looks like an updated Italian Renaissance mansion in a bustling business sector near the White House. Service is unpretentious but attentive, and the top two floors have day and night butler service. Luxuries such as cordless phones, Frette sheets, Bose radios, and bottled drinking water are found in every room. Children stay free in their parents' room, and the St. Regis Kids Program offers accredited baby-sitting, a small kids' video library, and cookies and milk on arrival. The Lespinasse restaurant, with renowned French cuisine, is cousin to the New York original. The outdoor pool is heated. ⊠ *923 16th St. NW, 20006,* ☎ *202/638–2626 or 800/325–3535,* FAX *202/638–4231. 179 rooms, 14 suites. Restaurant, lobby lounge, in-room safes,*

refrigerators, room service, pool, gym, business services, meeting room, parking (fee). AE, D, DC, MC, V. Metro: McPherson Square.

$$$ ★ 🏨 **Henley Park Hotel.** A Tudor-style building adorned with gargoyles, this National Historic Trust hotel has the cozy charm of an English country house. The highly acclaimed Coeur de Lion restaurant has a leafy atrium, stained-glass windows, and an American menu. The hotel lobby is warm and inviting, with a fireplace and grandfather clock. Rooms are decorated with Edwardian-style furnishings, and amply fitted with modern amenities. Some of the perks of staying here are shoe shines, morning delivery of the *Washington Post*, and weekday morning car service to any downtown destination. Tea is served each day at 4 PM. The hotel is a block from the Washington Convention Center, three blocks from Smithsonian museums, and five blocks from the MCI Sports Arena. ⊠ *926 Massachusetts Ave. NW, 20001*, ☎ *202/638–5200 or 800/222–8474*, FAX *202/638–6740*, WEB *www.henleypark. com. 96 rooms, 17 suites. Restaurant, bar, in-room data ports, in-room safes, minibars, room service, business services, parking (fee). AE, DC, MC, V. Metro: Metro Center or Gallery Place/Chinatown.*

$$$ ★ 🏨 **Hotel Washington.** Since opening in 1918, the Hotel Washington has been known for its view. Washingtonians bring visitors to the outdoor rooftop bar—open May to October—for cocktails and a panorama that includes the White House grounds and the Washington Monument. Now a National Landmark, the hotel sprang from the drawing boards of John Carrère and Thomas Hastings, who designed the New York Public Library. Guest rooms have 18th-century mahogany reproductions and Italian marble bathrooms. Rooms in the interior portion of the hotel are small. ⊠ *515 15th St. NW, 20004*, ☎ *202/638–5900*, FAX *202/638–1594*, WEB *www.hotelwashington.com. 344 rooms, 16 suites. 2 restaurants, bar, deli, lobby lounge, room service, hair salon, sauna, gym, laundry service, business services, parking (fee). AE, DC, MC, V. Metro: Metro Center.*

$$$ ★ 🏨 **Morrison-Clark Inn.** The elegant merger of two 1864 Victorian town houses, this inn functioned as the Soldiers, Sailors, Marines and Airmen's Club early in the 20th century. The antiques-filled public rooms have marble fireplaces, bay windows, 14-ft pier mirrors, and porch access, and one house has a 1917 Chinese Chippendale porch. Rooms have neoclassic, French country, or Victorian furnishings and offer comfy robes and VCRs. American cuisine with southern and other regional influences is served at the inn's highly regarded restaurant, which has a popular brunch. ⊠ *1015 L St. NW, 20001*, ☎ *202/898–1200 or 800/332–7898*, FAX *202/289–8576. 43 rooms, 13 suites. Restaurant, minibars, in-room data ports, room service, gym, laundry service, business services, parking (fee). AE, D, DC, MC, V. CP. Metro: Metro Center.*

$$$ 🏨 **Washington Renaissance Hotel.** Opposite the Washington Convention Center, a block from the MCI Center, and a 10-minute walk from the Smithsonian museums, the Renaissance was designed as a business hotel, with the requisite facilities and central location. Guests here have free access to the 10,000-square-ft fitness center and its lap pool. For an additional $20 per night, you become a member of the Renaissance Club, which includes complimentary breakfast, evening hors d'oeuvres in the Club lounge, coffeemakers, robes in your room, and morning newspaper delivery. The casual Florentine restaurant serves regional American cuisine. A food court is just outside the lobby. ⊠ *999 9th St. NW, 20001*, ☎ *202/898–9000 or 800/228–9898*, FAX *202/289–0947. 791 rooms, 10 suites. Restaurant, 2 bars, coffee shop, deli, in-room data ports, refrigerators, room service, indoor lap pool, sauna, health club, business services, parking (fee). AE, DC, MC, V. Metro: Chinatown.*

$$ ▥ **Marriott at Metro Center.** At its convenient downtown location, this hotel is near the White House, MCI Center, and the Smithsonian museums. The Marriott's virtues include a marble lobby, commissioned artwork, and the popular Metro Grille and Regatta Raw Bar—a handsome two-level mahogany, oak, brass, and marble facility that serves new American cuisine. Rooms are typical of others in the Marriott chain. ✉ *775 12th St. NW, 20005,* ☎ *202/737–2200,* ℻ *202/347–5886. 456 rooms, 3 suites. Bar, grill, room service, in-room data ports, indoor pool, sauna, health club, laundry service, business services, meeting room, parking (fee). AE, DC, MC, V. Metro: Metro Center.*

$ ▥ **Hostelling International-Washington D.C.** Well-kept, with bunk beds, a kitchen, small grocery, shared internet access, and a living room, this hostel was formerly the Washington International AYH-Hostel. Rooms are generally dormitory style, without private bathrooms, but families can have their own room if the hostel is not full. Towels and linens are provided at no additional fee. The maximum stay is 14 days and reservations are highly recommended. College-age travelers predominate, and July through August is the busiest period. ✉ *1009 11th St. NW, 20001,* ☎ *202/737–2333,* ℻ *202/737–1508. 270 beds. Coin laundry. MC, V. Metro: Metro Center.*

$ ▥ **Hotel Harrington.** One of Washington's oldest continuously operating hotels, the Harrington doesn't offer many frills, but it does have low prices and a prime location—right in the center of everything. It's very popular with springtime high school bus tours and with families who like the two-bedroom, two-bathroom deluxe family rooms. ✉ *436 11th St. NW, 20004,* ☎ *202/628–8140 or 800/424–8532,* ℻ *202/347–3924,* ᴡᴇʙ *www.hotelharrington.com. 236 rooms, 24 family rooms. Restaurant, pub, room service, coin laundry, meeting room, parking (fee). AE, D, DC, MC, V. Metro: Metro Center.*

Dupont Circle

$$$ ▥ **Radisson Barceló Hotel.** Guest rooms are spacious and have fluffy bedspreads and large sitting areas at the Barceló, a former apartment building near Dupont Circle and Georgetown. Spanish and Latin fare is served at the Gabriel restaurant, where the Sunday brunch spread—which includes delicacies like suckling pig, as well as traditional American favorites—is legendary. ✉ *2121 P St. NW, 20037,* ☎ *202/293–3100 or 800/333–3333,* ℻ *202/857–0134. 235 rooms, 65 suites. Restaurant, tapas bar, in-room data ports, room service, pool, gym, parking (fee). AE, D, DC, MC, V. Metro: Dupont Circle.*

$$-$$$ ▥ **Canterbury Hotel.** Both Theodore and Franklin Roosevelt lived in the Canterbury—then an apartment building—before moving into the White House. The 1901 building is on a quiet street near the embassies of Massachusetts Avenue and Dupont Circle. Rooms have 18th-century European reproduction furnishings, separate dressing areas, and queen-, double queen–, or king-size beds. The hotel serves a Continental breakfast, and offers free admission to the National Health Center, which is right around the corner. ✉ *1733 N St. NW, 20036,* ☎ *202/393–3000 or 800/424–2950,* ℻ *202/785–9581,* ᴡᴇʙ *www.canterburydc.com. 99 rooms. Restaurant, bar, in-room safes, kitchenettes, minibars, refrigerator, laundry service, business services, meeting room, parking (fee). AE, D, DC, MC, V. CP. Metro: Dupont Circle.*

$$-$$$ ▥ **Hotel Sofitel Washington.** Washington's only French boutique hotel ★ is comfortable, if somewhat worn around the edges. All rooms have a small work area, and because of the building's excellent hilltop location, many guest rooms have excellent views of Washington. The staff goes out of its way to be helpful, and children under 12 stay for free. The Trocadero Café serves three meals daily. ✉ *1914 Connecticut Ave. NW,*

20009, ☎ 202/797–2000 or 800/424–2464, FAX 202/462–0944. *107 rooms, 37 suites. Restaurant, bar, minibars, room service, gym, laundry service, parking (fee). AE, DC, MC, V. Metro: Dupont Circle.*

$$–$$$ ⌂ **Westin Fairfax.** The Gore family once owned this 1924 former apartment building, which was the childhood home of Al Gore. Now an intimate hotel, the Fairfax has an English hunt-club theme and complimentary butler service, and is close to Dupont Circle, Georgetown, and the Kennedy Center. Rooms have views of Embassy Row or Georgetown and the National Cathedral. Amenities include Garden Botanika toiletries and Starbucks coffee in the rooms. The renowned Jockey Club restaurant, with its half-timber ceilings, dark-wood paneling, and red-checker tablecloths, serves three meals daily. The Fairfax Bar is a cozy spot for a drink beside the fire, with piano entertainment some evenings. ✉ *2100 Massachusetts Ave. NW, 20008, ☎ 202/293–2100 or 800/325–3589, FAX 202/293–0641. 154 rooms, 59 suites. Restaurant, bar, in-room data ports, in-room safes, in-room VCRs, minibars, room service, massage, sauna, gym, meeting room, parking (fee). AE, DC, MC, V. Metro: Dupont Circle.*

$$ ⌂ **Washington Courtyard/Northwest by Marriott.** Excellent views of the skyline can be seen from many rooms in this hotel because of its elevation on upper Connecticut Avenue. In the compact but comfortable lobby, complimentary cookies and coffee are available each afternoon. ✉ *1900 Connecticut Ave. NW, 20009, ☎ 202/332–9300 or 800/842–4211, FAX 202/328–7039. 147 rooms. Restaurant, bar, lobby lounge, in-room data ports, pool, gym, baby-sitting, coin laundry, laundry service, meeting room, business services, parking (fee). AE, D, DC, MC, V. Metro: Dupont Circle.*

$–$$ ⌂ **Hotel Tabard Inn.** Three Victorian town houses were consolidated to form the Tabard, one of the oldest hotels in D.C. Although the wooden floorboards are creaky, the hotel exudes a quaint charm and well-worn Victorian and American Empire pieces fill the interior. Room size and facilities vary considerably—one guest room alternates as a private dining room, many rooms share bathrooms—along with prices. Passes are provided to the nearby YMCA, which has extensive fitness facilities. The contemporary restaurant, with a cozy courtyard, is popular with locals. ✉ *1739 N St. NW, 20036, ☎ 202/785–1277, FAX 202/785–6173,* WEB *www.tabardinn.com. 40 rooms, 25 with bath. CP. Restaurant, bar, lobby lounge, laundry, business services. AE, D, DC, MC, V. Metro: Dupont Circle.*

$ ⌂ **Adams Inn.** Think cozy and rustic and you've captured the essence of this European-style bed-and-breakfast in the heart of the city. Spread throughout three residential town houses, the inn is near Adams-Morgan, the zoo, and Dupont Circle. The rooms are small but comfortable and Victorian in style. Many rooms share baths, but those that do have a sink in the room. A shared kitchen and limited garage parking are available. Rooms don't have phones, but there are pay phones available in the lobby and the reception staff takes messages. ✉ *1744 Lanier Pl. NW, 20009, ☎ 202/745–3600 or 800/578–6807, FAX 202/319–7958,* WEB *www.adamsinn.com. 27 rooms (16 with private baths, 11 with shared baths). Breakfast room, coin laundry, parking (fee). AE, DC, MC, V. CP. Metro: Woodley Park/Zoo.*

$ ⌂ **Braxton Hotel.** A favorite among the youth and backpack sets, the Braxton Hotel is a good value and is just six blocks from the White House. Room sizes vary considerably—some are quite small. All rooms have cable TV, VCR, and refrigerator. ✉ *1449 Rhode Island Ave. NW, 20005, ☎ 202/232–7800 or 800/350–5759, FAX 202/265–3725,* WEB *www.braxtonhotel.com. 62 rooms. In-room data ports, parking (fee). AE, MC, V. CP. Metro: Dupont Circle or McPherson Square.*

$ ⊞ **Windsor Inn.** On tree-lined New Hampshire Avenue, dotted with small gardens and picturesque apartment buildings, this cozy bed-and-breakfast is in one of Washington's most attractive neighborhoods. Built in the 1920s but remodelled since, the Windsor is listed on the national Register of Historic Places and features some original art deco design elements in the lobby. The Phillips Collection and the restaurants and shops of Dupont Circle are all within six blocks. The White House is one Metro stop away, and Georgetown is two stops. The three-story inn is actually two buildings, and neither has an elevator. Rooms are small but pleasant, and have some amenities expected of larger hotels, like hair dryers and a morning newspaper. Afternoon sherry is served in the downstairs lobby and guests are welcome to browse in the library. All rooms have private baths. ✉ *1842 16th St. NW, 20009,* ☎ *202/667–0300 or 800/423–9111,* FAX *202/667–4503. 36 rooms, 10 suites. Lobby lounge. AE, D, DC, MC, V. CP. Metro: Dupont Circle.*

Georgetown

$$$$ ⊞ **Four Seasons Hotel.** Impeccable service and a wealth of wonderful
★ amenities have made pampering guests an art form at this perennial favorite with celebrities, hotel connoisseurs, and families. The hotel overlooks the C&O Canal and Rock Creek at the White House edge of Georgetown. Rich mahogany paneling, antiques, spectacular flower arrangements, and extensive greenery abound. Rooms are spacious and bright, with fine marble baths (some with sunken tubs) and original artwork. CD players, PCs, and exercise equipment are available for in-room use. An expansive state-of-the-art fitness center offers personal trainers, yoga and exercise classes. There are special programs for children. The Garden Terrace restaurant has live music six days a week and serves a popular Sunday brunch and daily afternoon tea. The formal Seasons restaurant offers traditional dishes with an elegant twist. ✉ *2800 Pennsylvania Ave. NW, 20007,* ☎ *202/342–0444 or 800/332–3442,* FAX *202/342–1673. 200 rooms, 60 suites. 2 restaurants, lobby lounge, in-room safes, room service, pool, hair salon, sauna, health club, concierge, business services, parking (fee). AE, DC, MC, V. Metro: Foggy Bottom.*

$$–$$$ ⊞ **Georgetown Inn.** With an atmosphere reminiscent of a gentleman's sporting club, this quiet, federal-era, redbrick hotel has an 18th-century flavor. Guest rooms are large and have Colonial-style decor. The hotel is in the heart of historic Georgetown, near shopping, dining, galleries, and theaters. Free passes to a nearby fitness center are provided. The Daily Grill restaurant serves American cuisine. ✉ *1310 Wisconsin Ave. NW, 20007,* ☎ *202/333–8900 or 800/424–2979,* FAX *202/625–1744,* WEB *www.georgetowninn.com. 86 rooms, 10 suites. Restaurant, bar, in-room data ports, room service, parking (fee). AE, DC, MC, V. Metro: Foggy Bottom.*

$$–$$$ ⊞ **Latham Hotel.** Many of the immaculate, beautifully decorated rooms at this small European-style hotel on Georgetown's fashionable main avenue have treetop views of "George's town," the Potomac River, and the C&O Canal. The hotel is a favorite of diplomats. The polished brass and glass lobby leads to Citronelle, one of the city's best French restaurants. There's a La Madeleine coffee shop on-site. ✉ *3000 M St. NW, 20007,* ☎ *202/726–5000 or 800/368–5922,* FAX *202/337–4250,* WEB *www.latham-hotel.com. 122 rooms, 21 suites. Restaurant, bar, coffee shop, in-room data ports, room service, pool, parking (fee). AE, DC, MC, V. Metro: Foggy Bottom.*

$$ ⊞ **Georgetown Suites.** If you consider standard hotel rooms cramped and overpriced, you'll find this establishment a welcome surprise. Consisting of two buildings a block apart in the heart of Georgetown, the hotel has suites of varying sizes. All have large kitchens with dishwashers and microwaves and separate sitting rooms. ⊠ *1111 30th St. NW, 20007,* ☎ *202/298–7800 or 800/348–7203,* ꜰꜰ *202/333–5792,* ᴡᴇʙ *www.georgetownsuites.com. 216 suites. Gym, coin laundry, laundry service, parking (fee). AE, DC, MC, V. CP. Metro: Foggy Bottom.*

$$ 🖭 **Holiday Inn Georgetown.** On the edge of Georgetown, the Holiday Inn is a short walk to dining, shopping, Dumbarton Oaks, the National Cathedral, and Georgetown University. Many of the guest rooms have a scenic view of the Washington skyline. There's complimentary coffee every morning in the lobby. ⊠ *2101 Wisconsin Ave. NW, 20007,* ☎ *202/338–4600,* ꜰꜰ *202/338–4458. 296 rooms, 4 suites. Restaurant, bar, no-smoking floor, room service, pool, gym, coin laundry, business services, meeting room, parking (fee). AE, DC, MC, V. Metro: Foggy Bottom.*

Southwest

$$$ 🖭 **Loews L'Enfant Plaza.** An oasis of calm above a Metro stop and a shopping mall, this hotel is two blocks from the Smithsonian museums and has spectacular views of the river, the Capitol, and monuments. Like other hotels in the Loews chain, this one is comfortably furnished and the staff is well-trained and efficient. Business travelers in particular take advantage of its proximity to several government agencies (USDA, USPS, USIA, and DOT). All rooms have coffeemakers, and both bathrooms and bedrooms have TVs and phones. Members of the Loews First club get rooms with fax machines, morning newspapers, and other extras. ⊠ *L'Enfant Plaza SW, 20024,* ☎ *202/484–1000 or 800/223–0888,* ꜰꜰ *202/646–4456. 348 rooms, 22 suites. Restaurant, 2 bars, in-room VCRs, minibars, room service, indoor pool, health club, business services, parking (fee). AE, DC, MC, V. Metro: L'Enfant Plaza.*

$$–$$$ 🖭 **Holiday Inn Capitol.** One block from the National Air and Space Museum, this large hotel is family friendly yet well equipped for business travelers. The downtown sightseeing trolley stops here, and you can buy discount tickets for NASM's IMAX movies at the front desk. With the purchase of a drink, you can enjoy an all-you-can-eat buffet from 4:30 to 6:30. ⊠ *550 C St. SW, 20024,* ☎ *202/479–4000 or 800/465–4329,* ꜰꜰ *202/488–4627. 505 rooms, 24 suites. Restaurant, bar, food court, in-room data ports, no-smoking floor, room service, pool, gym, coin laundry, meeting room, parking (fee). AE, D, DC, MC, V. Metro: L'Enfant Plaza.*

$ 🖭 **Channel Inn.** The only hotel on Washington's waterfront, this property overlooks the Washington Channel, the marina, and the Potomac River. Each room has a small balcony. All are decorated with either Laura Ashley or similar-style fabrics and have a European feel. Public areas and meeting rooms have a nautical motif with mahogany panels and marine artifacts. The terrace allows scenic cocktail quaffing, and dining in warm weather. The Mall, Smithsonian, Treasury, and several other government offices are nearby. Access to a local health club is free. ⊠ *650 Water St. SW, 20024,* ☎ *202/554–2400 or 800/368–5668,* ꜰꜰ *202/863–1164,* ᴡᴇʙ *www.channelinn.com. 100 rooms, 4 suites. Restaurant, bar, café, pool, meeting room, free parking. AE, D, DC, MC, V. Metro: Waterfront.*

Northwest/Upper Connecticut Avenue

$$$$ 🖭 **Omni Shoreham Hotel.** An immense facility with seven ballrooms, this hotel has hosted the world's rich and famous since 1930, when its art deco- and Renaissance-style lobby opened its doors for business.

It's still a busy site, with black-tie political events in its famed Regency ballroom many nights of the week. Rooms have cherry-wood furniture and marble-floor baths with phones and hair dryers. The hotel is a moderate walk from Rock Creek Park, Adams-Morgan, and the National Zoo. ⊠ *2500 Calvert St. NW, 20008,* ☎ *202/234–0700 or 800/843–6664,* FAX *202/756–5145. 812 rooms, 24 suites. Restaurant, bar, deli, in-room data ports, minibars, room service, pool, gym, dry cleaning, laundry service, parking (fee). AE, D, DC, MC, V. Metro: Woodley Park.*

$$$ ⊞ **Marriott Wardman Park.** With over a thousand rooms, this indomitable redbrick Victorian structure is the grand dame of Washington hotels. Off Connecticut Avenue, the Marriott has spectacular views of Rock Creek Park, and is a half-mile from Adams-Morgan and the National Zoo. Guest rooms and public areas of the older 10-story section are traditionally furnished. Rooms in the newer convention-ready main complex are contemporary, with chrome and glass touches and in-room data ports. ⊠ *2660 Woodley Rd. NW, 20008,* ☎ *202/328–2000 or 800/228–9290,* FAX *202/234–0015,* WEB *www.wardmanpark. com. 1,338 rooms, 125 suites. 2 restaurants, bar, coffee shop, pub, room service, 2 pools, spa, health club, baby-sitting, laundry service, business services, convention center, meeting room, parking (fee). AE, DC, MC, V. Metro: Woodley Park.*

$–$$ ⊞ **Jurys Normandy Inn.** On a quiet street in the embassy area of Con-
★ necticut Avenue lies this small, quaint European-style hotel, formerly the Doyle Normandy. Rooms are cozy, have coffeemakers, and are attractively decorated with Colonial reproduction furniture. Each Tuesday evening a wine-and-cheese reception is held for guests. You can select a book from the small library and read by the fireplace in the lobby while enjoying the complimentary coffee and tea in the morning and afternoon. ⊠ *2118 Wyoming Ave. NW, 20008,* ☎ *202/483–1350 or 800/842–3729,* FAX *202/387–8241,* WEB *www.jurysdoyle.com. 75 rooms. Cafe, in-room data ports, in-room safes, refrigerators, library, parking (fee). AE, D, MC, V. CP. Metro: Dupont Circle.*

$ ⊞ **Windsor Park Hotel.** The rooms are tiny and the hallways small, but the location of this hotel at the foot of Kalorama Circle overlooking Rock Creek Park can't be beat. Visitors who like to walk can easily get to the National Zoo, Dupont Circle, and Adams-Morgan, all within a mile of the hotel. Street parking can be difficult, but a reasonably priced garage is two blocks away. ⊠ *2116 Kalorama Rd. NW, 20008,* ☎ *202/483–7700 or 800/247–3064,* FAX *202/332–4547,* WEB *www.windsorparkhotel.com. 38 rooms, 5 suites. Refrigerator, in-room data ports, business services. AE, DC, MC, V. CP. Metro: Woodley Park.*

West End/Foggy Bottom

$$$$ ⊞ **Park Hyatt.** Original artworks, some by Picasso, Matisse, and Calder, grace the guest rooms and public spaces of this elegant and luxurious modern hotel, about four blocks from the eastern end of Georgetown, just off M Street. Rooms have built-in armoires, goose-down duvets, and specially commissioned artwork. Guests can enjoy the Rendez-Vous Day Spa. The Melrose restaurant, which specializes in seafood, features a Picasso at its entryway and has courtyard dining beside a cascading fountain. ⊠ *1201 24th St. NW, 20037,* ☎ *202/789–1234 or 800/228–9000,* FAX *202/457–8823. 93 rooms, 131 suites. Restaurant, café, lobby lounge, refrigerator, room service, pool, hair salon, hot tub, massage, sauna, spa, steam room, health club, business services, parking (fee). AE, DC, MC, V. Metro: Foggy Bottom-GWU.*

$$$$ ⊞ **Swissötel Washington Watergate.** The famed hotel was back in the
★ headlines in 2001, when First Lady Laura Bush chose its tony Aquarelle
restaurant as the site of her first official dinner party. It's a favorite of
Washingtonians and visitors alike, thanks to its river view and its sophisticated Euro-Asian cuisine. In the hotel proper, the lobby sets a genteel tone with its classic columns, Asian rugs on checkerboard marble,
subdued lighting, and soothing classical music. The hotel is on the Potomac River, across the street from the Kennedy Center and a short
walk from the State Department and Georgetown. Originally intended
as apartments, the guest rooms are large, and all have walk-in closets,
fax machines, and either full kitchens or wet bars. There's complimentary
limousine service weekdays 7 AM–10 AM. ⊠ *2650 Virginia Ave. NW,
20037,* ☎ *202/965–2300 or 800/424–2736,* FAX *202/337–7915. 104
rooms, 146 suites. Restaurant, bar, in-room safes, refrigerators, room
service, indoor pool, health club, parking (fee). AE, DC, MC, V. Metro:
Foggy Bottom.*

$$$$ ⊞ **Washington Monarch.** Contemporary and traditional meet at this
★ stylish hotel at the Georgetown end of downtown Washington. The
glassed lobby and about a third of the bright, airy rooms overlook the
central courtyard and gardens—a popular spot for weddings. The informal Bistro restaurant serves contemporary American cuisine and offers courtyard dining. The Colonnade room hosts a Sunday champagne
brunch. The deluxe fitness center is one of the best in the city. ⊠ *2401
M St. NW, 20037,* ☎ *202/429–2400 or 877/222–2266,* FAX *202/457–
5010,* WEB *www.monarchdc.com. 406 rooms, 9 suites. Restaurant, bar,
café, lobby lounge, in-room data ports, in-room safes, minibars, room
service, indoor lap pool, sauna, steam room, health club, parking (fee).
AE, DC, MC, V. Metro: Foggy Bottom.*

$$–$$$$ ⊞ **Clarion Hampshire Hotel.** In a quiet neighborhood of office build-
ings, embassies, and other fine hotels, the Hampshire Hotel is close to
Dupont Circle as well as shops and restaurants. Many rooms have ex-
cellent views of the city, Rock Creek Park, and Georgetown. All rooms
have microwave ovens. The adjoining L'Etoile Restaurant is open and
sunny, with outdoor dining in season. Free passes to the nearby YMCA
are available. ⊠ *1310 New Hampshire Ave. NW, 20036,* ☎ *202/296–
7600 or 800/368–5691,* FAX *202/293–2476. 82 rooms. Restaurant,
bar, café, in-room data ports, in-room safes, kitchenettes (some), re-
frigerators, business services, meeting room, parking (fee). AE, D,
DC, MC, V. Metro: Dupont Circle.*

$$$ ⊞ **Embassy Suites.** Plants cascade over balconies under a skylight in
this modern hotel's atrium, which is filled with classical columns, plas-
ter lions, wrought-iron lanterns, waterfalls, and tall palms. Within walking distance of Georgetown, the Kennedy Center, and Dupont Circle,
Embassy Suites is suited to business travelers and families alike. Each
spacious two-room suite has a wet bar, coffeemaker, and microwave
oven. A cooked-to-order breakfast is complimentary, and beverages are
free at the nightly manager's reception. The Italian restaurant, Panevino,
serves lunch and dinner. ⊠ *1250 22nd St. NW, 20037,* ☎ *202/857–
3388 or 800/362–2779,* FAX *202/293–3173. 318 suites. Restaurant, bar,
in-room data ports, refrigerators, room service, indoor pool, health club,
laundry service, business services, parking (fee). AE, D, DC, MC, V.
BP. Metro: Foggy Bottom or Dupont Circle.*

$$ ⊞ **Doubletree Guest Suites.** On this picturesque stretch of New Hamp-
shire Avenue dotted with row houses, you might not realize at first how
close you are to the Kennedy Center and Georgetown. The all-suite
hotel has a tiny lobby, but its suites have full kitchens, separate bed-
rooms, and living-dining areas with desks, dining tables, and sofa
beds. The rooftop pool provides a place to relax after sightseeing in
the summer. Guests receive chocolate-chip cookies upon arrival and

have privileges at a nearby health club. ⊠ *801 New Hampshire Ave. NW, 20037,* ☎ *202/785–2000 or 800/222–8733,* FAX *202/785–9485. 101 suites. In-room data ports, kitchenettes, room service, outdoor pool, coin laundry, dry cleaning, business services, parking (fee). AE, D, DC, MC, V. Metro: Foggy Bottom.*

$$ ⊞ **George Washington University Inn.** This boutique-style hotel is in a quiet neighborhood a few blocks from the Kennedy Center, the State Department, and George Washington University. Wrought-iron gates lead through a courtyard up to the hotel's front entrance, where beveled glass doors open into a small lobby floored in gray marble. Rooms vary in size and configuration and have Colonial-style furniture. Zuki Moon, a Japanese noodle house and tea garden, is off the lobby. The GWU fitness center is free for hotel guests. ⊠ *824 New Hampshire Ave. NW, 20037,* ☎ *202/337–6620 or 800/426–4455,* FAX *202/298– 7499,* WEB *www.gwuinn.com. 48 rooms, 31 suites, 16 efficiencies. Restaurant, in-room data ports, kitchenettes, microwaves, refrigerators, laundry service, meeting room, parking (fee). AE, D, DC, MC, V. Metro: Foggy Bottom.*

$$ ⊞ **One Washington Circle Hotel.** The combination of elegant rooms and facilities and a coveted location makes this hotel a relative bargain. All accommodations are suites that feel like well-furnished apartments, with separate bedrooms, living rooms, dining areas, and some full kitchens. Every suite has a balcony. The American-style West End Cafe is popular with locals who come for the food and the live music. ⊠ *1 Washington Circle NW, 20037,* ☎ *202/872–1680 or 800/424–9671,* FAX *202/ 223–3961,* WEB *www.onewashingtoncirclehotel.com. 151 suites. Restaurant, bar, kitchenettes (some), minibars, refrigerators, room service, pool, gym, piano, coin laundry, laundry service, meeting room, parking (fee). AE, D, DC, MC, V. Metro: Foggy Bottom.*

Suburban Maryland

$$$ ⊞ **Hyatt Regency Bethesda.** The sights of downtown Washington are about 15 minutes by Metro from this hotel atop the Bethesda Metro station on Wisconsin Avenue, the main artery between Bethesda and Georgetown. The atrium lobby has ferns and glass elevators. Some rooms have fax machines. An adjacent plaza has a small ice rink, open in winter, and a huge indoor food court. Many restaurants and shops are within walking distance. ⊠ *1 Bethesda Metro Center, on the 7400 block of Wisconsin Ave., Bethesda, MD 20814,* ☎ *301/657–1234 or 800/233– 1234,* FAX *301/657–6453. 371 rooms, 10 suites. Bar, café, lobby lounge, in-room data ports, indoor pool, gym, laundry service, business services, convention center, meeting room, parking (fee). AE, DC, MC, V. Metro: Bethesda.*

$–$$$ ⊞ **Marriott Residence Inn Bethesda Downtown.** In the heart of downtown Bethesda, this all-suites hotel caters primarily to business travelers who stay for several nights. However, if you're looking for an affordable home-away-from-home, this is a great option. There are fully equipped kitchens—complete with standard-size refrigerator and dishwasher, plates, and utensils—and comfortable furnishings in the one- and two-bedroom suites. You can also enjoy a variety of complimentary services such as grocery shopping, breakfast buffet, and evening cocktail and dessert receptions. A number of restaurants are within walking distance. ⊠ *7335 Wisconsin Ave., Bethesda, MD 20814,* ☎ *301/ 718–0200 or 800/331–3131,* FAX *301/913–0197. 187 suites. In-room data ports, pool, sauna, gym, coin laundry, airport shuttle, parking (fee). AE, D, DC, MC, V. CP.*

$$ ▥ **Holiday Inn Chevy Chase.** Two blocks from the Friendship Heights Metro on the D.C. border, this comfortable hotel is in the heart of the upscale Chevy Chase shopping district. Dining options are plentiful— the Avenue Deli and Julian's restaurant are in the hotel, nearby Chevy Chase Pavilion and Mazza Gallerie malls have family-style restaurants, and you'll find a wealth of gourmet choices one Metro stop away in Bethesda or a 10-minute drive down Wisconsin Avenue into Georgetown. A large outdoor swimming pool is set near the hotel's beautiful rose garden terrace, a popular spot for weddings. ✉ *5520 Wisconsin Ave., Chevy Chase, MD 20815,* ☎ *301/656–1500,* FAX *301/656–5045. 214 rooms, 10 suites. Restaurants, bar, deli, room service, pool, gym, coin laundry, business services, meeting room, parking (fee). AE, D, DC, MC, V. Metro: Friendship Heights.*

$–$$ ▥ **Bethesda Court Hotel.** Bright burgundy awnings frame the entrance to this comfortable, intimate, three-story Marriott property that has a lovely, well-tended, European-style courtyard. The hotel, two blocks from the Bethesda Metro and set back from busy Wisconsin Avenue, offers a relaxed environment. Rooms have amenities such as coffeemakers and fax machines. An evening tea with cookies and chocolates is complimentary, as are limousine service and shuttles to the National Institutes of Health. ✉ *7740 Wisconsin Avenue, Bethesda, MD 20814,* ☎ *301/656–2100 or 800/874–0050,* FAX *301/986–0375,* WEB *www.bethesdacourtwashdc.com. 75 rooms, 1 suite. In-room data ports, in-room safes, refrigerators, gym, coin laundry, free parking. AE, D, DC, MC, V. CP.*

$–$$ ▥ **Bethesda Ramada Hotel and Conference Center.** Just south of the National Institutes of Health and the Naval Medical Center, this hotel is particularly popular with government employees and business travelers. But its heavily discounted weekend rates attract vacationers who don't mind being just outside of D.C. as well. Rooms are bright and cheery, in rich navy with gold accents. The hotel has an outdoor Olympic-size swimming pool and a washer, dryer, and microwave on each floor. The popular Chatters Restaurant and Sports Bar has wide-screen TVs, a pool table, a jukebox, and seasonal outdoor dining. ✉ *8400 Wisconsin Ave., Bethesda, MD 20814,* ☎ *301/654–1000 or 800/272–6232,* FAX *301/986–1715. 160 rooms. Restaurant, in-room data ports, pool, gym, coin laundry, meeting room, parking (fee). AE, D, DC, MC, V. CP. Metro: Medical Center.*

$–$$ ▥ **Holiday Inn Bethesda.** Slightly more upscale in its appearance and services than its namesake in Chevy Chase, overnight stays at this inn promise comfort and convenience. Club members get a complimentary buffet breakfast and can stay on the concierge floor, where select services are offered. The hotel provides a free shuttle to the nearby Metro, the National Institutes of Health, and the Naval Medical Center. ✉ *8120 Wisconsin Ave., Bethesda, MD 20814,* ☎ *301/652–2000 or 877/888–3001,* FAX *301/652–4525. 269 rooms, 6 suites. Restaurant, bar, in-room data ports, pool, gym, coin laundry, meeting room, parking (fee). AE, D, DC, MC, V.*

$ ▥ **American Inn of Bethesda.** At the north end of downtown Bethesda, the American Inn is five blocks from the Metro and is within walking distance of restaurants and nightclubs. Rooms at this budget-friendly hotel are clean, well-furnished, and bright. The hotel houses Guapo's restaurant, which serves moderately priced Tex-Mex fare. The hotel provides a free shuttle to the National Institutes of Health and the Naval Hospital. ✉ *8130 Wisconsin Ave., Bethesda, MD 20814,* ☎ *301/656– 9300 or 800/323–7081,* FAX *301/656–2907,* WEB *www.american-inn. com. 75 rooms, 1 suite. Restaurant, bar, breakfast room, refrigerator, pool, coin laundry, laundry service, business services, meeting room, free parking. AE, D, DC, MC, V. CP. Metro: Bethesda.*

Suburban Virginia

$$$$ ★ **Ritz-Carlton Pentagon City.** The 18-story Ritz-Carlton at Pentagon City is more convenient to downtown Washington than many D.C. hotels. Guest rooms have mahogany furniture and lots of natural light. Public areas are decorated in a Virginia hunt country motif. Many upper rooms on the Potomac side have views of the monuments across the river. The lobby lounge serves meals and has an entrance to the Fashion Centre shopping mall, which has cinemas, a food court, 150 shops, and an underground Metro station. ⊠ *1250 S. Hayes St., Arlington, VA 22202,* ☎ *703/415–5000 or 800/241–3333,* ℻ *703/415–5060. 345 rooms, 21 suites. Restaurant, bar, in-room safes, minibars, room service, indoor lap pool, sauna, health club, laundry service, business services, convention center, meeting room, parking (fee). AE, DC, MC, V. Metro: Pentagon City.*

$$–$$$ ★ **Morrison House.** The architecture, parquet floors, crystal chandeliers, decorative fireplaces, and furnishings of Morrison House are so faithful to the style of the federal period (1790–1820) that it's often mistaken for a renovation of an historic building rather than one built in 1985. The hotel blends Early American charm with modern conveniences. Some rooms have fireplaces, and all have four-poster beds. The popular Elysium Restaurant, recently named among the best hotel eateries by Washingtonian magazine, serves American contemporary cuisine. The hotel is in the heart of Old Town Alexandria, seven blocks from the train and Metro stations. ⊠ *116 S. Alfred St., Alexandria, VA 22314,* ☎ *703/838–8000 or 800/367–0800,* ℻ *703/684–6283,* 🕸 *www.morrisonhouse.com. 42 rooms, 3 suites. 2 restaurants, bar, in-room data ports, in-room VCRs, room service, parking (fee). AE, DC, MC, V. Metro: King Street.*

$$ **Crystal City Marriott.** A business hotel in the heart of Crystal City, close to Ronald Reagan National Airport and the Pentagon, this Marriott is among a cluster of office buildings. The Smithsonian and Mall are just minutes away by Metro. The lobby, with its lush plants, marble floor, and art deco fixtures, is more luxurious than the rooms, which are tidy and have traditionally styled furniture. ⊠ *1999 Jefferson Davis Hwy., Arlington, VA 22202,* ☎ *703/413–5500 or 800/228–9290,* ℻ *703/413–0192. 345 rooms, 12 suites. Restaurant, bar, room service, indoor pool, sauna, health club, coin laundry, laundry service, business services, meeting room, airport shuttle, parking (fee). AE, D, DC, MC, V. Metro: Crystal City.*

$$ **Embassy Suites Old Town Alexandria.** Across the railroad station and tracks from Alexandria's landmark George Washington Masonic Temple sits this modern all-suite hotel. The large sunny atrium lobby has hanging foliage, waterfalls, and gazebos. If you're a train buff, request a suite overlooking the historic Alexandria train station, where passenger and freight trains pass. The passenger station and Metro are about 100 yards away across the street. There is a playroom for children. A free shuttle transports guests to the scenic Alexandria riverfront, which has shops and restaurants. A cooked-to-order breakfast is complimentary, as is the cocktail reception every evening. ⊠ *1900 Diagonal Rd., Alexandria, VA 22314,* ☎ *703/684–5900 or 800/362–2779,* ℻ *703/684–1403. 268 suites. Restaurant, in-room data ports, refrigerator, indoor pool, hot tub, sauna, gym, laundry service, business services, meeting room, parking (fee). AE, D, DC, MC, V. BP. Metro: King Street.*

$$ **Holiday Inn Arlington at Ballston.** You can get in and out of Washington quickly from this hotel, two blocks from a Metro station. Especially comfortable for business travelers, rooms have spacious work spaces, plus coffee and tea makers. Tourists can take advantage of

nearby sites, including Arlington Cemetery, the Newseum, Iwo Jima, and downtown monuments and museums. ⊠ *4610 N. Fairfax Dr., Arlington, VA 22203,* ☎ *703/243–6630,* FAX *703/527–2677. 219 rooms, 2 suites. Restaurant, bar, in-room data ports, room service, pool, coin laundry, gym, business services, free parking. AE, D, DC, MC, V. Metro: Ballston.*

$$ 🖭 **Key Bridge Marriott.** A short walk across the Key Bridge from Georgetown, this Marriott is near a Metro stop for easy access to Washington's major sights. The hotel provides a shuttle to the station three blocks away. Rooms on the Potomac side have excellent Washington views, as does the rooftop restaurant. ⊠ *1401 Lee Hwy., Arlington, VA 22209,* ☎ *703/524–6400 or 800/228–9290,* FAX *703/524–8964. 588 rooms, 22 suites. 2 restaurants, 2 bars, lobby lounge, room service, indoor pool, barbershop, hair salon, health club, coin laundry, laundry service, business services, meeting room, parking (fee). AE, D, DC, MC, V. Metro: Rosslyn.*

$$ 🖭 **Marriott Residence Inn Pentagon City.** The view across the Potomac of the D.C. skyline and the monuments is magnificent from this all-suite high-rise. Adjacent to the Pentagon, it's one block from the up-scale Pentagon City Fashion Centre mall, which has cinemas, a food court, 150 shops, and a Metro stop. All rooms are suites and have full kitchens with dishwashers, microwaves, ice makers, coffeemakers, toasters, dishes, and utensils. Complimentary services include grocery shopping, daily newspaper, breakfast, light dinner Monday to Wednesday, dessert buffet on Thursday evening, and transportation to Ronald Reagan National Airport. ⊠ *550 Army Navy Dr., Arlington, VA 22202,* ☎ *703/413–6630,* FAX *703/418–1751. 299 suites. In-room data ports, kitchenettes, microwaves, no-smoking rooms, indoor pool, hot tub, gym, coin laundry, laundry service, business services, meeting room, airport shuttle, parking (fee). AE, D, DC, MC, V. BP. Metro: Pentagon City.*

$ 🖭 **Best Western Pentagon.** In the shadow of the world's largest office building, this hotel has free shuttle service to three nearby Metro stops and the attractions around them. Three two-story buildings have outside entrances and conventional motel rooms. The tower section has a new restaurant and meeting rooms on the ground floor, and brand-new furnishings in the guest rooms, many of which have nice views. ⊠ *2480 S. Glebe Rd., Arlington, VA 22206,* ☎ *703/979–4400 or 800/ 426–6886,* FAX *703/685–0051. 326 rooms. Restaurant, bar, in-room data ports, in-room safes, refrigerators, room service, pool, gym, laundry service, airport shuttle, free parking. AE, D, DC, MC, V. Metro: Pentagon City, Crystal City, or Ronald Reagan National Airport.*

$ 🖭 **Days Inn Crystal City.** On Route 1 between the Pentagon and National Airport, this eight-floor hotel is only four Metro stops from the Smithsonian. There is free shuttle service to nearby shops and Ronald Reagan National Airport. The Crystal City Underground—with its many shops and restaurants and a Metro stop—is a very short walk away. The hotel holds Days Inn's highest quality rating for service and cleanliness. ⊠ *2000 Jefferson Davis Hwy. (Rte. 1), Arlington, VA 22202–3698,* ☎ *703/920–8600,* FAX *703/920–2840. 242 rooms, 3 suites. Restaurant, bar, in-room data ports, room service, pool, gym, laundry service, airport shuttle, car rental, free parking. AE, D, DC, MC, V. Metro: Crystal City.*

$ 🖭 **Holiday Inn Rosslyn.** Comfortable and budget-friendly, this 17-story hotel is just two blocks from the Rosslyn Metro and a leisurely ¾-mi stroll across Key Bridge to Georgetown with its restaurants and nightclubs. The Newseum, Fort Myer, and Arlington National Cemetery are all very close. Each rooms has a balcony, but the hotel's best feature may be the view of Washington's monuments from the Vantage Point restaurant's panoramic windows. ⊠ *1900 N. Fort Myer Dr., Arlington, VA 22209,* ☎ *703/807–2000 or 800/368–3408,* FAX *703/522–7480. 306 rooms, 28 suites. Restaurants, café, in-room data ports, in-room safes, indoor pool, health club, coin laundry, laundry service, business services, meeting room, free parking. AE, D, DC, MC, V. Metro: Rosslyn.*

$ 🏨 **Quality Inn Iwo Jima.** Two blocks from the Marine Corps War Memorial and half a mile from the Rosslyn Metro, this budget hotel offers easy access to Georgetown, the Pentagon, and Ronald Reagan National Airport. The older original section of the hotel has outside entrances and larger rooms with double-sink bathrooms. The newer high-rise section has business-class rooms with work tables, data ports, and 25-inch television sets. For a small deposit, your pet can stay, too. ⊠ *1501 Arlington Blvd. (Rte. 50), Arlington, VA 22209,* ☎ *703/524–5000 or 800/228–5151,* FAX *703/522–5484. 141 rooms. Restaurant, bar, room service, 2 pools (1 indoor), salon, gym, laundry service, free parking. AE, D, DC, MC, V. Metro: Rosslyn.*

$ 🏨 **Travelodge Cherry Blossom.** A modestly priced, three-story lodging, this hotel is less than 2 mi from the Pentagon and Pentagon City Fashion Centre mall. Two Metro stations are nearby and the hotel can also be reached by a city bus that stops out front. HBO is included, and microwaves are available on request. Rincome, a Thai restaurant, is on the premises, and more than 50 other restaurants are within five blocks. ⊠ *3030 Columbia Pike, Arlington, VA 22204,* ☎ *703/521–5570,* FAX *703/271–0081. 76 rooms. Restaurant, bar, kitchenettes, refrigerators, room service, gym, pool, laundry service, free parking. AE, D, DC, MC, V. CP. Metro: Pentagon.*

4 NIGHTLIFE AND THE ARTS

Washington's after-dark offerings run the gamut from comedy clubs to brew pubs, military bands to hard-core music, opera to experimental theater. The Kennedy Center, in Foggy Bottom, is the grande dame of arts happenings, while the revitalized Seventh Street arts district offers up art galleries, the venerable Shakespeare Theatre, and the MCI Center. Some of the city's liveliest and most popular nightspots are in Adams-Morgan, and the U Street corridor, once devastated by riots in the '60s.

THE ARTS

By John F. Kelly

Updated by
Karyn-Siobhan
Robinson

HISTORICALLY, THE CAPITAL'S main claim to fame has been its role as the nation's center of political power. But in the past 20 years, D.C. has gone from being a cultural desert to a thriving arts center—a place where national artists develop new works. The Kennedy Center is a world-class venue, home of the National Symphony Orchestra (NSO), now conducted by Leonard Slatkin, and host to Broadway shows, ballet, modern dance, opera, and more. Lines wrap around the block at the National Theatre for such big hit musicals as *Rent* and *Chicago*. Washington even has its own "off-Broadway": a half dozen or so plucky theaters scattered around the city offer new works and new twists on old works. Several art galleries present highly regarded chamber music series. And the service bands from the area's numerous military bases ensure an endless supply of John Philip Sousa–style martial music as well as rousing renditions of more contemporary tunes.

Several publications have calendars of entertainment events. The *Washington Post* "Weekend" section comes out on Friday, and its "Guide to the Lively Arts" is printed daily. On Thursday, look for the *Washington Times* "Weekend" section and the free weekly *Washington CityPaper*. Also consult the "City Lights" section in the monthly *Washingtonian* magazine.

One local festival of note is the **Washington Art-O-Matic,** an all-volunteer, month-long celebration of the arts that showcases the work of hundreds of local artists, including painters, sculptors, filmmakers, writers, dancers, poets, and musicians. Started in 2000 with more than 700 participants, the event switches venues and dates each year. Check the Web site or call for information about the 2002 festival (☎ 202/661–7589, WEB www.artomatic.org).

Tickets

Tickets to most events are available by calling or visiting each theater's box office, or through the following ticket agencies.

Ticketmaster takes phone charges for events at most venues around the city. You can purchase Ticketmaster tickets in person at all Hecht's department stores. No refunds or exchanges are allowed. ☎ *202/432–SEAT or 410/481–SEAT,* WEB *www.ticketmaster.com.*

TicketPlace sells half-price, day-of-performance tickets for select shows; a "menu board" lists available performances. There's a 10% service charge per order. TicketPlace is also a full-price Ticketmaster outlet. It's closed on Sunday and Monday, but tickets for performances on those days are sold on Saturday. ⊠ *Old Post Office Pavilion, 1100 Pennsylvania Ave. NW,* ☎ *202/842–5387. Metro: Federal Triangle.*

Tickets.com takes reservations for events at Arena Stage, Center Stage, Ford's Theatre, the Holocaust Museum, the 9:30 Club, and Signature Theater. It also has outlets in selected Olsson's Books & Records. ⊠ ☎ *703/218–6500,* WEB *www.tickets.com.*

Concert Halls

Concert halls tend to focus on music, but many present performances of all types. It's not uncommon for a venue to present modern dance one week, a rock or classical music concert another week, and a theatrical performance the next.

Cramton Auditorium. This 1,500-seat auditorium on the Howard University campus regularly presents jazz, gospel, and R&B concerts. It is also the site of many special events. ⊠ *2455 6th St. NW,* ☎ *202/806-7194.*

DAR Constitution Hall. The 3,700-seat Constitution Hall hosts visiting musicians who perform everything from jazz to pop to rap. ⊠ *18th and C Sts. NW,* ☎ *202/628-4780.*

George Mason University. The GMU campus in suburban Virginia is home to the glittering, ambitious Center for the Arts complex. Music, ballet, and drama performances regularly take place in the 1,900-seat concert hall, the 500-seat proscenium Harris Theater, and the intimate 150-seat Black Box Theater. Also on campus is the 9,500-seat Patriot Center, site of pop acts and sporting events. ⊠ *Rte. 123 and Braddock Rd., Fairfax, VA,* ☎ *703/993-8888, 703/993-3000, or 202/432-7328.*

John F. Kennedy Center for the Performing Arts. Any search for cultured entertainment should start here, whether you want to see an international symphony orchestra, a troupe of dancers, a Broadway musical, engaging children's theater, or a comedic whodunit. The "KenCen" is actually five stages under one roof: the Concert Hall, home of the National Symphony Orchestra (NSO); the 2,200-seat Opera House, the setting for ballet, modern dance, opera, and large-scale musicals; the Eisenhower Theater, usually used for drama; the Terrace Theater, a Philip Johnson–designed space that showcases chamber groups and experimental works; and the Theater Lab, home to cabaret-style performances (since 1987 the audience-participation hit mystery *Shear Madness* has been playing there). You can also catch a free performance every evening at 6 PM on the Millennium Stage in the center's Grand Foyer. ⊠ *New Hampshire Ave. and Rock Creek Pkwy. NW,* ☎ *202/467-4600 or 800/444-1324.*

Lisner Auditorium. A 1,500-seat theater on the campus of George Washington University, Lisner Auditorium is the setting for pop, classical, and choral music shows as well as modern dance performances and musical theater. ⊠ *21st and H Sts. NW,* ☎ *202/994-6800.*

MCI Arena. In addition to being the home of the Washington Capitals hockey and Washington Wizards basketball teams, this new, 19,000-seat arena also hosts concerts, ice-skating events, and the circus. Parking can be a problem, but the arena is conveniently situated near several Metro lines. ⊠ *601 F St. NW,* ☎ *202/628-3200.*

Merriweather Post Pavilion. In Columbia, Maryland, an hour's drive north of Washington, Merriweather Post is an outdoor pavilion with some covered seating. In warmer months it hosts big-name pop acts. ⊠ *Broken Land Pkwy., Exit 18B off Rte. 21 N, Columbia, MD,* ☎ *301/982-1800 concert information; 301/596-0660 off-season.*

National Gallery of Art. Free concerts by the National Gallery Orchestra, conducted by George Manos, and performances by visiting recitalists and ensembles are held in the venerable West Building's West Garden Court on Sunday evening from October to June. Most performances highlight classical music, though April's American Music Festival often features jazz. Entry is first-come, first-serve, with doors opening at 6 PM and concerts starting at 7. ⊠ *6th St. and Constitution Ave. NW,* ☎ *202/842-6941 or 202/842-6698.*

Nissan Pavilion at Stone Ridge. Cellar Door Productions, the country's largest concert promoter, built this 25,000-seat venue in rural Virginia, about an hour from downtown Washington, to host all types of music. ⊠ *7800 Cellar Door Dr., Bristow, VA,* ☎ *703/754-6400 or 202/432-7328.*

Smithsonian Institution. The Smithsonian presents a rich assortment of music—both free and ticketed. Jazz, musical theater, and popular standards are performed in the National Museum of American History. In the museum's third-floor Hall of Musical Instruments, musicians periodically play instruments from the museum's collection. The Smithsonian Associates sponsors programs that offer everything from a cappella groups to Cajun zydeco bands; all events require tickets and locations vary. The annual Smithsonian's Folk Life festival, held on the Mall, is one of the city's most anticipated events. The dates for 2002 are June 26–June 30 and July 3–July 7. ✉ *1000 Jefferson Dr. SW, Smithsonian Castle:* ☎ *202/357–2700; Smithsonian Associates:* ☎ *202/357–3030,* WEB *www.si.edu.*

USAirways Arena. The area's top venue for big-name pop, rock, and rap acts seats 20,000. ✉ *1 Harry S. Truman Dr., Landover, MD,* ☎ *301/350–3400 or 202/432–7328.*

Wolf Trap Farm Park. Just off the Dulles Toll Road, about a half hour from downtown, Wolf Trap is the only national park dedicated to the performing arts. On its grounds is the Filene Center, an outdoor theater that is the scene of pop, jazz, opera, ballet, and dance performances each June through September. On performance nights, Metrorail operates a $3.50 round-trip shuttle bus between the West Falls Church Metro station and the Filene Center. The fare is exact change only, and the bus leaves 20 minutes after the show, or no later than 11 PM, whether the show is over or not. The rest of the year, the intimate, indoor Barns at Wolf Trap hosts folk, jazz, rock, chamber, opera, and other music. For tickets, call Tickets.com. ✉ *1551 Trap Rd., Vienna, VA,* ☎ *703/255–1900; 703/938–2404 Barns at Wolf Trap.*

Dance

Dance Place. A studio theater that presented its first performance in 1980, Dance Place hosts a wide assortment of modern and ethnic dance shows most weekends. It also conducts dance classes daily. ✉ *3225 8th St. NE,* ☎ *202/269–1600.*

Joy of Motion. A dance studio by day, Joy of Motion is the home of several area troupes that perform in the studio's Jack Guidone Theatre by night, including City Dance Ensemble (modern), the Spanish Dance Ensemble (flamenco), and JazzDanz.dc (you guessed it, jazz). Two additional studios in Dupont Circle (✉ *1643 Connecticut Ave. NW,* ☎ *202/387–0911*) and Bethesda (✉ *7702 Woodmont Ave., Bethesda, MD,* ☎ *301/986–0016*) offer classes only. ✉ *5207 Wisconsin Ave. NW,* ☎ *202/362–3042,* WEB *www.joyofmotion.org.*

Washington Ballet. Between September and May this company presents classical and contemporary ballets—including works by such choreographers as George Balanchine, Choo-San Goh, and artistic director Septime Webre—at the Kennedy Center and the Warner Theatre. Each December the Washington Ballet performs *The Nutcracker.* ☎ *202/362–3606.*

Film

AMC Union Station 9. On Capitol Hill, AMC Union Station 9 has nine screens showing mainstream, first-run movies; validated, three-hour parking is available at an adjacent lot. ✉ *Union Station,* ☎ *202/842–3757.*

American Film Institute. More than 700 movies—including contemporary and classic foreign and American films—are shown each year at the American Film Institute's theater in the Kennedy Center. Filmmakers and actors are often present to discuss their work. ✉ *Kennedy Center, New Hampshire Ave. and Rock Creek Pkwy. NW,* ☎ *202/785–4600.*

Arlington Cinema 'N' Drafthouse. A suburban Virginia alternative to movie theaters in the capital, Arlington Cinema 'N' Drafthouse has table seating and serves various libations along with pizza, buffalo wings, nachos, and other snacks during its films. You must be 21 or over or have a parent with you to attend. ⊠ *2903 Columbia Pike, Arlington, VA,* ☎ *703/486–2345.*

Filmfest DC. An annual citywide festival of international cinema, the DC International Film Festival, or Filmfest, as it is affectionately known, takes place in late April and early May. Films are shown at various venues throughout the city. You can purchase tickets in advance over the phone; otherwise, ticket sales and seating are on a first-come, first-serve basis—and some films *do* sell out. ⊠ *Box 21396, 20009,* ☎ *202/724–5613.*

General Cinema at Mazza Gallerie. Right near the D.C.-Maryland border is the only movie theater in the area with stadium seating and all-digital sound. The seats are cushy and some armrests even retract to create love seats. In the smaller Club Cinema, moviegoers enjoy leather seats, a full-service bar, and sandwiches and snacks. But be forewarned, pampering like this doesn't come cheap: tickets are $9.75 for the main theater, $12.50 for the Club Cinema. ⊠ *5300 Wisconsin Ave. NW, 3rd floor,* ☎ *202/537–9551.*

Hirshhorn Museum. If you love avant-garde and experimental film, check out the weekly movies—often first-run documentaries, features, and short films—shown here for free. Children's movies are screened most Saturday mornings at 11. ⊠ *7th and Independence Ave. SW,* ☎ *202/357–2700.*

Loews Cineplex Uptown. You don't find many like this old beauty anymore: one huge, multiplex-dwarfing screen; art deco flourishes instead of a bland, boxy interior; a wonderful balcony; and—in one happy concession to modernity—crystalline Dolby sound. ⊠ *3426 Connecticut Ave. NW,* ☎ *202/966–5400.*

National Archives. Historical films are shown here daily. Check the calendar of events for listings. ⊠ *Constitution Ave. between 7th and 9th Sts. NW,* ☎ *202/501–5000.*

National Gallery of Art, East Building. Free classic and international films (they often complement exhibits) are shown in this museum's large auditorium. You can pick up a film calendar at the museum. ⊠ *Constitution Ave. between 3rd and 4th Sts. NW,* ☎ *202/737–4215.*

National Geographic Society. Free educational films with a scientific, geographic, or anthropological focus are shown here weekly. ⊠ *17th and M Sts. NW,* ☎ *202/857–7588.*

Visions Cinema Bistro Lounge. Independent, foreign, and art films dominate the only independently owned theater in the city. In the Bistro, look for yummy Mediterranean, Middle Eastern, and Indian tapas-style foods alongside more standard movie time fare. Sit at a table or take your snacks into the red-wall lounge, where you can nosh while gazing at the silent films running near a full bar. ⊠ *1927 Florida Ave. NW at 20th St.,* ☎ *202/667–0090.*

Art Galleries

Washington has three main gallery districts, though small art galleries can be found all over the city in converted houses and storefronts. Many galleries close on Sunday and Monday or keep unusual hours, so it's best to call ahead. For a comprehensive review of current and future exhibits, pick up a copy of *Galleries* magazine, available in some galleries or by subscription (☎ 301/270–0180).

Downtown

The downtown art scene is concentrated on 7th Street between D and I streets. Redevelopment has meant that many artists have had to move their working studios from here to more affordable digs. Fortunately, the galleries, which bring foot traffic to area businesses, have managed to maintain a foothold. On the third Thursday of each month, the galleries extend their hours and offer light refreshments from 6 PM to 8 PM.

The building at 406 7th Street houses several galleries: The **David Adamson Gallery** (⊠ 406 7th St. NW, ☎ 202/628–0257) shows prints, paintings, and ceramics. **Numark Gallery** (⊠ 406 7th St. NW, ☎ 202/628–3810) specializes in prints and works on paper. There's a varied collection at the **Artists' Museum** (⊠ 406 7th St. NW, ☎ 202/638–7001). And the **Touchstone Gallery** (⊠ 406 7th St. NW, ☎ 202/347–2787) showcases minimalist paintings and photography. A stone's throw away is the eclectic **Zenith Gallery** (⊠ 413 7th St. NW, ☎ 202/783–2963), where you can find indoor, outdoor, and monumental sculpture made from bronze, steel, wood, and ceramics, as well as a wide selection of three-dimensional mixed media works. Around the corner, the **Wilson Arts Center** (⊠ 501–505 E St. NW, ☎ 202/628–1663) features local painters and sculptors. **projectspace** (⊠ 625 E St. NW, ☎ 202/639–1714) often ties in installations, films, and performances with exhibits.

Dupont Circle

The area has close to 30 galleries. On "First Fridays," the joint open house held on the first Friday of each month, the streets are filled with wine-and-cheese–loving gallery hoppers. Check out www.artgalleriesdc.com for information on all events.

America, Oh Yes! Home to one of the most extensive folk art collections in the country, this gallery is known for its reasonable prices. Art by more than 165 self-taught artists from all over America is shown in a constantly changing inventory. ⊠ *1700 Connecticut Ave., Suite 300 NW,* ☎ *202/483–9644.*

Anton Gallery. Look for Asian-influenced art in this collection of contemporary painting, sculpture, photography, mixed-media installations, and works on paper by national and international artists. Paintings by Tom Nakashima are regularly featured. ⊠ *2108 R St. NW,* ☎ *202/328–0828.*

Burdick Gallery. John Burdick's cozy gallery focuses on Inuit Art and sculpture and works on paper by Canadian Eskimos. ⊠ *1609 Connecticut Ave. NW,* ☎ *202/986–5682.*

Burton Marinkovich Fine Art. You'll know you've reached this gallery when you spot the small front yard ornamented with two distinctive sculptures by Emily Mason and Leonard Cave. The gallery has works on paper by modern and contemporary masters, including Bleckner, Diebenkorn, Hockney, Kandinsky, Matisse, Miró, Motherwell, Picasso, and others. Rare modern illustrated books and British linocuts from the Grosvenor School are also specialties. ⊠ *1506 21st St. NW,* ☎ *202/296–6563.*

Gallery K. H. Marc Moyens and Komei Wachi have devoted a lifetime to amassing a sizeable collection of contemporary art. Their spacious gallery holds a large inventory, including such internationally known artists as Andy Warhol, Robert Motherwell, and Jackson Pollock. ⊠ *2010 R St. NW,* ☎ *202/234–0339.*

Tartt Gallery. The emphasis here is on 19th- and early 20th-century vintage photography and American contemporary folk art. ⊠ *2114 R St. NW,* ☎ *202/332–5652.*

Georgetown

Many of Georgetown's galleries are on side streets away from the main commercial strip. The work tends to focus more on established artists favored by serious collectors.

Addison Ripley. This well-respected gallery exhibits contemporary work by local artists, including painter Manon Cleary and sculptor John Drayfuss. ⊠ *1670 Wisconsin Ave. NW,* ☎ *202/338–5180.*

Creighton-Davis. Collectors with deep pockets can pick up a Matisse at this art powerhouse, which has also been known to carry Whistler. ⊠ *Georgetown Park Mall, 3222 M St. NW,* ☎ *202/333–3050.*

Galleries 1054 (⊠ 1054 31st St. NW) brings six distinct galleries together under one roof. With its focus on avant-garde art, **eklektikos** (☎ 202/342–1809) is one of the more daring, and exciting, galleries in the city, while **Fraser** (☎ 202/298–6450) prides itself on presenting accessible art. **Gallery Okuda International** (☎ 202/625–1054) showcases Japanese art. **Alla Rogers** (☎ 202/333–8595) features Eastern European art. **Georgetown Art Guild** (☎ 202/625–1470) shows international artists. And **Veerhoff Galleries** (☎ 202/338–6456) presents a mix of Washington-based and other American artists.

Georgetown Gallery of Art. This cozy gallery off the beaten path features paintings by Pablo Picasso, Honore Daumier, and Marc Chagall, but emphasizes the work of British sculptor Henry Moore. ⊠ *3235 P St. NW,* ☎ *202/333–6308.*

Hemphill Fine Arts. Nestled alongside the C & O Canal, this gem of a gallery shows established artists such as Jacob Kainen and William Christenberry. ⊠ *1027 33rd St. NW,* ☎ *202/342–5610.*

Spectrum. Thirty artists, most of them female, form this cooperative gallery, which specializes in abstract and representational art. ⊠ *1132 29th St. NW,* ☎ *202/333–0954.*

Worth a Special Trip

Torpedo Factory Art Center. Created through the joint effort of a group of local artists and the City of Alexandria in 1974, this center has 84 working studios, eight group studios, and six galleries. ⊠ *105 North Union St., Old Town, Alexandria, VA,* ☎ *703/838–4565.*

Music

Chamber Music

Corcoran Gallery of Art. Hungary's Takacs String Quartet and the Cleveland Quartet are among the chamber groups that appear in the Corcoran's Musical Evening Series, one Friday each month from October to May (there are also some summer offerings). Concerts are followed by a reception with the artists. ⊠ *17th St. and New York Ave. NW,* ☎ *202/639–1700.*

Folger Shakespeare Library. The library's internationally acclaimed resident chamber music ensemble, the Folger Consort, regularly presents a selection of instrumental and vocal pieces from the medieval, Renaissance, and Baroque periods. The season runs from October to May. ⊠ *201 E. Capitol St. SE,* ☎ *202/544–7077.*

National Academy of Sciences. Free performances are given fall through spring in the academy's 670-seat auditorium, which has almost perfect acoustics. Both the National Musical Arts Chamber Ensemble and the United States Marines Chamber Orchestra perform regularly. ⊠ *2100 C St. NW,* ☎ *202/334–2436.*

Phillips Collection. Duncan Phillips's mansion is more than an art museum. From September through May the long, paneled music room hosts Sunday-afternoon recitals. Chamber groups from around the world perform. Concerts begin at 5 PM; arrive early for decent seats. ⊠ *1600 21st St. NW,* ☎ *202/387–2151.*

Choral Music

Basilica of the National Shrine of the Immaculate Conception. Choral and church groups frequently perform in this impressive venue. ⊠ *Michigan Ave. and 4th St. NE*, ☏ *202/526–8300*.

Choral Arts Society of Washington. The 180-voice Choral Arts Society choir performs a varied selection of classical pieces at the Kennedy Center from September to June. Three Christmas sing-a-longs are scheduled each December. ☏ *202/244–3669*.

Washington National Cathedral. Choral and church groups frequently perform in this grand cathedral. Admission is usually free. ⊠ *Wisconsin and Massachusetts Aves. NW*, ☏ *202/537–6200*.

Opera and Classical

In Series. Trademark cabaret, experimental chamber opera, performance-art productions, and Spanish musical theater (also known as *zarzuela*) are among the hallmarks of this burgeoning nonprofit company, which performs at various venues around the city. ☏ *202/237–9834*.

Opera Theater of Northern Virginia. During each of its three seasons (October, January–February, and May) this company stages an opera, sung in English, at an Arlington, VA community theater. Each December the company also presents a one-act opera especially for young audiences. ☏ *703/528–1433*.

Summer Opera Theater Company. An independent professional troupe, the Summer Opera Theater Company stages one opera in June and one in July. ⊠ *Hartke Theater, Catholic University, 620 Michigan Ave. NE*, ☏ *202/526–1669*.

Washington Opera. Eight operas—presented in their original languages with English supertitles—are performed each season (October–March) in the Kennedy Center's Opera House and Eisenhower Theater. Performances are often sold out to subscribers, but you can purchase returned tickets an hour before curtain time. Standing-room tickets go on sale at the Kennedy Center box office each Saturday at 10 AM for the following week's performances. ☏ *202/295–2400 or 800/876–7372*.

Orchestra

National Symphony Orchestra. The season at the Kennedy Center is from September to June. In summer the NSO performs at Wolf Trap and gives free concerts at the Carter Barron Amphitheatre and, on Memorial Day and Labor Day weekends and July 4, on the West Lawn of the Capitol. The cheapest way to hear the NSO perform in the Kennedy Center Concert Hall is to get $13 second-tier side seats. ☏ *202/416–8100*.

Performance Series

Armed Forces Concert Series. From June to August, service bands from all four military branches perform Monday, Tuesday, Thursday, and Friday evenings on the East Terrace of the Capitol and several nights a week at the Sylvan Theater on the Washington Monument grounds. The traditional band concerts include marches, patriotic numbers, and some classical music. The air-force celebrity series features popular artists such as Earl Klugh and Keiko Matsui. The bands often perform free concerts at other locations throughout the year. ☏ *202/767–5658 Air Force; 703/696–3718 Army; 202/433–2525 Navy; 202/433–4011 Marines*.

Carter Barron Amphitheatre. On Saturday and Sunday nights from mid-June to August this lovely, 4,250-seat outdoor theater in Rock Creek Park hosts pop, jazz, gospel, and rhythm-and-blues artists such as Chick Corea and Nancy Wilson. The National Symphony Orchestra also performs, and for two weeks in June the Shakespeare Theatre presents a free play by the Bard. ⊠ *16th St. and Colorado Ave. NW,* ☎ *202/426–6837.*

District Curators. This independent, nonprofit organization presents adventurous contemporary performers from around the world in spaces around the city, mostly in summer (June–August). Much of the group's season is encompassed by its Jazz Arts Festival. Past artists have included Laurie Anderson, Philip Glass, the World Saxophone Quartet, and Cassandra Wilson. ☎ *202/723–7500.*

Ft. Dupont Summer Theater. When it comes to music in Washington, even the National Park Service gets in on the act. The NPS presents national and international jazz artists at 8:30 on Friday and Saturday evenings from July to August at the outdoor Ft. Dupont Summer Theater. Wynton Marsalis, Shirley Horne, and Ramsey Lewis are among the artists who have performed free concerts. ⊠ *Minnesota Ave. and Randall Circle SE,* ☎ *202/426–7723.*

Sylvan Theater. Military bands from all four branches usually perform alfresco at the Sylvan Theater from June to August, Tuesday, Thursday, Friday, and Sunday nights at 8 PM. Schedules are subject to change. ⊠ *Washington Monument grounds,* ☎ *202/426–6841.*

Transparent Productions. Composed of a small group of dedicated jazz connoisseurs, this nonprofit presenting organization regularly brings acclaimed avant-garde jazz musicians to intimate clubs and university stages. Past performers have included the Ethnic Heritage Ensemble, bassist William Parker, and saxophonist Anthony Braxton. Tickets are usually in the $10 range, with 100% of the revenues going directly to the artists. ☎ *202/232–5061.*

Washington Performing Arts Society. This independent nonprofit organization books high-quality classical music, jazz, modern dance, and gospel and performance art into halls around the city. Past artists include Alvin Ailey American Dance Theater, Wynton Marsalis, Yo-Yo Ma, the Chieftains, the vocal group Sweet Honey in the Rock, and Cecilia Bartoli. ☎ *202/833–9800.*

Theater and Performance Art

Commercial Theaters

Arena Stage. The city's most-respected resident company (established in 1950), this was also the first outside New York to win a Tony award. It presents a wide-ranging season in its three theaters: the Fichandler Stage, the proscenium Kreeger, and the cabaret-style Old Vat Room. ⊠ *6th St. and Maine Ave. SW,* ☎ *202/488–3300.*

Ford's Theatre. Looking much as it did when President Lincoln was shot at a performance of *Our American Cousin,* Ford's hosts both dramas and musicals, many with family appeal. Dickens's *A Christmas Carol* is presented each holiday season. ⊠ *511 10th St. NW,* ☎ *202/ 347–4833.*

Lincoln Theatre. From the 1920s to the 1940s, the Lincoln hosted the same performers as the Cotton Club and the Apollo Theatre in New York City: Cab Calloway, Lena Horne, Duke Ellington. Today the 1,250-seater shows films and welcomes such acts as the Count Basie Orchestra and the Harlem Boys and Girls Choir. ⊠ *1215 U St. NW,* ☎ *202/328–6000.*

National Theatre. Destroyed by fire and rebuilt four times, the National Theatre has operated in the same location since 1835. It presents touring Broadway shows. From September through April, look for free children's shows on Saturday, and free Monday night shows that run the gamut from Asian dance to performance art to a cappella cabarets. ⊠ *1321 Pennsylvania Ave. NW,* ☎ *202/628–6161.*

Shakespeare Theatre. Five plays—three by the Bard and two classics from his era—are staged each year by the acclaimed Shakespeare The-

atre troupe in a state-of-the-art, 450-seat space. For two weeks each
June the company offers a free play under the stars at Carter Barron
Amphitheatre. ⊠ *450 7th St. NW,* ☎ *202/547–1122.*

Warner Theatre. One of Washington's grand theaters, this 1924 building hosts road shows, dance recitals, pop music, and the occasional
comedy act. ⊠ *13th and E Sts. NW,* ☎ *202/783–4000.*

Small Theaters and Companies

Often performing in churches and other less-than-ideal settings, Washington's small theaters and companies offer some beautifully staged
and acted plays and musicals that can be every bit as enthralling as—
and often more daring than—their blockbuster counterparts. In the past
few years there has been a veritable explosion of new companies,
many of which tackle difficult, controversial, and specialized subjects.
All compete fiercely for the Helen Hayes Award, Washington's version
of the Tony. Several acclaimed alternative stages are on 14th Street NW
and near Dupont Circle; take a cab after dark.

District of Columbia Arts Center. Known by area artists as DCAC, this
cross-genre space shows changing exhibits in its gallery and presents
avant-garde performance art and experimental plays in its small black-
box theater. ⊠ *2438 18th St. NW,* ☎ *202/462–7833.*

Folger Shakespeare Library. Look for three to four productions a year
of Shakespeare or Shakespeare-influenced works, all staged in the library's little jewel box of a theater. With room for 250, the theater is
a replica of the in-yard theaters popular in Shakespeare's time. ⊠ *201
E. Capitol St. SE,* ☎ *202/544–7077.*

Gala Hispanic Theatre. This company produces Spanish classics as
well as contemporary and modern Latin American plays in both Spanish and English. ⊠ *1021 7th St. NW,* ☎ *202/234–7174.*

Glen Echo Park. The National Park Service has transformed this former amusement park into a thriving arts center. The Adventure Theater produces traditional plays and musicals every weekend. Plays are
aimed at children ages four to 12, and families can spread out on car-
peted steps. At the Puppet Co. Playhouse, skilled puppeteers manipu-
late a variety of puppets in classic plays and stories Wednesday–Sunday.
⊠ *7300 MacArthur Blvd. NW, Glen Echo, MD,* ☎ *301/492–6282,
301/320–5331 Adventure Theater; 301/320–6668 Puppet Co.*

Imagination Stage (BAPA). In White Flint Mall, Imagination Stage presents shows like *The Secret Garden* and *Cinderella* for children ages
four to 12. Reservations are strongly recommended. ⊠ *11301 Rockville
Pike, Kensington, MD,* ☎ *301/881–5106.*

Olney Theatre. Musicals, comedies, and summer stock are presented in
a converted barn, one hour from downtown in the Maryland countryside. ⊠ *2001 Olney–Sandy Spring Rd., Olney, MD,* ☎ *301/924–3400.*

Signature Theatre. This plucky group performs in a 136-seat black-
box theater in a converted bumper-plating facility in suburban Virginia.
Sondheim is a favorite with Signature, and Signature is said to be a favorite of Sondheim's, too. ⊠ *3806 S. Four Mile Run Dr., Arlington,
VA,* ☎ *703/820–9771.*

Source Theatre. The 125-seat Source Theatre presents established plays
with a sharp satirical edge and modern interpretations of classics.
Every July and August, Source hosts the Washington Theater Festival,
a series of new plays, many by local playwrights. ⊠ *1835 14th St. NW,*
☎ *202/462–1073.*

Studio Theatre. This small, independent company has an eclectic season of classic and offbeat plays. With two 200-seat theaters, the Mead
and the Milton, as well as the 50-seat Secondstage (home to particularly experimental works), it is one of the busiest groups in the city. ⊠
1333 P St. NW, ☎ *202/332–3300.*

Washington Stage Guild. After its home of several decades—historic Carroll Hall—was demolished, the Washington Stage Guild moved in with the Source Theater. The Guild performs classics as well as more contemporary works, and Shaw is a specialty. ✉ *1835 14th St. NW,* ☎ *240/582–0050.*

Woolly Mammoth. Unusual, imaginatively produced shows have earned Woolly Mammoth good reviews and favorable comparisons to Chicago's Steppenwolf. Bounced from its beloved location at Logan Circle, at presstime the company was temporarily sharing space at the Kennedy Center's American Film Institute (AFI) Theater and other locations. ☎ *202/393–3939,* WEB *www.woollymammoth.net.*

NIGHTLIFE

Washington's nightlife includes watering holes, comedy clubs, discos, and intimate musical venues that cater to a variety of customers—from proper political appointees to blue-collar regulars in from the 'burbs. Many places are clustered in key areas, making a night of bar-hopping relatively easy. Georgetown has dozens of bars, nightclubs, and restaurants on M Street east and west of Wisconsin Avenue and on Wisconsin Avenue north of M Street. Along the 18th Street strip in Adams-Morgan, bordered by Columbia Road and Florida Avenue, you'll find several small live-music clubs, ethnic restaurants, and bars. West of Florida Avenue, the U Street corridor—which several publications have called one of the hippest neighborhoods in the country—appeals to young people looking for musical entertainment from hip-hop to alternative rock to reggae. On a stretch of Pennsylvania Avenue between 2nd and 4th streets, you'll find a half dozen Capitol Hill bars. And for a happenin' happy hour, head to the intersection of 19th and M streets NW, which is near the lawyer- and lobbyist-filled downtown.

D.C. may be a two-party town, but Washington audiences tend not to draw party lines when it comes to music. This means that you can hear funk at a rock club, blues at a jazz club, and calypso at a reggae club. Washington was the birthplace of hard-core, a socially aware form of punk rock music that has influenced young bands throughout the country. Go-go—an infectious, rhythmic music that mixes elements of rap, rhythm and blues, and funk—is another homegrown art form. Live punk and go-go shows can get rowdy, and the best place for curious out-of-towners to experience these sounds is at an outdoor summer music event.

The city's formerly sleepy suburbs have emerged in the past few years to gain a nightlife of their own. Downtown Bethesda has a vibrant restaurant and club scene. In Northern Virginia, where a plethora of exciting bars and clubs render once-necessary trips to the city moot, the beautiful people have a strong and resilient presence. Much of the suburban growth can be traced to Washington's Metro system, which now runs until 2 AM on weekend nights. Club-hoppers find plenty to do in the areas surrounding the Clarendon and Ballston Metro stations in Virginia and the Bethesda stop in Maryland.

To check out the local scene, consult Friday's "Weekend" section in the *Washington Post* and the free weekly *Washington CityPaper.* The free *Metro Weekly* and *Women in the Life* magazines offer insights on gay and lesbian nightlife. It's also a good idea to call clubs ahead of time to find out what's on. Reservations are advised for comedy clubs; places where reservations are essential are noted below.

Most bars in D.C. have cover charges for live bands and DJs, generally on the weekends. Expect to pay anywhere from $5 to $15 for most dance clubs. Jazz and comedy clubs often have higher cover charges along with drink minimums. Last call in D.C. is 2 AM, and most bars and clubs close by 3 AM on the weekends and between midnight and 2 AM during the week. The exceptions are after-hours dance clubs and bars with kitchens that stay open late.

Acoustic, Folk, and Country Clubs

Washington has a very active folk scene. For information on different folk events—from *contra* (a form of folk) dancing to storytelling to open singing—call the recorded information line of the **Folklore Society of Greater Washington** (☎ 202/546–2228).

Birchmere. This is one of the best places this side of the Blue Ridge Mountains to hear acoustic folk and bluegrass. Audiences come to listen, and the management politely insists on no distracting chatter. ⊠ *3701 Mt. Vernon Ave., Alexandria, VA,* ☎ *703/549–7500.*

Soho Tea and Coffee. Quality singer-songwriters share the stage with poets and writers at Soho's open mike the second and fourth Wednesdays of every month, in addition to featured performances throughout the month. Other pluses: the café serves as a gallery space with changing monthly exhibits, stays open very late, and serves breakfast all day along with its regular menu of light fare. ⊠ *2150 P St. NW,* ☎ *202/463–7646.*

Bars and Lounges

Brickskeller. This is *the* place to go when you want something more exotic than a Bud Lite. More than 900 brands of beer are for sale—from Central American lagers to U.S. microbrewed ales. Servers actually have to go to "beer school" to land a job here. ⊠ *1523 22nd St. NW,* ☎ *202/293–1885.*

Capital City Brewing Company. In the New York Avenue location of this microbrewery, a gleaming copper bar dominates the airy room; metal steps lead up to where the brews—from bitters to bocks—are made. Consult the brew master's chalkboard to see what's on tap. The fabulous Postal Square location on Massachusetts Avenue has five 30-keg copper serving vessels in the center of the restaurant and a gorgeous vault door left over from the days when the building was a post office. ⊠ *1100 New York Ave. NW,* ☎ *202/628–2222;* ⊠ *2 Massachusetts Ave. NE,* ☎ *202/842–2337.*

Carpool. Andy Warhol meets General Motors is how *Billiards Digest* described this former-garage-turned-bar. Enjoy a brew and shoot a game of pool in the relaxed atmosphere, where casual clothes rule. Food is available from Rocklands, home to some of the best barbecue in the metro area. Carpool has 16 pool tables, four dartboards, and a cigar room with a walk-in humidor. ⊠ *4000 Fairfax Dr., Arlington, VA,* ☎ *703/532–7665.*

Chi Cha Lounge. Groups of stylish young patrons relax on sofas and armchairs—enjoying a menu of Andean appetizers, homemade sangria, and cocktails—while Latin jazz plays in the background. It gets packed on weekends, so come early to get a coveted sofa along the back wall, where it's easier to see—and be seen. Sunday through Thursday, for a small price, you can indulge in a Turkish water pipe filled with imported honey-cured tobacco. ⊠ *1624 U St. NW,* ☎ *202/234–8400.*

Dr. Dremo's Tap House. Key to the new feel of this former auto dealership are the snug nooks, de rigeur couches, and huge 6- by 9-foot TV (sneak downstairs for a peak). The bar features nine microbrews from the Bardo Brewery and 10 pool tables, two of which are outdoors.

The pub-style menu features nachos, bratwurst, and Italian sausage. ⊠ *2001 Clarendon Blvd., Arlington, VA,* ☎ *703/528–4660.*

Dragonfly. This ultra-hip bar features minimalist white and chrome furnishings and sleek, mod, '60s bar stools. Projections of kung-fu movies provide a pleasant distraction from the assemblage of youthful beautiful people. The bar serves sushi, but the food here is more fashion accessory than nourishment. ⊠ *1215 Connecticut Ave. NW,* ☎ *202/ 331–1715.*

Dubliner. Snug paneled rooms, thick Guinness, and nightly live entertainment make Washington's premier Irish pub popular among Capitol Hill staffers. ⊠ *520 N. Capitol St. NW,* ☎ *202/737–3773.*

Fishmarket. There's something different in just about every section of the Fishmarket—a multilevel, multiroom space in Old Town Alexandria—from piano-bar crooner to ragtime piano shouter to guitar strummer. The operative word here is *boisterous.* If you really like beer, order the largest size; it comes in a glass big enough to wash your face in. ⊠ *105 King St., Alexandria, VA,* ☎ *703/836–5676.*

Galaxy Hut. Holiday lights out front mark this small yet intimate bar that hosts breaking bands from the area. The bar also features an ever-changing display of intriguing outsider art. ⊠ *2711 Wilson Blvd., Arlington, VA,* ☎ *703/525–8646.*

Hawk 'n' Dove. The regulars at this friendly bar—set in a neighborhood dominated by the Capital and the Library of Congress—include politicos, lobbyists, and well-behaved marines from a nearby barracks. ⊠ *329 Pennsylvania Ave. SE,* ☎ *202/543–3300.*

Iota. The bands at Iota tend to play alt-country or stripped-down rock. The refreshingly unpretentious crowd comes mainly because they're simply fans of good music. Expect to fight your way to the bar—it gets crowded quickly. ⊠ *2832 Wilson Blvd., Arlington, VA,* ☎ *703/ 522–8340.*

Mimi's American Bistro. One of Dupont Circle's newest hotspots, Mimi's has swiftly become a neighborhood sensation. Some of the city's most talented performers work here as "singing servers." Expect to be mesmerized by their renditions of beloved standards, campy torch songs, and fun pop tunes. The bar gets packed quickly and the coveted plush couch (with an intimate view of the tiny stage) is rarely vacant. ⊠ *2120 P St. NW,* ☎ *202/464–6464.*

Ozio Restaurant & Lounge. There are four stories of hip coolness in this popular martini and cigar lounge. A humidor graces the first floor, along with cozy plush couches and art-deco decor. Three more floors feature dancing and VIP service for the multi-ethnic, upscale crowd. Long lines of sharply dressed hipsters stretch in front on weekends. Dig out your Manolo Blahniks—looks count here. ⊠ *1813 M St. NW,* ☎ *202/822–6000.*

Sign of the Whale. The best hamburger in town is available at the bar of this well-known post-preppie–neo-yuppie haven. ⊠ *1825 M St. NW,* ☎ *202/785–1110.*

Uncle Jed's Roadhouse. Who knew that downtown Bethesda had such a laid-back, down-to-earth bar? Well, it seems everyone. Expect long lines on the weekends at this fun-filled roadhouse. Jukeboxes blare rock and country, arcade games roar, and big screen TVs blast. Wind down from the fun with a brew and some down-home food; don't miss the ribs. ⊠ *7525 Old Georgetown Rd., Bethesda, MD,* ☎ *301/913–0026.*

Yacht Club. Enormously popular with well-dressed, 35-plus singles, this suburban Maryland lounge is the brainchild of irrepressible entrepreneur Tommy "The Matchmaker" Curtis, who measures his success by the number of engagements and marriages spawned here. At last count it was in the vicinity of 118. The bar is closed Sunday–Tuesday. ⊠ *8111 Woodmont Ave., Bethesda, MD,* ☎ *301/654–2396.*

Comedy Clubs

The number of comedy groups in Washington that welcome, indeed rely on, the zany suggestions of audience members has mushroomed. These improvisation groups pop up at various venues, performing in the laughs-at-any-cost style of Chicago's Second City troupe, but many disappear as quickly as they appeared.

Capitol Steps. The musical political satire of the Capitol Steps, a group of current and former Hill staffers, is presented in the high-tech, 600-seat amphitheater of the Ronald Reagan Building and International Trade Center every Friday and Saturday at 7:30 PM, and occasionally at other spots around town. ✉ *Ronald Reagan Building and International Trade Center, 1300 Pennsylvania Ave. NW,* ☎ *703/683–8330, Capitol Steps.*

Comedy Connection. The Comedy Connection at the Arts Theater hosts comics every Friday and Saturday. Comedians such as Martin Lawrence, Tommy Davidson, and Jimmie Walker call the Connection home when in town. (Note: no tennis shoes allowed; there is a two-item minimum in addition to the cover charge.) ✉ *312 Main St., Laurel, MD,* ☎ *301/490–1993.*

ComedySportz. Two teams of improv artists go to work to make you laugh on Friday and Saturday nights. ☎ *703/486–4242 for locations and times.*

Gross National Product. After years of spoofing Republican administrations with such shows as *Man Without a Contra,* then aiming its barbs at the Democrats in *Clintoons* and *All the President's Women,* the satirical comedy troupe Gross National Product was most recently performing *Son of a Bush.* ☎ *202/783–7212 for location and reservations.*

Improv. A heavyweight on the Washington comedy scene, the Improv is descended from the club that sparked the stand-up boomlet in New York City and across the country. Name headliners are common. ✉ *1140 Connecticut Ave. NW,* ☎ *202/296–7008.*

WIT! The Washington Improv Theater (WIT) presents its irreverent humor to sellout crowds at area theaters and clubs. Refreshingly, the troupe's comedy tends not to focus strictly on beltway politics, and relies heavily on audience suggestions. ☎ *202/244–8630 for location and reservations.*

Dance Clubs

Washington's dance clubs seem to be constantly re-creating themselves. A club might offer heavy "industrial" music on Wednesday, host a largely gay clientele on Thursday, and thump to the sounds of '70s disco on Friday. Those who like to club-hop will find five club hubs: Georgetown; Adams-Morgan; U Street; the intersection of 18th and M streets, just south of Dupont Circle; and along 9th Street NW near Metro Center.

Chelsea's. At this elegant Georgetown club near the C&O Canal, the DJs trot the globe. Depending on the night, dancers pulse to the rhythms of Arabic, Latin, or Iranian music. Call ahead to find out each night's theme. ✉ *1055 Thomas Jefferson St. NW,* ☎ *202/298–8222.*

Habana Village. No matter what the temperature outside, it's always balmy inside Habana Village. The tiny dance floor is packed nightly with couples moving to the latest salsa and merengue tunes. When it's time to cool down, you can head to one of several lounges in this converted four-story town house and relax in a wicker chair surrounded by potted palms. Be sure to order a *mojito,* the house special made of white rum, sugar, and fresh crushed mint leaves. ⊠ *1834 Columbia Rd. NW,* ☎ *202/462–6310.*

Platinum. Known for years as the Bank, this upscale dance venue always keeps up with the trends. Now the multi-level club with three dance floors and a VIP lounge bills itself as a sushi bar, and the DJs play techno, house, and Latin music. That may change in six months, but there's guaranteed to be some kind of party happening. ⊠ *915 F St. NW,* ☎ *202/393–3555.*

Polly Esther's. Polly Esther's is the Hard Rock Cafe of dance clubs, with outlets in New York, Miami, downtown D.C., and yes, even Rockville, Maryland. Focusing on popular '70s and '80s tunes and catering to a crowd barely old enough to remember the tail end of the disco era, the club provides an unpretentious good time, especially for groups. You can sing out loud to your favorite Bee Gees song while striking a John Travolta pose, and no one will look twice (though you'll be noticed if you wear tennis shoes or a baseball cap, which aren't considered appropriate attire). ⊠ *605 12th St. NW,* ☎ *202/737–1970;* ⊠ *1370 Rockville Pike, Rockville, MD,* ☎ *301/881–7340.*

Republic Gardens. On any given night, scores of young black professionals flock to Republic Gardens to meet, drink, network, and dance. Party people love the club's beautiful interior, delicious Caribbean-influenced nouvelle cuisine, and mix of hip-hop and classic soul tunes. But even wallflowers can appreciate the pool tables and big screen TVs showing sports events. It's best to dress up and leave the tennis shoes at home. ⊠ *1355 U St. NW,* ☎ *202/232–2710.*

The Spot. This downtown nightclub near the FBI building consistently draws a crowd of young professionals and partygoers. The four floors and six rooms have DJs spinning a different type of music—everything from Top 40 to Latin pop to '70s disco to house music—in each. Dressing up is recommended. The club is open Wednesday and Friday–Sunday. ⊠ *932 F St. NW,* ☎ *202/262–0321.*

State of the Union. State draws a young, eclectic crowd dressed in the requisite wide-leg jeans of today's casually hip. Patrons tend to be serious music fans who come to dance or hold down a spot at the bar while the city's best DJs spin a mix of house music, hip-hop, jungle, and classic R&B. ⊠ *1357 U St. NW,* ☎ *202/588–8926.*

Zei. Pronounced "zee," this New York–style dance club in a former electric power substation draws an international crowd that includes everything from dark-suited "hiplomats" to affluent exchange students. The relentless thump of high-energy Euro-pop complements a decor that includes a wall of television sets that peer down on the proceedings. Tennis shoes aren't considered appropriate here. ⊠ *1415 Zei Alley NW (14th St. between H and I Sts. NW),* ☎ *202/842–2445.*

Gay and Lesbian Dance Clubs

Badlands. One of the best things about Badlands is that it's open on weeknights when other clubs are closed. Men will find a definite meat-market vibe here, but with less attitude than at larger nightclubs. ⊠ *1415 22nd St. NW,* ☎ *202/296–0505.*

Chaos. You could walk right by this basement-level restaurant/nightclub if it weren't for all the gorgeous guys spilling up the stairs into the street on Fridays and Saturdays. A young, chic lesbian crowd takes over the club on Wednesday, and Thursday is Latin night. ⊠ *1633 Q St. NW,* ☎ *202/232–4141.*

Hung Jury. You can count on the women at the Hung Jury to make the most of the dance floor, where you're just as likely to hear the innuendo-laden lyrics of rapper Lil' Kim as you are an upbeat Top 40 dance track. ⊠ *1819 H St. NW,* ☎ *202/785–8181.*

Ziegfeld's. This club tries to offer something for everyone and has a mixed clientele (mostly gay men and straight women). Half the club is dedicated to drag shows, male strippers, and go-go boys, while on the other side of the club patrons dance to the latest house tracks. ✉ *1345 Half St. SE,* ☎ *202/554–5141.*

Jazz and Blues Clubs

The **D.C. Blues Hotline** (☎ 202/828–3028) is a clearinghouse for information on upcoming shows, festivals, and jam sessions in the metropolitan area. In addition to the hot line, it has a monthly newsletter and a Web site.

Blues Alley. The restaurant turns out creole cooking, while cooking on stage you'll find such nationally known performers as Nancy Wilson, Joshua Redman, and Stanley Turrentine. You can come for just the show, but those who come for a meal get better seats. ✉ *1073 Wisconsin Ave. NW (entrance in rear),* ☎ *202/337–4141.*

Columbia Station. This place is a neighborhood favorite, with good food and great music. Amber lights illuminate the brass instrument–theme artwork adorning the walls. The nightly live music usually consists of a quality local jazz band and sometimes blues. Either way, there's usually an electric bass, rather than an upright, to help pound out tunes funky enough for dancing. ✉ *2325 18th St. NW,* ☎ *202/462–6040.*

HR-57 Center for the Preservation of Jazz and Blues. Known locally as HR-57, this hotspot isn't really a club or a lounge, but a nonprofit cultural center. The warm, inviting center features D.C.'s hottest local musicians Wednesday through Sunday. Bring your own bottle— HR-57 doesn't serve liquor. ✉ *1610 14th St. NW,* ☎ *202/667–3700.*

Takoma Station Tavern. In the shadow of the Metro stop that lends it its name, the Takoma Station Tavern hosts such local favorites as Marshall Keys and Keith Killgo, with the occasional nationally known artist stopping by to jam. The jazz happy hours starting at 6:30 Wednesday through Friday pack the joint. There's reggae on Saturday and comedy on Sunday. (Sneakers and athletic wear are not allowed.) ✉ *6914 4th St. NW,* ☎ *202/829–1999.*

Twin's Lounge. This venerable jazz standby recently relocated from its longtime Georgia Avenue home to the burgeoning U Street corridor— once known as the "Black Broadway." Twin sisters Kelly and Maze Tesfaye have made the cozy, second floor space a haven for some of D.C.'s strongest straight-ahead players, as well as for groups from New York City. The club's menu offers tasty Ethiopian appetizers along with staples like nachos, wings, and burgers. ✉ *1344 U St. NW,* ☎ *202/ 234–0072.*

219 Basin Street Lounge. Jazz combos perform Tuesday through Saturday in this attractive Victorian-style bar, across the Potomac in Old Town Alexandria and above the 219 Restaurant. Musicians from local service bands often stop by to sit in. ✉ *219 King St., Alexandria, VA,* ☎ *703/549–1141.*

Vegas Lounge. This sweet dive bar is the home of Dr. Blues, and he doesn't allow any soft-jazz-bluesy-fusion in his house. Even during the weekly open-jam session, it's strictly no-nonsense wailing guitar rhythms by seasoned local players. ✉ *1415 P St. NW,* ☎ *202/483–3971.*

Rock and Pop Clubs

Black Cat. This is the place to see the latest local bands as well as a few up-and-coming indie stars from such labels as TeenBeat and Dischord Records. Occasionally, you can see MTV acts like alternative rockers Sleater-Kinney, white-boy-funkster G. Love, or jazz-based rappers the

Roots. The post-punk crowd whiles away the time in the Red Room, a side bar with pool tables, an eclectic jukebox, and no cover charge. ⊠ *1831 14th St. NW,* ☏ *202/667–7960.*

Metro Cafe. Stop by this Gen X venue to hear good-quality emerging bands and an eclectic range of artists, from alternative rock to jump blues to hip-hop and funk. The walls are dark red, the lights are dim, and the changing selection of art is eccentric. Metro Cafe is also home to the, ahem, unusual theater troupe Cherry Red Productions. Known for productions such as *Romeo & Juliatric* and *Seven Deadly Dwarves,* Cherry Red is "committed to delivering quality adult-oriented B-theatre." ⊠ *1522 14th St. NW,* ☏ *202/518–7900, 202/675–3071 Cherry Red.*

Nation. As one of the largest venues for alternative and rock music in Washington (it holds 1,000 people), Nation brings in such bands as David Bowie, the Fugees, and Jamiroquai. Depending on the act, tickets are available at Ticketmaster or the door. On a separate side of the club, you can gyrate to a mix of mostly alternative dance music. On Friday night this warehouse space becomes "Sting," a massive rave featuring the latest permutations of techno and drum-and-bass music. ⊠ *1015 Half St. SE,* ☏ *202/554–1500.*

9:30 Club. This trendy club books an eclectic mix of local, national, and international artists (most of which fall into the alternative-music category—from Third Eye Blind and Ani DiFranco to Lucky Dube and Macy Gray). The club has a balcony on three sides and a large dance floor in front of the stage, so you can see the show from almost anywhere. Vegetarian food catered from Planet X helps provide much-needed nourishment after you've been standing several hours. Get tickets at the door or through Tickets.com. ⊠ *815 V St. NW,* ☏ *202/393–0930.*

Velvet Lounge. Squeeze up the narrow stairway and check out the eclectic local and national bands that play at this unassuming little joint. Indie mainstays like Adam West are regulars, but you'll also find acclaimed up-and-comers like The Bastard Sons of Johnny Cash. The bar books bands that play psychobilly, alt-country, indie pop . . . you name it, it's here. ⊠ *915 U St. NW,* ☏ *202/462–3213.*

5 OUTDOOR ACTIVITIES AND SPORTS

In and around the capital you can explore by bike, run amid historic buildings and memorials, head for an afternoon of fishing, sail up the Potomac, and enjoy golf and duckpin bowling. Washington and nearby Baltimore have plenty of pro teams that provide entertainment. But be prepared: Redskins fans sell their souls—or at least their cars—to get tickets, and games are sold out months in advance.

By John F. Kelly

Updated by
Mitchell Tropin

W ASHINGTON'S 69 SQUARE MILES form a fantastic recreational backyard. There are hundreds of grassy spaces—from the mammoth Rock Creek Park, with miles of trails for bikers, runners, joggers, and walkers, to the National Mall, where you can spike a volleyball with the monuments as a backdrop. Sports fans have a glut of professional teams on their doorstep, not to mention two spectacular stadiums: FedEx Field, where the Washington Redskins play; and the showcase MCI Center, where you can catch the NBA Wizards, the NHL Capitals, the WNBA Mystics, a host of Division 1 college basketball teams, and the Washington Power pro lacrosse team, which joined the D.C. sports scene in 2001. The Robert F. Kennedy Stadium, showcases some of the greatest soccer teams from Europe and Latin America, along with D.C. United—perennial Major Soccer League powerhouse—and 2001 newcomer the Washington Freedom, of the Women's United Soccer Association.

PARTICIPANT SPORTS

Bicycling

The numerous trails in the District and its surrounding areas are well maintained and clearly marked.

For scenery, you can't beat the 89-mi **C&O Canal Towpath** that starts in Georgetown and runs along the C&O Canal into Maryland. You could pedal to the end of the canal, 184 mi away in Cumberland, MD, but most cyclists stop at Great Falls, 15 mi from where the canal starts. The towpath, an occasionally bumpy gravel-and-packed surface, passes through wooded areas of the C&O Canal National Historical Park. You can see 19th-century locks from the canal's working days and, if you are particularly lucky, you may catch a glimpse of mules pulling a canal barge. Information on the towpath and surrounding areas can be found online at WEB www.nps.gov/choh.

Suited for bicyclists, walkers, rollerbladers, and strollers, the paved **Capital Crescent Trail** stretches along the old Georgetown Branch, a B&O Railroad line that was completed in 1910 and saw its last train in 1985. The 7½-mi route runs from Georgetown near Key Bridge to central Bethesda at Bethesda and Woodmont Avenues. At most trail entrances there are kiosks with brochures and maps. The trail picks up again at Bethesda and Woodmont Avenues at a well-lighted tunnel near Thyme Square Restaurant (⊠ 4735 Bethesda Ave.) and continues into Silver Spring. The 3½-mi stretch from Bethesda to Silver Spring is gravel surface. The Georgetown Branch Trail, as this section is officially named, connects with the Rock Creek Trail, which goes to Rockville in the north and Memorial Bridge past the Washington Monument in the south. On weekends when the weather's nice, all sections of the trails are crowded. For more information call the Capital Crescent Coalition at ☎ 202/234–4874.

Cyclists interested in serious training might try the 3-mi loop around the golf course in **East Potomac Park** at Hains Point, the southern most area of the park (entry is near the Jefferson Memorial). It is a favorite training course for dedicated local racers and would-be triathletes. Restrict your workouts to the daytime; the area is not safe after dark. At press time renovation of the Hains Point area was scheduled to continue through the summer of 2002, so some roads may be closed. For current conditions, contact the National Park Service's East Potomac Park Office at ☎ 202/485–9874.

Each day, bicyclists cruise **The Mall** amid the endless throngs of runners, walkers, and tourists. There is relatively little traffic and bikers can take in some of Washington's landmarks, such as the Washington Monument, the Reflecting Pool, and the Vietnam Memorial and some of the city's more interesting architecture, such as the Smithsonian Castle and the Hirshhorn "Concrete Donut." A pleasant loop route begins at the Lincoln Memorial, going north past the Washington Memorial, turning around at the Tidal Basin. Along the way, there are small fountains and parks if you want to take a break or get a drink of water.

The **Mount Vernon Trail,** across the Potomac in Virginia, has two sections. The northern part is 3½ mi long and begins near the causeway across the river from the Kennedy Center that heads to Theodore Roosevelt Island and passes Ronald Reagan National Airport and on to Old Town Alexandria. This section features slightly rolling hills and almost no interruptions for traffic, making it a delightful, but challenging, biking route. Even relatively inexperienced bikers will enjoy the trail, which gives wonderful views of the Potomac. From the trail, you can take a bridge to Theodore Roosevelt Island, a relatively undeveloped area with beautiful trees. To access the trail from the District, take the Theodore Roosevelt Bridge or the Rochambeau Memorial Bridge, also known as the 14th Street Bridge. South of the airport, the trail runs down to the Washington Marina. The final mile of the trail's northern section meanders through protected wetlands before ending in the heart of Old Town Alexandria. The trail's 9-mi southern section extends along the Potomac from Alexandria to Mount Vernon.

Rock Creek Park covers an area from the edge of Georgetown to Montgomery County, MD. The bike path is asphalt and has a few challenging hills, but it is mostly flat and a biker can go several miles without having to stop for cars. The 15 mi of dirt trails are best for hiking. The roadway is closed to traffic on weekends. There are separate northern parts of the trail that begin in Bethesda and Silver Spring. The two sections merge around the Washington, D.C. line. Many bikers gather at this point and follow the trail on a path that goes past the Washington Zoo and eventually runs toward the Lincoln Memorial and Kennedy Center.

Information
The **Washington Area Bicyclist Association** (✉ 733 15th St. NW, Ste. 1030, 20005, ☎ 202/628–2500) has information and publications about cycling in the nation's capital. *The Greater Washington Area Bicycle Atlas,* in particular, is an invaluable resource.

Rentals
Big Wheel Bikes (✉ 1034 33rd St. NW, ☎ 202/337–0254), near the C&O Canal Towpath, rents multispeed bikes for $25 per day and $15 for three hours. A second location is near the Capital Crescent Trail (✉ 6917 Arlington Rd., Bethesda, MD, ☎ 301/652–0192). If you are in Virginia and want to ride on the Mount Vernon Trail, there is a location in Alexandria (✉ 2 Prince St., Alexandria, VA, ☎ 703/739–2300). **Bikes USA** (✉ 1506-C Belle View Blvd., Alexandria, VA, ☎ 703/768–3444) is a bike store near the Mount Vernon Trail in Alexandria. **Bike the Sites** (☎ 202/966–8662) is a tour company that offers three-hour, 8-mi guided tours of downtown Washington. Costs range from $35 to $55, and bike rental is included. Reservations are available. **Blazing Saddles** (✉ 1001 Pennsylvania Ave., NW, ☎ 202/544–0055) rents all types of bikes, including tandems, and offers self-guided tours of Washington. Bikes are $5 to $9 per hour and $25 to $45 per day.

City Bikes (✉ 2501 Champlain St., NW, ☎ 202/265–1564) is in Adams-Morgan near the Woodley Park Metro Station, and offers easy access to Rock Creek Park. You can get a multispeed bike for $20 for two hours and $25 per day. Reservations are available.

Fletcher's Boat House (✉ 4940 Canal Rd., at Reservoir Rd., ☎ 202/244–0461), next to the C&O Towpath and Capital Crescent Trail, rents fixed-gear bikes for $8 per hour and $12 per day.

Griffin Cycle is in Bethesda near the Capital Crescent Trail and the Bethesda Metro station. Multispeed bikes are $15 per day and $10 for each additional day. (✉ 4940 Canal Rd., at Reservoir Rd., ☎ 301/656–6188).

Thompson's Boat Center (✉ 2900 Virginia Ave. NW, at the corner of Virginia Ave. and Rock Creek Pkwy., behind Kennedy Center, ☎ 202/333–4861) allows easy access to the Rock Creek Trail and the C&O Towpath and is close to the monuments. Multispeed bikes are $8 per hour and $25 per day. Fixed-gear bikes are $8 per hour and $12 per day.

Washington Sailing Marina (✉ 1 Marina Dr., ☎ 703/548–9027) rents multispeed bikes for $6 per hour and $22 per day. Fixed-gear bikes are $4 per hour and $16.50 per day. The marina is on the Mount Vernon Trail off the George Washington Parkway, south of Ronald Reagan National Airport.

Boating and Sailing

The Chesapeake Bay is one of the great sailing basins of the world. For some scenic and historical sightseeing, take a day trip to Annapolis, MD, the home of the U.S. Naval Academy. The popularity of boating and the many boating businesses in Annapolis make it one of the best civilian sailing centers on the East Coast.

A world-renowned school and charter company, **Annapolis Sailing School** (✉ 601 6th St., Annapolis, MD, ☎ 410/267–7205) is a good choice for lessons and rentals.

Some of the best white-water kayakers and canoeists in the country call Washington home. On weekends they practice below Great Falls in **Mather Gorge,** a canyon carved by the Potomac River just north of the city, above Chain Bridge. The water is deceptive and dangerous—only top-level kayakers should consider a run here. It is safe, however, to watch the experts at play from a post above the gorge. For information, call the ranger station at Great Falls, VA (☎ 703/285–2965), or Great Falls, MD (☎ 301/299–3613).

Canoeing, sailing, and powerboating are all popular in the Washington, D.C. area. Several places rent boats along the **Potomac River** north and south of the city. You can dip your oars just about anywhere along the river—go canoeing in the C&O Canal, sailing in the widening river south of Alexandria, or even kayaking in the raging rapids at Great Falls, a 30-minute drive from the capital.

Rentals

The **Belle Haven Marina** (✉ George Washington Pkwy., ☎ 703/768–0018), south of Reagan National Airport and Old Town Alexandria, rents three types of sailboats: Sunfish are $27 for two hours during the week and $32 for two hours on the weekend; Hobie Cat–style sailboats and Flying Scots are $42 for two hours during the week and $48 for two hours during the weekend. Rentals are available from mid-May to September.

Fletcher's Boat House (✉ 4940 Canal Rd., at Reservoir Rd., ☎ 202/244–0461), just north of Georgetown, rents 17-ft rowboats for $17 per day.

Thompson's Boat Center (✉ 2900 Virginia Ave., NW, at the corner of Virginia Ave. and Rock Creek Pkwy. behind Kennedy Center, ☎ 202/333–4861) is near Georgetown and beautiful Theodore Roosevelt Island. The center rents canoes for $8 per hour and $22 per day. Single kayaks are $8 per hour and $24 per day, and double kayaks are $10 per hour and $30 per day. Rowing sculls are available, but you must demonstrate prior experience and an appropriate skill level.

Tidal Basin (✉ 1501 Maine Ave. SW, ☎ 202/479–2426), in front of Jefferson Memorial, rents paddleboats beginning in April and usually ending in September, depending on how cold the water gets. The entrance is on 1501 Maine Avenue SW, on the east side of the Tidal Basin. From around April until September you can rent two-passenger boats at $8 per hour and four-passenger boats at $16 per hour.

The **Washington Sailing Marina** (✉ George Washington Pkwy., south of Ronald Reagan National Airport, ☎ 703/548–9027) rents sailboats from around mid-May to September, or until the water gets too cold. Sunfish are $10 per hour, Island 17's are $17 per hour, and the larger Flying Scots are $19 per hour. There is a two-hour minimum rental for all boats.

Bowling and Duckpin Bowling

The mid-Atlantic region is the birthplace of duckpin bowling, and among its last remaining bastions. The balls and pins are smaller than those in the standard tenpin version of bowling. John McGraw, who later went on to become a Hall of Fame baseball manager with the New York Giants, invented duckpin bowling in Baltimore at the turn of the century as a way to keep his players in shape during the off-season. Though this species of bowling—also known as "the ducks"—is by all accounts endangered, there are still several duckpin alleys in the area. Local enthusiasts also are trying to preserve remaining duckpin centers.

The 40 lanes at **AMF College Park** (✉ 9021 Baltimore Blvd., College Park, MD, ☎ 301/474–8282) are open 9 AM–11 PM weekdays, and until 1 AM on Friday and Saturday. Games are $2.50 to $3.75. Shoe rental is $2.50. **Bowl America Westwood** (✉ 5353 Westbard Ave., Bethesda, MD, ☎ 301/654–1320) has 14 duckpin and 20 tenpin lanes, open daily 9 AM to 11 PM. Games are $1.80 to $3.50. Shoe rental is $2.50. The **Falls Church Bowling Center** (✉ 400 South Maple St., Falls Church, VA, ☎ 703/533–8131) has 32 lanes, open 9 AM to 10 PM Monday through Thursday, 10 AM to 10 PM Friday, 11 AM to 10 PM Saturday, and 12 PM to 7 PM Sunday. Games cost $2.75. Shoe rental is $1.25. **White Oak Lanes** (✉ 11207 New Hampshire Ave., Silver Spring, MD, ☎ 301/593–3000) has 24 lanes, and is open 9 AM to 11 PM weekdays and Sunday, and 9 AM to 1 AM Saturday. Games are $2.50 during the week and $3 on the weekend. Shoe rental is $1.50 on weekdays and $2 on weekends.

Fishing

The **Potomac River** is something of an environmental success story. Once dangerously polluted, it has rebounded. Now largemouth bass, striped bass, shad, and white and yellow perch are all down there somewhere, willing to take your bait. Simply renting a boat and going fishing in Washington is complicated because this stretch of the Potomac is divided among the three jurisdictions of Virginia, Maryland, and the District of Columbia. It isn't always easy to determine in whose water you're fishing or which licenses you should have. The solution: hire a guide.

A 5-mi stretch of the Potomac River—roughly from the Wilson Memorial Bridge in Alexandria south to Ft. Washington National Park—is one of the country's best spots for largemouth-bass fishing. It has, in fact, become something of an East Coast mecca for anglers in search of this particular fish. The area around Fletcher's Boat House on the C&O Canal is one of the best spots for perch.

Information

Nationally known fishing writer **Gene Mueller** has a column that appears three times a week in the *Washington Times*. He gladly takes readers' telephone calls Thursday mornings (☎ 202/636–3268). The **"Fish Lines"** column in Friday's *Washington Post* "Weekend" section, written by Gary Diamond, outlines where the fish are biting, from the Potomac to the Chesapeake Bay.

Tackle Shop and Guides

Run by nationally known fisherman and conservationist Ken Penrod, **Life Outdoors Unlimited** (☎ 301/937–0010) is an umbrella group of the area's best freshwater fishing guides. For about $250 a day a guide sees to all your needs, from tackle to boats, and tells you which licenses are required. All of the guides are pros, who teach novices and guide experts. You might be asked to leave a message; calls are usually returned the same evening.

Golf

Serious golfers must resign themselves to driving out of the city to find a worthwhile course. None of the three public courses in town could be considered first-rate. Still, people line up to play here and at about 50 other local public courses, sometimes arriving as early as 2 AM to snare a tee time. Some courses allow you to call ahead to reserve a time.

Public Courses in the District

The claim to fame of the flat, wide, and featureless **East Potomac Park Golf Course** (⊠ 972 Ohio Dr. SW, ☎ 202/554–7660) is that professional golfer and Washington resident Lee Elder got his start here. The course is 6,303 yards, and par-72. Two 9-hole courses and a driving range are on the property, as well as one of the country's oldest miniature golf courses—open only in summer. Greens fees are $15 for 18 holes and $9 for nine on weekdays—on weekends it's $19 and $12.25, respectively. The course is at Hains Point on the eastern side of the park, near the Jefferson Memorial.

The par-72, 6,300-yard **Langston Golf Course** (⊠ 2600 Benning Rd. NE, at 26th St., ☎ 202/397–8638) is popular despite poorly maintained greens and fairways. Holes 8 and 9, by the Anacostia River, are challenging. Greens fees are $13.50 for 18 holes on weekdays, $9 for 9; weekends it's $17 and $10.50, respectively.

A tight, rolling, well-treed back nine makes the 4,798-yard, par-65 **Rock Creek Park Golf Course** (⊠ 16th and Rittenhouse Sts., NW, ☎ 202/882–7332) the most attractive public course in the capital. The front nine holes are easy, but the back nine are challenging. Greens fees are $15 for 18 holes and $9 for nine on weekdays; weekend fees are $19 and $12.25.

Public Courses in Nearby Suburbs

Maryland's 6,209-yard, par-72 **Enterprise Golf Course** (⊠ 2802 Enterprise Rd., Mitchellville, MD, ☎ 301/249–2040) is reputedly the best-manicured public course in the area. Its well-landscaped layout gives it a country-club feel. The fee for 18 holes is $40 weekdays and $45 weekends. About 30 minutes by car from downtown Washington, the course is near the Beltway in Prince George's County.

Extremely long and winding, the 6,732-yard, par-72 **Northwest Park Golf Course** (⊠ 15701 Layhill Rd., Wheaton, MD, ☎ 301/598–6100) makes for slow play. It is immaculately groomed and has a short nine course. It's about a half hour from town. The fee for 18 holes is $21 weekdays, $26 weekends; the short-9 course is $13 and $16, respectively.

To squeeze in a round of golf on the way to or from Dulles Airport, try **Penderbrook Golf Club** (⊠ 3700 Golf Trail La., Fairfax, VA, ☎ 703/ 385–3700), a short but imaginative 5,927-yard, par-71 course. The 5th, 11th, 12th, and 15th holes are exceptional. The fees for 18 holes are $55 Monday through Thursday, and $69 Friday through Sunday. Penderbrook is off West Ox Road and Route 50.

Designed by Ault, Clark & Associates, **Pleasant Valley Golfers' Club** (⊠ 4715 Pleasant Valley Rd., Chantilly, VA, ☎ 703/631–7902) has a 6,957-yard, par-72, 18-hole course that is pristinely landscaped with hills, hardwood trees, wildflowers, native-grass meadows, and water features. Greens fees are $60 Monday through Thursday, $70 Friday, and $85 on weekends. The club is off Route 50, south of Dulles Airport.

Though heavily wooded, the well-maintained 6,871-yard, par-71 **Reston National Golf Course** (⊠ 11875 Sunrise Valley Dr., Reston, VA, ☎ 703/620–9333) is not too difficult for the average player. It is about a half-hour drive from downtown Washington. Greens fees for 18 holes are $65 weekdays and $85 weekends.

Renowned architect Dan Maples designed **South Riding Golf Course** (⊠ 43237 Golf View Dr., South Riding, VA, ☎ 703/327–3673), an 18-hole, 7,100-yard, par-72 course off Route 50, south of Dulles Airport. Greens fees are $60 Monday through Thursday, $70 Friday, and $85 weekends.

Health Clubs

All health clubs require that you be a member—or at least a member of an affiliated club—to use their facilities. Some hotels have made private arrangements with neighboring health clubs to enable guests to use the club's facilities, sometimes at a daily rate. If you belong to a member club of the **International Health, Racquet & Sportsclub Association (IHRSA)** (☎ 617/951–0055 or 800/228–4772, FAX 617/951–0056), you can pay by the day to use the facilities at a member club in Washington, provided that it is at least 50 mi from your home club. To access the facilities, bring your club membership card and an IHRSA "passport" from your home club. The IHRSA does not supply passports.

Guests at any Washington-area hotel may use the fabulous **Fitness Company West End** (⊠ 2401 M St., NW, ☎ 202/457–5070) facilities at the Monarch Hotel for $20 per day—$10 for Washington Monarch guests. Show your hotel-room key to the center's employees to get in. The **National Capital YMCA** (⊠ 1711 Rhode Island Ave. NW, ☎ 202/ 862–9622) has basketball, weights, racquetball, squash, swimming, exercise equipment, and more. Some downtown hotels offer their guests free one-day passes. Members of an out-of-town Y show their membership card and pay a daily fee of $7 to $10, depending on the time of day, and their guests are allowed in for $15 to $20.

Hiking

Hikes and nature walks are listed in the Friday "Weekend" section of the *Washington Post*. Several area organizations sponsor outings: The **Potomac-Appalachian Trail Club** (⊠ 118 Park St., SE, Vienna, VA

22180, ☎ 703/242–0965) sponsors hikes—usually free—on trails from Pennsylvania to Virginia, including the C&O Canal and the Appalachian Trail. The **Sierra Club** (☎ 202/547–2326) offers a variety of regional outings; call for details.

A self-guided nature trail winds through **Woodend** (✉ 8940 Jones Mill Rd., Chevy Chase, MD 20815, ☎ 301/652–9188; 301/652–1088 for recent bird sightings, ⓦ www.audubonnaturalist.org/woodend.htm), a verdant 40-acre estate in Chevy Chase, MD, and around the suburban Maryland headquarters of the local **Audubon Naturalist Society.** The estate was designed in the 1920s by Jefferson Memorial architect John Russell Pope and has a mansion, also called Woodend, on its grounds. You're never very far from the trill of birdsong here, as the Audubon Society has turned the place into something of a private nature preserve, forbidding the use of toxic chemicals and leaving some areas in a wild, natural state. Programs include wildlife identification walks, environmental education programs, and a weekly Saturday bird walk September through June. A bookstore stocks titles on conservation, ecology, and birds. The grounds are open daily sunrise to sunset and admission is free.

A 1,460-acre refuge in Alexandria, **Huntley Meadows Park** (✉ 3701 Lockheed Blvd., Alexandria, VA, ☎ 703/768–2525) is a birder's delight. You can spot more than 200 species of fowl—from ospreys to owls, egrets, and ibis. Much of the park is wetlands, a favorite of aquatic species. A boardwalk circles through a marsh, enabling you to spot beaver lodges, and 4 mi of trails wend through the park, making it likely you'll see deer, muskrats, and river otters as well. The park is usually open daily dawn to dusk.

Horseback Riding

Lessons and trail rides are offered year-round at the **Rock Creek Park Horse Center** (✉ Military and Glover Rds., NW, ☎ 202/362–0117). The guided trail rides—for beginning riders ages 12 and up—are an hour long. Hours of operation vary with the season.

Ice-Skating

You can rent skates at all the rinks listed.

The indoor rink at **Cabin John Park** (✉ 10610 Westlake Dr., Rockville, MD, ☎ 301/365–0585) is in the Maryland suburb of North Bethesda and is open year-round. The **Mount Vernon Recreation Center** (✉ 2017 Belle View Blvd., Alexandria, VA, ☎ 703/768–3222) has an indoor rink that is open all year. It is convenient if you are staying in the lower half of Washington, D.C. The **National Gallery of Art Ice Rink** (✉ Constitution Ave. NW, between 7th and 9th Sts., ☎ 202/289–3361) is surrounded by the gallery's Sculpture Garden, which is filled with extraordinary art sculptures on meticulously landscaped gardens. The art deco design of the rink makes it one of the most popular outdoor winter sites in Washington. In the spring, the rink becomes a fountain. The prime location of the **Pershing Park Ice Rink** (✉ Pennsylvania Ave. and 14th St., NW, ☎ 202/737–6938), just a few blocks from the White House, makes it one of Washington's most popular places to skate.

Running

Running is one of the best ways to see the city, and downtown Washington and nearby northern Virginia offer several scenic trails. It can be dangerous to run at night on the trails, although the streets are fairly well lit. Even in daylight, it's best to run in pairs when venturing beyond public areas or heavily used sections of trails. Most city streets are safe for runs alone during the day, especially around government buildings, museums, and monuments, where there is additional police protection. Group runs and weekend races around Washington are listed in the Friday "Weekend" section of the *Washington Post*. You can also check the Thursday calendar of events in the *Washington Times*. Comprehensive listings of running and walking events are posted online by the *Washington Running Report* at www.runwashington.com and *RacePacket* at www.racepacket.com. Another reliable source on the Web for races and casual running gatherings is the Montgomery County Road Runners—the nation's third-largest running club—at www. mcrrc.org.

The 89-mi-long **C&O Canal Towpath** in the C&O National Historical Park is a favorite of runners and cyclists. The path is mostly gravel and dirt, making it easy on a runner's knees and feet. The most popular loop—from a point just north of the Key Bridge in Georgetown to Fletcher's Boat House—is about 4 mi round-trip. Information on the towpath and surrounding areas can be found online at WEB www. nps.gov/choh.

The most popular running route in Washington is the 4½-mi loop on **The Mall** around the Capitol and past the Smithsonian museums, the Washington Monument, the Reflecting Pool, and the Lincoln Memorial. At any time of day, hundreds of runners, speed walkers, bicyclists, and tourists make their way along the gravel pathways. For a longer run, veer south of the Mall on either side of the Tidal Basin and head for the Jefferson Memorial and East Potomac Park, the site of many races.

Across the Potomac in Virginia is the **Mount Vernon Trail,** a favorite with Washington runners. The 3½-mi northern section begins near the pedestrian causeway leading to Theodore Roosevelt Island (directly across the river from the Kennedy Center) and goes past Ronald Reagan National Airport and on to Old Town Alexandria. You can get to the trail from the District by crossing either the Theodore Roosevelt Bridge at the Lincoln Memorial or the Rochambeau Memorial Bridge, also known as the 14th Street Bridge, at the Jefferson Memorial. South of the airport, the trail runs down to the Washington Marina. The final mile of the trail's northern section meanders through protected wetlands before ending in the heart of Old Town Alexandria. The trail's longer southern section—approximately 9 mi—takes you along the banks of the Potomac from Alexandria all the way to George Washington's home, Mount Vernon.

Rock Creek Park has 15 mi of trails, a bicycle path, a bridle path, picnic groves, playgrounds, and a boulder-strewn rolling stream, from which it gets its name. The creek isn't safe or pleasant for swimming. Starting one block south of the corner of P and 22nd Streets on the edge of Georgetown, Rock Creek Park runs all the way to Montgomery County, MD. The most popular run in the park is a trail along the creek from Georgetown to the National Zoo—about a 4-mi loop. In summer there's considerable shade, and there are water fountains at an exercise station along the way. The roadway is closed to traffic on weekends.

Information and Organizations

Tuesday and Thursday evenings at 6:30 PM, you can join the **Capitol Hill Runners** (☎ 301/283–0821) on a 6- to 8-mi run, which begins at the reflecting pool at the base of the Capitol's west side. Most Sunday mornings, the **Fleet Feet Sports Shop** (1841 Columbia Rd. NW, 20011, ☎ 202/387–3888) in Adams-Morgan sponsors informal runs through

Rock Creek Park and other areas. The shop's owner, Phil Fenty, leads the runs. The courses change at Phil's discretion and usually go from 5 to 7 mi. Call the **Gatorade and Road Runners Club of America Hotline** (☎ 703/683–7722) for general information about running and racing in the Washington area.

Swimming

Washington has no beaches. If you want to swim, your best bet is to stay at a hotel with a pool. Health-club pools are open only to members, though the downtown YMCA has a pool and welcomes members of out-of-town Ys—for a fee. The District of Columbia maintains 6 public indoor pools and 19 large outdoor pools, as well as 15 outdoor pools that are smaller, but still fun for children. For information and a list of public facilities, contact the **D.C. Department of Recreation Aquatics Department** (⊠ 1230 Taylor St. NW, 20011, ☎ 202/576–6436).

Tennis

The District maintains 123 outdoor courts, but because some are in seedy parts of town, check on the neighborhood in question before heading out. Contact the **D.C. Department of Recreation** (⊠ 3149 16th St. NW, 20010, ☎ 202/673–7646) for a list of city-run courts and information about specific courts. **Hains Point** (⊠ East Potomac Park, ☎ 202/554–5962) has outdoor tennis courts, as well as courts under a bubble for wintertime play. Fees run from $5 to $30.75 an hour depending on the time, the season, and whether it's an indoor or outdoor court. Make court reservations as early as possible—up to one week in advance. To reach Haines Point, take 15th St. south to the Tidal Basin and then follow signs to East Potomac Park. At press time (fall 2001), renovation of the Haines Point area was scheduled to continue through the summer of 2002, with possible road closures. For current conditions, contact the National Park Service's East Potomac Park Office (☎ 202/234–4874). **Rock Creek Tennis Center** (⊠ 16th and Kennedy Sts., NW, ☎ 202/722–5949) has clay and hard courts. Fees range from $5 to $30.75 per hour depending on the time, the season, and whether you're playing indoors or out. You can make reservations up to a week in advance.

Volleyball

Possibly the most idyllic non-coastal volleyball venue you'll ever find, the **Underpass Volleyball Courts** (⊠ 26th St. Circle NW, between Rock Creek Pkwy. and Independence Ave., ☎ 202/619–7225) are 11 public courts in the shadow of the Lincoln Memorial and Washington Monument and bordering the Potomac River. The courts are in an unnamed park area that is run cooperatively by the National Park Service and the D.C. Government, with six of the courts reserved for organizations granted permits through the city, and the remaining five available on a first-come, first-use basis.

SPECTATOR SPORTS

Many sporting events—hockey, basketball, lacrosse, and figure skating, to name a few—take place at the modern **MCI Center** (⊠ 601 F St., NW, ☎ 202/628–3200, WEB www.mcicenter.com). The perennially popular Washington Redskins play at **FedEx Field** (Arena Drive, Landover, ☎ 301/276–6070, WEB www.redskins.com). **RFK Stadium** (⊠ 2400 E. Capitol St. NE, at 22nd St.) has become a mecca for professional soccer and hosts several international matches. For information on RFK

Stadium events call ☏ 202/628–3200. You can buy tickets for most major sporting events at the stadium from **Ticketmaster** (☏ 202/432–7328; 410/481–7328; and 800/551–7328 outside D.C. and Baltimore areas).

Baseball

Washington doesn't have a professional baseball team, so fans go to Baltimore and root for the **Baltimore Orioles** (✉ 333 W. Camden St., Baltimore, MD, ☏ 410/685–9600; 888/848–BIRD for TicketMaster). The team plays in beautiful Oriole Park at Camden Yards, which seats 48,000. Tickets range from $9 for spots in the bleachers to $35 for club level. Special light-rail train service from Washington's Union Station is offered by Maryland's Mass Transit Administration (☏ 410/539–5000, www.mtamaryland.com).

The **Bowie Baysox** (✉ Prince George's County Stadium, Rtes. 50 and 301, Bowie, MD, ☏ 301/805–6000), the Orioles' Class AA farm team, play in a 10,000-seat stadium in suburban Prince George's County, MD, about 45 minutes by car from Washington. Tickets range from $5 to $15 and children ages 5 and under get in free.

Head north of Washington up I–270 in Maryland to see the Oriole Class A **Frederick Keys** (✉ Harry Grove Stadium, 6201 New Design Rd. Frederick, MD, ☏ 301/662–0013) in action. To reach the stadium, look for the Market St. exit from Route 70 or 270. Tickets range from $5 to $11, and children ages 5 and under get in free.

To see the Toronto Blue Jays Class A **Hagerstown Suns** (✉ Municipal Stadium, 274 E. Memorial Blvd., Hagerstown, MD, ☏ 301/791–6266), take I–270 north into Maryland. Tickets range from $3 to $7.50.

About an hour south of Washington is the home of the **Potomac Cannons** (✉ G. Richard Pfitzner Stadium, 7 County Complex Ct., Woodbridge, VA, ☏ 703/590–2311), the St. Louis Cardinals' Class A affiliate. Tickets range from $5 to $10. Take Exit 158B off of Prince William Parkway and look for the sign that says Manassas; drive 8 mi and take a right onto County Complex Court.

Basketball

Of the Division I men's college basketball teams in the area, the best known is the **Georgetown University Hoyas** (☏ 202/687–HOYA box office; 202/432–7328 TicketMaster), former NCAA national champion. Most home games are played at the MCI Center. You can purchase tickets at the MCI Center box office at 6th and F streets. The **University of Maryland Bulldogs** (☏ 800/462–TERP or 301/314–7070) is a national basketball powerhouse. Its games are played in College Park, MD.

Other Division I teams include: the **American University Eagles** (☏ 202/885–3267); the **George Mason University Patriots** (☏ 703/993–3000); the **George Washington University Colonials** (☏ 703/993–3270); the **Howard University Bison** (☏ 202/806–7198); and the Navy team at the **U.S. Naval Academy** (☏ 410/268–6060).

The WNBA's **Washington Mystics** play at the Metro-accessible MCI Center in downtown Washington. Ticket prices range from $8 to $37.50 and can be purchased at the MCI Center box office at 6th and F streets or from TicketMaster (☏ 202/432–7328). The WNBA's women's basketball season runs from late May to August.

The NBA's **Washington Wizards** play from October to April at the Metro-accessible MCI Center in downtown Washington. Every now and then, the team's new president of basketball operations and athlete of the century, Michael Jordan, shows up in the owner's box. Ticket prices range from $19 to $85 and can be purchased at the MCI Center box office at 6th and F Streets or from TicketMaster (☎ 202/432–7328).

Football

In this football-crazy town, tickets for the **Washington Redskins** (☎ 301/276–6050) are a scarce commodity. Though the team has the largest football stadium in the NFL, all 80,000 seats at FedEx Field are held by season-ticket holders. Occasionally you can find tickets advertised in the classifieds of the *Washington Post*—at top dollar of course. Tickets for pre-season Redskins games, played at FedEx Field in August, are easier to get.

Colleges around the capital offer an excellent alternative to booked-solid Redskins games. Teams from **Howard University** (☎ 202/806–7198), the **University of Maryland** (☎ 301/314–7070), and the **U.S. Naval Academy** (☎ 410/268–6068) in Annapolis, MD, play full schedules September through November.

Hockey

The **Washington Capitals** play October through April. Home games are played in the MCI Center (☎ 202/266–2350). The Caps have become one of pro hockey's best teams. Tickets range from $20 to $75 and can be purchased at the MCI Center box office at 6th and F streets or from TicketMaster (☎ 202/432–7328).

Horse Racing

Maryland has a long-standing affection for the ponies. You can watch and wager on thoroughbreds at **Laurel Park** (⊠ Rte. 198 and Race Track Rd., Laurel, MD, ☎ 301/725–0400) from January through March, July and August, and October through December. Race days are usually Wednesday–Sunday. Simulcast wagering is available year-round, every day but Tuesday.

On the third Saturday in May the Preakness Stakes is run at Baltimore's **Pimlico Race Course** (⊠ Hayward and Winner Aves., Baltimore, MD, ☎ 410/542–9400). The course has thoroughbred racing from early April to late June. Race days are usually Wednesday through Sunday. Simulcast wagering is available year-round, every day but Tuesday.

Harness racing is just outside the Beltway at **Rosecroft** (⊠ 6336 Rosecroft Dr., Fort Washington, MD, ☎ 301/567–4000). Race days are usually Thursday through Saturday, and the season runs from February to mid-December.

A little over an hour from downtown, just across the West Virginia border from Maryland and near scenic Harper's Ferry, **Charles Town Races** (⊠ U.S. Route 340, Charles Town, WV, ☎ 800/795–7001) offers bettors who lose on the ponies the chance to win it back at the slot machines. Races are year-round, with evening post times Thursday through Saturday and afternoon post times on Sunday. There is no live racing Monday through Wednesday, but simulcast wagering is available daily.

Lacrosse

Washington's entry in the Professional Lacrosse League is the **Washington Power** (☎ 202/628–3200 or 202/432–SEAT TicketMaster), which plays at the MCI Center. Ticket prices range from $10 to $150.

You can buy tickets at the MCI Center at 6th and F Streets or through TicketMaster.

Polo

A scenic one-hour drive from downtown, in the heart of Virginia horse country, is the **Great Meadow Polo Club** (✉ 5089 Old Tavern Rd., Plains, VA, ☎ 540/253–5156), where arena polo—a smaller-scale, more fan-friendly version of the hockey-on-horses pastime—is played each Friday night from June 2 to September 1. Games start at 7 PM, weather permitting, but many arrive early to people-watch and to tailgate, both of which are at least as important to the polo culture as the competition. Admission is $15 per carload.

Soccer

D.C. United (✉ RFK Stadium, 2400 E. Capitol St. SE, ☎ 202/547–3134; 202/432–SEAT TicketMaster) is consistently one of the best Major League Soccer (U.S. pro soccer) teams. International matches are often played on the grass field, now dedicated exclusively to soccer play. Games are April through September. You can buy tickets, which range from $12 to $37, at the RFK Stadium ticket office or through Ticket-Master.

Representing D.C. in the the professional women's soccer league—the WUSA—the **Washington Freedom** (✉ RFK Stadium, 2400 E. Capitol St. SE, ☎ 202/547–3134; 202/432–SEAT TicketMaster) features some of the players from the U.S. Olympic and World Cup teams. The Freedom plays at RFK Stadium April through August. Tickets range from $12 to $37 and are available at the RFK Stadium ticket office or through TicketMaster.

6 SHOPPING

From vinyl microminis to power suits, from karma beads to diamonds, Washington has a variety of merchandise for shoppers of all political stripes. There are both clean-cut and funky shopping districts in the city, as well as some stalwart department stores and small malls; suburban malls have the well-known department stores. On the discount scene, several major outlet centers are within a 45-minute drive.

By Deborah
Papier

Updated by
Robin
Dougherty

AFRICAN MASKS LIKE THOSE that inspired Picasso; kitchenware as objets d'art; bargains on apparel by Christian Dior, Hugo Boss, and Burberry; paisley scarves from India; American and European antiques; books of every description; handicrafts from almost two dozen Native American tribes; music boxes by the thousands; busts of U.S. presidents; textiles by the score; fine leather goods—all this and more can be found in the nation's capital.

Discriminating shoppers can find satisfaction at Filene's Basement (the Boston-based fashion discounter) or at upscale malls on the city's outskirts. Many of the smaller one-of-a-kind shops have survived urban renewal, the number of designer boutiques is on the rise, and interesting specialty shops and minimalls can be found all over town. Weekdays, downtown street vendors offer a funky mix of jewelry; brightly patterned ties; buyer-beware watches; sunglasses; and African-inspired clothing, accessories, and art. Of course, T-shirts and Capital City souvenirs are always in plentiful supply, especially on the streets ringing *the* Mall.

Store hours vary greatly, so it's best to call ahead. In general, Georgetown stores are open late and on Sunday; stores downtown that cater to office workers close at 6 PM and may not be open at all on weekends. Some stores extend their hours on Thursday. Sales tax is 6%, and major credit cards and traveler's checks are accepted virtually everywhere. Each shop's listing below includes the nearest Metro station, although some may be as far as a 15- to 20-minute walk; we do not list Metro stops for the few stores that have no Metro within walking distance.

Blitz Tours

With so many historical and cultural sights in D.C., you may find yourself struggling to fit everything in. To maximize your precious shopping hours, consider following one of these three itineraries or, if you're a power shopper, a combination thereof. If you'd rather work in some shopping with your sightseeing, note that the stores throughout the chapter are organized by neighborhood for easy planning.

Clothing and Antiques

When it comes to fashion, **Georgetown** is the place to go. You might want to start at 2000 Pennsylvania Avenue, a cluster of clothing stores and eateries just a few blocks from the Foggy Bottom Metro. From the Metro it's a 10- to 15-minute walk: cross Washington Circle and head up Pennsylvania Avenue (the numbered cross streets will be going up) to M Street, where Georgetown begins with a row of antiques shops. Wisconsin Avenue—where you can find designer boutiques as well as trendy, youth-oriented retailers—intersects M Street. Fortify yourself at one of the area's many restaurants before heading to **upper Wisconsin Avenue** on the D.C.-Maryland border. The bus, which runs every 7–10 minutes, will take you here (or back downtown) for $1.10, or you can hop in a cab. Upscale merchants such as Saks, Cartier, and Tiffany are located at the northern reaches of this neighborhood. Two midsize malls, Mazza Gallerie and Chevy Chase Pavilion, contain a wealth of clothing shops, ranging from Ann Taylor to Talbots and Neiman Marcus. Filene's Basement and T. J. Maxx offer brand-name bargains, and Lord & Taylor is right around the corner on Western Ave. Book and music browsers may want to stop in at Border's. When you're done, the convenient Friendship Heights Metro on the Red Line will bring you back into the city.

Markets

A few blocks from the Metro stop of the same name, Eastern Market in **Capitol Hill** offers an eclectic array of culinary delights indoors and the wares of artists and artisans outdoors. The weekend flea market presents nostalgia by the crateful, and vendors are willing to negotiate prices. Open every Sunday from March through December, the **Georgetown** flea market—at the intersection of 34th Street and Wisconsin Avenue NW—has a well-deserved reputation as an antiquer's heaven. As a result, however, prices tend to be higher here than elsewhere. Come early in the morning for the best finds. **Takoma Park,** on the Metro's Red Line, has an excellent weekend farmers' market in the warmer months. Seasonal street festivals with vendors and musical performances complement the area's cluster of quaint shops, which are open year-round.

Retro and Eclectic Finds

Across the street from the Woodley Park Metro you'll find a shop or two selling original works of art, antiques, and vintage jewelry. From here walk to the corner of Connecticut Avenue and Calvert Street. Turn left and cross the Duke Ellington Bridge—which offers a great view of forested Rock Creek Park—into **Adams-Morgan,** where there are one-of-a-kind ethnic jewelry shops, fun restaurants, vintage-clothing stores, and hip boutiques. Shop your way down 18th Street to Florida Avenue. Turn left to walk toward **U Street,** where more vintage clothing and antique furniture await. Or turn right and walk to Connecticut Avenue. A left turn will lead you downhill to **Dupont Circle** and its assortment of funky book, music, and gift shops.

Adams-Morgan

Scattered among the dozens of Latin, Ethiopian, and Caribbean restaurants in this most bohemian of Washington neighborhoods are a score of eccentric shops. If quality is what you seek, **Adams-Morgan** is a minefield; tread cautiously. Still, for the bargain hunter it's great fun. If bound for a specific shop, you may wish to call ahead to verify hours. Adams-Morganites are often not clock-watchers, although you can be sure a weekend afternoon stroll will find a good representation of the shops open and a few hours of great browsing. ⊠ *18th St. NW, between Columbia Rd. and Florida Ave. Metro: Woodley Park or Dupont Circle.*

Specialty Stores

ANTIQUES AND COLLECTIBLES

Chenonceau Antiques. The mostly American 19th- and 20th-century pieces on this shop's two floors were selected by a buyer with an exquisite eye. Merchandise includes beautiful 19th-century paisley scarves from India and Scotland, and 1920s glass lamps. ⊠ *2314 18th St. NW,* ☎ *202/667–1651. Closed weekdays. Metro: Woodley Park.*
Miss Pixie's. Two levels of well-chosen collectibles include gorgeous parasols and umbrellas, antique home furnishings, glass- and silverware, vintage clothes, and hardwood bed frames. The low prices should keep your attention. ⊠ *1810 Adams Mill Rd. NW,* ☎ *202/232–8171. Metro: Woodley Park.*

BOOKS

Idle Time Books. This used bookstore sells "rare to medium rare" books with plenty of meaty titles in all genres, especially out-of-print literature. ⊠ *2410 18th St. NW,* ☎ *202/232–4774. Metro: Woodley Park.*
Yawa. Featuring a large collection of African and African-American fiction and nonfiction, magazines, and children's books, Yawa also sells ethnic jewelry, crafts, and greeting cards. ⊠ *2206 18th St. NW,* ☎ *202/ 483–6805. Metro: Woodley Park.*

HOME FURNISHINGS

Skynear and Company. The owners of this extravagant shop travel the world to find the unusual. Their journeys have yielded a treasure-trove of rich textiles, furniture, and home accessories—all for the art of living. ✉ 2122 18th St. NW, ☎ 202/797–7160. Metro: Dupont Circle.

MEN'S AND WOMEN'S CLOTHING

Kobos. Anyone looking to add traditional ethnic dress to their wardrobe may appreciate this shop's rainbow of clothing and accessories, all imported from West Africa. ✉ 2444 18th St. NW, ☎ 202/332–9580. Metro: Woodley Park.

Niagara. Tucked inside the DC CD music store, this compact boutique offers ultrahip vintage and contemporary clothes. ✉ 2423 18th St. NW, ☎ 202/332–7474. Closed Mon.–Tues. Metro: Woodley Park.

MUSIC

DC CD. The club crowd loves this upstart music store, attracted by late hours and a wide selection of indie, rock, hip-hop, alternative, and soul. The knowledgeable staff often opens packages, allowing customers to listen before they buy. ✉ 2423 18th St. NW, ☎ 202/588–1810. Metro: Woodley Park.

SHOES

Shake Your Booty. Trend-conscious Washingtonians come here for modish leather boots and platform shoes. ✉ 2324 18th St. NW, ☎ 202/518–8205. Closed Tues. Metro: Woodley Park.

WOMEN'S CLOTHING

Khismet Wearable Art Showroom. Owner Millée Spears fills her colorful shop with traditional garments from West Africa as well as her own original designs. Spears, who lived in Ghana, uses ethnic-print fabrics to create garments that are suitable for both work and an evening out and will custom design if desired. ✉ 1800 Belmont Rd. NW, ☎ 202/234–7778. ☉ Open weekends and by appointment. Metro: Dupont Circle.

Capitol Hill/Eastern Market

As the Capitol Hill area has become gentrified, unique shops and boutiques have sprung up, many clustered around the redbrick structure known as **Eastern Market.** Inside are produce and meat counters, plus the Market Five art gallery; outside are a farmers' market (on Saturday) and a flea market (on weekends). Along 7th Street you'll find a number of small shops, selling everything from art books to handwoven rugs to antiques and knickknacks. ✉ 7th and C Sts. SE. Metro: Eastern Market, Union Station, or Capitol South.

Mall

Union Station. This delightful shopping enclave, resplendent with marble floors and gilded, vaulted ceilings, is nestled inside a working train station. You'll find several familiar retailers, including Jones New York, Aerosole, Swatch, and Ann Taylor, as well as a bookstore and a multiplex cinema. The east hall, reminiscent of London's Covent Garden, is filled with vendors of expensive and ethnic wares in open stalls. Christmas is an especially pleasant time to shop here. ✉ Massachusetts Ave. NE near N. Capitol St., ☎ 202/371–9441. Metro: Union Station.

Specialty Stores

ANTIQUES AND COLLECTIBLES

Antiques on the Hill. This store has the feel of an old thrift shop where *nothing* is ever thrown away. From floor to roof, knickknacks of every kind fill the shelves. The center of the floor is filled with furniture, and light fixtures hang from every available spot on the ceiling. ✉ *701 N. Carolina Ave. SE,* ☎ *202/543–1819. Closed Mon. Metro: Eastern Market.*

BOOKS

Bird-in-Hand Bookstore & Gallery. This quirky store specializes in books on art and design and also carries exhibition catalogs. ✉ *323 7th St. SE,* ☎ *202/543–0744. Closed Sun.–Mon. Metro: Eastern Market.*

Capital Hill Books. Pop into this inviting store to browse through a wonderful collection of out-of-print history books and modern first editions. ✉ *657 C St. SE,* ☎ *202/544–1621. Metro: Eastern Market.*

Fairy Godmother. This store specializes in books for youngsters, from infancy through young adulthood. It also sells puppets, toys, craft sets, and audiotapes for those long summer-vacation car rides. ✉ *319 7th St. SE,* ☎ *202/547–5474. Metro: Eastern Market.*

Trover Books. Newshounds can come here to find the latest political volumes and out-of-town newspapers. ✉ *221 Pennsylvania Ave. SE,* ☎ *202/547–2665. Metro: Capitol South.*

CRAFTS AND GIFTS

Appalachian Spring. Appalachian Spring's two Washington stores (*see also* Georgetown, *below*) sell traditional and contemporary American-made crafts, including quilts, jewelry, weavings, pottery, and blown glass. ✉ *Union Station,* ☎ *202/682–0505. Metro: Union Station.*

Silk Road/Woven History. These connected stores sell handmade treasures from small villages around the world. Silk Road sells home furnishings, gifts, clothing, and accessories made in mountain communities in South America and Asia as well as such contemporary items as aromatherapy candles from not-so-rural Greenwich Village in New York. Woven History's rugs are made the old-fashioned way, with vegetable dyes and hand-spun wool. ✉ *311–315 7th St. SE,* ☎ *202/543–1705. Metro: Eastern Market.*

FOOD AND WINE

Schneider's of Capitol Hill. Specializing in fine wines, this Capitol Hill shop tempts with myriad international wines and spirits. ✉ *300 Massachusetts Ave. NE,* ☎ *202/543–9330. Closed Sun. Metro: Union Station.*

WOMEN'S CLOTHING

Forecast. If you favor classic, contemporary styles, Forecast should be in your future. It sells silk sweaters and wool blends in solid, muted tones that won't quickly fall out of fashion. ✉ *218 7th St. SE,* ☎ *202/ 547–7337. Closed Mon. Metro: Eastern Market.*

Downtown

The domain of the city's many office workers, downtown tends to shut down at 5 PM sharp with the exception of the larger department stores. Old **downtown** is where you'll find Hecht's and sundry specialty stores; established chains such as Ann Taylor and Gap tend to be concentrated near Farragut Square. Avoid the lunch-hour crowds to ensure more leisurely shopping. ✉ *North of Pennsylvania Ave. between 7th and 18th Sts., up to Connecticut Ave. below L St. Metro: Archives/Navy Memorial, Farragut North and West, Foggy Bottom, Gallery Place, McPherson Square, or Metro Center.*

Department Stores

Hecht's. Bright and spacious, this Washington favorite has sensible groupings and attractive displays that make shopping easy on both the feet and the eyes. The clothing sold ranges from conservative to trendy, with the men's department assuming increasing importance. Cosmetics, lingerie, and housewares are also strong departments. ⊠ *12th and G Sts. NW,* ☎ *202/628–6661. Metro: Metro Center.*

Malls

Old Post Office Pavilion. This handsome shopping center, located in an historic 19th-century post office building, hasn't grown into the popular spot that developers hoped it would two decades ago. Plans are afoot to convert the space into a hotel or other enterprise, but until that happens, you can enjoy about a dozen food vendors and 17 shops. An observation deck in the building's clock tower offers an excellent view of the city. ⊠ *1100 Pennsylvania Ave.,* ☎ *202/289–4224. Metro: Federal Triangle.*

Shops at National Place. The Shops takes up three levels, one devoted entirely to food stands. Although mainly youth-oriented (this is a good place to drop off teenagers weary of the Smithsonian and more in the mood to buy T-shirts), Perfumania and clothing stores such as Casual Corner and August Max have branches here, too. Those in search of presidential souvenirs may find the White House Gift Shop quite handy. ⊠ *13th and F Sts. NW,* ☎ *202/662–1250. Metro: Metro Center.*

Specialty Stores

BOOKS

Borders. In addition to a large selection of books and magazines, Borders also sells recorded music, has a coffee bar, and regularly presents free films and jazz performances. ⊠ *1801 K St. NW (entrance at 18th and L Sts. NW),* ☎ *202/466–4999. Metro: Farragut North.*

Chapters. This "literary bookstore" eschews cartoon collections and diet guides, filling its shelves with serious contemporary fiction, classics, and poetry. The store hosts author readings regularly, so check the schedule if you're spending a few days in town. ⊠ *1512 K St. NW,* ☎ *202/347–5495. Metro: McPherson Square.*

Olsson's Books & Records. The store stocks a large and varied collection of books and a good selection of classical and folk records, tapes, and CDs. Hours vary significantly from store to store. In addition to the downtown locations, there are branches in Dupont Circle (⊠ *1307 19th St. NW,* ☎ *202/785–1133)* and Georgetown (⊠ *1239 Wisconsin Ave. NW,* ☎ *202/338–9544).* ⊠ *1200 F St. NW,* ☎ *202/347–3686; Metro: Metro Center.* ⊠ *418 7th St. NW,* ☎ *202/638–7610; Metro: Archives/Navy Memorial.*

CRAFTS AND GIFTS

Al's Magic Shop. For professional magicians, aspiring kids, and amateur pranksters, Al's has offered a full line of cards, tricks, magic wands, and mind games for more than 55 years. Proprietor Al Cohen counts Doug Henning and David Copperfield among his customers, although it's the regulars who ask to see him perform. ⊠ *1012 Vermont Ave. NW,* ☎ *202/789–2800. Metro: McPherson Square.*

Discovery Channel Store. Shopping is just one of the many activities at this half store, half museum. You can also play high-tech interactive games, walk through the fuselage of a B-25 bomber, or stand awestruck before a 42-ft cast of the world's largest T-rex. Items for sale include everything from telescopes and science kits to authentic amber jewelry. After browsing, consider slipping into the on-site theater to see the movie *Destination DC* before heading out on the store's 1½-hour "Discover Historic Downtown D.C." tour, available weekends from March to November for $8 per person. ⊠ *601 F St. NW,* ☎ *202/639–0908. Metro: Gallery Place/Chinatown.*

Fahrney's. What started out as a pen bar and repair shop in 1929—a place to fill your fountain pen before setting out for work—is today, a wonderland for anyone who loves a good writing instrument, offering pens in silver, gold, and lacquer by the world's leading manufacturers. ⊠ *1317 F St. NW, ☎ 202/628–9525. Metro: Metro Center.*

Indian Craft Shop. Handicrafts, such as jewelry, pottery, sand paintings, weavings, and baskets from more than 45 Native American tribes—including Navajo, Pueblo, Zuni, Cherokee, Lakota, and Seminole—are at your fingertips here . . . as long as you have a photo ID to enter the federal building. Items range from inexpensive (as little as $5) jewelry on up to collector-quality art pieces at more than $1,000. ⊠ *Dept. of Interior, 1849 C St. NW, Room 1023, ☎ 202/208–4056. Closed weekends. Metro: Farragut West.*

Music Box Center. Listen to a total of 500 melodies on more than 1,500 music boxes at this exquisite—and unusual—specialty store. The latest irresistible item is a Harry Potter music box that plays "That's What Friends Are For." ⊠ *1920 I St. NW, ☎ 202/783–9399. Metro: Farragut West.*

FOOD AND WINE

Dean & Deluca. This outlet of the popular New York gourmet market features coffees and teas, chocolates, and other good reasons to take a break from shopping. ⊠ *1299 Pennsylvania Ave. NW, ☎ 202/628–8155. Metro: Metro Center.*

JEWELRY

Pampillonia Jewelers. Here you'll find traditional designs in 18-karat gold and platinum as well as eye-catching contemporary designs. The selection for men is particularly good. ⊠ *1213 Connecticut Ave. NW, ☎ 202/628–6305. Metro: Farragut North.*

Tiny Jewel Box. Despite its name, this shop offers three floors of precious and semi-precious wares, including works by well-known designers and unique gifts. ⊠ *1147 Connecticut Ave. NW, ☎ 202/393–2747. Metro: Farragut North.*

MEN'S AND WOMEN'S CLOTHING

Britches of Georgetown. The larger of two Washington branches (the other is in Georgetown), this store has a wide selection of traditional but trend-conscious men's clothing. In addition to the store's private label, you'll find menswear by St. Andrews and Hickey Freeman. ⊠ *1776 K St. NW, ☎ 202/347–8994. Metro: Farragut North.*

Brooks Brothers. This venerable clothier has been issuing its discreet "Brooks Brother, Makers" label since 1818. Men with classic tastes—grey wool suits; navy blazers; chinos; dignified formal wear; and of course the original, glorious, 5-trillion thread count cotton dress shirt—can always take comfort here. And these days, so can women, with a selection of classic casual and work clothes for her. ⊠ *1201 Connecticut Ave. NW, ☎ 202/659–4650. Metro: Farragut North.*

Burberry. Burberry made its reputation with the still-popular trench coat, but this British company also manufactures traditional men's and women's indoor apparel and accessories. ⊠ *1155 Connecticut Ave. NW, ☎ 202/463–3000. Metro: Farragut North.*

J. Press. Like its flagship store, founded in Connecticut in 1902 as a custom shop for Yale University, this Washington outlet is a resolutely traditional clothier: Shetland and Irish wool sport coats are a specialty. ⊠ *1801 L St. NW, ☎ 202/857–0120. Metro: Farragut North.*

REJUVENATION

Andre Chreky Salon. Housed in an elegantly renovated, four-story Victorian town house, this salon offers complete services—hair, nails, facials, waxing, massage, and makeup. And because it's a favorite of the Washington elite, you might just overhear a tidbit or two on who's going to what black-tie function with whom. Adjacent whirlpool pedicure chairs allow two friends to get pampered simultaneously. While you splurge on a treatment, enjoy complimentary espresso and pastries (mornings) or wine and live piano music (evenings). ⊠ *1604 K St, NW,* ☎ *202/293–9393. Metro: Farragut North.*

The Healthy Back Store. To get the knots out quickly, stop here for a seated 15-, 20-, or 30-minute shoulder rub by a certified massage therapist. The shop also sells such products as handheld back-rub aids to get to those hard-to-reach spots and ergonomic chairs designed to release back stress and relieve aches and pains. ⊠ *1741 14th St. NW,* ☎ *202/393–2225. Closed weekends. Metro: Metro Center.*

Victoria's Day Spa. What this spa lacks in fancy amenities it more than makes up for in homespun appeal and comparatively low prices. Special services include paraffin manicures, pedicures, and body wraps as well as seaweed masks and body wraps. ⊠ *1926 I St. NW,* ☎ *202/254–0442. Metro: Farragut West.*

SHOES

Church's. Church's is a top-notch English company whose handmade men's shoes are noted for their comfort and durability. ⊠ *1820 L St. NW,* ☎ *202/296–3366. Metro: Farragut North.*

Parade of Shoes. The house label at this discount women's shoe store features knockoffs of designer labels and classically styled Italian imports. During seasonal clearances, shoes are often marked down as low as $20 a pair. ⊠ *1020 Connecticut Ave. NW,* ☎ *202/872–8581. Metro: Farragut North.*

WOMEN'S CLOTHING

Ann Taylor. Young professional women head here for classy yet trendy fashions, including accessories and a small but excellent selection of shoes. Other locations include Mazza Gallerie (⊠ 5300 Wisconsin Ave., ☎ 202/244–1940), Georgetown Park (⊠ 3222 M St. NW, ☎ 202/338–5290), and Union Station (⊠ Massachusetts Ave. NE, near N. Capitol St., ☎ 202/371–8010). ⊠ *1720 K St. NW,* ☎ *202/466–3544. Metro: Farragut West.*

Chanel Boutique. The Willard Hotel annex is the place to find handbags, perfume, couture fashions, and other goodies from this legendary house of fashion. ⊠ *1455 Pennsylvania Ave. NW,* ☎ *202/638–5055. Metro: Metro Center.*

Earl Allen. Earl Allen offers conservative but distinctive dresses and sportswear, wearable art, and one-of-a-kind items—much of it made exclusively for this store. ⊠ *1825 I St. NW,* ☎ *202/466–3437. Closed weekends. Metro: Farragut West.*

Rizik Bros. This Washington institution offers both designer clothing and expert advice. The sales staff is trained to find just the right style from their inventory. Take the elevator up from the northwest corner of Connecticut Avenue and L Street. ⊠ *1100 Connecticut Ave. NW,* ☎ *202/223–4050. Metro: Farragut North.*

Dupont Circle

You might call **Dupont Circle** a younger, hipper version of Georgetown—almost as pricey and not quite as well kept, with more apartment buildings than houses. Its many restaurants, offbeat shops, and specialty book and record stores lend it a distinctive, cosmopolitan air. The street scene here is more urban than Georgetown's, with bike messengers and chess aficionados filling up the park while shoppers frequent the many coffee shops and stores. ⊠ *Connecticut Ave. between M and S Sts. Metro: Dupont Circle.*

Specialty Stores

ANTIQUES AND COLLECTIBLES

Geoffrey Diner Gallery. This shop is a must for hard-core antiques shoppers on the hunt for 19th-century American wares. ⊠ *1730 21st St. NW,* ☎ *202/483–5005. Metro: Dupont Circle.*

Marston Luce. The focus is on French country furniture, but Marston Luce also carries home and garden accessories, including weather vanes, stone carvings from building facades, and decorative cast-iron work. ⊠ *1314 21st St. NW,* ☎ *202/775–9460. Metro: Dupont Circle.*

BOOKS

Kramerbooks. This cozy bookstore was well loved even before its management refused to reveal Monica Lewinsky's book purchases to the independent prosecutor. Open 24 hours on weekends, it shares space with a café that has late-night dining and weekend entertainment; be prepared for a smoke-filled room. The stock is small but well selected. ⊠ *1517 Connecticut Ave. NW,* ☎ *202/387–1400. Metro: Dupont Circle.*

Lambda Rising. Dupont Circle's gay bookstore is a major player in the area, featuring novels by gay and lesbian writers and other books of interest to the gay community. ⊠ *1625 Connecticut Ave. NW,* ☎ *202/ 462–6969. Metro: Dupont Circle.*

Lammas Books. This store offers a selection of music by women, as well as women's and lesbian literature. ⊠ *1607 17th St. NW,* ☎ *202/ 775–8218. Metro: Dupont Circle.*

Mystery Books. Mystery lovers are bound to drool when they see this shop's selection of detective, crime, suspense, and spy fiction—the richest in town. Gift basket delivery is available to any place in the United States. ⊠ *1715 Connecticut Ave. NW,* ☎ *202/483–1600; 800/955– 2279 gift and book orders. Metro: Dupont Circle.*

Second Story Books. A mecca for bibliophiles that encourages hours of browsing, this used-books and -records emporium stays open late. ⊠ *2000 P St. NW,* ☎ *202/659–8884. Metro: Dupont Circle.*

CHILDREN'S CLOTHING

Kid's Closet. If filling a little one's closet is on your list, stop here for quality contemporary children's clothing, shoes, and toys. ⊠ *1226 Connecticut Ave. NW,* ☎ *202/429–9247. Metro: Dupont Circle (south exit).*

CRAFTS AND GIFTS

Beadazzled. This appealing shop stocks a dazzling array of ready-to-string beads and jewelry as well as books on crafts history and techniques. ⊠ *1507 Connecticut Ave. NW,* ☎ *202/265–2323. Metro: Dupont Circle.*

KITCHENWARE

Coffee & the Works. Coffee and tea lovers can find every amenity in this charmingly cluttered shop, from flavored brews to colorful ceramic pots. Also on hand is an eclectic assortment of kitchen gadgets, magnets, and other paraphernalia. ⊠ *1627 Connecticut Ave. NW,* ☎ *202/ 483–8050. Metro: Dupont Circle.*

SHOES

Shoe Scene. The fashionable, moderately priced shoes for women found here are imported from Europe. ⊠ *1330 Connecticut Ave. NW,* ☎ *202/659–2194. Metro: Dupont Circle.*

WOMEN'S CLOTHING

Betsy Fisher. Catering to women of all ages in search of contemporary styles, this store stocks one-of-a-kind accessories, duds, and jewelry. ⊠ *1224 Connecticut Ave. NW,* ☎ *202/785–1975. Metro: Dupont Circle (south exit).*

Secondi. The city's finest consignment shop, Secondi's well-chosen selection of women's designer and casual clothing, accessories, and shoes represents labels such as Donna Karan, Prada, Ann Taylor, and Coach. ✉ *1702 Connecticut Ave. NW,* ☎ *202/667–1122. Metro: Dupont Circle.*

Georgetown

Georgetown remains Washington's favorite shopping area. This is the capital's center for famous citizens, as well as for restaurants, bars, night-clubs, and trendy shops. Although Georgetown is not on a subway line (the nearest Metro, Foggy Bottom, is a 10- to 15-minute walk from the shops) and parking is difficult at best, people still flock here. National chains are beginning to overtake the specialty shops that first gave the district its allure, but the historic neighborhood is still charming, and its street scene lively. In addition to housing tony antiques, elegant crafts, and high-style shoe and clothing boutiques, Georgetown offers wares that attract local college students and young people: books, music, and fashions from familiar names like Banana Republic and Urban Outfitters. ✉ *Intersection of Wisconsin Ave. and M St.; most stores lie to the east and west on M St. and to the north on Wisconsin. Metro: Foggy Bottom.*

Mall

Shops at Georgetown Park. Near the hub of the Georgetown shopping district, at the intersection of Wisconsin Avenue and M Street, is this posh tri-level mall, designed like a Victorian ice-cream parlor inside. The pricey clothing and accessory boutiques and the ubiquitous chain stores (such as Victoria's Secret), as well as the upscale toy store FAO Schwarz, draw international visitors in droves. Next door is a branch of Dean & Deluca, New York's premier gourmet food store. ✉ *3222 M St. NW,* ☎ *202/298–5577. Metro: Foggy Bottom.*

Specialty Stores

ANTIQUES AND COLLECTIBLES

Georgetown Antiques Center. The center, in a Victorian town house, has two dealers who share space: Cherub Gallery specializes in Art Nouveau and Art Deco, and Michael Getz Antiques sells fireplace equipment and silverware. ✉ *2918 M St. NW,* ☎ *202/337–2224 Cherub Gallery; 202/338–3811 Michael Getz Antiques. Metro: Foggy Bottom.*

Miller & Arney Antiques. English, American, and European furniture and accessories from the 17th, 18th, and early 19th centuries give Miller & Arney Antiques a museum-gallery air. Asian porcelain adds splashes of color. ✉ *1737 Wisconsin Ave. NW,* ☎ *202/338–2369. Metro: Foggy Bottom.*

Old Print Gallery. Here you'll find the capital's largest collection of old prints, with a focus on maps and 19th-century decorative prints (including Washingtoniana). ✉ *1220 31st St. NW,* ☎ *202/965–1818. Closed Sun. Metro: Foggy Bottom.*

Opportunity Shop of the Christ Child Society. This Georgetown thrift store sells second-hand clothing and good-quality household goods. Consigned fine antiques, crystal, and silver at moderate prices are available on the second floor. ✉ *1427 Wisconsin Ave. NW,* ☎ *202/333–6635. Closed Sun.–Mon. Metro: Foggy Bottom.*

Susquehanna. With three rooms upstairs, four rooms downstairs, and a garden full of benches, urns, and tables, Susquehanna is the largest antiques shop in Georgetown. Paintings cover every inch of wall space, though the shop specializes in American and English furniture. ✉ *3216 O St. NW,* ☎ *202/333–1511. Metro: Foggy Bottom.*

BOOKS

Barnes & Noble. This expansive three-story chain store, housed in a former warehouse, has a coffee bar along with countless books, magazines, and CDs from around the world. ⊠ *3040 M St. NW,* ☎ *202/ 965–9880. Metro: Foggy Bottom.*

Bridge Street Books. This charming bookshop on antiques row stocks a good selection of literature and fine arts books. ⊠ *2814 Pennsylvania Ave. NW,* ☎ *202/965–5200. Metro: Foggy Bottom.*

Old Forest Bookshop. Small and cozy, this used bookshop specializes in art, literature, and history. It also carries a small selection of jazz, blues, and classical vinyl records. ⊠ *3145 Dumbarton St. NW,* ☎ *202/ 965–3842. Metro: Foggy Bottom.*

CRAFTS AND GIFTS

American Studio. One-of-a-kind functional and nonfunctional pieces fill this wonderful place—tea kettles, corkscrews, glassware, and jewelry—all by international designers. ⊠ *2906 M St. NW,* ☎ *202/965– 3273. Metro: Foggy Bottom.*

Appalachian Spring. The largest of this chain's four outlets (there are two suburban shops and another one in Union Station), Appalachian Spring has a wide selection of traditional and contemporary American-made crafts: quilts, jewelry, weavings, pottery, and blown glass. ⊠ *1415 Wisconsin Ave. NW,* ☎ *202/337–5780.*

HOME FURNISHINGS

A Mano. The store's name is Italian for "by hand," and it lives up to its name, stocking colorful hand-painted ceramics, hand-dyed tablecloths, blown glass stemware, and other home accessories by Italian and French artisans. ⊠ *1677 Wisconsin Ave. NW,* ☎ *202/298–7200.*

Little Caledonia. Nine rooms are crammed with thousands of unusual and imported items for the home. Candles, cards, fabrics, bedside tables, lamps, and china round out the stock of decorative home accessories. ⊠ *1419 Wisconsin Ave. NW,* ☎ *202/333–4700.*

JEWELRY

Blanca Flor. The specialty here is elegant, high-quality silver jewelry, mostly from Mexico. ⊠ *3066 M St. NW,* ☎ *202/944–5051. Metro: Foggy Bottom.*

LEATHER GOODS

Coach Store. Coach carries a complete (and expensive) line of well-made leather handbags, briefcases, belts, and wallets. ⊠ *1214 Wisconsin Ave. NW,* ☎ *202/342–1772. Metro: Foggy Bottom.*

MEN'S AND WOMEN'S CLOTHING

Britches of Georgetown. The smaller of two branches, with the other downtown, this Britches carries an extensive selection of traditional but trend-conscious designs in natural fibers for men. ⊠ *1247 Wisconsin Ave. NW,* ☎ *202/338–3330. Metro: Foggy Bottom.*

Commander Salamander. This funky outpost sells trendy clothes for the alternative set—punk kids and ravers. Sifting through the assortment of leather, chains, toys, and candy-color makeup is as much entertainment as it is shopping. The store is open till 10 PM on weekends. ⊠ *1420 Wisconsin Ave. NW,* ☎ *202/337–2265. Metro: Foggy Bottom.*

REJUVENATION

efx SPA. The retail space up front sells soaps, lotions, cosmetics, and nail polishes in trendy colors. Behind the glass door, the spa offers an array of services in its "skin gym": facials, waxing, massage, and oxygen treatments. Efx's Dupont Circle location also offers products, but no spa services (⊠ 1745 Connecticut Ave. NW, ☎ 202/462–1300). ⊠ *3059 M St. NW,* ☎ *202/965–1300. Metro: Foggy Bottom.*

L'Occitane. This French chain is known for its fine botanical fragrances, soaps, and toiletries ranging from classic lavender, rose, and vanilla scents to the more exotic lotus flower and green tea. ⊠ *3106 M St. NW,* ☎ *202/337–6001. Metro: Foggy Bottom.*

Roche Salon. On the Georgetown waterfront, this salon showcases owner Dennis Roche, who has been featured in *Vogue, Harper's Bazaar,* and *Glamour* magazines. Many believe he is the city's best source for the latest hair-coloring techniques. ⊠ *3050 K St. NW,* ☎ *202/775–0003.*

Sephora. Better than any department store perfume or cosmetic counter, this candy store of beauty products offers hundreds of fine fragrances, bath products, and cosmetics from all over the world. Sephora also carries its own line of beauty products, all exquisitely packaged and quite affordable. The black-clad salespeople are pleasantly low-key. ⊠ *3065 M St. NW,* ☎ *202/338–5644. Metro: Foggy Bottom.*

SHOES

Prince & Princess. This retailer carries a full line of men's shoes and boots, including Timberland and Sebago. For women, the selection includes strappy party shoes, chunky platforms, and stylish pumps from designers such as Via Spiga and Nine West. ⊠ *1400 Wisconsin Ave. NW,* ☎ *202/337–4211. Metro: Foggy Bottom.*

Shake Your Booty. The Georgetown location of this Adams-Morgan venue carries trendy, must-have footwear for women who believe that shoes, not diamonds, are a girl's best friend. ⊠ *3225 M St. NW,* ☎ *202/333–6524.*

WOMEN'S CLOTHING

Betsey Johnson. The fanciful frocks here are favorites of the young and restless. ⊠ *1319 Wisconsin Ave. NW,* ☎ *202/338–4090. Metro: Foggy Bottom.*

Phoenix. Here you'll find contemporary clothing in natural fibers by designers such as Eileen Fisher and Flax, as well as jewelry and art pieces (fine and folk) from Mexico. ⊠ *1514 Wisconsin Ave. NW,* ☎ *202/338–4404.*

U Street

In the '30s and '40s, **U Street** was known for its classy theaters and jazz clubs. After decades of decline following the 1968 riots, the neighborhood has been revitalized. Although the area is far from gentrified, U Street's mainstay is its devoted community, a mix of multiethnic young adults and older, working-class African-Americans. In 1997, the *Utne Reader* declared U Street one of the hippest neighborhoods in the country, and the label still applies. At night the neighborhood's club scene comes alive. During the day, the street scene is more laid-back, with more locals than tourists occupying the few lunch spots and distinctive array of shops. ⊠ *U St. between 12th and 17th Sts. Metro: U Street/Cardozo.*

Specialty Stores

ANTIQUES AND COLLECTIBLES

Good Wood. This friendly shop sells vintage and antique wood furniture—including wonderful 19th-century pieces—along with stained glass and other decorative items. ⊠ *1428 U St. NW,* ☎ *202/986–3640. Metro: U Street/Cardozo.*

Millennium. This eclectic shop offers a unique blend of housewares, clothing, records, books, and furniture—all of which it has dubbed "20th-century antiques." Depending on the week, you might find Bakelite silverware or an eight-track tape player. ⊠ *1528 U St. NW,* ☎ *202/483–1218. Metro: U Street/Cardozo.*

Weathered Classics. If your idea of a "weathered classic" is a 19th-century bed or dining room set, this is the place to go. ✉ *1517 U St. NW,* ☎ *202/238–0404. Metro: U Street/Cardozo.*

BOOKS

Sisterspace and Books. Sisterspace specializes in books written by and appealing to African-American women. In addition to titles by authors such as Iyanla Vanzant, Maya Angelou, and Toni Morrison, the store offers seminars on everything from money and health to spirituality and creative fulfillment. ✉ *1515 U St. NW,* ☎ *202/332–3433. Metro: U Street/Cardozo.*

HOME FURNISHINGS

Home Rule. At this upscale home-furnishings store, you might find unique kitchen cabinets or an eye-catching vanity for your bathroom. ✉ *1807 14th St. NW,* ☎ *202/797–5544. Metro: U Street/Cardozo.*
Zawadi. The name means "gift" in Swahili, but you may want to buy up the beautiful African art, home accessories, and jewelry for yourself. ✉ *1524 U St. NW,* ☎ *202/232–2214. Metro: U Street/Cardozo.*

MEN'S AND WOMEN'S CLOTHING

Meeps Fashionette. Catering to fans of true shabby-chic and campy glamour, this shop stocks a wide selection of vintage clothes from the '50s through the '80s. ✉ *1520 U St. NW,* ☎ *202/265–6546. Closed Mon.–Wed. Metro: U Street/Cardozo.*
Trade Secrets. The textured wool, velvet, and silk designs in African-inspired patterns sold here seem almost too pretty to wear. Almost. ✉ *1515 U St. NW, lower level,* ☎ *202/667–0634. Closed Mon. Metro: U Street/Cardozo.*

Wisconsin Avenue

A major shopping district, upper **Wisconsin Avenue** straddles the Maryland border. Between the malls, department stores, and chic, small boutiques, this area has everything you could want to buy. ✉ *Wisconsin Ave. between Jennifer St. NW and Western Ave. Metro: Friendship Heights.*

Department Stores

Filene's Basement. To really appreciate the bargains here, do some window-shopping in Mazza Gallerie before entering this store from the mall. In addition to big savings on men's and women's clothing by well-regarded designers such as Hugo Boss and Christian Dior, Filene's has discounts on shoes, perfume, housewares, and accessories. ✉ *Mazza Gallerie, 5300 Wisconsin Ave. NW,* ☎ *202/966–0208. Metro: Friendship Heights.*
Lord & Taylor. Lord & Taylor lets the competition be all things to all people while it focuses on classic men's, women's, and children's clothing by such designers as Anne Klein and Ralph Lauren. ✉ *5255 Western Ave. NW,* ☎ *202/362–9600. Metro: Friendship Heights.*
Neiman Marcus. If price is an object, this is definitely not the place to shop. Headquartered in Dallas, Neiman Marcus caters to customers who value quality above all. The carefully selected merchandise includes couture clothes, furs, precious jewelry, crystal, and silver. ✉ *Mazza Gallerie, 5300 Wisconsin Ave. NW,* ☎ *202/966–9700. Metro: Friendship Heights.*
Saks Fifth Avenue. Though technically just over the Maryland line, Saks is nonetheless a Washington institution. It has a wide selection of European and American couture clothes; other attractions are the shoe, jewelry, fur, and lingerie departments. ✉ *5555 Wisconsin Ave.,* ☎ *301/ 657–9000. Metro: Friendship Heights.*

Malls

Chevy Chase Pavilion. Across from Mazza Gallerie is the newer, similarly upscale Chevy Chase Pavilion. Its women's clothing stores range from Steilmann European Selection (which carries Karl Lagerfeld's sportier KL line) to Express. Specialty shops include Pottery Barn and Country Road Australia. ✉ *5335 Wisconsin Ave. NW,* ☎ *202/686–5335. Metro: Friendship Heights.*

Mazza Gallerie. The four-level Mazza Gallerie is anchored by the ritzy Neiman Marcus department store and the discount department store Filene's Basement. Other stores include Williams-Sonoma for kitchenware and Villeroy & Boch for housewares, as well as Ann Taylor, Pampillonia Jewelers, and Kron Chocolates. ✉ *5300 Wisconsin Ave. NW,* ☎ *202/966–6114. Metro: Friendship Heights.*

Specialty Stores

BOOKS

Politics and Prose. With a wide selection of topical novels and literary nonfiction as well as provocative author readings almost every night, this bookstore–coffeehouse lives up to its name. The nearest Metro is 15 minutes away. ✉ *5015 Connecticut Ave. NW,* ☎ *202/364–1919. Metro: Friendship Heights.*

Travel Books & Language. One of the largest specialty bookshops of its kind in the country, Travel Books & Language boasts an enormous stock of travel guides, cookbooks, travel narratives, maps, and language-study workbooks and audio tapes, not to mention an accommodating and knowledgeable staff. ✉ *4437 Wisconsin Ave. NW,* ☎ *202/237–1322. Metro: Tenleytown/American University.*

CHILDREN'S CLOTHING

Full of Beans. This boutique sells updated classic styles, mostly in natural fibers. Sizes range from infants to boys' size 10 and girls' size 14. ✉ *5502 Connecticut Ave. NW,* ☎ *202/362–8566.*

FOOD AND WINE

Calvert Woodley Liquors. This liquor store carries not only an excellent selection of wine and hard liquor, but also a wide range of cheese and other foods to go with your drink. ✉ *4339 Connecticut Ave. NW,* ☎ *202/966–4400. Metro: Van Ness–UDC.*

Rodman's Discount Foods and Appliances. The rare store that carries wine, cheese, and space heaters, Rodman's is a fascinating hybrid of K-Mart and Dean & Deluca. The appliances are downstairs, the imported peppers and chocolates upstairs. It's also a working drugstore, where you can have a prescription filled or pick up some sinus medicine, bath bubbles, or a pair of sunglasses. ✉ *5100 Wisconsin Ave. NW,* ☎ *202/363–3466. Metro: Friendship Heights.*

GIFTS

Wake Up Little Suzi. Clocks shaped like dogs and cats, silver jewelry, funky switch-plate covers, and idiosyncratic ceramics are all here in this boutique of whimsical yet useful gifts. ✉ *3409 Connecticut Ave. NW,* ☎ *202/244–0700. Metro: Cleveland Park.*

JEWELRY

Charles Schwartz & Son. This full-service jeweler specializes in precious stones in traditional and modern settings. Fine watches are also offered. ✉ *Mazza Gallerie, 5300 Wisconsin Ave. NW,* ☎ *202/363–5432. Metro: Friendship Heights.*

MEN'S AND WOMEN'S CLOTHING

Brooks Brothers. The oldest men's store in America, Brooks Brothers has sold traditional formal and casual clothing since 1818. It is the largest men's specialty store in the area and has a small women's department as well. ✉ *5504 Wisconsin Ave. NW,* ☎ *301/654–8202. Metro: Friendship Heights.*

Catch Can. Local shoppers come here for the great sales on comfortable clothing made from bright fabrics and ethnic-inspired prints. Visitors any time of year come for the selection of one-of-a-kind gifts for the house and closet, including stationery, furniture, and ceramics. ✉ *5516 Connecticut Ave. NW,* ☎ *202/686–5316.*

Micmac. At this gem of a boutique you'll find clothes by Issey Miyake and fab Arche shoes. Eye-catching displays make you want to buy one of everything. ✉ *5301 Wisconsin Ave. NW,* ☎ *202/362–6834. Metro: Friendship Heights.*

REJUVENATION

Georgette Klinger Skin Care Salon. The doyenne of spas, Georgette Klinger specializes in skin care but can also pamper you with a full range of services, from massage to manicures. Treatments are pricey, but regular patrons say they're well worth it. ✉ *5345 Wisconsin Ave. NW,* ☎ *202/686–8880. Metro: Friendship Heights.*

TOYS

Child's Play. Despite the name, toys are serious business in this shop. An attentive staff helps you sort through the large selection, which includes building toys, computer software, art supplies, and classic games. ✉ *5536 Connecticut Ave. NW,* ☎ *202/244–3602.*

Tree Top Toys. This store specializes in plush dolls, European toys, and children's books. ✉ *3301 New Mexico Ave. NW,* ☎ *202/244–3500.*

Maryland/Virginia

Although it's a bit of a trek, some of the best shopping is found on the outskirts of the city in Maryland and Virginia. Most malls are close to a Metro station, though a few are best reached by car. The Takoma Park area, on the D.C./Maryland border, offers a concentration of charming antiques, clothing, and gift shops. *By car: take George Washington Pkwy., I–495 (the Beltway).*

Malls and Outlets

City Place. The off-price Nordstrom Rack and other discount shops such as Burlington Coat Factory and Marshall's are clustered in this mall in downtown Silver Spring, a 20-minute ride on the Metro from downtown D.C. ✉ *8661 Colesville Rd., Silver Spring, MD,* ☎ *301/589–1091. Metro: Silver Spring.*

Fashion Centre at Pentagon City. Just across the river in Virginia, a 10-minute ride on the Metro from downtown, is this four-story mall (including a food court) with Macy's at one end and Nordstrom at the other. In between are such shops as Liz Claiborne and the Coach Store. ✉ *1100 S. Hayes St., Arlington, VA,* ☎ *703/415–2400. Metro: Pentagon City.*

Potomac Mills. This mile-long mall off I–95, 30 minutes by car from the District, bills itself as Virginia's most popular attraction. There are some 220 discount and outlet stores here, including Nordstrom Rack, T. J. Maxx, Saks Off Fifth, and Linens 'N Things. Swedish furniture giant IKEA is also here. ✉ *2700 Potomac Mills Circle, Woodbridge, VA,* ☎ *703/490–5948.*

Tysons Corner Center and Galleria at Tysons II. Anchored by Bloomingdale's and Nordstrom, Tysons Corner Center also houses 238 other retailers. Next door, the Galleria at Tysons II has 125 retailers, including Saks Fifth Avenue, Neiman Marcus, and Macy's. No matter when you go, be prepared to fight some of the area's heaviest traffic. *Tysons Corner Center:* ✉ *1961 Chain Bridge Rd.,* ☎ *703/893–9400. Galleria:* ✉ *2001 International Dr.,* ☎ *703/827–7730.*

White Flint Mall. The big stores at this upscale mall are Bloomingdale's and Lord & Taylor; other stores include the Coach Store, Sharper Image, and Eddie Bauer. A free shuttle bus is available from the Metro. ⊠ *11301 Rockville Pike, North Bethesda, MD,* ☎ *301/231–7467. Metro: White Flint.*

Specialty Stores

ANTIQUES AND COLLECTIBLES

Takoma Underground. Descend the stairs to find yourself in a treasure chest of vintage clothing, jewelry, books, collectibles, antique house-wares, and esoterica. ⊠ *7000 B Carroll Ave., Takoma, MD,* ☎ *301/ 270–6380. Metro: Takoma.*

CRAFTS AND GIFTS

Arise. Primarily a purveyor of Asian artifacts, antiques, and furniture, Arise also carries its own label of vibrant cotton and silk leisure cloth-ing, as well as an astounding collection of kimonos. ⊠ *6925 Willow St. NW,* ☎ *202/291–0770. Metro: Takoma.*

MEN'S AND WOMEN'S CLOTHING

Amano. Not to be confused with the gift shop A Mano, this laid-back boutique sells sophisticated, funky clothing that you can wear to work or relax in at home. Accessories include cloth briefcases, cartoon-char-acter lunchboxes, silk scarves, hats, shoes, and tie-dyed socks. ⊠ *7030 Carroll Ave., Takoma, MD,* ☎ *301/270–1140. Metro: Takoma.*
Glad Rags. This fun vintage clothing shop often features wacky sales. One sidewalk sale had customers layering like crazy since they could purchase everything they could put on all at once for a flat fee of $20. ⊠ *7306 Carroll Ave., Takoma, MD,* ☎ *301/891–6870.*

MUSICAL INSTRUMENTS

House of Musical Traditions. If you're looking for a dulcimer or a sitar, or want to learn the difference between bluegrass and blues guitar, this nationally regarded shop carries uncommon instruments as well as books and recordings. ⊠ *7040 Carroll Ave., Takoma, MD,* ☎ *301/270–9090.*

REJUVENATION

Jolie, the Day Spa and Hair Design. Busy Washington women don't mind leaving the city behind for an appointment at Jolie. The day spa has 15 private treatment rooms and a full gamut of services—body treat-ments, massage, facials, hair, nails, and makeup. ⊠ *7200 Wisconsin Ave., Bethesda, MD,* ☎ *301/986–9293. Metro: Bethesda.*

7 SIDE TRIPS

When you've had your fill of museums and monuments, you can take a mule-drawn boat from Georgetown along the historic C&O Canal or kayak in the spray of the stunning Great Falls. Or venture out of D.C. to set sail in Annapolis; visit Mount Vernon, George Washington's family home; or tour the Civil War battlefields in Fredericksburg.

By Michael
Dolan

Updated
by CiCi
Williamson

W **ITHIN AN HOUR OF WASHINGTON, D.C.,** are numerous
popular sights relating to our first president, naval history, Colonial events, and famous battles. For an active
side trip, you can walk or bike along the path that parallels the Chesapeake & Ohio (C&O) Canal for 13 mi, past Glen Echo Park, to Great
Falls Tavern on the Maryland side of the Potomac. Sailing aficionados enjoy visiting the United States Naval Academy and getting out
on the water in Annapolis, a boating mecca. Mount Vernon, George
Washington's family home, is 16 mi from D.C.; two other interesting
plantation homes—Woodlawn and Gunston Hall—are nearby. History
buffs might also want to make a beeline for historic Fredericksburg to
learn about the important roles this and surrounding towns played in
the Revolutionary and Civil wars. The town's 40-block National Historic District contains more than 350 original 18th- and 19th-century
buildings. Fredericksburg is also known for its antiques shops and its
excellent, yet often reasonably priced, dining and lodging establishments.

Most of these side trips can be taken via trains, buses, and escorted
tours. The most convenient way to reach the sights in D.C.'s two
neighboring states, however, is in a car.

Pleasures and Pastimes

Historical Sights

Across the Potomac and Anacostia rivers in Maryland and Virginia are
places where pivotal events in our nation's history occurred. These states
also have abundant Colonial architecture—the real thing. Of utmost
importance to the shaping of the United States are spots dear to George
Washington: Mount Vernon; his boyhood home at Ferry Farm near
Fredericksburg; and the mansions of his relatives. Bayside Annapolis,
the country's first peacetime capital, is not to be missed for its naval
ties and port. A vast neighborhood of 18th-century architecture, which
includes 50 pre–Revolutionary War buildings, is also here.

Outdoor Adventures

Hikers traversing Virginia's rolling hills might find their senses over-
loaded by the beauty of flowering trees in spring or a palette of autumn leaves. Beside the Potomac's white-water rapids are Maryland
and Virginia's vast hiking areas in Great Falls parks.

Those who fish can stake out the numerous riverbanks and salty
shores. Bikers may ride for hundreds of miles on the area's excellent,
paved bicycle paths. One especially attractive route winds south along
the Virginia shore of the Potomac. From it, you can view Georgetown
and Washington's monuments on the opposite bank; Arlington National
Cemetery; Ronald Reagan National Airport; and Old Town Alexandria. Before ending at Mount Vernon, the route traverses wildlife sanc-
tuaries, and there are many excellent picnic spots along the way.

What's Where

C&O Canal and Great Falls Park

The C&O Canal and the twin parks of Great Falls—on the Maryland
and Virginia sides of the Potomac River 13 mi northwest of Georgetown—are part of the National Park system. The steep, jagged falls roar
into a narrow gorge, providing one of the most spectacular scenic attractions in the East. Canoeing, bicycling, and fishing are popular. Glen
Echo is a charming village of Victorian houses; Glen Echo Park is noted
for its whimsical architecture and its splendid 1921 Dentzel carousel.

Annapolis, Maryland

Annapolis, Maryland's capital, is a popular destination for oyster catchers and boating aficionados, and on warm, sunny days at the City Dock, boats moor against a redbrick background of waterfront shops and restaurants. Annapolis's enduring nautical reputation is strengthened by the presence of the United States Naval Academy, whose handsomely uniformed students can often be seen on the city streets. One of the country's largest assemblages of 18th-century architecture, with no fewer than 50 pre-Revolutionary buildings, the academy recalls the city's days as a major port.

Frederick, Maryland

Maryland's second-largest city is less than an hour away from Washington, D.C., and has one of the best-preserved historic districts in Maryland. There are several unique museums in Frederick as well a Civil War battlefield. The city and its environs are also a mecca for antiques shopping.

Potomac Plantations

Three splendid examples of plantation architecture remain on the Virginia side of the Potomac, just 15 mi south of the District. Easily visited in a day, these riverfront mansions offer a look into a way of life long gone. Mount Vernon, one of the most popular sights in the area, was the home of George Washington; Woodlawn was the estate of Washington's granddaughter; and Gunston Hall was the residence of George Mason—patriot and author of the document on which the Bill of Rights was based.

Fredericksburg, Virginia

This compact city 50 mi south of Washington near the falls of the Rappahannock River figured prominently at crucial points in the nation's history, particularly during the Revolutionary and Civil wars. Fredericksburg, a popular day-trip destination for history buffs and antiques collectors, has a 40-block National Historic District containing more than 350 18th- and 19th-century buildings.

C&O CANAL NATIONAL HISTORIC PARK AND GREAT FALLS PARK

In the 18th and early 19th centuries, the Potomac River was the main transportation route between Cumberland, Maryland—one of the most important ports on the nation's frontier—and the seaports of the Chesapeake Bay. Tobacco, grain, whiskey, furs, iron ore, timber, and other commodities were sent down the Potomac to Georgetown and Alexandria, which served as major distribution points for both domestic and international markets.

Although it served as a vital link with the country's western territories, the Potomac had some drawbacks as a commercial waterway: rapids and waterfalls along the 190 mi between Cumberland and Washington originally made it impossible for traders to travel the entire distance by boat. Just a few miles upstream from Washington, the Potomac cascades through two such barriers—the breathtakingly beautiful Great Falls and the less dramatic but no less impassable Little Falls.

To help traders move goods between the eastern markets and the western frontier more efficiently, 18th-century engineers proposed that a canal with a series of elevator locks be constructed parallel to the river. The first Potomac canal system was built at the urging of George Washington, who actually helped found the Patowmack Company for this purpose. What obstacles this firm couldn't eliminate by dredging, it built canals (five of them) around. These improvements were completed in 1802 (after

Washington's death), but natural variations in the river's flow—sometimes too little, sometimes too much—still interrupted river traffic, and the project, although successful for a time, eventually failed.

Numbers in the margin correspond to points of interest on the C&O Canal National Historic Park and Great Falls Park map.

C&O Canal National Historic Park

West from Georgetown extending 13 mi to Great Falls Tavern.

The C&O Canal is considered to be the finest relic of America's canal-building era. Its route and structures are still almost entirely intact. Construction of the C&O Canal along the Maryland bank began in 1828, using the principles of the Erie Canal in New York. When construction ended in 1850, canals stretched from downtown Washington to Cumberland, Maryland, through 74 locks. The public rest room at the intersection of 17th Street and Constitution Avenue was originally a lock house of an earlier canal through Washington. The original plan to extend a canal to the Ohio River was superseded by the economic success of the Baltimore & Ohio (B&O) Railroad, which eventually put the canal out of business.

Ironically, construction of the C&O Canal and the B&O Railroad began on the same day, July 4, 1828. Initially, the C&O provided an economical and practical way for traders to move goods through the Washington area to the lower Chesapeake. During the mid-19th century, boats carried as many as a million tons of merchandise a year. The C&O Canal suffered a flood in late spring 1889 and couldn't recover from the financial disaster that ensued. Ownership then shifted to the B&O Railroad, which had been the largest stockholder, and operation continued until 1924, when another flood ended traffic. The railroad transferred ownership of the canal to the federal government in 1938 in satisfaction of a $2 million debt.

In the 1950s a proposal to build a highway over the canal near Washington was thwarted by residents of the Palisades—a neighborhood overlooking the waterway—and others concerned with the canal's history and legacy. Since 1971 the canal has been a national park, providing Washingtonians and visitors with a window into the past and a marvelous place to enjoy the outdoors. The towpath along the canal in

❶ Georgetown passes traces of that area's industrial past, such as the Godey Lime Kilns near the mouth of Rock Creek, as well as the fronts of numerous houses that date from 1810. At the Foundry Mall, you can start a tour of the area on foot, by bike, or—from April through late October—by mule-drawn boat.

At the **Georgetown Visitor Center,** National Park Service rangers and volunteers provide maps, information, and history relating to the canal. Mule-drawn canal boat rides depart from the center from about April 1 through late October. The one-hour ride costs $8. ✉ *1057 Thomas Jefferson St. NW,* ☎ *202/653–5190.* ☉ *Apr.–Oct., Wed.–Sun. 9–4:30; Nov.–Mar., weekends 10–4 (staffing permitting).*

❷ Fletcher's Boat House on the D.C. side of the Potomac, rents rowboats, canoes, and bicycles and sells tackle and D.C. fishing licenses. Here you can catch shad, perch, catfish, striped bass, and other freshwater species. Canoeing is allowed in the canal and, weather permitting, in the Potomac. There's a large picnic area along the riverbank. ✉ *4940 Canal Rd., at Reservoir Rd.,* ☎ *202/244–0461.* ☉ *Late Mar.–May, daily 7:30–7:30; June–Aug., daily 9–7:30; Sept.–Nov., daily 9–6:30; closed Dec.–early Mar. or during severe weather.*

❸ Chain Bridge, named for the chains that held up the original structure, links D.C. and Virginia. The bridge was built to enable cattlemen to bring

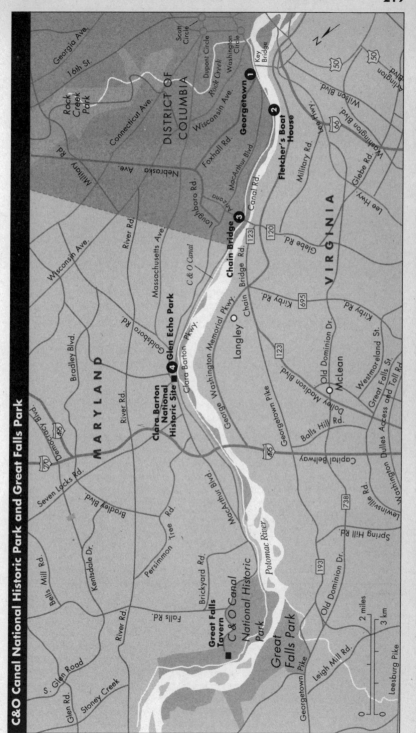

C&O Canal National Historic Park and Great Falls Park

Virginia herds to the slaughterhouses along the Maryland side of the Potomac. During the Civil War the bridge was guarded by Union troops stationed at earthen fortifications along what's now Potomac Avenue NW. The Virginia side of the river in the area around Chain Bridge is known for its good fishing and narrow rapids. ⊠ *Glebe Rd. (Rte. 120).*

The village of Glen Echo was founded in 1891 when brothers Edwin and Edward Baltzley, made wealthy by their invention of the eggbeater, fell under the spell of the Chautauqua movement, which started in New York in 1874 and promoted liberal education among the masses. The brothers sold land and houses to further their dream, but the Glen Echo Chautauqua movement lasted only one season. Their compound, **Glen Echo Park,** preserves the site of Washington's oldest amusement park (1911–68) and a stone tower from the earlier days of a Chatauqua Assembly. The National Park Service administers this 10-acre property and offers year-round dances Friday through Sunday in the 1933 Spanish Ballroom, classes in the arts, two children's theaters, two art galleries with ongoing exhibits, artist demonstrations, and a Children's Museum with environmental education workshops. You can also take a ride accompanied by calliope music on a 1921 Dentzel carousel May through September. ⊠ *7300 MacArthur Blvd. NW,* ☎ *301/492–6229; 301/492–6282 events hot line,* WEB *www.nps.gov/glec.* ⊠ *Park free, carousel ride 50¢, cost varies for dances.*

Beside Glen Echo Park's parking lot is the **Clara Barton National Historic Site,** a monument to the founder of the American Red Cross. The structure was built for her by the founders of Glen Echo, and she used it originally to store Red Cross supplies; later it became both her home and the organization's headquarters. Today the building is furnished with many of her possessions and period artifacts. Access is by 30- to 45-minute guided tour only. ⊠ *5801 Oxford Rd.,* ☎ *301/492–6245.* ⊠ *Free.* ☉ *Daily 10–4:45; tours begin on the hour from 10–4.*

Great Falls Tavern, in Maryland, has displays of canal history and photographs that show how high the river can rise. A platform on Olmsted Island, accessible from near the tavern, provides a spectacular view of the falls. On the canal walls are grooves worn by decades of friction from boat towlines. Mule-drawn canal boat rides ($8), about one hour round-trip, start here between April and November daily except Tuesdays. The tavern ceased food service long ago, so if you're hungry, head for the snack bar a few paces north. ⊠ *11710 MacArthur Blvd.,* ☎ *301/299–3613 or 301/767–3714.* ⊠ *$4 per vehicle, $2 per person without vehicle (good for 3 days at both Great Falls Park and C&O Canal National Historic Park).* ☉ *Nov.–Mar., daily 9–4:30; Apr.–Oct. daily 9–5.*

Great Falls Park, Virginia

23 mi northwest from Georgetown.

Part of the National Park System, Great Falls Park is on the Virginia side of the Potomac, across the river from C&O Canal National Historic Park. Great Falls Park consists of 800 acres and is a favorite place for outings. The steep, jagged falls roar into the narrow Mather Gorge—a spectacular scene. There are stunning views of the Potomac here, and a marker shows the river's high-water marks. The sites that overlook the falls date from the early 20th century, when the land was a private amusement park and visitors arrived by train. Fifteen mi of trails lead past the old Patowmack Canal and among the boulders along the edge of the falls.

Swimming, wading, overnight camping, and alcoholic beverages are prohibited, but you can fish (a Virginia, Maryland, or D.C. license is required for anglers 16 and older), climb rocks (climbers must register at the visitor center beforehand), or—if you're an experienced boater with your own equipment—go white-water kayaking (*below* the falls only). As is true all along this stretch of the river, the currents are deadly. Despite frequent signs and warnings, visitors occasionally dare the water and drown.

A tour of the **Great Falls Park Visitor Center and Museum** takes 30 minutes. Staff members also conduct park walks year-round; the visitor center tour and guided park walks are included in the price of admission. You're encouraged to take self-guided tours along well-marked trails, including one that follows the route of the old Patowmack Canal; the visitor center provides maps for the various trails. ⊠ *Rte. 738 (Old Dominion Dr.),* ☎ *703/285–2966,* WEB *www.nps.gov/gwmp/ grfa/index.htm.* ⊠ *$4 per vehicle, $2 per person without vehicle (good for 3 days at both Great Falls Park and C&O Canal National Historic Park); annual park pass $15.* ☉ *7 AM–dark; visitor center Nov.– Mar., daily 10–4; Apr.–May and Oct., daily 10–5; June–Sept. weekdays 10–5; weekends 10–6. Hours are subject to change.*

C&O Canal National Historic Park and Great Falls Park A to Z

CAR TRAVEL
To reach Great Falls Park, take the scenic and winding Route 193 (Exit 13 off Route 495, the Capital Beltway) to Route 738 (Old Dominion Drive), and follow the signs. It takes about 25 minutes to drive to the park from the Beltway. C&O Canal National Historic Park is along the Maryland side of the Potomac and is accessible by taking Canal Road or MacArthur Boulevard from Georgetown or by taking Exit 41 off the Beltway and then following the signs to Carderock. There are several roadside stops accessible from the southbound lanes of Canal Road where you can park and visit restored canal locks and lock houses.

OUTDOORS AND SPORTS
The C&O Canal National Historic Park and its towpath are favorite destinations for joggers, bikers, and canoeists. The path has a slight grade, which makes for a leisurely ride or hike. Most recreational bikers consider the 13 mi from Georgetown to Great Falls Tavern an easy ride; you only need to carry your bike for one short stretch of rocky ground near Great Falls. You can also take a bike path that parallels MacArthur Boulevard and runs from Georgetown to Great Falls Tavern. Storm damage has left parts of the canal dry, but many segments remain intact and navigable by canoe. You can rent rowboats, canoes, or bicycles at Fletcher's Boat House, just upriver from Georgetown.
➤ CONTACTS: **Fletcher's Boat House** (⊠ 4940 Canal Rd., at Reservoir Rd., ☎ 202/244–0461).

TOURS
Between April and November, mule-drawn canal boats leave for roughly one-hour trips from the Foundry Mall on Thomas Jefferson Street NW, half a block south of M Street in Georgetown. Reservations are not required; ticket sales ($8) begin two hours before each trip. Floods sometimes affect canal boat trips, so call the National Park Service office (☎ 202/653–5190 or 301/299–2026) to check.

ANNAPOLIS, MARYLAND

In 1649 a group of Puritan settlers moved from Virginia to a spot at the mouth of the Severn River, where they established a community called Providence. Lord Baltimore—who held the royal charter to settle Maryland—named the area around this town Anne Arundel County, after his wife; in 1684 Anne Arundel Town was established across from

Providence on the Severn's south side. Ten years later, Anne Arundel Town became the capital of Maryland and was renamed Annapolis—for Princess Anne, who later became queen. It received its city charter in 1708 and became a major port, particularly for the export of tobacco. In 1774 patriots here matched their Boston counterparts (who had thrown their famous tea party the previous year) by burning the *Peggy Stewart,* a ship loaded with taxed tea. Annapolis later served as the nation's first peacetime capital (1783–84).

Today, "Crabtown," as the city is nicknamed, is a picturesque place to stroll, shop, relax, study, or dine. It has a large assemblage of 18th-century architecture, including 50 pre–Revolutionary War buildings—more surviving Colonial buildings than any other place in the country. Maryland is the only state in which the homes of all its signers of the Declaration of Independence still exist. The houses are all in Annapolis, and you can tour three of the four—the homes of Charles Carroll, Samuel Chase, and William Paca.

Although it has long since been overtaken by Baltimore as the major Maryland port, Annapolis is still a popular pleasure-boating destination. On warm sunny days, the waters off City Dock become center stage for an amateur show of powerboaters maneuvering through the heavy traffic. Annapolis's enduring nautical reputation derives largely from the presence of the United States Naval Academy, whose handsomely uniformed midshipmen throng the city streets in white uniforms during the summer and navy blue in winter. April and October commercial boat shows attract national attention.

Numbers in the text correspond to numbers in the margin and on the Annapolis, Maryland, map.

A Good Tour

You can see Annapolis in a single well-planned day. To get maps, schedules, and information about guided tours all year round, it's best to begin your walking tour at the **Annapolis & Anne Arundel County Conference & Visitors Bureau** ①. Walk out the door of the visitor center then turn left at West Street and walk to **St. Anne's Church** ②, straight ahead a half block. The edifice incorporates walls from a former church that burned in 1858 and whose congregation has worshiped here continuously since 1692. Off Church Circle, take Franklin Street one block to the **Banneker-Douglass Museum** ③, which portrays African-American life in Maryland, and return to the circle after a visit. Continue around the circle to the Maryland Inn and walk to the end of Main Street—passing many boutiques and small restaurants—and the **Historic Annapolis Foundation Museum Store** ④, where you can rent audiotapes for self-guided walking tours. Farther down, past the Market House, which has many places to stop for a snack, look down to see the **Kunta Kinte Plaque** ⑤, a three-sided obelisk and plaque beyond Market Square; commemorating the 1767 arrival of the slave immortalized in Alex Haley's *Roots.* On the other side of City Dock in front of the Harbor Master's office, there's an **information booth** ⑥ where you can get maps and information from April to October.

To see the **Charles Carroll House** ⑦, return to Market Square and walk down Compromise Street. Turn right at St. Mary's Street, which dead-ends at Duke of Gloucester Street (the house is across this street, behind St. Mary's Church). The house is birthplace and city home of the only Catholic to sign the Declaration of Independence. Retrace your steps and turn right at Market Square onto Randall Street. Walk two blocks to the Naval Academy wall and turn right, entering the gate to the **United States Naval Academy** ⑧ and its Armel-Leftwich Visitor Center. Here you can join a tour or continue solo through the academy grounds where future U.S. Navy and Marine Corps officers are trained. Walk toward the Naval Academy Chapel dome and turn right on Buchanan Road and again at the Tecumseh statue, figurehead of the USS *Delaware,* to visit the academy's dormitory, Bancroft Hall. Return to Tecumseh and take the curvy walkway to the left to the chapel. From the chapel entrance the Naval Academy Museum is to the left a half block in Preble Hall.

From the museum, leave through Gate 3 to your right and walk to the **Hammond-Harwood House** ⑨, described as one of the most beautiful in Colonial America, and the **Chase-Lloyd House** ⑩, both designed by Colonial America's foremost architect, William Buckland. The two homes are across the street from each other in the second block of Maryland Avenue. Continue on Maryland Avenue a block to Prince George Street; turn left and walk a block to the **William Paca House and Garden** ⑪, home of a former Maryland governor and signer of the Declaration of Independence. Retrace your route and continue a block past Maryland Avenue to the campus of **St. John's College** ⑫, a liberal arts institution known for its Great Books curriculum, directly ahead at the College Avenue end of Prince George Street. After touring the campus, follow College Avenue away from the Naval Academy wall to North Street and go one block up to the **Maryland State House** ⑬ in the middle of State Circle, the oldest state capitol in continuous legislative use and the only one in which the U.S. Congress has sat. Free tours are given daily at 11 and 3. After touring the capitol, stop and visit the **Thurgood Marshall Memorial** ⑭ in State House Square, close to Bladen Street and College Avenue. The native Marylander was the first African-American Supreme Court Justice. After leaving the memorial, turn back toward State Circle and turn right, exiting State Circle via School Street. Notice the beautiful wrought iron fencing that surrounds Government House, a Georgian mansion with sculpture gardens that's the home of Maryland's governor. Walk down School Street, which leads back to Church Circle and West Street where the tour began. From here you can drive to the **Maryland State Archives** ⑮, where you can search for family history or do historical research. It's on the right as you leave downtown on Rowe Boulevard, heading toward Route 50. Farther west on U.S. Route 50 is **London Town House and Garden** ⑯, Maryland's largest archaeological excavation where digging goes on in search of the lost town of London. The public can participate in the dig on scheduled dig days. Docents lead tours of a three-story brick home built there in 1760. To get here from Route 50, take Exit 22 onto Highway 665 and turn right onto Highway 2 south; cross the South River Bridge and turn left at Mayo Road; in less than a mile, turn left onto Londontown Road and follow it 1 mi to the site.

TIMING

Walking this route will take about an hour. Budget another half hour each for tours of the smaller historic homes and an hour each for the Paca and Hammond-Harwood houses. The Naval Academy deserves about two hours, plus another half hour if you visit the museum. The capitol takes a quarter hour to see. The drive to the Maryland Archives takes about 5 minutes; it's another 15 minutes to London Town. Plan on 1½ hours to take the tour and/or wander the grounds.

Sights to See

❶ **Annapolis & Anne Arundel County Conference & Visitors Bureau.** Start your visit at Annapolis's main visitors center in the Historic District. Here you can pick up maps and brochures or begin a guided tour. ⊠ *26 West St.,* ☎ *410/280–0445.* ☯ *Daily 9–5.*

224

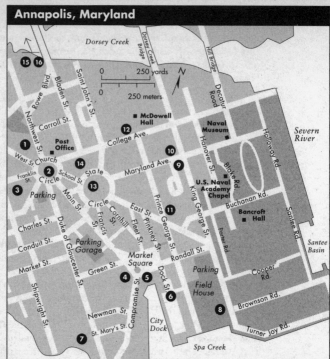

Annapolis, Maryland

❸ **Banneker-Douglass Museum.** This museum, in a former church, has changing exhibits, lectures, films, and literature that convey a picture of the African-American experience in Maryland. It's named for Benjamin Banneker—a Maryland astronomer, surveyor, and mathematician who lived during the 18th and 19th centuries—and Frederick Douglass, the 19th-century abolitionist, politician, and writer. ⊠ *84 Franklin St.,* ☎ *410/216–6180.* ⌨ *Free.* ☉ *Tues.–Fri. 10–3, Sat. noon–4.*

❼ **Charles Carroll House.** This birthplace and city home of the only Catholic to sign the Declaration of Independence has 18th-century terraced gardens that overlook Spa Creek. The Marylander was one of the wealthiest men in Colonial America. The restored 1720 house contains a wine cellar that was added in the 19th century. ⊠ *107 Duke of Gloucester St.,* ☎ *410/269–1737,* ᴡᴇʙ *www.carrollhouse.com.* ⌨ *$4.* ☉ *Fri. and Sun. noon–4, Sat. 10–2; other times by appointment.*

❿ **Chase-Lloyd House.** William Buckland, a prominent Colonial architect, built the Chase-Lloyd House, with its gracefully massive facade—sheer except for a center third beneath the pediment. In 1774 the tobacco planter and revolutionary Edward Lloyd IV completed work begun five years earlier by Samuel Chase, a signer of the Declaration of Independence and future Supreme Court justice. The first floor is open to the public and contains more of Buckland's handiwork, including a parlor mantelpiece with tobacco leaves carved into the marble. (Buckland was famous for his interior woodwork; you can see more of it in the **Hammond-Harwood House** across the street and in George Mason's Gunston Hall in Lorton, Virginia.) The house is furnished in a mixture of 18th-, 19th-, and 20th-century pieces, and its staircase parts dramatically around an arched triple window. For more than 100 years the house has served as a home for elderly women. You can tour the first floor; the ladies live upstairs. ⊠ *22 Maryland Ave.,* ☎ *410/ 263–2723.* ⌨ *$2.* ☉ *Mar.–Dec., Mon.–Sat. 2–4.*

★ ❾ **Hammond-Harwood House.** Ninety percent of this home is original. One of the finest examples of Colonial five-part Georgian architecture (a single block with two connecting rooms and wings on each side) in America, the Hammond-Harwood House is the only verifiable full-scale example of William Buckland's work. It was also his final project, as he died in 1774—the year the house was completed. Exquisite moldings, cornices, and other carvings appear throughout (note especially the garlands of roses above the front doorway—described as one of the most beautiful in Colonial America). All were part of what was meant to be a manorial wedding present from Matthias Hammond, a planter and revolutionary, to his fiancée, who jilted him before the house was finished. Hammond died a bachelor in 1784. The Harwoods took over the house toward the turn of the 19th century. Today it's furnished with 18th-century pieces, and the garden is tended with regard to period authenticity. Tours leave on the half hour; the last begins at 3:30. ✉ *19 Maryland Ave.,* ☎ *410/269–1714.* 🎟 *$5; $10 combination ticket with William Paca House.* ⊙ *Mon.–Sat. 10–4, Sun. noon–4.*

❹ **Historic Annapolis Foundation Museum Store.** The Historic Annapolis Foundation operates its museum store in a warehouse that held supplies for the Continental Army during the Revolutionary War. Here you can shop, check out a diorama of the city's 18th-century waterfront, and rent taped narrations for walking tours. ✉ *77 Main St.,* ☎ *410/ 268–5576,* WEB *www.hasmuseumstore.com.* 🎟 *Free.* ⊙ *Daily 10–5.*

❻ **Information Booth.** From April to October the information booth on City Dock, adjacent to the harbormaster's office, is open and stocked with maps and brochures. ✉ *Dock St. parking lot,* ☎ *410/280–0445.*

NEED A BREAK? The reconstructed **Market House Pavilion** (✉ City Dock), a collection of about 20 market stalls in the center of Market Square, sells baked goods, fast food, and seafood (prepared or to cook at home). There's no seating; set up your picnic anywhere on the dock.

❺ **Kunta Kinte Plaque and Alex Haley Memorial.** The three-sided obelisk and plaque beyond Market Square at the head of City Dock commemorates the 1767 arrival of the African slave immortalized in Alex Haley's *Roots*. The Haley Memorial is a tribute to the author.

⑯ **London Town House and Gardens** Maryland's largest archaeological site, this National Historic Landmark is on the South River, just minutes by car from Annapolis. The three-story brick house at London Town, built by William Brown in 1760, shares a dramatic waterfront setting with 8 acres of woodland gardens. Archaeological work here continues in search of the lost town of London—40 dwellings, shops, and taverns that made up a 17th-century tobacco port that slowly began to decline and disappear (the buildings were abandoned and left to decay) in the 18th century. From May to September, visitors can join the dig the third Saturday of the month. Docents conduct 30–45-minute house tours; allow more time to wander the grounds. From March to December, house tours leave on the hour (last tour is at 3); January and February tours are by appointment only. ✉ *839 Londontown Rd., Edgewater 21037,* ☎ *410/222–1919.* 🎟 *$6.* ⊙ *Mar.–Dec., Mon.–Sat. 10–4, Sun. noon–4; Jan.–Feb. by appointment only.*

⑮ **Maryland State Archives.** Genealogists use the public search room for family history and historical research. Collections include original public records, church records, newspapers, photographs, and maps. In the lobby are changing exhibits and a gift shop. ✉ *350 Rowe Blvd.,* ☎ *410/260–6400,* WEB *www.mdarchives.state.md.us.* 🎟 *Free.* ⊙ *Tues.– Fri. 8–4:30, Sat. 8:30–noon and 1–4:30.*

⓭ Maryland State House. There are some fascinating facts associated with Maryland's capitol: completed in 1780, it has the nation's largest wooden dome and is the oldest state capitol in continuous legislative use; it's also the only one in which the U.S. Congress has sat (1783–84). It was here that General George Washington resigned as commander in chief of the Continental Army and where the Treaty of Paris was ratified, ending the Revolutionary War. Both events took place in the Old Senate Chamber, which is filled with intricate woodwork (featuring the ubiquitous tobacco motif) attributed to Colonial architect William Buckland. Also decorating this room is Charles Willson Peale's painting *Washington at the Battle of Yorktown,* considered the masterpiece of the Revolutionary War period's finest portrait artist. The Maryland Senate and House now hold their sessions in two other chambers in the building. Also on the grounds is the oldest public building in Maryland, the tiny redbrick **Treasury,** built in 1735. Nearby on Lawyers Mall is the impressive Thurgood Marshall Memorial. ⊠ *State Circle,* ☎ *410/974–3400.* ⊡ *Free.* ☉ *Daily 9–5; ½-hr tour daily at 11 and 3.*

❷ St. Anne's Church. St. Anne's Episcopal parish was founded in 1692; King William III donated the Communion silver. The first St. Anne's Church, built in 1704, was torn down in 1775. The second, built in 1792, burned down in 1858; however, parts of the walls survived and were incorporated into the present structure, which was built in 1859. The churchyard contains the grave of the last Colonial governor, Sir Robert Eden. ⊠ *Church Circle,* ☎ *410/267–9333.* ⊡ *Free.* ☉ *Daily 8–5:30.*

⓬ St. John's College. Here is the alma mater of Francis Scott Key, lyricist of *The Star Spangled Banner.* However, since 1937, the college has been best known as the birthplace of the Great Books curriculum, which includes reading the works of great authors from Homer to Freud. All students at the college follow the same curriculum for four years, and classes are conducted as discussions rather than lectures. Climb the gradual slope of the long, brick-paved path to the impressive golden cupola of **McDowell Hall,** the third-oldest academic building in the country, just as St. John's is the third-oldest college in the country (after Harvard and William and Mary, respectively). Founded as King William's School in 1696, it was chartered under its current name in 1784. St. John's was the home to the last living Liberty Tree (those designated trees under which the Sons of Liberty convened in order to hear patriot-orators plan the Revolution against England). Fatally wounded in a 1999 hurricane, the 400-year-old tree was removed; its progeny stands to the left of McDowell Hall. The **Elizabeth Myers Mitchell Art Gallery** (☎ 410/626–2556), on the east side of Mellon Hall, presents a variety of exhibits and special programs related to the fine arts. Down King George Street toward the water is the **Carroll-Barrister House,** now the college admissions office. The house was built in 1722 at Main and Conduit streets and was moved onto campus in 1957. Charles Carroll (not the signer of the Declaration but his cousin), who helped draft Maryland's Declaration of Rights, was born here. ⊠ *St. John's St. and College Ave.,* ☎ *410/263–2371.*

⓮ Thurgood Marshall Memorial. Born in Baltimore, Maryland, Thurgood Marshall was the first African-American Supreme Court Justice and was one of the 20th century's foremost leaders in the struggle for equal rights under the law. Marshall won the decision in Brown v. Board of Education of Topeka in which the Supreme Court in 1954 overturned the doctrine of "separate but equal." He was appointed as United States Solicitor General in 1965 and to the Supreme Court in 1967 by President Lyndon B. Johnson. The memorial is an 8-foot statue that depicts Marshall as a young lawyer. ⊠ *State House Square, bordered by Bladen St., School St., and College Ave.*

★ ❽ **United States Naval Academy.** Probably the most interesting and important site in Annapolis, the Naval Academy runs along the Severn River and abuts downtown Annapolis. Midshipmen enter from every part of the United States and many foreign countries to undergo rigorous study in subjects that range from literature to navigation to nuclear engineering. The academy, established in 1845 on the site of a U.S. Army fort, occupies 329 scenic waterfront acres. The centerpiece of the campus is the bright copper-clad dome of the interdenominational **U.S. Naval Academy Chapel.** Beneath it lies the crypt of the Revolutionary War naval officer John Paul Jones, who, in a historic naval battle with a British ship, uttered the inspirational words, "I have not yet begun to fight!"

Near the chapel in Preble Hall is the **U.S. Naval Academy Museum & Gallery of Ships** (✉ 118 Maryland Ave., ☎ 410/293–2108), which tells the story of the U.S. Navy with displays of model ships and memorabilia from naval heroes and fighting vessels. The U.S. Naval Institute and Bookstore is also in this building. This 85,000-member professional association has advanced scientific and literary knowledge of the sea services since 1873; publishes more than 500 books; and houses more than 450,000 historic images. Admission for the museum, institute, and bookstore is free; hours are Monday through Saturday from 9 to 5 and Sunday from 11 to 5.

The academy grounds are alive with hustle and bustle as midshipmen go to classes, conduct military drills, practice for or compete in intercollegiate and intramural sports, or leave campus—weekends usually— for "liberty." **Bancroft Hall** is one of the largest dormitories in the world (it houses the entire 4,000-member Brigade of Midshipmen). You may view a midshipman's room just inside the hall. Always subject to inspection, rooms here are quite a bit neater than the typical student's room. The **Statue of Tecumseh,** in front of Bancroft Hall, is a bronze replica of the USS *Delaware*'s wooden figurehead, "Tamanend." It's decorated by midshipmen for athletics events, and they pitch pennies in his quiver of arrows for good luck during exams. If you're there at noon in fair weather you can see midshipmen form up outside Bancroft Hall and parade to lunch to the beat of the Drum and Bugle Corps. ✉ *52 King George St.,* ☎ *410/263–6933,* WEB *www.navyonline.com.* ☞ *Grounds tour $6.* ☉ *Visitor center: Mar.–Dec., daily 9–5; Jan.–Feb., daily 9–4. Guided walking tours generally leave Mon.–Sat. 10–3 and Sun. 12:30–2:30; call ahead to confirm.*

★ ⓫ **William Paca House and Garden.** Paca (pronounced "PAY-cuh") was a signer of the Declaration of Independence and a Maryland governor from 1782 to 1785. His house was built in 1765, and its original garden was finished in 1772. Inside, the main floor (furnished with 18th-century antiques) retains its original Prussian-blue and soft-gray color scheme. The second floor contains a mixture of 18th- and 19th-century pieces. The adjacent 2-acre gentlemen's pleasure garden provides a longer perspective on the back of the house, plus worthwhile sights of its own: parterres (upper terraces), a Chinese Chippendale bridge, a pond, a wilderness area, and formal arrangements. An inn, Carvel Hall, once stood on the gardens. After the inn was demolished in 1965, it took eight years to rebuild the gardens, which are planted in 18th-century perennials. ✉ *186 Prince George St.,* ☎ *410/263–5553,* WEB *www.annapolis.org.* ☞ *House and garden $7, house only $5, garden only $4, combination ticket with Hammond-Harwood House $10.* ☉ *House and garden Mar.–Dec., Mon.–Sat. 10–4, Sun. noon–4; Jan.–Feb., Fri.–Sat. 10–4, Sun. noon–4.*

Dining and Lodging

In the beginning, there was crab—crab cakes, crab soup, whole crabs to crack. This Chesapeake Bay specialty is still found in abundance, but Annapolis has broadened its horizons to include eateries—many in the Historic District—that offer a variety of cuisines. Ask for a restaurant guide at the visitor center. There are many hostelries near the heart of the city—places where you can leave your car with a valet and stroll historic streets unencumbered. Other lodging options include chain motels a few miles outside town (some of which offer free transportation to the downtown historic area) and area B&Bs. For lodging reservations, call **Annapolis Accommodations** (☎ 410/280–0900 or 800/715–1000) or **Annapolis Bed & Breakfast Association** (☎ 410/295–5200, WEB www.annapolisbandb.com). For price category charts, *see* Dining and Lodging *in* Smart Travel Tips A to Z

$$$–$$$$ ✕ **Ristorante Piccola Roma.** Amid the sophisticated black and white decor of the cozy "Little Rome" Restaurant, you can feast on authentic Italian food. Silva Recine prepares the recipes—specialties are *antipasti, insalate,* pasta, veal, and fish—and supervises the fine dining staff. ⊠ *200 Main St.,* ☎ *410/268–7898. AE, D, DC, MC, V.*

$$$–$$$$ ✕ **Treaty of Paris Restaurant.** Period reproduction furniture and fabrics decorate this handsome, 18th-century dining room. Dinner specialties include such Continental dishes as beef Wellington as well as seafood choices like crab imperial, twin lobster tails, and crab cakes. The adjacent King of France Tavern has live jazz Friday and Saturday evenings (cover charge). ⊠ *Maryland Inn, 16 Church Circle,* ☎ *410/263–2641. AE, D, DC, MC, V.*

$$–$$$$ ✕ **Middleton Tavern Oyster Bar and Restaurant.** Horatio Middleton began operating this "inn for seafaring men" in 1750; Washington, Jefferson, and Franklin were among its patrons. Today, two fireplaces, wood floors, paneled walls, and a nautical theme give it a cozy charm. Seafood tops the menu; the Maryland crab soup and broiled Chesapeake Bay rockfish are standouts. Be sure to try the tavern's own microbrewed Middleton Pale Ale, perhaps during happy hour or during a weekend blues session in the upstairs piano bar. The restaurant also has a solid brunch menu on weekends as well as seating in an outdoor café in good weather. ⊠ *City Dock at Randall St.,* ☎ *410/263–3323. AE, D, DC, MC, V.*

$$–$$$$ ✕ **Phillips Annapolis Harbor.** Enjoying a panoramic view of the harbor, this newest eatery on the city dock belongs to a group of popular local restaurants whose forte is Maryland-style seafood. The building is sun-filled via skylights and a glassed all-season room. There's also a piano bar lounge. Specialties here include buckets of mussels, clams on the halfshell, lump crab cocktail, seafood platters, and Eastern Shore stew. ⊠ *12 Dock St.,* ☎ *410/990-9888. AE, D, DC, MC, V.*

$$–$$$$ ✕ **Rams Head Tavern.** A traditional English-style pub is also home to the Fordham Brewing Company. The Rams Head serves better-than-usual tavern fare, such as spicy shrimp salad, crab cakes, and beer-battered shrimp, as well as more than 170 beers—26 on draft—from around the world. If you want to do more than just sample beer, you can take a brewery tour and see how it's made. The menu has daily specials and Sunday brunch is served. The Rams Head Tavern On Stage seats 215 in a nightclub atmosphere for nationally known entertainment by folk, rock, jazz, country, and bluegrass groups. Dinner-show combo specials are offered, and the menu offers light fare. ⊠ *33 West St.,* ☎ *410/268–4545. AE, D, DC, MC, V.*

$$–$$$ ✕ **Café Normandie.** Ladderback chairs, wooden beams, skylights, and a four-sided fireplace give this French restaurant a homey look. Out of the open kitchen—with its blue and white ceramic tiles—comes what may well be the best French onion soup in America, made daily from scratch. Puffy omelets, crepes, and seafood dishes are other specialties. The restaurant's brunch (Friday through Sunday) offers American and French dishes, including poached eggs in ratatouille, eggs Benedict,

seafood omelets, pancakes, waffles, and house-made croissants and muffins. ⊠ *185 Main St.,* ☎ *410/263–3382. AE, D, DC, MC, V.*

$$–$$$ ✕ **Carrol's Creek.** You can walk, catch a water taxi from City Dock, or drive over the Spa Creek drawbridge to this local favorite in Eastport. Whether you dine indoors or out, the view of historic Annapolis and its harbor is spectacular. All-you-can-eat Sunday brunch is of special note, as are the seafood specialties. A four-course *prix fixe* crab or bay dinner is offered. ⊠ *410 Severn Ave.,* ☎ *410/263–8102. AE, D, DC, MC, V.*

$$–$$$ ✕ **Fred's Tiffany Room Restaurant.** A favorite of locals for 40 years, Fred's specializes in lump crabmeat specialties, seafood, and Mediterranean cuisine. The dining rooms are lit with antique Tiffany fixtures, Old Master–style paintings hang on the brick walls, and booths and tables are laid with white linens. ⊠ *Rte. 2 at Sommerville Rd. (near Parole Plaza),* ☎ *410/224–2386; 800/773–3477. AE, DC, MC, V.*

$–$$$ ✕ **Corinthian Restaurant.** This stylishly elegant dining room has a relaxed ambience and award-winning food. Crab cakes and aged prime rib are good choices. There are also daily specials using fresh ingredients from local growers. ⊠ *Loews Annapolis Hotel, 126 West St.,* ☎ *410/263–1299. AE, D, DC, MC, V.*

$$$ 🏨 **Annapolis Marriott Waterfront.** You can practically fish from your room at the city's only waterfront hotel. Rooms have modern decor with mauve quilted bedspreads; all rooms have either balconies over the water or large windows with views of the harbor or the historic district. The outdoor bar by the harbor's edge is popular in nice weather. ⊠ *80 Compromise St., 21401,* ☎ *410/268–7555 or 800/336–0072,* ℻ *410/269–5864,* 🖳 *www.annapolismarriott.com. 150 rooms. Restaurant, 2 bars, in-room data ports, no-smoking rooms, gym, boating, laundry service, concierge, business services, meeting rooms, parking (fee). AE, D, DC, MC, V.*

$$ 🏨 **Governor Calvert House** This old historic home facing the state capitol was built in 1727 and lived in by two former Maryland governors, both named Calvert. During its 1984 expansion, workers discovered a "hypocaust" or greenhouse heating system in the basement (you can view it through a section of the floor). Rooms in the historic section are furnished with period antiques; newer rooms have period reproductions. The Governor Calvert House is one of the three Historic Inns of Annapolis. The Treaty of Paris Restaurant, the Drummer's Lot Pub, and the King of France Tavern serve all three inns. Colonial tea time is held on Wednesdays from 3 to 4. ⊠ *58 State Circle, 21401,* ☎ *410/263–2641 or 800/847–8882,* ℻ *410/268–3813,* 🖳 *www.annapolisinns.com. 55 rooms. In-room data ports, no-smoking rooms, laundry service, concierge, business services, meeting rooms, parking (fee). AE, D, DC, MC, V.*

$$ 🏨 **Loews Annapolis Hotel.** Although its redbrick exterior blends with the surrounding historic architecture, this hotel's interior is airy, spacious, and modern. Step onto the lobby's herringbone parquet floor and be soothed by the celadon green-and-sand color scheme. Guest rooms—done in beige fabrics in a variety of textures and shades—are no less comforting and have such amenities as coffeemakers and terry robes. The Plaza Club floors (fifth and sixth) have a well-appointed lounge. A complimentary breakfast is served in the restaurant for concierge guests. The Corinthian restaurant serves elegant cuisine, and the Weather Rail Bar & Grill has happy-hour specials and serves light-fare lunch and dinner. A free hotel shuttle bus takes you anywhere you want to go in Annapolis. ⊠ *126 West St., 21401,* ☎ *410/263–7777 or 800/235–6397,* ℻ *410/263–0084,* 🖳 *www.loewsannapolis.com. 210 rooms, 7 suites. 2 restaurants, bar, in-room data ports, minibars, no-smoking floors, room service, hair salon, gym, laundry service, concierge, concierge floor, business services, meeting rooms, airport shuttle, parking (fee). AE, D, DC, MC, V.*

$$ **Maryland Inn.** Eleven delegates of the 1786 U.S. Congress stayed here. Many of the guest rooms date back to the Revolutionary era, while the wooden porches and marble-tiled lobby are vintage Victorian. Mahogany furniture and a velvet wing chair rest on aqua carpeting in guest rooms. Neutral bedspreads, floral wallpaper and draperies, and many antique furnishings complete the decor. Antique radiators heat the rooms. Some rooms have kitchenettes, sitting suites, or whirlpools. The Maryland Inn is one of the three Historic Inns of Annapolis; registration takes place at the ☞ **Governor Calvert House.** Dine at the inn's Treaty of Paris Restaurant, chill out in the downstairs Drummer's Lot Pub, or enjoy food and entertainment in the King of France Tavern. Colonial tea time is held on Wednesdays from 3 to 4. ✉ *16 Church Circle (the entrance is on Main Street)., 21401,* ☎ *410/263–2641 or 800/847–8882,* 𝖥𝖠𝖷 *410/268–3813,* 𝖶𝖤𝖡 *www.annapolisinns.com. 34 rooms, 10 suites. Restaurant, 2 pubs, in-room data ports, kitchenettes (some), no-smoking rooms, gym, laundry service, concierge, business services, meeting rooms, parking (fee). AE, D, DC, MC, V.*

$$ 🏨 **Robert Johnson House.** One of the three Historic Inns of Annapolis, this hostelry is actually three cleverly integrated 18th-century houses. The front overlooks the state capitol. Guest rooms are furnished with 19th-century antiques, four-poster beds, and draperies matching the pattern of the wallpaper. Registration is at the ☞ **Governor Calvert House.** The Treaty of Paris Restaurant, the Drummer's Lot Pub, and the King of France Tavern serve all three Historic Inns. ✉ *23 State Circle, 21401,* ☎ *410/263–2641 or 800/847–8882,* 𝖥𝖠𝖷 *410/268–3813,* 𝖶𝖤𝖡 *www.annapolisinns.com. 29 rooms. In-room data ports, no-smoking rooms, laundry service, parking (fee). AE, D, DC, MC, V.*

$–$$ 🏨 **Sheraton–Barcelo Hotel.** Traffic and parking in downtown Annapolis can be difficult, especially on weekends and during good weather. Adjacent to the Annapolis Mall and Westfield Shoppingtown, in the midst of numerous chain restaurants, is this large, newly redecorated hostelry with a free shuttle bus to and from the historic downtown. Previously known as the Wyndham Garden, the Sheraton's lobby is outfitted with marble floors, fresh flowers and ferns, and two sitting areas among marble columns. The café is adjacent to the lobby. Rooms are furnished with blond woods, geometric carpeting, and burgundy-printed bedspreads. A free shuttle bus leaves hourly to and from the historic downtown. ✉ *173 Jennifer Rd., 21401,* ☎ *410/266–3131 or 888/627–8980,* 𝖥𝖠𝖷 *410/266–6247. 197 rooms. Café, lobby lounge, in-room data ports, no-smoking rooms, room service, indoor pool, gym, business center, meeting rooms, free parking. AE, D, DC, MC, V.*

$ 🏨 **Best Western Annapolis.** This two-story motel is a good value for the money. Set away from traffic intersections but just 3 mi from the U.S. Naval Academy, it's a well-maintained hostelry. Guest rooms are entered from the parking lot and are decorated in forest green with quilted floral bedspreads. There's an outdoor covered deck for enjoying breakfast or your own picnic *al fresco.* From U.S. 50, take exit 22 and follow the signs to Riva Road north. The motel is in a business park on your left. ✉ *2520 Riva Rd., 21401,* ☎ *410/224–2800 or 800/638–5179,* 𝖥𝖠𝖷 *410/266–5539,* 𝖶𝖤𝖡 *www.bestwestern.com. 142 rooms. Gym, free parking. AE, D, DC, MC, V. CP.*

Annapolis A to Z

BUS TRAVEL TO AND FROM ANNAPOLIS
Bus service between Washington, D.C. and Annapolis is geared toward commuters rather than vacationers. Weekday mornings and afternoons, buses arrive at and depart from the Navy–Marine Corps Stadium parking lot, from College Avenue by the state buildings, and also

from St. John's College. On weekends Greyhound makes one trip daily, arriving at and departing from the stadium.

➤ BUS INFORMATION: **Dillons Bus Service** (☎ 800/827–3490 or 410/647–2321, WEB www.dillonbus.com). **Greyhound** (☎ 800/231–2222, WEB www.greyhound.com). **MTA** (☎ 800/543–9809 or 410/539–5000, WEB www.marylandmta.com).

CAR TRAVEL

The drive (east on U.S. 50, to the Rowe Boulevard exit) normally takes 35–45 minutes from Washington. During rush hour (weekdays 3:30–6:30 PM), however, it takes about twice as long.

PARKING

Parking spots on Annapolis's historic downtown streets are scarce, but you can pay $4 ($8 for recreational vehicles) to park at the Navy–Marine Corps Stadium (to the right of Rowe Boulevard as you enter town from Route 50), and ride a shuttle bus downtown for 75¢. Parking is also available at garages on Main Street and Gott's Court (adjacent to the visitor center); on weekdays parking is free for the first hour and $1 an hour thereafter; on weekends it costs $4 a day.

TOURS

BOAT TOURS

When the weather's good, Chesapeake Marine Tours, Inc. runs cruises that last from 40 minutes to 7½ hours and go as far as St. Michael's on the eastern shore of the bay, where there's a maritime museum, yachts, dining, and boutiques. Prices range from $6 to $35.

➤ FEES AND SCHEDULES: **Chesapeake Marine Tours, Inc.** (✉ City Dock, ☎ 410/268–7600 or 301/261–2719).

BUS TOURS

Discover Annapolis Tours leads one-hour narrated minibus tours ($12) that introduce you to the history and architecture of Annapolis. Tours leave from the visitor center daily April through November and most weekends December through March.

➤ FEES AND SCHEDULES: **Discover Annapolis Tours** (✉ 31 Decatur Ave., ☎ 410/626–6000).

WALKING TOURS

The Historic Annapolis Museum Store rents two self-guided (with audiotapes and maps) walking tours: "Historic Annapolis Walk with Walter Cronkite" and "Historic Annapolis African-American Heritage Audio Walking Tour." The cost for each is $5.

Several tours leave from the visitor center at 26 West Street. On Annapolis Walkabout tours ($8), experts on historic buildings take you around the historic district and the U.S. Naval Academy. Tours are held weekends from April to October.

Guides from Three Centuries Tours wear Colonial-style dress and take you to the state house, St. John's College, and the Naval Academy. The cost is $9. Tours depart daily April through October at 10:30 from the visitor center and at 1:30 from the information booth, City Dock.

➤ FEES AND SCHEDULES: **Annapolis Walkabout** (✉ 223 S. Cherry Grove Ave., ☎ 410/263–8253). **Historic Annapolis Museum Store** (✉ 77 Main St., ☎ 410/268–5576). **Three Centuries Tours** (✉ 48 Maryland Ave., ☎ 410/263–5401, FAX 410/263–1901).

FREDERICK, MARYLAND

Just 45 miles outside the District of Columbia are the rolling farmlands and Appalachian foothills of Maryland's second-largest city, Frederick. Founded in 1745, it has one of the best-preserved historic districts in Maryland, topped only by Annapolis. Frederick was in the path of the Civil War Battles of Antietam, Monocacy, and South Mountain, and was in a see-saw of occupation between Confederate and Union forces. The city would have been destroyed in 1864 had the local government not come up with a ransom of $200,000 to Confederate general Jubal Early to spare the town.

The historic downtown with its many church spires occupies a grid of one-way streets that traverse Carroll Creek. One of the bridges across the creek is painted with a large-scale mural celebrating the spirit of the community. There are several museums and homes to tour, and it's an excellent area for antiques shopping, both in Frederick and in nearby towns. Just 8 mi east is New Market, billed as "the Antique Capital of Maryland."

An easy day trip can be made from the Washington area, or visitors may choose to spend the night at a historic bed-and-breakfast or a chain motel. A side trip from Frederick is the quaint, historic town of Harper's Ferry, W.V., 27 miles to the south.

The most direct route to the Frederick Visitor's Center—a good place to pick up free maps and begin touring the area—is to take I-270 into the city, where it becomes Highway 15 North. Exit at Rosemont Avenue and follow the signs to the visitor's center. There has been some long-term construction at the Patrick Street interchange; if this exit is open, take Patrick Street East.

Sights to See

Barbara Fritchie House and Museum. This modest brick cottage was home to patriot Fritchie, who bravely defied Confederate troops from her second-floor window. The daring woman, in her 90s at the time, refused to remove her American flag and shouted at the soldiers parading by her house. Winston Churchill and Franklin Roosevelt were visitors here, and John Greenleaf Whittier wrote a poem about her. ⊠ *154 W. Patrick St.,* ☎ *301/698–0630.* ☜ *$2.* ☺ *Apr.–Sept., Mon. and Thurs.–Sat. 10–4; Oct.–Nov., Sat. 10–4, Sun. 1–4.*

NEED A
BREAK?   Any time, any day, drop by the **Frederick Coffee Company** (⊠ Shab Row/Everedy Square, 100 East St., ☎ 301/698–0039 or 800/822–0806) for pastries, soup, sandwiches, quiche, dessert, and—of course—a wide variety of coffees and other beverages. As you walk in the door of this former 1930s gas station, inhale the heady fragrance of beans roasting in front of you.

Historical Society of Frederick County. A gracious 1820s Federal-style mansion depicts the homefront during the Civil War. Docent-led tours of the society's building include a room that shows the building was used as a female orphanage for 70 years. The downstairs library is invaluable to those doing genealogical research or seeking background for historical novels. The society's bookstore is across the street. ⊠ *24 East Church St.,* ☎ *301/663–1188,* 𝖶𝖤𝖡 *www.fwp.net/hsfc.* ☜ *$2.* ☺ *Jan. 15–Dec., Mon.–Sat. 10–4, Sun. 1–4.*

Monocacy National Battlefield. The Civil War battle fought here—although won by the Confederates—is important because it delayed and prevented them from capturing Washington, D.C. The **visitor center** (☎ 301/662–3515, 𝖶𝖤𝖡 www.nps.gov/mono/home.html) is housed in the fieldstone Gambrell's Mill and features an interactive computer program and electric map with commentary about the battle. Hours for the center from April through October are daily, 8 to 4:30 (it's open

Frederick, Maryland

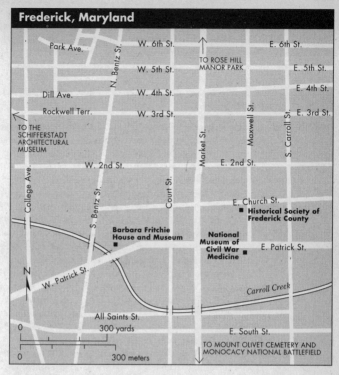

until 5:30 from Memorial Day to Labor Day); from November to March the center hours are Wednesday to Sunday, 8 to 4:30. Walking trails and a self-guided auto tour take you through the July 9, 1864 clash. ⊠ *4801 Urbana Pike (north of Exit 26 of I-270).*

Mount Olivet Cemetery. Among the 800 Confederate and Union soldiers killed during the Battle of Antietam are graves of Frederick's famous sons and daughters including Francis Scott Key and Barbara Fritchie. ⊠ *515 S. Market St.,* ☎ *301/662–1164.* ☉ *Daily dawn–dusk, chapel daily 8–5.*

National Museum of Civil War Medicine. This is the only known museum devoted to the study and interpretation of Civil War medicine. Housed in a historic building that served as a furniture store and funeral home from 1830 to 1978, it was used to embalm the dead from the Battle of Antietam in 1862. Exhibits include "Recruitment," "Camp Life," "Medical Evacuation," and "Veterinary Medicine." More than 3,000 artifacts are on display, including a Civil War ambulance and the only known surviving Civil War surgeon's tent. Photographs and a video help explain the story of medicine during this period. ⊠ *48 E. Patrick St.,* ☎ *301/695–1864,* WEB *www.civilwarmed.org.* ☒ *$6.50.* ☉ *Mon.– Sat. 10–5, Sun. 11–5. From Nov. 15–Mar. 15, museum closes at 4.*

Rose Hill Manor Park. The home of Maryland's first elected governor, Thomas Johnson, hosts two museums on the property. The **Children's Museum** specializes in historic educational tours targeted at elementary school ages. The **Farm Museum** offers self-guided tours featuring 19th- and 20th-century exhibits that include a farm kitchen, carpentry shop, harvesting equipment, and a separate carriage museum. ⊠ *1611 N. Market St.,* ☎ *301/694–1646 or 301/694–1648.* ☒ *Donation requested.* ☉ *Apr.–Oct., Mon.–Sat. 10–4, Sun. 1–4; Nov., Sat. 10–4, Sun. 1–4.*

Schifferstadt Architectural Museum. This structure, built in 1756, is one of the finest examples of German architecture in colonial America. Inside you can see original construction elements such as a vaulted cellar, a "wishbone" chimney, exposed hand-hewn oak beams, mud and straw insulation, and original hardware. An authentic 18th-century garden complements the story of everyday farm life. ⊠ *1110 Rosemont Ave.,* ☎ *301/663–3885.* ⬚ *$2.* ⊙ *Apr.–mid-Dec., Tues.–Sat. 10–4, Sun. noon–4.*

Dining and Lodging

$$$-$$$$ ✕ **John Hagan's Tavern.** Built in 1785, this fieldstone structure with its original wooden floors has always been a tavern or restaurant. Staff wear period dress, and all desserts and breads are made on the premises. Specialties on the Mid-Atlantic regional menu with an early-American influence include house-smoked salmon, duck, and quail; Maryland-style roast chicken with lump-crabmeat sauce; and twin grilled duck breasts in a pear–orange confit. ⊠ *5018 Old National Pike, Braddock Heights,* ☎ *301/371–9189. AE, D, DC, MC, V. Closed Mon.*

$$-$$$ ✕ **Province Restaurant.** This historic building has handmade quilts hanging on the brick walls of the original house, a garden dining room, and seasonal flower and herb gardens. The restaurant's name refers to the 1767 property deed when the area was still known as the "Province of Maryland." Specialties include the Province seafood sauté, veal *amontillado* (prepared with fine, dry sherry), *mire poix* (sautéed fragrant vegetables), braised lamb shank, and Parisian *poulet* (chicken finished with Brie and sautéed mushrooms). ⊠ *129–131 N. Market St.,* ☎ *301/663–1441. AE, D, DC, MC, V. Closed Mon.*

$$-$$$ ✕ **Tauraso's.** A wood oven emanating the distinctive essence of pizza greets diners approaching the reservations desk. This wood-paneled, white-tablecloth trattoria specializes in pasta dishes, poultry, steaks, seafood, and pizzas. A favorite appetizer is Tauraso's own homemade seafood sausage. The restaurant has a bar, separate dining room, and a garden patio open seasonally. ⊠ *6 East St.,* ☎ *301/663–6000. AE, D, DC, MC, V.*

$-$$ ✕ **Brewer's Alley.** Frederick's first brew pub was once a town hall and market building. The eatery is clean and bright, and copper brewing pots gleam next to the bar and wooden tables. Substantial main dishes, such as jumbo-lump Maryland crab cakes, double-thick pork chops, steaks, and ribs are available as well as starters, salads, specialty sandwiches, pasta, and pizza. Several varieties of beers are made on the premises. ⊠ *124 North Market St.,* ☎ *301/631–0089. AE, D, DC, MC, V.*

$-$$ ✕🖫 **Catoctin Inn and Conference Center.** Antiques, books, family pictures, and heirlooms decorate this large house built in 1790. The atmosphere is cozy and its well-worn original floors attest to the traffic that has come and gone in this inn a few miles south of Frederick. Some rooms have working fireplaces and hot tubs. The inn's restaurant is open to the public for lunch and dinner ($$-$$$, closed Monday). Maryland crab soup, hickory-smoked duck, crusted rack of lamb, and bacon-wrapped pork are all specialties of the house. ⊠ *3619 Buckeystown Pike, Buckeystown, 21717,* ☎ *301/874–5555 or 800/730–5550,* 𝔽𝔸𝕏 *301/831–8102,* 𝚆𝙴𝙱 *www.catoctininn.com. 11 rooms, 3 cottages, 2 suites. Restaurant, in-room VCRs, refrigerators, outdoor hot tub, business services, meeting rooms, airport shuttle. AE, D, DC, MC, V.*

$ ✕🖫 **Turning Point Inn.** This lovely Edwardian-era estate built in 1910 is a B&B as well as an excellent restaurant ($$$) open to the public for dinner and Sunday brunch. The large guest rooms have antique reproduction furniture and private baths. There are several dining rooms, one with an enclosed patio overlooking the gardens of the six-acre estate. The main-floor common-area rooms have Queen Anne and other antique furnishings. Specialties of the restaurant include lobster bisque, crispy sea bass, crab cakes, pheasant served two ways, roasted venison, and spicy seafood. ⊠ *3406 Urbana Pike (at Exit 26 off I–270), 21701,* ☎ *301/874–2421 or 301/831–8232,* WEB *www.bbonline.com/md/ turningpoint/. Restaurant, 5 rooms, 2 cottages. Bar. D, MC, V.*

$$$ 🖬 **Tyler Spite Inn.** This federal-style mansion retells some history in its furnishings. The check-in desk was used by Gen. MacArthur when signing a peace treaty in the Philippines. A 10-ft-high pier mirror from the old Frederick train station is the one President Lincoln used to adjust his top hat before giving a lecture to the townspeople following the Battle of Antietam. The Chippendale-style mahogany and ebony grand piano was made in Baltimore for Francis Scott Key, author of the national anthem. Of the five guest rooms in two adjacent 19th-century homes, seven have working fireplaces. The large rooms are beautifully decorated in colors, fabrics, and wallpaper indicative of the era. Lodging price includes room tax, a generous breakfast, and an extensive afternoon tea. ⊠ *112 West Church St., 21701,* ☎ *301/831–4455. 5 rooms. Pool. MC, V. CP.*

Frederick, Maryland A to Z

To research prices, get advice from other travelers, and book travel arrangements, visit www.fodors.com.

BUS TRAVEL TO AND FROM FREDERICK
Greyhound runs daily buses between Frederick and Washington, D.C. Buses leave every two or three hours; call for schedules. The trip takes about an hour.

➤ Bus Information: **Greyhound** (☎ 301/663–3311, WEB www.greyhound.com).

BUS TRAVEL WITHIN FREDERICK
Frederick's historic area is compact and visitors can walk to most attractions. Otherwise, Frederick Transit runs frequent buses on all downtown streets and arteries.

➤ Bus Information: **Frederick Transit** (☎ 301/694–2065).

CAR TRAVEL
It's easiest to drive to Frederick. From Washington, the trip takes about 45 minutes. Drive north on I–270 from the Beltway I–495. The highway number changes to I–70. Frederick has several exits. To reach the historic area, use exit 56 and follow Patrick Street west toward downtown.

TAXIS
➤ Taxi Companies: **City Cab Co.** (☎ 301/662–2250).

TOURS
The Frederick Tour & Carriage Company offers horse-drawn carriage rides through the city's historic district on weekends by reservation ($4.50 for one hour). The company also offers historic walking and ghost tours.

Costumed guides lead 90-minute walking tours ($4.75) through the historic district on weekends and holidays from April through December, with an additional Friday tour June through September, leaving at 1:30. May through October, ghost tours ($7) are offered Friday and Saturday "after dark." Tours leave from the Frederick Visitor's Center (call for information).

➤ Fees and Schedules: **Frederick Tour & Carriage Company** (☎ 301/ 694–7433, WEB www.frederickcarriage.com). **Frederick Visitor Center** (⊠ 19 East Church St., ☎ 301/228–2888 or 800/999–3613).

VISITOR INFORMATION
The Frederick Visitor Center is open daily 9–5 and offers brochures, walking-tour maps, and guided 90-minute tours. The Tourism Council of Frederick County can mail you brochures about the area.

➤ TOURIST INFORMATION: **Frederick Visitor Center** (✉ 19 East Church St., ☎ 301/228–2888 or 800/999–3613). **Tourism Council of Frederick County** (☎ 301/228–2888 or 800/999–3613, WEB www.visitfrederick.org).

MOUNT VERNON, WOODLAWN, AND GUNSTON HALL

Long before Washington was planned, the shores of the Potomac had been divided into plantations by wealthy traders and gentleman farmers. Most traces of the Colonial era were obliterated as the capital grew in the 19th century, but several splendid examples of plantation architecture remain on the Virginia side of the Potomac, just 15 mi or so south of D.C. In just one day you can easily visit three such mansions: Mount Vernon, the home of George Washington and one of the most popular sites in the area; Woodlawn, the estate of Washington's step-granddaughter; and Gunston Hall, the home of George Mason, author of the document on which the Bill of Rights was based. On hillsides overlooking the river, these estates offer magnificent vistas and bring a bygone era to vivid life.

Numbers in the margin correspond to points of interest on the Mount Vernon, Woodlawn, and Gunston Hall map.

Mount Vernon

★ ❶ *16 mi southeast of Washington, D.C.; 8 mi south of Alexandria, VA.*

Mount Vernon and the surrounding lands had been in the Washington family for nearly 90 years by the time George inherited it all in 1761. Before taking over command of the Continental Army, Washington was a yeoman farmer managing the 8,000-acre plantation, of which more than 3,000 acres were under cultivation. He also oversaw the transformation of the main house from an ordinary farm dwelling into what was, for the time, a grand mansion.

The red-roofed house is elegant though understated, with an yellow pine exterior that's been painted and coated with layers of sand to resemble white-stone blocks. The first-floor rooms are quite ornate, especially the formal large dining room, with its molded ceiling decorated with agricultural motifs. Throughout the house are other, smaller symbols of the owner's eminence, such as a key to the main portal of the Bastille—presented to Washington by the Marquis de Lafayette—and Washington's presidential chair. As you tour the mansion, guides are stationed throughout the house to describe the furnishings and answer questions.

The real treasure of Mount Vernon is the view from around back: beneath a 90-ft portico, George Washington's contribution to architecture—the home's dramatic riverside porch—overlooks an expanse of lawn that slopes down to the Potomac. In springtime the view of the river (a mile wide where it passes the plantation) is framed by the blossoms of redbud and dogwood. Protocol requires United States Navy and Coast Guard ships to salute when passing the house. Although not required, foreign naval vessels often salute, too.

You can stroll around the estate's 500 acres and three gardens, visiting the workshops, the kitchen, the carriage house, the greenhouse, the slave quarters, and—down the hill toward the boat landing—the tomb of George and Martha Washington. There's also a pioneer farmer site: a 4-acre hands-on exhibit with a reconstruction of George Washington's 16-sided treading barn as its centerpiece. Among the souvenirs sold at the plantation are stripling boxwoods that began life as clip-

Mount Vernon, Woodlawn, and Gunston Hall

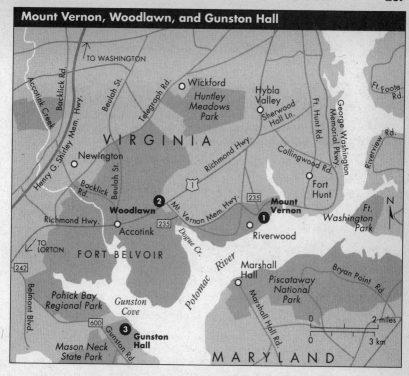

pings from bushes planted in 1798, the year before Washington died. A tour of house and grounds takes about two hours.. There's a limited number of wheelchairs available at the main gate. Private, evening candlelight tours of the mansion with staff dressed in 18th-century costumes can be arranged. ⊠ *Southern end of George Washington Pkwy., Mount Vernon, VA,* ☎ *703/780–2000; 703/799–8606 evening tours;* FAX *703/799–8609.* ▨ *$9.* ⊙ *Mar. and Sept.–Oct., daily 9–5; Apr.–Aug., daily 8–5; Nov.–Feb., daily 9–4.*

Woodlawn

❷ *3 mi west of Mount Vernon, 15 mi south of Washington, D.C.*

Woodlawn occupies a piece of ground that was originally part of the Mount Vernon estate; even today you can see traces of the bowling green fronting Washington's home from Woodlawn. The house was built for Washington's step-granddaughter, Nelly Custis, who married his favorite nephew, Lawrence Lewis. (Lewis was summoned to Mount Vernon from Fredericksburg to assist his uncle with his papers and his many guests.)

The Lewises' home, completed in 1805, was designed by William Thornton, a physician and amateur architect from the West Indies who drew up the original plans for the U.S. Capitol. Like Mount Vernon, the Woodlawn house is constructed wholly of native materials, including the clay for its bricks and the yellow pine used throughout its interior. In the tradition of southern riverfront mansions, Woodlawn has a central hallway that provides a cool refuge in summer. At one corner of the passage is a bust of George Washington set on a pedestal so the crown of the head is at 6 ft 2 inches—Washington's actual height. The bust and pedestal were constructed so they could go outside, sink 2 inches into the ground, and then be the same height as Washington. The music room has a ceiling that's approximately 2 ft higher than any other in the house, built that way to improve the acoustics for the harp and harpsichord recitals that the Lewises and their children enjoyed.

After Woodlawn passed out of the Lewis family's hands it was owned by a Quaker community, which established a meetinghouse and the first integrated school in Virginia here. Subsequent owners included the playwright Paul Kester and Senator and Mrs. Oscar Underwood of Alabama. The property was acquired by the National Trust for Historic Preservation in 1957, which had been operating it as a museum since 1951. Every March, Woodlawn hosts an annual needlework exhibit with over 700 items on display.

Also on the grounds of Woodlawn is the **Pope-Leighey House.** Frank Lloyd Wright designed this "Usonian" modernistic home as a means of providing affordable housing for people of modest means. It was built in 1940 and moved here from Falls Church, Virginia, in 1964. ⊠ *9000 Richmond Hwy., Mount Vernon, VA,* ☎ *703/780–4000,* WEB *www.nthp.org/mail/sitesmain.htm.* ⊠ *$6, Mar. $7; combination ticket for Woodlawn and Pope-Leighey House $10.* ☉ *Mar.–Dec. daily 10– 5 (no guided tours in Mar. due to annual needlework show); tours leave every ½ hr (last tour at 4:30).*

Gunston Hall

❸   *12 mi south of Woodlawn, 25 mi south of Washington, D.C.*

Gunston Hall Plantation—like Mount Vernon, located on the Potomac River—was the home of a lesser-known George. George Mason was a gentleman farmer, colonel of the Fairfax militia, and author of the Virginia Declaration of Rights, the model for the U.S. Bill of Rights, which called for freedom of the press, tolerance of religion, and other fundamental democratic principles. Mason was a framer of the Constitution but refused to sign the final document because it didn't stop the importation of slaves, adequately restrain the powers of the federal government, or include a bill of rights. Mason's objections spurred the movement for the inclusion of the Bill of Rights into the Constitution.

Mason's home, Gunston Hall, was built circa 1755. The Georgian-style mansion features some of the finest hand-carved ornamented interiors in the country, demonstrating the talent of the 18th century's foremost architect, William Buckland, who also designed the Hammond-Harwood and Chase-Lloyd houses in Annapolis. Gunston Hall is built of native brick, black walnut, and yellow pine. The style of the time demanded absolute balance in all structures, hence the false door set into one side of the center hallway. The house's interior, with its carved woodwork in styles from Chinese to Gothic, has been meticulously restored, with paints made from the original formulas and carefully carved replacements for the intricate mahogany medallions in the moldings. Restored outbuildings include a kitchen, dairy, laundry, and smokehouse. A schoolhouse has also been reconstructed on the property.

The formal gardens, currently under excavation by a team of archaeologists, are famous for their boxwoods—some now 12 ft high, thought to be among the oldest in the country and planted during George Mason's time. The Potomac is visible past the expansive deer park. Also on the grounds is an active farmyard with award-winning historic livestock and crops. Special programs—such as history lectures and hearth cooking demonstrations—are offered throughout the year. A tour of Gunston Hall takes a minimum of 45 minutes; tours begin at the visitor center, which includes a museum and gift shop. ⊠ *10709 Gunston Rd., Mason Neck, VA,* ☎ *800/811–6966 or 703/550–9220,* WEB *www.gunstonhall.org.* ⊠ *$7.* ☉ *Daily 9:30–5; first tour at 10, last tour at 4:30.*

Mount Vernon, Woodlawn, and Gunston Hall A to Z

BIKE TRAVEL

An asphalt bicycle path leads from the Virginia side of Memorial Bridge (across from the Lincoln Memorial), past Ronald Reagan National Airport, and through Alexandria all the way to Mount Vernon. The trail is steep in places, but bikers in moderately good condition can make the 16-mi trip in less than two hours. You can rent bicycles at several locations in Washington.

BOAT TRAVEL

The *Potomac Spirit* makes a pleasant trip from Washington down the Potomac to Mount Vernon. Tickets include admission to the estate. You can take lunch, dinner, and Sunday brunch cruises on the *Spirit of Washington*, which also departs from Washington but doesn't go quite as far as Mount Vernon. Tickets include your meal and, on the dinner and brunch cruises, live entertainment. Prices range from $26.50 to $72.45, depending on the meal served (if any) and the day of the week.

➤ BOAT INFORMATION: *Potomac Spirit* and *Spirit of Washington* (⊠ Pier 4, 6th and Water Sts. SW, ☎ 202/554–8000, boat reservations).

BUS TRAVEL

For Mount Vernon, you can take Fairfax County Connector Bus 101 or 102 marked MT. VERNON (50¢) from Huntington. Buses leave about once an hour—more often during rush hour—and operate weekdays 6:30 AM–9:15 PM, Saturday 7:20 AM–7:36 PM, and Sunday 9:21 AM–6:43 PM.

For Woodlawn, take Bus 105 (FT. BELVOIR; 50¢). Buses operate weekdays 6 AM–11:10 PM and weekends 6:48 AM–7:05 PM. Schedules for these lines are posted at the Huntington Metrorail station. Buses returning to the station have the same numbers but are marked HUNTINGTON.

➤ BUS INFORMATION: **Fairfax County Connector** (☎ 703/339–7200).

CAR TRAVEL

To reach Mount Vernon from the Capital Beltway (Route 495), take Exit 1 and follow the signs to George Washington Memorial Parkway southbound. Mount Vernon is about 8½ mi south. From downtown Washington, cross into Arlington on either Key Bridge, Memorial Bridge, or the 14th Street Bridge and drive south on the George Washington Memorial Parkway past Ronald Reagan National Airport through Alexandria straight to Mount Vernon. The trip from Washington takes about a half hour.

For Woodlawn, travel southwest on Route 1 to the second Route 235 intersection (the first leads to Mount Vernon). The entrance to Woodlawn is on the right at the traffic light. From Mount Vernon, travel northwest on Route 235 to the Route 1 intersection; Woodlawn is straight ahead through the intersection.

To visit Gunston Hall, travel south on Route 1, 9 mi past Woodlawn to Route 242; turn left there and go 3½ mi to the plantation entrance.

SUBWAY TRAVEL

From downtown D.C., Arlington, or Alexandria you can take the Yellow Line train to the Huntington Metrorail station ($1.50–$2.50, depending on the time of day and point of origin), from which you must take a bus.

TOURS

Gray Line runs half-day trips to Mount Vernon (with a stop in Alexandria), departing daily at 8:30 AM (and 2 PM in the summer) from Union

Station. A ticket is $25 and includes admission to the mansion and grounds.

Tourmobile offers trips to Mount Vernon, April through October daily at 10 AM, noon, and 2 PM, from Arlington Cemetery and the Washington Monument. Reservations must be made in person 30 minutes in advance at the point of departure, and the $22 ticket includes admission to the mansion. A two-day combination ticket for Mount Vernon and several sites in Washington is available for $40.

➤ FEES AND SCHEDULES: **Gray Line** (☎ 301/386–8300). **Tourmobile** (☎ 202/554–5100, WEB www.tourmobile.com).

FREDERICKSBURG, VIRGINIA

Just 50 mi south of Washington on I–95, near the falls of the Rappahannock River, Fredericksburg is a popular day-trip destination for history buffs. The town's National Historic District contains the house George Washington bought for his mother, Mary; the Rising Sun Tavern; and Kenmore, the magnificent 1752 plantation home of George Washington's sister. The town is a favorite with antiques collectors, who enjoy cruising the dealers' shops along Caroline Street on land once favored by Indian tribes as fishing and hunting ground.

Although its site was visited by explorer Captain John Smith as early as 1608, the town of Fredericksburg wasn't founded until 1728. Established as a frontier port to serve nearby tobacco farmers and iron miners, Fredericksburg took its name from England's crown prince at the time, and the streets still bear names of his family members: George, Caroline, Sophia, Princess Anne, Hanover, William, and Amelia.

George Washington knew Fredericksburg well, having grown up just across the Rappahannock on Ferry Farm—his residence from age 6 to 19. The myths about chopping down a cherry tree and throwing a coin (actually a rock) across the Rappahannock—later described as the Potomac—refer to this period of his life. In later years Washington often visited his mother here on Charles Street.

Fredericksburg city prospered in the decades after independence, benefiting from its location midway along the 100-mi route between Washington and Richmond—an important intersection of railroad lines and waterways. When the Civil War broke out in 1861, Fredericksburg became the linchpin of the Confederate defense of Richmond and, as such, the inevitable target of Union assaults.

The short drive across the Rappahannock to George Washington's Ferry Farm, Chatham Manor, and Belmont is well worth it to see where our first president grew up, tour the beautiful residences, and enjoy their splendid views of all of Fredericksburg.

Numbers in the text correspond to numbers in the margin and on the Fredericksburg, Virginia, map.

Downtown Fredericksburg

Fredericksburg, a modern commercial town, includes a 40-block National Historic District with more than 350 original 18th- and 19th-century buildings. No play acting here—residents live in the historic homes and shop in the quaint stores, noted for their large number of antiques.

A Good Tour

Begin at the **Fredericksburg Visitor Center** ① to get maps or directions or to join a tour. Walk northwest on Caroline Street three blocks to the **Hugh Mercer Apothecary Shop** ②, where you can see tools used in

18th- and 19th-century medicine, passing numerous antiques shops and boutiques along the way. Continue another three blocks to the **Rising Sun Tavern** ③, a house built by George Washington's brother Charles that was a popular taproom where patriots conversed over eat and drink. Walk back to Lewis Street, turn right, and walk two blocks to the **Mary Washington House** ④, purchased by her famous son, where George's mother spent the last 17 years of her life. Continue on Lewis Street and turn right on Washington Avenue to the **Kenmore** ⑤ entrance. This home of George's sister contains rooms that have been called some of the most beautiful in America. To see the **Mary Washington Grave and Monument** ⑥, at a spot on her daughter's property where Mrs. Washington liked to read, turn right on Washington Avenue and walk two blocks. Then turn around and walk back down Washington four blocks to the **Confederate Cemetery** ⑦, the final resting place for more than 2,000 Confederate soldiers, including some generals. From the cemetery take William Street east (back toward the center of town) four blocks to Charles Street and turn right to the **James Monroe Museum and Memorial Library** ⑧, where the fifth president of the United States practiced law in the 1780s. Return to the corner of Charles and William and walk a block to Princess Anne Street. The **Fredericksburg Area Museum and Cultural Center** ⑨, on the far right corner, explores the story of the area from prehistoric times through the Revolutionary and Civil wars to the present. Walk one more block along Princess Anne to the **George Washington Masonic Museum** ⑩, where George became a Mason. To return to the visitor center, turn left on Hanover and right on Caroline Street. To view the **Mary Washington College Galleries** ⑪, it's best to drive unless you want to walk almost a mile from where you are now. Drive five blocks on Caroline Street and turn left on Amelia. Follow Amelia and turn left on Washington Avenue. One block later, turn right onto William Street. At College Avenue, turn right and drive ½ mi to the gallery on your right. Parking (on College Avenue and two reserved spots in the staff lot at the corner of College and Thornton Street) may be tight on weekdays when the college is in session. The galleries display paintings, drawings, sculptures, photography, ceramics, and textiles by art faculty, students, and contemporary artists.

TIMING

A walking tour through the town proper takes three to four hours; battlefield tours will take at least that long. (The Park Service's tape cassettes last about 2 ½ hours for an automobile tour.) A self-guided tour of the Mary Washington College galleries takes about 30 minutes. Spring and fall are the best times to tour Fredericksburg on foot, but because Virginia weather is temperate intermittently in winter, you may find some suitable walking days then. Summers—especially August—can be hot, humid, and not very pleasant for a long walk.

Sights to See

⑦ **Confederate Cemetery.** This cemetery contains the remains of more than 2,000 soldiers (most of them unknown) as well as the graves of Generals Dabney Maury, Seth Barton, Carter Stevenson, Daniel Ruggles, Henry Sibley, and Abner Perrin. ✉ *1100 Washington Ave., near Amelia St.* ⊙ *Daily dawn–dusk.*

⑨ **Fredericksburg Area Museum and Cultural Center.** In an 1816 building once used as a market and town hall, this museum's six permanent exhibits tell the story of the area from prehistoric times through the Revolutionary and Civil wars to the present. Displays include dinosaur footprints from a nearby quarry, Native American artifacts, an 18th-century plantation account book with an inventory of slaves, and other Confederate memorabilia. The first and third floors have chang-

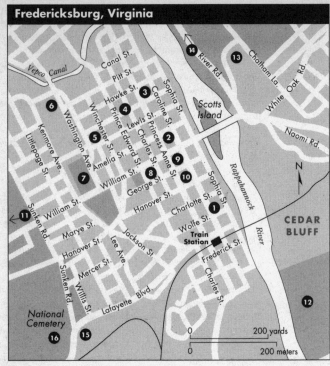

Fredericksburg, Virginia

ing exhibits. ⊠ *907 Princess Anne St.,* ☎ *540/371–3037,* WEB *www. famcc.org.* ≋ *$4.* ⊙ *Mar.–Nov., Mon.–Sat. 9–5, Sun. 1–5; Dec.–Feb., Mon.–Sat. 10–4, Sun. 1–4.*

❶ Fredericksburg Visitor Center. Beyond the usual booklets, pamphlets, and maps, this visitor center has passes that enable you to park for a whole day in what are usually two-hour zones as well as money-saving passes to city attractions ($19.75 for entry to seven sights; $13.75 for four sights). Before beginning your tour, you may want to see the center's ten-minute orientation slide show. The center building itself was constructed in 1824 as a residence and confectionery; during the Civil War it was used as a prison. ⊠ *706 Caroline St.,* ☎ *540/373–1776 or 800/678–4748,* WEB *www.fredericksburg.com/community/tourism.html.* ⊙ *Labor Day– Memorial Day, daily 9–5; Memorial Day–Labor Day, daily 9–7.*

NEED A BREAK?
> Have an old-fashioned malt in **Goolrick's Pharmacy** (⊠ 901 Caroline St., ☎ 540/373–9878), a 1940s drugstore with a soda fountain. In addition to malts and egg creams, Goolrick's serves light meals weekdays 8:30–7 and Saturday 8:30–6. **Virginia Deli** (⊠ 101 William St., ☎ 540/371–2233) offers breakfast, specialty sandwiches, and Virginia favorites Monday–Saturday 8–5 and Sunday 9–5.

❿ George Washington Masonic Museum. Our first president was "raised," or became a Master Mason, in Lodge No. 4 AF and AM in 1752. The lodge museum now contains memorabilia and relics relating to his membership, including an original Gilbert Stuart portrait of him. ⊠ *803 Princess Anne St.,* ☎ *540/373–5885.* ≋ *$2.* ⊙ *By appointment.*

❷ Hugh Mercer Apothecary Shop. Offering a close-up view of 18th- and 19th-century medicine, including instruments and procedures, Hugh Mercer

Apothecary Shop was established in 1771 by Dr. Mercer, a Scotsman who served as a brigadier general of the Continental Army (he was killed at the Battle of Princeton). Dr. Mercer might have been more careful than other Colonial physicians, but his methods will make you cringe. A costumed hostess explicitly describes amputations and cataract operations before the discovery of anesthetics. You can also hear about therapeutic bleeding and see the gruesome devices used in Colonial dentistry. ⊠ *1020 Caroline St., at Amelia St.,* ☎ *540/373–3362.* 🖅 *$4.* ☉ *Mar.–Nov., Mon.–Sat. 9–5; Sun. 11–5; Dec.–Feb., Mon.–Sat. 10–4; Sun. 12–4.*

8 **James Monroe Museum and Memorial Library.** This tiny one-story building—on the site where Monroe, who became the fifth president of the United States, practiced law from 1787 to 1789—contains many of Monroe's possessions, collected and preserved by his family until the present day. They include a mahogany dispatch box used during the negotiation of the Louisiana Purchase and the desk on which Monroe signed the doctrine named for him. ⊠ *908 Charles St.,* ☎ *540/654–1043.* 🖅 *$4.* ☉ *Mar.–Nov., daily 9–5; Dec.–Feb., daily 10–4.*

★ **5** **Kenmore.** Kenmore was built in 1775 on a 1,300-acre plantation owned by Colonel Fielding Lewis, a patriot, merchant, and brother-in-law of George Washington, though it was named Kenmore by a later owner. Lewis sacrificed his fortune to operate a gun factory and otherwise supply General Washington's forces during the Revolutionary War. As a result, his debts forced his widow to sell the home following his death. The plaster moldings in the ceilings are outstanding and even more ornate than those at Mount Vernon. It's believed that the artisan responsible for the ceilings worked frequently in both homes, though his name is unknown, possibly because he was an indentured servant. The furnishings, which include a large standing clock that belonged to Mary Washington, are original 18th-century Virginia furniture with two pieces that belonged to Fielding and Betty Washington Lewis. In the beautiful dining room is a portrait of Betty, who strongly resembles her famous brother. The subterranean Crowningshield museum on the grounds includes family portraits and changing exhibits of Fredericksburg life. After the 60-minute tour, you're served tea and ginger cookies baked according to a Washington family recipe. ⊠ *1201 Washington Ave.,* ☎ *540/373–3381,* 🌐 *www.kenmore.org.* 🖅 *$6.* ☉ *Mar.–Dec., Mon.–Sat. 10–5, Sun. noon–5.*

11 **Mary Washington College Galleries.** The Ridderhof Martin Gallery hosts exhibitions of art from various cultures and historical periods. In Melchers Hall, the duPont Gallery displays paintings, drawing, sculpture, photography, ceramics, and textiles by art faculty, students, and contemporary artists. ⊠ *College Ave.,* ☎ *540/654–2120.* 🖅 *Free.* ☉ *During college sessions, Mon., Wed., and Fri. 10–4, weekends 1–4.*

6 **Mary Washington Grave and Monument.** A 40-ft granite obelisk, dedicated by President Grover Cleveland in 1894, marks the final resting place of George's mother at "Meditation Rock," a place on her daughter's property where Mrs. Washington liked to read. It replaced a previous marble monument cornerstone laid by President Andrew Jackson in 1833, which was damaged by the Civil War bombardment of Fredericksburg.

4 **Mary Washington House.** George purchased this modest white-painted house for his mother in 1772. She spent the last 17 years of her life here, tending the charming garden where her boxwood still flourishes and where many a bride and groom now exchange their vows. Inside, displays include Mrs. Washington's "best dressing glass"—a silver-over-tin mirror—and her teapot, as well as period furniture. The kitchen and its spit are original. Tours begin on the back porch with a history of the house. From there you can see the brick sidewalk leading to Kenmore, the home of Mrs. Washington's only daughter. ✉ *1200 Charles St.,* ☎ *540/373–1569.* 💲 *$4.* ⏰ *Mar.–Nov., Mon.–Sat. 9–5, Sun. 11–5; Dec.–Feb., Mon.–Sat. 10–4, Sun. 12–4.*

❸ Rising Sun Tavern. In 1760 George Washington's brother Charles built as his home what became the Rising Sun Tavern, a watering hole for such patriots as the Lee brothers; Patrick Henry, the five-term Governor of Virginia who said, "Give me liberty or give me death"; and future presidents Washington and Jefferson. A "wench" in period costume leads a tour without stepping out of character. From her perspective you watch the activity—day and night, upstairs and down—at this busy institution. In the taproom you're served spiced tea. ✉ *1304 Caroline St.,* ☎ *540/371–1494.* 💲 *$4.* ⏰ *Mar.–Nov., Mon.–Sat. 9–5, Sun. 11–5; Dec.–Feb., Mon.–Sat. 10–4, Sun. 12–4.*

Around Fredericksburg

Surrounding the town of Fredericksburg are historic sites and beautiful vistas where, in 1862, Union forces looked menacingly over the peaceful little place with conquest on their mind. Today you see only the lively Rappahannock and beautiful homes on a lovely drive across the river.

A Good Drive

From downtown Fredericksburg, drive east on William Street (Route 3) across the Rappahannock River 1 mi to **George Washington's Ferry Farm** ⑫, on the right. Living here from age 6 to 19, Washington received his formal education and taught himself surveying. Park (free) and see the site with its exhibits and ongoing archaeological excavations. Return on Route 3 toward Fredericksburg and turn right at the signs to **Chatham Manor** ⑬, just east of the river. This Georgian mansion—now a museum—built by noted plantation owner William Fitzhugh overlooks the Rappahannock River and the town of Fredericksburg. Fitzhugh's contemporaries George Washington and Thomas Jefferson frequently slept and dined here. From Chatham Manor take River Road (Route 607) about a mile along the river, crossing U.S. 1 (Jefferson Davis Highway) to Route 1001 and **Belmont** ⑭, a 1790s spacious Georgian house furnished with a rich collection of antiques and paintings of the 20th-century artist Gari Melchers. Return to Route 1 via Route 1001 and turn right (south) and cross the river. Turn left on Princess Anne Street (Business 1, 17, and 2) and go 1½ mi to the train station. This takes you past many old homes, churches, the main business district, and the museum. Turn right on Lafayette Boulevard; the **Fredericksburg/Spotsylvania National Military Park** ⑮ and **National Cemetery** ⑯ are ½ mi ahead on the right. Exhibits, films, and ranger-led tours describe Fredericksburg's role in the Civil War. In the cemetery are buried 15,000 Union casualties, most of whom were never identified.

TIMING

Allow 5 minutes to drive to Ferry Farm and 10 minutes each to drive to Belmont and Chatham Manor. A tour of Belmont takes about an hour, as does Chatham Manor if you tour the museum and gardens. The battlefields of Wilderness, Chancellorsville, and Spotsylvania Court House are each within 15 mi of Fredericksburg. It can take one to several hours to tour each one, depending on your level of interest. At the Fredericksburg Battlefield Visitor Center, allow an hour or two—there's a 12-minute slide show, a small museum, and frequent walking tours.

Sights to See

⑭ Belmont. The last owner of this 1790s Georgian-style house was American artist Gari Melchers, who chaired the Smithsonian Commission to establish the National Gallery of Art in Washington; his wife, Corinne, deeded the 27-acre estate and its collections to Virginia. Belmont is now a public museum and a Virginia National Historic Landmark administered by Mary Washington College. You can take a one-hour tour of the spacious house, which is furnished with a rich collection of antiques. Galleries in the stone studio, built by Melchers in 1924, house the largest repository of his work. An orientation movie is shown in the reception area, formerly the carriage house. ⊠ *224 Washington St., Belmont Hills, VA,* ☎ *540/654–1015.* ⌂ *$4.* ☉ *Mar.–Nov., Mon.–Sat. 10–5, Sun. 1–5; Dec.–Feb., Mon.–Sat. 10–4, Sun. 1–4.*

⑬ **Chatham Manor.** A fine example of Georgian architecture, Chatham Manor was built between 1768 and 1771 by William Fitzhugh on a site overlooking the Rappahannock River and the town of Fredericksburg. Fitzhugh, a noted plantation owner, frequently hosted such luminaries of his day as George Washington and Thomas Jefferson. During the Civil War, Union forces commandeered the house and converted it into a headquarters and hospital. President Abraham Lincoln conferred with his generals here; Clara Barton (founder of the American Red Cross) and poet Walt Whitman tended the wounded. After the war, the house and gardens were restored by private owners and eventually donated to the National Park Service. The home itself is now a museum housing exhibits spanning several centuries. Concerts are often held here in summer. ⊠ *120 Chatham La., Falmouth, Fredericksburg, VA,* ☎ *540/373–4461.* ⌂ *$4 (includes Fredericksburg/Spotsylvania National Military Park).* ☉ *Daily 9–5.*

★ ⑮ **Fredericksburg/Spotsylvania National Military Park.** The 9,000-acre park actually includes four battlefields and three historic buildings, all accessible for a single admission price. At the Fredericksburg and Chancellorsville visitor centers you can learn about the area's role in the Civil War by watching two 12-minute slide shows (one at each facility) and by viewing displays of soldiers' art and battlefield relics. In season, park rangers lead walking tours. The centers offer tape-recorded tour cassettes ($2.75 rental, $4.25 purchase) and maps that show how to reach hiking trails at the Wilderness, Chancellorsville (where General Stonewall Jackson was mistakenly shot by his own troops), and Spotsylvania Court House battlefields (all within 15 mi of Fredericksburg). Just outside the Fredericksburg battlefield park visitor center is Sunken Road, where from December 11 to 13, 1862, General Robert E. Lee led his troops to a bloody but resounding victory over Union forces attacking across the Rappahannock (there were 18,000 casualties on both sides). Much of the stone wall that hid Lee's sharpshooters has been rebuilt, but 100 yards from the visitor center, part of the original wall overlooks the statue *The Angel of Marye's Heights,* by Felix de Weldon (sculptor of the famous *Marine Corps War Memorial* statue in Arlington, Virginia). This memorial honors Sergeant Richard Kirkland, a South Carolinian who risked his life to bring water to wounded foes; he later died at the Battle of Chickamauga. ⊠ *Fredericksburg Battlefield Visitor Center, Lafayette Blvd. and Sunken Rd.,* ☎ *540/373–6122;* ⊠ *Chancellorsville Battlefield Visitor Center, Rte. 3 W (Plank Rd.),* ☎ *540/786–2880.* ⌂ *$4 (includes all 4 battlefields, Chatham Manor, and other historic buildings).* ☉ *Visitor centers daily 9–5; driving and walking tours daily dawn–dusk.*

⑫ **George Washington's Ferry Farm.** But for the outcries of historians and citizens, a Wal-Mart store would have been built on this site of our first president's boyhood home. The land was saved by the Historic Kenmore Foundation, and the discount store found a location farther out on the same road. Ferry Farm is just across the Rappahannock River from downtown Fredericksburg. Living here from age 6 to 19, Washington received his formal education and taught himself surveying while *not* chopping a cherry tree or throwing a dollar across the Rappahannock. The mainly archaeological site, now with exhibits and ongoing excavations, became a major artillery base and river-crossing site for Union forces during the Battle of Fredericksburg. ⊠ *Rte. 3 E, 268 Kings Hwy. at Ferry Rd., Fredericksburg, VA 22405,* ☎ *540/370–0732,* WEB *www.kenmore. org.* ⊡ *$2.* ☉ *Feb. 21–Dec. 30, Mon.–Sat. 10–5, Sun. noon–5; Jan. 2–Feb. 20, Mon.–Fri. by group reservation only, Sat. 10–4, Sun. noon–4.*

⑯ **National Cemetery.** The National Cemetery is the final resting place of 15,000 Union casualties, most of whom were never identified. ⊠ *Lafayette Blvd. and Sunken Rd.,* ☎ *540/373–6122.* ☉ *Daily dawn–dusk.*

Dining and Lodging

For price category charts, *see* Dining and Lodging *in* Smart Travel Tips A to Z.

$$$–$$$$ ✕ **Claiborne's.** The walls of this swank eatery in the 1910-era Fredericksburg train station are hung with historic train photographs. Solid, classic meals of steaks, chops, and seafood are in keeping with the classy dark green-and-navy color scheme and the mahogany-and-brass bar. ⊠ *200 Lafayette Blvd.,* ☎ *540/371–7080,* WEB *www.claibornesrestaurant. com. AE, DC, MC, V. No lunch Mon.–Sat., no dinner Sun.*

$$–$$$$ ✕ **The Riverview.** There's a view of the Rappahannock River and Chatham Manor from both the dining room, with its cozy fireplace, and the brick patio—a lovely place to eat in summer. The Riverview specializes in Angus beef (particularly prime rib) and seafood, and has been a favorite with locals for years. ⊠ *1101 Sophia St.,* ☎ *540/373–6500. AE, D, DC, MC, V.*

$$–$$$ ✕ **La Petite Auberge.** Housed in a pre-Revolutionary brick general store, this white-tablecloth restaurant actually has three dining rooms in varied decor, as well as a small bar. They specialize in house-cut beef, French onion soup, and seafood with a continental accent. A prix-fixe ($14) three-course dinner is served from 5:30 to 7 Mon.–Thurs. ⊠ *311 William St.,* ☎ *540/371–2727. AE, D, MC, V. Closed Sun.*

$$–$$$ ✕ **Risorante Renato.** This family-owned restaurant, decorated with lace curtains, red carpeting, and walls covered with paintings, specializes in Italian cuisine, including veal and seafood. ⊠ *422 William St.,* ☎ *540/371–8228. AE, MC, V. No lunch weekends.*

$$ ✕ **Merriman's Restaurant & Bar.** Orange walls and bright paintings are clues that this restaurant isn't mired in the past. The eclectic menu features delicious ethnic dishes, innovative new American food, classic Virginia seafood, and desserts made fresh daily. ⊠ *715 Caroline St.,* ☎ *540/371–7723. AE, D, DC, MC, V.*

$$ ✕ **Smythe's Cottage & Tavern.** Taking a step into this cozy dining room—once a blacksmith's house—is like taking a step back in time. The decor is Colonial; the lunch and dinner menus, classic Virginia: seafood pie, quail, stuffed flounder, peanut soup, and Smithfield ham biscuits. ⊠ *303 Fauquier St.,* ☎ *540/373–1645. MC, V. Closed Tues.*

$–$$ ✕ **Sammy T's.** A tin ceiling, high wooden booths, and wooden ceiling fans contribute to the homey, turn-of-the-20th-century atmosphere here. Swivel captain's stools sit at the bar, which is stocked with nearly 50 brands of beer. Vegetarian dishes, healthy foods, and homemade soups and breads share the menu with hamburgers and dinner platters. There's a separate no-smoking section around the corner, but the chumminess in the main dining room is worth chancing the smoke. ⊠ *801 Caroline St.,* ☎ *540/371–2008. AE, D, MC, V.*

$ 🏨 **Fredericksburg Colonial Inn.** This 1920s motel with moss-green siding and forest-green awnings conceals a lobby staircase reminiscent of the one in *Gone with the Wind's* Tara. Indeed, rooms are furnished with authentic antiques and appointments from the Civil War period, and the lobby has an old-time upright piano. The complimentary breakfast includes beverages, cereal, and homemade breads. Smoking isn't allowed anywhere in the inn. Carriage rides along the streets of Fredericksburg are available (fee). ⊠ *1707 Princess Anne St., 22401,* ☎ *540/371–5666,* FAX *540/371–5884,* WEB *www.fcil.com. 30 rooms. Refrigerators, free parking. AE, MC, V.*

$ 🏨 **Hampton Inn.** This may be a typical chain motel, but it's neat and clean, and the extensive Continental breakfast is complimentary. Because it's on a main artery in a busy retail area, ask for a room facing the interior courtyard. Local phone calls from your room are free, as is the HBO. Several restaurants are a short walk away. ⊠ *2310 William St. 22401 (Exit 130-A off I–95),* ☎ *540/371–0330,* FAX *540/371–1753. 166 rooms. In-room data ports, pool, coin laundry, meeting rooms, free parking. AE, D, DC, MC, V.*

$ 🏨 **Richard Johnston Inn.** This elegant B&B was constructed in the late 1700s and served as the home of Richard Johnston, mayor of Fredericksburg from March 1809 to March 1810. Guest rooms—each with a private bath—are decorated with period antiques and reproductions; three rooms have TV. The aroma of freshly baked breads and muffins entices you to breakfast in the large Federal-style dining room set with fine china, silver, and linens. The inn is just across from the visitor center and two blocks from the train station. ⊠ *711 Caroline St., 22401,* ☎ *540/899–7606. 6 rooms, 2 suites. Free parking. AE, MC, V.*

$ 🏨 **WyteStone Suites.** Located in the vicinity of a small outlet mall, several restaurants, and the Spotsylvania County Tourism Office, this modern, all-suite hotel is 2 mi from the historic area. Each suite has king or double beds with quilted bedspreads, a microwave and refrigerator, a sofa bed in the living room, and cable TV. All rooms are entered from inside walkways around the 6-story atrium with indoor pool. An extensive hot breakfast is included in the price. ⊠ *4615 Southpoint Pkwy. 22407 (Take Exit 126 off I–95, bear right onto U.S. 1 South, and turn left onto Southpoint Pkwy. to the hostelry on the right),* ☎ *540/891–1112 or 800/794–5005,* FAX *540/891–5465. 85 suites. In-room data ports, indoor pool, coin laundry. AE, D, DC, MC, V. BP.*

Fredericksburg A to Z

To research prices, get advice from other travelers, and book travel arrangements, visit www.fodors.com.

BUS TRAVEL TO AND FROM FREDERICKSBURG

Greyhound buses depart several times a day from Washington to Fredericksburg. A round-trip ticket is $16–$18, but a ticket doesn't guarantee a seat (riders sometimes wait in long lines for seats). Buses stop at a station on Alternate Route 1, about 2 mi from the center of town; taxis and a cheap regional bus service are available there. Unfortunately, the waiting room is not open late at night.

➤ Bus Information: **Greyhound** (☎ 202/289–5160 or 800/231–2222).

BUS TRAVEL WITHIN FREDERICKSBURG

You can ride FRED, the city's excellent little bus, for only 25 cents. Six lines—red, yellow, blue, orange, green, and purple—serve the region and stop at all historic sites as well as shopping malls and other modern areas of the city from 7:30 AM to 8:30 PM. To see schedules and maps, visit their Web site.

➤Bus Information: **FRED** (☎ 540/372–1222, WEB www.efredericksburg. com/transit).

CAR TRAVEL

To drive to Fredericksburg from the District, take I–95 South to Route 3 (Exit 130-A), turn left, and follow the signs. The drive takes about an hour one-way—except during rush hour, when it's about 1½ hours.

TOURS

The tour coordinator at the Fredericksburg Visitor Center can arrange tours of the city as well as of battlefields and other historic sites. Reservations are required. The Fredericksburg Department of Tourism (in the visitor center) publishes a booklet that includes a short history of Fredericksburg and a self-guided tour covering 29 sights.

Fredericksburg Carriage Tours depart from the visitor center for leisurely paced, narrated tours of downtown Fredericksburg in horse-drawn carriages. Tours last about 45 minutes and cost $10.

You can take a 75-minute narrated tour of Fredericksburg's most important sights on the Trolley. Tours, which are conducted April through November, cost $12.50 and leave from the visitor center daily at 10, noon, 1:30, and 3:30 June through October, and daily at 11 and 1:30 in April, May, and November.

➤ FEES AND SCHEDULES: **Fredericksburg Carriage Tours** (☎ 540/752–5567). **Fredericksburg Visitor Center** (✉ 706 Caroline St., ☎ 540/373–1776 or 800/678–4748, FAX 540/372–6587). **Trolley** (☎ 540/898–0737).

TRAIN TRAVEL

Trains depart for Fredericksburg several times daily from Washington's Union Station, Alexandria, and several commuter stops; the trip takes an hour or less. The Fredericksburg railroad station is two blocks from the historic district at Caroline Street and Lafayette Boulevard. A round-trip ticket from Washington costs about $40 on Amtrak. The Virginia Rail Express offers workday commuter service with additional stops near hotels in Crystal City, L'Enfant Plaza, and elsewhere. A round-trip ticket from Washington's Union Station costs about $14.

➤ TRAIN INFORMATION: **Amtrak** (☎ 202/484–7540 or 800/872–7245). **Virginia Rail Express** (VRE; ☎ 800/743–3873, WEB www.vre.org/).

VISITOR INFORMATION

➤ TOURIST INFORMATION: **Fredericksburg Visitor Center** (✉ 706 Caroline St., ☎ 540/373–1776 or 800/678–4748, FAX 540/372–6587).

8 BACKGROUND AND ESSENTIALS

Portraits of Washington, D.C.

Smart Travel Tips A to Z

Map of Washington, D.C.

Map of Washington, D.C. Area

Map of Washington, D.C. Metro System

EDIFICE TREKS

Washington probably produces more words than any other city in the world. Politicians orate, pundits speculate, and commentators narrate. But Washington's words have a peculiarly fleeting quality. They're copied into notebooks, transferred to computer screens, then set into type and bound into reports that are filed on shelves and forgotten. They're printed in newspapers that yellow and turn to dust. Words are spat out in sound bytes on the evening news, then released into the ether, lost forever. In the wordy war of politics, a paper trail is something best avoided.

But there is a stone trail in Washington, too: The words someone felt were important enough not just to commit to parchment, paper, or videotape but to engrave in sandstone, marble, or granite. On the buildings of Washington are noble sentiments and self-serving ones, moving odes and contemplative ones.

A reading tour of Washington's inscriptions amounts to a classical education. The inscriptions, lofty in position and tone, are taken from the Bible, from the Greeks and Romans, from poets and playwrights, from presidents and politicians. When viewing Washington's inscriptions, soaking up what is in most cases a perfect union of poesy and architecture, it's easy to see why the words "edifice" and "edify" spring from the same root.

Lesson one starts in Union Station, that great Beaux Arts bathhouse on Capitol Hill. Architect Daniel Burnham's 1908 train station is encrusted with carvings that do everything from romantically outline the development of the railroad to offer lessons in both humility and hospitality.

On the western end of the shining white Vermont granite structure, above the entrance to the Metro, is written (in all capital letters, as most inscriptions are):

He that would bring home the wealth of the Indies must carry the wealth of the Indies with him. So it is in travelling. A man must carry knowledge with him if he would bring home knowledge.

A bit heavy to digest when dashing for the Metroliner on a rainy Monday morning, but worth mulling over once a seat is found.

At the other end of the station is the perfect sentiment for the returning hero:

Welcome the coming, speed the parting guest. Virtue alone is sweet society. It keeps the key to all heroic hearts and opens you a welcome in them all.

These are just two of the half dozen inscriptions on Union Station. Above allegorical statues by Louis (brother of Augustus) Saint-Gaudens that stand over the main entrance are inscriptions celebrating the forces that created the railroads, including this set singing the praises of fire and electricity:

Fire: greatest of discoveries, enabling man to live in various climates, use many foods, and compel the forces of nature to do his work. Electricity: carrier of light and power, devourer of time and space, bearer of human speech over land and sea, greatest servant of man, itself unknown. Thou has put all things under his feet.

So inspirational were these and the other Union Station inscriptions that the Washington Terminal Company, operators of the station, once distributed free pamphlets imprinted with them. This probably saved more than a few sore necks.

Union Station's inscriptions were selected by Charles William Eliot, who was president of Harvard University. According to John L. Andriot's "Guide to the Inscriptions of the Nation's Capital," Eliot borrowed from such sources as the Bible, Shakespeare, Alexander Pope, and Ralph Waldo Emerson. Eliot also penned his own epigrams, a seemingly modest skill until you start to wonder what you'd come up with when confronted with a big blank wall that will bear your words forever.

Eliot wrote the two inscriptions on the City Post Office right next to the station. The inscriptions, facing Massachusetts Avenue, describe the humble letter carrier as a:

Carrier of news and knowledge, instrument of trade and industry, promoter of mutual acquaintance of peace and of goodwill among men and nations . . . and a . . . Messenger of sympathy and love, servant of parted friends, consoler of the lonely, bond of scattered family, enlarger of the common life.

It's said that President Woodrow Wilson edited these inscriptions, unaware that the Ivy League wordsmith Eliot had written them. Like all good editors, Wilson improved them.

Rocks and Hard Places

Behind every inscription in Washington is the person who carved it, the man or woman who put chisel or pneumatic drill to stone and, with a sharp eye and a steady hand, made the most lasting of impressions.

Ann Hawkins is one such carver. (You can admire her chisel work throughout the National Gallery of Art. She did the names on the Patrons' Permanent Fund in the east building, a roll call of philanthropists.)

"There are two comments I get from people who watch me carve, and they make perfect symmetry," says Hawkins. "Half the people say, 'Oh, that looks so tedious. You must have a lot of patience.' But I also get 'That looks *fun*.' And they wish they could do it."

Hawkins studied for four years before she could carve well enough to take her first paying commission. She's been carving professionally since 1982, and in that time she's decided that stones are "living, breathing things." And each one is different. Sandstone is soft. Slates can be brittle and hard, with knots in them almost like wood. White Vermont marble feels sugary and crumbles a bit at the first stroke. Tennessee pink marble is chunky and firm.

There are a lot of things a stone carver has to take into account before striking the first blow, Hawkins says. "The nature of the stone, the light the inscription will receive, the weathering of the stone, how large the letters will be, what distance they'll be viewed from."

The most important part of carving, she says, is the layout of the inscription. The letters must be spaced correctly, not bunched too tightly together as if they were typeset, but spread comfortably and handsomely. The inscription must look as if it is *of* the stone, not *on* the stone.

Hawkins draws the letters on paper that—"after being measured from every direction" to make sure it's straight—is taped to the stone over sheets of typewriter carbon paper. She then outlines the inscription, transferring it to the stone. With a tungsten-carbide-tip chisel she starts hammering, sometimes working her way around the edges of the letter, sometimes starting in the center and working out. She turns and shifts the blade, roughing the letter in at first, then finishing it, aiming for the perfect V-shape indentation that is the mark of a hand-carved inscription. (Inscriptions that are machine-sandblasted through a stencil have a round center.) As with everything from squash to Frisbee, it's all in the wrist.

If the inscription is outside, the sun will provide the contrast necessary for the letters to be read. As the rays rake across the inscription, the shadows will lengthen, making the words pop. If the inscription is indoors, Hawkins paints the inside of the letters with a lacquer that's mixed with pigment, deepening the color of the stone.

Triangular Logic

If a walk around Washington's inscriptions is a classical education, a perambulation of Federal Triangle is the civics lesson. The limestone cliffs of the Triangle, stretching from their base at 15th Street down Pennsylvania and Constitution avenues, are inscribed with mottoes that immediately conjure up a nobler time.

The walls fairly sing with inscriptions, enjoining passersby to be eternally vigilant (it's *the price of liberty; Study the past,* says the National Archives), and to heed Thomas Jefferson and *Cultivate peace and commerce with all* (on the Commerce Building and an example of one of the tenets of good epigram selection— try to work the name of the building into at least one inscription).

The Federal Triangle inscriptions also provide justification for the buildings that they decorate and government departments they praise. The inscription on the Internal Revenue Service headquarters on Constitution Avenue is not Dante's *Abandon all hope ye who enter here* but Oliver Wendell Holmes's *Taxes are what we pay for a civilized society*—just in case you were wondering what you were paying for every April 15.

Likewise, on the Justice Department we have:

Justice is the great interest of man on earth. Wherever her temple stands there is a foundation for social security, general happiness and the improvement and progress of our race.

While Justice certainly has its share of letters (including this bit of Latin: *Lege atque ordine omnia fiunt*—"By law and order all is accomplished"), the award for the most verbose structure must go to the Commerce Department Building. Stretched out along 14th Street, eight stories up and spread out over hundreds of feet, is this edifying ode:

The inspiration that guided our forefathers led them to secure above all things the unity of our country. We rest upon government by consent of the governed and the political order of the United States is the expression of a patriotic ideal which welds together all the elements of our national energy promoting the organization that fosters individual initiative. Within this edifice are established agencies that have been created to buttress the life of the people, to clarify their problems and coordinate their resources, seeking to lighten burdens without lessening the responsibility of the citizen. In serving one and all they are dedicated to the purpose of the founders and to the highest hopes of the future with their local administration given to the integrity and welfare of the nation.

It's a mouthful. But it's also redolent of a time that seems almost hopelessly naive now, a time when we could use words like "national energy" and "purpose of the founders" without smirking. This passage and two other long ones were created especially for the building, composed, it is believed, by Royal Cortissoz, for 50 years the influential art critic of the *New York Tribune* (and author of this much pithier epigram from the Lincoln Memorial: *In this temple as in the hearts of the people for whom he saved the union the memory of Abraham Lincoln is enshrined forever*).

You can imagine Washingtonians in the 1930s watching as the inscriptions were going up in Federal Triangle, trying to guess what would be said, as if a huge game of hangman were being played. At least one Washingtonian wasn't thrilled with what he saw. In 1934, when the giant Commerce Department Building was in its final stages of construction, one Thomas Woodward wrote a letter to a friend in the Department of Justice, expressing his dismay. The letter was addressed to Charles W. Eliot II, son of the Harvard president who composed the Union Station and City Post Office epigrams. The younger Eliot forwarded the letter of complaint to Charles Moore, chairman of the Commission of Fine Arts, the body responsible—then as now—for reviewing the design of government building projects. Moore allowed as how his commission hadn't been consulted on the inscriptions. The younger Eliot followed up with a salvo of his own to Moore, stating that the inscriptions "seem to be thoroughly bromidic and uninteresting—a lost opportunity."

Eliot had a point. The Commerce Department inscriptions are lecturing rather than inspirational, long and sour rather than short and sweet. Moore must have forgotten that he once wrote: "Inscriptions are an art in themselves. They should be monumental and express in few words a great sentiment."

Still, there can be poetry in even the longest of inscriptions. Consider this moving sentiment, carved on the hemicycle of the Post Office Department Building, facing 14th Street:

The Post Office Department, in its ceaseless labors, pervades every channel of commerce and every theatre of human enterprise, and while visiting as it does kindly, every fireside, mingles with the throbbings of almost every heart in the land. In the amplitude of its beneficence, it ministers to all climes, and creeds, and pursuits, with the same eager readiness and with equal fullness of fidelity. It is the delicate ear trump through which alike nations and families and isolated individuals whisper their joys and their sorrows, their convictions and their sympathies to all who listen for their coming.

What is it about the Post Office that inspires the most poignant inscriptions? And to whom do we talk about getting "ear trump" back into common usage?

Oops . . .

What do you do if you're a stone carver and you make a mistake? After all, the expression "carved in stone" isn't much good if fixing a typo on a chunk of marble is as easy as depressing the backspace key. Ann

Hawkins: "If I got a chip, there are epoxy resins I could apply. . . . It's very rare to make a mistake, unless you do something stupid."

On big projects, boo-boos can be lopped out entirely, the offending block of stone cut out and replaced with a "dutchman," a fresh piece that's inserted like a patch and—one hopes—carved correctly. There's no dutchman in what is perhaps the city's most obvious mistake. Inscribed in three sections on the north wall of the Lincoln Memorial is Abraham Lincoln's second inaugural address. Twenty lines down in the first block of words is a phrase that concludes: "WITH HIGH HOPES FOR THE EUTURE." The poor stone carver added an extra stroke to the *F*, transforming it into an *E*. Because the inscription is inside—away from the sunshine and its shadows—it would be virtually unreadable if the insides of the letters weren't painted black. And so, the bottom stroke of the *E* was left unpainted, making the best of a bad situation.

Back to the Stone Age

The capital's official buildings, monuments, and memorials urge us in various ways to remember the past or strive toward a more perfect future. None of the blank verse, mottoes, or maxims, though, are as moving as what appears on a V-shape set of black granite panels set into the ground near the Lincoln Memorial. The inscription isn't made up of words at all, but it's as moving as any sonnet.

Etched into the stone of the Vietnam Veterans Memorial are the names of the more than 58,000 Americans killed in that war. The names weren't carved high atop a pediment out of reach but were sandblasted delicately into the wall. Washington's other inscriptions might be meant to provide edification from a distance, but this memorial is designed to be touched, its inscriptions traced with unsteady fingers. And behind the names we see ourselves, reflected in the stone as true as any mirror.

Which leads us to the state of stone carving in Washington today. Most newer buildings in Washington aren't graced with inscriptions. While a building named after a famous American might once have warranted an inscribed quotation from that person, today we have the James Forrestal Federal Building and the William McChesney Martin Jr. Federal Reserve Board Building with nary a peep from either gentleman.

Gone, too, is the specially commissioned aphorism meant to enlighten or fire. Inscriptions like those on the Justice and Commerce department buildings—whether you consider them quaint optimism or naive bluster—are in short supply these days.

After all, our time isn't like the 1930s, the period of Washington's big inscription boom. This is supposed to be the time of little, quiet government, not big, loud government. Why should government buildings assault the eyes of pedestrians and motorists with jingoistic slogans and propagandist mottoes? Shouldn't the feds just get out of our hair?

Perhaps, but somehow when we were willing not only to stand behind our words but carve them immutably into the living stone, it suggested we believed in them a little more, thought them worth remembering, no matter how self-evident or self-aggrandizing they seemed.

We don't seem to do much of that anymore. Maybe it's time to read the writing on the walls.

— John F. Kelly

THE FEDERAL GOVERNMENT: HOW OUR SYSTEM WORKS

The Federal government is a major employer, an important landlord, and a source of contracts, contacts, and conversation for Washingtonians. It's a patron of the arts and a provider for the needy. To some, pervasive government is what's wrong with Washington. To others, it's what's right.

The federal government occupies some of the choicest real estate in town yet pays no taxes to the District of Columbia. On the other hand, although citizens of the District *do* pay taxes, they could not vote until some 20 years ago. This has changed; now they can help elect the president, but still they have only a nonvoting delegate in Congress.

In Washington, the "separation of powers" doctrine becomes more than just a phrase in the Constitution. A visit here gives you a chance to see the legislative, executive, and judicial branches of government in action, to see how the system of checks and balances works. As Boswell put it, you have an opportunity, "instead of thinking how things may be, to see them as they are."

The Legislative Branch

In Pierre-Charles L'Enfant's 18th-century plan for the city of Washington, the U.S. Capitol and the White House were just far enough away from each other on Pennsylvania Avenue to emphasize the separation of powers between the legislative and executive branches. L'Enfant chose Jenkins Hill as the site for the Capitol; it's the focal point of an area now called Capitol Hill.

Guided tours of the Capitol leave from the Rotunda almost continuously from 9 AM to 3:45 PM daily throughout the year. The Senate side of the Capitol faces Constitution Avenue, while the House side can be approached from Independence Avenue.

Drop by the office of your senator or representative to pick up passes to the Visitors Galleries. Without a pass, you aren't permitted to watch the proceedings. There are two Senate office buildings at 1st Street and Constitution Avenue NE, named, respectively, for former senators Everett Dirksen and Richard Russell. A third, honoring Senator Philip A. Hart, is at 2nd Street and Constitution Avenue NE.

The House office buildings, named for former Speakers Joseph Cannon, Nicholas Longworth, and Sam Rayburn, are located in that order along Independence Avenue between 1st Street SE and 1st Street SW. It's generally agreed by residents and visitors alike that the Rayburn Building is the least attractive and, at $75 million, one of the most expensive structures in the city.

According to the Constitution, "the Congress shall assemble at least once in every year, and such meeting shall begin at noon on the 3rd day of January, unless they shall by law appoint a different day." In the years before air-conditioning, Congress usually recessed in the summer and reconvened in the fall. Today, however, with congressional calendars more crowded and air-conditioning commonplace, sessions frequently last much longer. It's not unusual for the House and/or Senate to sit through the summer and well into the fall.

Congressional sessions usually begin at noon; committee meetings are generally held in the morning. Check the *Washington Post*'s "Today in Congress" listings to find out what is going on.

Don't be surprised to see only a handful of senators or members of Congress on the floor during a session. Much congressional business dealing with constituent problems is done in committees or in offices. When a vote is taken during a session, bells are rung to summon absent members to the floor.

To save time, many members of Congress make the brief trip between their offices and the Capitol on the congressional subway. Visitors may ride, too. The Senate restaurant in the Capitol—famed for its bean soup—is open to the public at all times. Cafeterias in the Rayburn, Longworth, and Dirksen office buildings are also open to visitors. Watch the hours, however. From 11:30 AM to 1:15 PM, only members of Congress and their staffs are admitted.

There are two senators from each state, who are elected for six-year terms; the 435 members of the House serve for two years. Rank-and-file senators and members receive an annual salary of $145,100.

The Executive Branch

The White House is at 1600 Pennsylvania Avenue NW, the most prestigious address in the country. However, its first occupant, Abigail Adams, was disappointed in the damp, drafty "President's Palace." She complained that it had "not a single apartment finished" and "not the least fence, yard, or other convenience without." On the other hand, Thomas Jefferson found the house "big enough for two emperors, one Pope, and the grand lama"—and still unfinished.

When Franklin Delano Roosevelt became president in 1932, the entire White House staff consisted of fewer than 50 people. Today, approximately 1,800 people work for the executive office of the president. They are crammed into offices in the east and west wings of the White House and in the ornate Executive Office Building (formerly the State, War, and Navy Building) adjacent to the White House to the west on Pennsylvania Avenue.

The president's annual salary is $400,000; the vice president receives $186,300. They're elected for a four-year term. If the president dies or becomes incapacitated, the vice president is next in line of succession. He is followed, in order, by the speaker of the House of Representatives; the president pro tempore of the Senate;

the secretaries of state, treasury, and defense; the attorney general; the postmaster general; and the secretaries of the interior, agriculture, commerce, labor, health and human services, housing and urban development, transportation, energy, education, and veterans affairs.

The Judicial Branch

Traditionally, the opening session of the Supreme Court, on the first Monday in October, marks the beginning of Washington's social season, and the quadrennial inaugural festivities add to the excitement. The inaugural week in January usually includes a star-studded gala, as well as receptions honoring the new president, vice president, and their spouses.

The Supreme Court meets from October through June in a Corinthian-column white-marble building at 1st Street and Maryland Avenue NE. Until 1935, the justices used various rooms in the Capitol. For a while, in the 19th century, they met in taverns and boardinghouses. You can see the Old Supreme Court Chamber on the ground floor of the Capitol.

Approximately 5,000 cases are submitted for appeal each year, and the justices choose about 3%—roughly 160 cases in all—those that raise constitutional questions or affect the life or liberty of citizens.

Justice Felix Frankfurter said, "The words of the Constitution are so unrestricted by their intrinsic meaning or by their history or by tradition or by prior decisions that they leave the individual Justice free, if indeed they do not compel him, to gather meaning not from reading the Constitution but from reading life."

In the courtroom, the nine black-robed justices are seated in high-back black leather chairs in front of heavy red velvet draperies. Lawyers for each side present their oral arguments, with the justices often interjecting questions or comments. Generally, the court sits for two weeks and then recesses for two weeks to do research and write opinions.

They are on the bench Monday, Tuesday, and Wednesday from 10 to noon and from 1 to 3 from October through April, and they usually hear about four cases a day. During this first part of the term, the justices meet privately every Wednesday afternoon and all day Friday to discuss the cases they have heard that week and to take a preliminary vote on decisions.

The chief justice assigns different members to write the opinions. If the chief justice is on the minority side in a particular case, however, the senior justice in the majority assigns the opinion. Any justice may write his or her own opinion, agreeing or disagreeing with the majority. During the remainder of the term, in May and June, the justices usually meet every Thursday to decide on releasing their opinions.

Monday is "Decision Day," probably the most interesting time to visit the Supreme Court. That is when the justices announce their decisions and read their opinions.

Throughout the year, in the courtroom, staff members give a brief lecture about the court Monday through Friday, every hour on the half hour from 9:30 AM to 3:30 PM. Lectures are not given on holidays or on days when the justices are on the bench hearing cases.

Supreme Court justices are appointed by the president with the advice and consent of the Senate. They serve for life or, as the Constitution says, "during good behavior."

Associate justices receive $178,300 per year; the chief justice's salary is $186,300. After 10 years of service, justices may resign or retire with full pay.

Lobbyists

Virtually every special-interest group in the country, as well as a sprinkling of foreign governments, is represented by someone who "lobbies" for its cause in Washington—some say that the word comes from President Grant's time. He used to escape the White House for brandy and a cigar in the lobby of the Willard Hotel, where interested parties would try to bend his ear. Today's lobbyists frequently conduct their business over luncheons, cocktails, and dinners, as well as on the golf courses or tennis courts of suburban country clubs.

Lobbyists' backgrounds are as diverse as the causes they represent. They are usually lawyers, public relations executives, or former congressional staff members. Many were once members of Congress or high government officials from all over the United States who have developed "Potomac fever"; that is, they do not return home but find being a Washington representative the ideal way to continue to influence public policy.

Sometimes, it appears that every group is well represented here except the average citizen. Under those circumstances, if you have a pet project, discuss it with your senator or member of Congress—he or she is your lobbyist. In doing so—like Washington's highly skilled and well-paid lobbyists—you would simply be exercising your First Amendment rights to express your beliefs and influence your government.

— Betty Ross

Portraits

ESSENTIAL INFORMATION

ADDRESSES

Although it may not appear so at first glance, there's a system to addresses in D.C., albeit a bit confusing. The city is divided into the four quadrants of a compass (NW, NE, SE, SW), with the U.S. Capitol building at the centerpoint of the compass. If someone tells you to meet them at 6th and G, ask them to specify the quadrant, because there are actually four different 6th and G intersections (one per quadrant). Within each quadrant, numbered streets run north–south, and lettered streets run east–west (the letter J is skipped). The streets form a fairly simple grid—for instance, 900 G Street NW is the intersection of 9th and G Streets in the NW quadrant of the city. Likewise, if you count the letters of the alphabet, skipping J, you can get a good approximation of an address for a numbered street or diagonal state-named avenue. For instance, 1200 Connecticut Ave. NW is close to M Street, M being the 12th letter of the alphabet if you skip J. All the city avenues are named after U.S. states and run diagonally. If all that's too much to keep track of, you can usually find a helpful resident, police officer, or uniformed business district representative to lend a hand.

AIR TRAVEL TO AND FROM
WASHINGTON, D.C.

BOOKING

When you book **look for nonstop flights** and **remember that "direct" flights stop at least once.** Try to avoid connecting flights, which require a change of plane. For more booking tips and to check prices and make online flight reservations, log on to www.fodors.com.

CARRIERS

All major airlines fly into BWI, Ronald Reagan National, and Dulles airports, except America West, which doesn't fly into Dulles.

Of the smaller airlines, Air Tran flies to Dulles and Midwest Express flies to Dulles and Reagan National. Southwest has service to BWI.

➤ MAJOR AIRLINES: **Air Canada** (☎ 888/422–7533, WEB www.aircanada.ca). **America West** (☎ 800/235–9292, WEB www.americawest.com). **American** (☎ 800/433–7300, WEB www.aa.com). **Continental** (☎ 800/525–0280, WEB www.continental.com). **Delta** (☎ 800/221–1212, WEB www.delta.com). **Northwest** (☎ 800/225–2525, WEB www.nwa.com). **United** (☎ 800/241–6522, WEB www.united.com). **US Airways** (☎ 800/428–4322, WEB www.usairways.com).

➤ SMALLER AIRLINES: **Air Tran** (☎ 800/825–8538, WEB www.airtran.com). **Midwest Express** (☎ 800/452–2022, WEB www.midwestexpress.com). **Southwest** (☎ 800/435–9792, WEB www.southwest.com).

CHECK-IN & BOARDING

Assuming that not everyone with a ticket will show up, airlines routinely overbook planes. When this happens, airlines ask for volunteers to give up their seats. In return, these volunteers usually get a certificate for a free or discounted flight and are rebooked on the next flight out. If there aren't enough volunteers, the airline must choose who will be denied boarding. The first to get bumped are passengers who checked in late and those flying on discounted tickets, so **get to the gate and check in as early as possible,** especially during peak periods.

Always **bring a government-issued photo I.D. to the airport.** You may be asked to show it before you are allowed to check in.

CUTTING COSTS

The least expensive airfares to Washington, D.C. must usually be purchased in advance and are non-refundable. It's smart to **call a number of airlines, and when you are quoted a good price, book it on the spot, or ask for a 24-hour courtesy reservation**—the same fare may not be available the next day. Always **check different routings** and look into using different airports. Travel agents, especially low-fare specialists (☞ Discounts & Deals), are helpful.

Consolidators are another good source. They buy tickets for scheduled international flights at reduced rates from the airlines, then sell them at prices that beat the best fare available directly from the airlines, usually without restrictions. Carefully read the fine print detailing penalties for changes and cancellations, and **confirm your consolidator reservation with the airline.**

➤ CONSOLIDATORS: **Cheap Tickets** (☎ 800/377–1000). **Discount Airline Ticket Service** (☎ 800/576–1600). **Unitravel** (☎ 800/325–2222). **Up & Away Travel** (☎ 212/889–2345). **World Travel Network** (☎ 800/409–6753).

ENJOYING THE FLIGHT

For more legroom, **request an emergency-aisle seat.** Don't sit in the row in front of the emergency aisle or in front of a bulkhead, where seats may not recline. If you have dietary concerns, **ask for special meals when booking.** These can be vegetarian, low-cholesterol, or kosher, for example. On long flights, try to maintain a normal routine, to help fight jet lag. At night, **get some sleep.** By day, **eat light meals, drink water** (not alcohol), and **move around the cabin** to stretch your legs. For additional jet-lag tips consult *Fodor's FYI: Travel Fit & Healthy* (available at bookstores everywhere).

FLYING TIMES

A flight to D.C. from New York takes a little less than an hour. It's about 1½ hours from Chicago, 3 hours from Denver, and 5 hours from San Francisco. Those flying from London can expect a trip of about 6 hours.

HOW TO COMPLAIN

If your baggage goes astray or your flight goes awry, complain right away. Most carriers require that you **file a claim immediately.**

➤ AIRLINE COMPLAINTS: U.S. Department of Transportation **Aviation Consumer Protection Division** (✉ C-75, Room 4107, Washington, DC 20590, ☎ 202/366–2220, WEB www.dot.gov/airconsumer). **Federal Aviation Administration Consumer Hotline** (☎ 800/322–7873).

AIRPORTS & TRANSFERS

The major gateways to D.C. include **Ronald Reagan National Airport,** in Virginia, 4 mi south of downtown Washington; **Dulles International Airport,** 26 mi west of Washington; and **Baltimore-Washington International (BWI) Airport,** in Maryland, about 30 mi northeast of Washington. At this writing, the status of Reagan National, which was closed indefinitely following the September 2001 terrorist attacks on the Pentagon and New York's World Trade Center, is unknown.

➤ AIRPORT INFORMATION: **Baltimore-Washington International Airport** (BWI; ☎ 410/859–7100, WEB www.bwiairport.com). **Dulles International Airport** (☎ 703/572–2700, WEB www.mwaa.com). **Ronald Reagan National Airport** (☎ 703/417–8000, WEB www.mwaa.com).

TRANSFERS BY BUS

Dulles and National airports are served every half hour (hourly on weekends) by **Washington Flyer.** The ride from Dulles to downtown takes 45 minutes and from National 20 minutes. Both cost $16 ($26 round-trip). The bus takes you to the Washington Convention Center at 11th Street and New York Avenue NW, where you can board a free shuttle bus that serves downtown hotels. The bus will also transport you from your hotel to the Convention Center to catch the main airport bus on your return journey. Fares may be paid in cash or with Visa or MasterCard; children under age six ride free.

Reagan National, Dulles, and BWI airports are served by **SuperShuttle**, which will take you to a specific hotel or residence. Make reservations at the ground transportation desk. Fares vary depending on the destination. The 20-minute ride from Reagan National to downtown averages $9–$13; the 45-minute ride from Dulles runs $22–$25; the 65-minute ride from BWI averages $28–$30; drivers accept major credit cards in addition to cash.

➤ BUS INFORMATION: **SuperShuttle** (☎ 800/258–3826 or 202/296–6662, WEB www.supershuttle.com). **Washington Flyer** (☎ 703/685–1400, WEB www.washfly.com).

TRANSFERS BY LIMOUSINE

Private Car has a counter at BWI Airport and charges approximately $70 plus a 15% tip for up to four passengers traveling from there to downtown; or call ahead to have a car waiting for you at Reagan National (approximately $45 plus 15% tip) or Dulles (approximately $85 plus 15% tip).

➤ LIMOUSINE INFORMATION: **Private Car** (☎ 800/685–0888).

TRANSFERS BY METRO

If you're coming into Ronald Reagan National Airport, have little to carry, and are staying at a hotel near a subway stop, it makes sense to take the Metro downtown. The station is within walking distance of the baggage claim area, but a free airport shuttle stops outside each terminal and brings you to the National Airport station. The Metro ride downtown takes about 20 minutes and costs $1–$2, depending on the time of day and your end destination.

TRANSFERS BY TAXI

Expect to pay about $14 to get from Ronald Reagan National Airport to downtown, $45–$50 from Dulles, and $55–$60 from BWI. Unscrupulous cabbies prey on out-of-towners, so if the fare strikes you as astronomical, get the driver's name and cab number and threaten to call the **D.C. Taxicab Commission.** A $1.50 airport surcharge is added to the total at all airports.

➤ TAXI INFORMATION: **D.C. Taxicab Commission** (☎ 202/645–6018).

TRANSFERS BY TRAIN

Free shuttle buses carry passengers between airline terminals and the train station at BWI Airport. **Amtrak** and **Maryland Rail Commuter Service (MARC)** trains run between BWI and Washington's Union Station from around 6 AM to 10 PM. The cost of the 45-minute ride is $20–$32 on an Amtrak train, $5 on a MARC train (weekdays only).

➤ TRAIN INFORMATION: **Amtrak** (☎ 800/872–7245, WEB www.amtrak.com). **Maryland Rail Commuter Service** (MARC; ☎ 800/325–7245, WEB www.mtamaryland.com).

BIKE TRAVEL

D.C. is a fairly bike-friendly city. Except for the ire provoked by the sometimes reckless riding of local bike messengers, cars and bicycles coexist peacefully, although it's best to avoid riding during rush hour, if possible. Several bicycle shops in the city that rent and repair bikes can be found in the local yellow pages. On weekends and holidays, sections of Rock Creek Park are closed to motorists, making it safe for bikers, rollerbladers, and walkers alike. Also, the Metro system allows riders to bring bicycles aboard the last car of trains during non-rush hours. Bicycles are not allowed on the Metro during Independence Day or other holidays and special events when large crowds are expected. The Washington Area Bicyclists Association has information on local bike laws, where to ride, and maps of bike trails on its Web site.

➤ BIKE INFORMATION: **Washington Area Bicyclists Association** (☎ 202/628–2500, WEB www.waba.org).

BUS TRAVEL

Washington is a major terminal for Greyhound Bus Lines. The company also has stations in nearby Silver Spring, Maryland, and in Arlington and Springfield, Virginia.

➤ BUS INFORMATION: **Greyhound Bus Lines** (✉ 1005 1st St. NE, ☎ 202/289–5160 or 800/231–2222, WEB www.greyhound.com).

PAYING

You can purchase your ticket 10 days in advance via the Internet, or pay for your ticket in the station before you board the bus. Greyhound accepts all major credit cards and cash.

BUS TRAVEL WITHIN D.C.

The red, white, and blue Washington Metropolitan Area Transit Authority (WMATA) Metrobuses crisscross the city and nearby suburbs. Free bus-to-bus transfers, good for two hours, are available on buses. In Metro stations rail-to-bus transfers must be picked up before boarding the train. There is a transfer charge (25¢ on regular Metrobus routes and $1.15 on express routes) when boarding the bus. Transfers are free for senior citizens. There are no bus-to-rail transfers.

FARES & SCHEDULES

All bus rides within the District are $1.10. Routes run from 5:30 AM–midnight on weekdays and from 8 AM–2:00 AM on weekends. All-day passes are available on the bus for $2.50. Complete bus and Metro maps for the metropolitan D.C. area, which note museums, monuments, theaters, and parks, can be purchased for $1.50 at Metro Center or map stores. Call the WMATA for schedule and route information. It's open weekdays 6 AM to 10:30 PM, and weekends 8 AM to 10:30 PM.

➤ INFORMATION: **Washington Metropolitan Area Transit Authority** (WMATA; ☎ 202/637–7000; 202/628–8973 or 202/638–3780 TDD).

PAYING

Buses require exact change, or tokens available for purchase inside the Metro Center train station sales office, open weekdays from 7:30 AM–6:30 PM.

BUSINESS HOURS

BANKS

Banks are generally open weekdays 9–3. On Friday many stay open until 5 or close at 2 and open again from 4 to 6.

MUSEUMS & SIGHTS

Museums are usually open daily 10–5:30; some have later hours on Thurs-day. Many private museums are closed Monday or Tuesday, and some museums in government buildings are closed weekends. The Smithsonian often sets extended spring and summer hours for some of its museums.

SHOPS

Stores are generally open Monday–Saturday 10–6. Some have extended hours on Thursday and many open Sunday anywhere from 10 to noon and close at 5 or 6.

CAMERAS & PHOTOGRAPHY

With so much pomp and circumstance in D.C., there's no dearth of photo opportunities. But how do you make your pictures of oft-photographed memorials and ceremonies unique? When shooting structures, look at postcards to see what the pros have done. Snap a few shots from the same angle and with the same light as the commercial photos, and then add your own flourishes through different perspectives, juxtapositions, and light/reflections.

For monuments and buildings, take a few shots in which you zoom in on particular elements. Try to capture details with light coming from the side so they have more definition. Put your zoom lens away and experiment with a wide-angle lens for up-close (perhaps even upward) shots of building exteriors; look for dramatic lines and angles. Then step back and take a few straightforward, sweeping shots. For parades or ceremonies, arrive early and find a spot with clear sight lines (a hill, steps of a nearby building, a balcony). Zoom in on reactions in the crowd, particularly the expressions on children's faces. Try shooting distinctive uniforms or costumes; look for items in the procession that express its theme.

For additional tips, consult the *Kodak Guide to Shooting Great Travel Pictures* (available at bookstores everywhere).

EQUIPMENT PRECAUTIONS

Always **keep your film and tape out of the sun.** Carry an extra supply of batteries, and **be prepared to turn on your camera or camcorder** to prove to security personnel that the device is real. Always **ask for hand inspection of film,** which becomes clouded after repeated exposure to airport X-ray machines, and **keep videotapes away from metal detectors.**

➤ PHOTO HELP: **Kodak Information Center** (☎ 800/242–2424).

CAR RENTAL

Rates in Washington, D.C., begin at $37 a day and $131 a week for an economy car with air-conditioning, an automatic transmission, and unlimited mileage. This does not include tax on car rentals, which is 8%.

➤ MAJOR AGENCIES: **Alamo** (☎ 800/327–9633; 020/8759–6200 in the U.K.). **Avis** (☎ 800/331–1212; 800/331–1084 in Canada; 02/9353–9000 in Australia; 09/525–1982 in New Zealand). **Budget** (☎ 800/527–0700; 0144/227–6266 in the U.K.). **Dollar** (☎ 800/800–4000; 0124/622–0111 in the U.K., where it is known as Sixt; 02/9223–1444 in Australia). **Hertz** (☎ 800/654–3131; 800/263–0600 in Canada; 020/8897–2072 in the U.K.; 02/9669–2444 in Australia; 09/256–8690 in New Zealand). **National** (☎ 800/227–7368; 0845/722–2525 in the U.K., where it is known as National Europe).

CUTTING COSTS

To get the best deal, **book through a travel agent who will shop around.** Also **price local car-rental companies,** although the service and maintenance may not be as good as those of a major player. Remember to ask about required deposits, cancellation penalties, and drop-off charges if you're planning to pick up the car in one city and leave it in another. If you're traveling during a holiday period, also make sure that a confirmed reservation guarantees you a car.

Do **look into wholesalers,** companies that do not own fleets but rent in bulk from those that do and often offer better rates than traditional car-rental operations.

INSURANCE

When driving a rented car you are generally responsible for any damage to or loss of the vehicle as well as for any property damage or personal injury that you may cause. Before you rent see what coverage your personal auto-insurance policy and credit cards already provide.

For about $15 to $20 per day, rental companies sell protection, known as a collision- or loss-damage waiver (CDW or LDW), that eliminates your liability for damage to the car.

In most states you don't need a CDW if you have personal auto insurance or other liability insurance.

REQUIREMENTS & RESTRICTIONS

In Washington you must be 25 to rent a car, although some companies allow employees of major corporations to rent at a younger age. You'll pay extra for child seats (about $3 per day), which are compulsory for children under five, and for additional drivers (about $5 per day). Non-U.S. residents will need a reservation voucher, a passport, a driver's license, and a travel policy that covers each driver, when picking up a car.

SURCHARGES

Before you pick up a car in one city and leave it in another, **ask about drop-off charges or one-way service fees,** which can be substantial. Note, too, that some rental agencies charge extra if you return the car before the time specified in your contract. To avoid a hefty refueling fee, **fill the tank just before you turn in the car,** but be aware that gas stations near the rental outlet may overcharge.

CAR TRAVEL

A car is often a drawback in Washington. Traffic is horrendous, especially at rush hours, and driving is often confusing, with many lanes and some entire streets changing direction suddenly during rush hour. Even longtime residents carry maps in their cars to help navigate confusing traffic circles and randomly arranged one-way streets. The traffic lights sometimes stymie visitors; most don't hang down over the middle of the streets but stand at the sides of intersections. Radar detectors are illegal in Washington, D.C., and Virginia.

EMERGENCY SERVICES

Dial 911 to report accidents on the road and to reach police, the highway patrol, or the fire department. For police non-emergencies, dial 311.

➤ CONTACTS: **U.S. Park Police** (☎ 202/619–7300).

GASOLINE

At press time, gasoline cost $1.60–$2 per gallon.

LAY OF THE LAND

Interstate 95 skirts D.C. as part of the Beltway, the six- to eight-lane highway that encircles the city. The eastern half of the Beltway is labeled both I–95 and I–495; the western half is just I–495. If you are coming from the south, take I–95 to I–395 and cross the 14th Street Bridge to 14th Street in the District. From the north, stay on I–95 south. Take the exit to Washington, which will place you onto the Baltimore-Washington (B-W) Parkway heading south. The B-W Parkway will turn into New York Avenue, taking you into downtown Washington, DC.

Interstate 66 approaches the city from the southwest. You can get downtown by taking I–66 across the Theodore Roosevelt Bridge to Constitution Avenue.

Interstate 270 approaches Washington from the northwest before hitting I–495. To get downtown, take I–495 east to Connecticut Avenue south, toward Chevy Chase.

PARKING

Parking in Washington is an adventure; the police are quick to tow away or immobilize with a "boot" any vehicle parked illegally. (If you find you've been towed from a city street, call ☎ 202/727–5000 or log on to www.dmv.washingtondc.gov.) Since the city's most popular sights are within a short walk of a Metro station anyway, **it's best to leave your car at the hotel.** Touring by car is a good idea only if you're considering visiting sights in Maryland or Virginia.

Most of the outlying, suburban Metro stations have parking lots, though these fill quickly with city-bound commuters. If you plan to park in one of these lots, arrive early, armed with lots of quarters. Private **parking lots downtown are expensive,** charging as much as $6 an hour and $17 a day. There's free, two-hour parking around the Mall on Jefferson Drive and Madison Drive, though these spots are always filled. You can park free—in some spots all day—in parking areas off Ohio Drive near the Jefferson Memorial and south of the Lincoln Memorial on Ohio Drive and West Basin Drive in West Potomac Park.

RULES OF THE ROAD

Unless indicated by a sign, right turns at red lights are allowed in D.C. All passengers are required to wear a seat belt. Infants up to 1 year of age and under 20 pounds must be strapped into a rear-facing car seat in the back seat. Children both over age 1 and weighing 20 to 40 pounds must also use a car seat in the back seat, though it can face the front. Children cannot sit in the front seat of a car until they are at least 4 years old and weigh over 80 pounds.

CHILDREN IN WASHINGTON, D.C.

Washington may seem to be mainly for grown-ups, but it has many attractions that appeal to the younger set. *Fodor's Around Washington, D.C. with Kids* (available in bookstores everywhere) can help you plan your days together.

If you are renting a car, don't forget to **arrange for a car seat** when you reserve. For general advice about traveling with children, consult *Fodor's FYI: Travel with Your Baby* (available in bookstores everywhere).

BABY-SITTING

Most large hotels and those with concierges can arrange baby-sitting (or even the opportunity to have sitters take your children sightseeing) with a D.C.-area child-care agency. These agencies perform in-depth interviews and background checks of all their sitters, and some provide references. Rates average about $14 an hour (usually with a four-hour

Smart Travel Tips A to Z

minimum) for one child, with additional children about $1 more per hour. Some agencies charge more to sit for additional, nonrelated children; some also charge a daily fee of about $25 above and beyond the cost of the sitter. In addition, you may need to pay for the sitter's transportation and/or parking costs. Agencies can usually arrange last-minute child care, but advance notice is appreciated. **Mothers' Aides Inc.** counts teachers amongst its sitters. **White House Nannies** has been in business since 1985 and charges a $125 initial registration fee.

➤ AGENCIES: **Mothers' Aides Inc.** (✉ Box 7088, Fairfax Station, VA 22039, ☎ 703/250–0700 or 301/424–6000). **White House Nannies** (✉ 7200 Wisconsin Ave., Suite 409, Bethesda, MD 20814, ☎ 301/652–8088 or 800/270–6266).

FLYING

Experts agree that it's a good idea to use safety seats aloft for children weighing less than 40 pounds. Airlines set their own policies: U.S. carriers usually require that the child be ticketed, even if he or she is young enough to ride free, since the seats must be strapped into regular seats. Do **check your airline's policy about using safety seats during takeoff and landing.** And since safety seats are not allowed just everywhere in the plane, get your seat assignments early.

When reserving, **request children's meals or a freestanding bassinet** if you need them. But note that bulkhead seats, where you must sit to use the bassinet, may lack an overhead bin or storage space on the floor.

LODGING

Most hotels in Washington allow children under a certain age to stay in their parents' room at no extra charge, but others charge for them as extra adults; be sure to **find out the cutoff age for children's discounts.** Note that major convention hotels (and those on Capitol Hill and the waterfront) don't see many families. It's best to choose a hotel downtown, in Foggy Bottom, uptown, or in Maryland or Virginia. Also, the closer your hotel is to a Metro stop, the quicker you can hit the sightseeing

trail. Consider a stay at an all-suite hotel. This will allow you to spread out and, if you prepare your meals in a kitchenette, keep costs down. A pool may well be essential for a stay with children, and game rooms are a plus.

In Georgetown, the deluxe Four Seasons Hotel offers children's menus and activities, a Tea Time for Tots program, milk and cookies, Web TV, and electronic games in every room. Georgetown Suites has spacious, apartmentlike accommodations. The Holiday Inn on the Hill is moderately priced and close to the Capitol, Union Station, and the Capital Children's Museum; baby-sitting is available nightly from 4 to 11 PM at a rate of $5 per child for kids 3–12 from Memorial Day–Labor Day in the hotel's Discovery Zone. In addition to Nintendo in every room, the Embassy Suites in Foggy Bottom provides "panda packages" with a stuffed panda, coloring books, zoo coupons, and other treats.

➤ BEST CHOICES: **Embassy Suites** (✉ 1250 22nd St. NW, ☎ 202/857–3388 or 800/362–2779). **Four Seasons Hotel** (✉ 2800 Pennsylvania Ave. NW, ☎ 202/342–0444 or 800/332–3442). **Georgetown Suites** (✉ 1111 30th St. NW, ☎ 202/298–7800 or 800/348–7203). **Holiday Inn on the Hill** (✉ 415 New Jersey Ave. NW, ☎ 202/638–1616 or 800/638–1116).

SIGHTS & ATTRACTIONS

Places that are especially appealing to children are indicated by a rubber duckie icon in the margin.

Consult the Friday *Washington Post* "Weekend" section. Its "Carousel" listings include information on plays, puppet shows, concerts, storytelling sessions, nature programs, and other events for families.

Also, don't forget to visit information desks. Many museums have exhibits designed for children and/or docents (trained guides) who conduct kid-friendly tours. In addition, many sights have special printed children's guides, allowing kids to take pencil in hand, for example, and go on "scavenger hunts" to pick out the shapes and patterns in modern artwork.

CONCIERGES

Concierges, found in many hotels, can help you with theater tickets and dinner reservations: a good one with connections may be able to get you seats for a hot show or prime-time dinner reservations at the restaurant of the moment. You can also turn to your hotel's concierge for help with travel arrangements, sightseeing plans, services ranging from aromatherapy to zipper repair, and emergencies. Always, **always tip** a concierge who has been of assistance (☞ Tipping).

CONSUMER PROTECTION

Whenever shopping or buying travel services in Washington, D.C., **pay with a major credit card** so you can cancel payment or get reimbursed if there's a problem. If you're doing business with a particular company for the first time, **contact your local Better Business Bureau and the attorney general's offices** in your own state and the company's home state, as well. Have any complaints been filed? Finally, if you're buying a package or tour, always **consider travel insurance** that includes default coverage (☞ Insurance).

➤ BBBs: **Council of Better Business Bureaus** (✉ 4200 Wilson Blvd., Suite 800, Arlington, VA 22203, ☎ 703/276–0100, FAX 703/525–8277, WEB www.bbb.org).

DINING

Washington hosts an international array of visitors and new residents, and this infusion of cultures means that you *can* find almost any type of food here, from Burmese to Ethiopian. The restaurants we list are the cream of the crop in each price category. Properties indicated by an ✗☎ are lodging establishments whose restaurant warrants a special trip.

Price categories are as follows for restaurants:

CATEGORY	COST*
$$$$	over $25
$$$	$18–$25
$$	$10–$18
$	under $10

per person for a main course at dinner, excluding sales tax (10% in D.C., 7.5% in VA, 5% in MD)

RESERVATIONS & DRESS

Reservations are always a good idea: we mention them only when they're essential or not accepted. Book as far ahead as you can, and reconfirm as soon as you arrive. We mention dress only when men are required to wear a jacket or a jacket and tie.

DISABILITIES & ACCESSIBILITY

The Metro has excellent facilities for visitors with vision and hearing impairments or mobility problems. Virtually all streets have wide, level sidewalks with curb cuts, though in Georgetown the brick-paved terrain can be bumpy. Most museums and monuments are accessible to visitors using wheelchairs.

The Washington, D.C., Convention and Tourism Corporation offers a free, 97-page publication full of sightseeing tips, maps, and contacts. The Washington MTA publishes a metro and bus-system guide. The Smithsonian publishes an access guide to all its museums; "Dial-a-Museum" lists museum hours and daily activities. All Smithsonian museums are open every day of the year except December 25th; admission is free. At press time, the National Portrait Gallery and the Smithsonian American Art Museum were closed for renovations through 2004.

➤ LOCAL RESOURCES: **Smithsonian** (☎ 202/357–2700; 202-357-2020 "Dial-a-Museum"; 202/357–1729 TDD, WEB www.si.edu). **Washington, D.C., Convention and Tourism Corporation** (☎ 202/789–7000, WEB www.washington.org). **Washington MTA** (☎ 202/637–7000).

RESERVATIONS

When discussing accessibility with an operator or reservations agent, **ask hard questions.** Are there any stairs, inside *or* out? Are there grab bars next to the toilet *and* in the shower/tub? How wide is the doorway to the room? To the bathroom? For the most extensive facilities meeting the latest legal specifications, **opt for newer accommodations.**

➤ COMPLAINTS: **Aviation Consumer Protection Division** (☞ Air Travel) for airline-related problems. **Civil**

Rights Office (⊠ U.S. Department of Transportation, Departmental Office of Civil Rights, S-30, 400 7th St. SW, Room 10215, Washington, DC 20590, ☎ 202/366–4648, FAX 202/366–9371) for problems with surface transportation. **Disability Rights Section** (⊠ U.S. Department of Justice, Civil Rights Division, Box 66738, Washington, DC 20035-6738, ☎ 202/514–0301 or 800/514–0301; 202/514–0301 TTY or 800/514–0301 TTY, FAX 202/307–1198) for general complaints.

TRAVEL AGENCIES

In the United States, the Americans with Disabilities Act requires that travel firms serve the needs of all travelers. Some agencies specialize in working with people with disabilities.

➤ TRAVELERS WITH MOBILITY PROBLEMS: **Access Adventures** (⊠ 206 Chestnut Ridge Rd., Rochester, NY 14624, ☎ 716/889–9096, dltravel@prodigy.net), run by a former physical-rehabilitation counselor. **Accessible Vans of the Rockies** (⊠ 2040 W. Hamilton Pl., Sheridan, CO 80110, ☎ 303/806–5047 or 888/837–0065, FAX 303/781–2329, WEB www.access-able.com/avr/avrockies.htm). **CareVacations** (⊠ 5-5110 50th Ave., Leduc, Alberta T9E 6V4, ☎ 780/986–6404 or 877/478–7827, FAX 780/986–8332, WEB www.carevacations.com), for group tours and cruise vacations. **Flying Wheels Travel** (⊠ 143 W. Bridge St., Box 382, Owatonna, MN 55060, ☎ 507/451–5005 or 800/535–6790, FAX 507/451–1685, thq@ll.net, WEB www.flyingwheels.com).

➤ TRAVELERS WITH DEVELOPMENTAL DISABILITIES: **Sprout** (⊠ 893 Amsterdam Ave., New York, NY 10025, ☎ 212/222–9575 or 888/222–9575, FAX 212/222–9768, sprout@interport.net, WEB www.gosprout.org).

DISCOUNTS & DEALS

Be a smart shopper and **compare all your options** before making decisions. A plane ticket bought with a promotional coupon from travel clubs, coupon books, and direct-mail offers may not be cheaper than the least expensive fare from a discount ticket agency. And always keep in mind that what you get is just as important as what you save.

DISCOUNT RESERVATIONS

To save money, **look into discount reservations services** with toll-free numbers, which use their buying power to get a better price on hotels, airline tickets, even car rentals. When booking a room, always **call the hotel's local toll-free number** (if one is available) rather than the central reservations number—you'll often get a better price. Always ask about special packages or corporate rates.

➤ AIRLINE TICKETS: ☎ 800/FLY–4–LESS. ☎ 800/FLY–ASAP.

➤ HOTEL ROOMS: **Accommodations Express** (☎ 800/444–7666, WEB www.accommodationsexpress.com). **Central Reservation Service (CRS)** (☎ 800/548–3311). **Hotel Reservations Network** (☎ 800/964–6835, WEB www.hoteldiscounts.com). **Quickbook** (☎ 800/789–9887, WEB www.quickbook.com). **RMC Travel** (☎ 800/245–5738, WEB www.rmcwebtravel.com). **Steigenberger Reservation Service** (☎ 800/223–5652, WEB www.srs-worldhotels.com). **Turbotrip.com** (☎ 800/473–7829, WEB www.turbotrip.com).

PACKAGE DEALS

Don't confuse packages and guided tours. When you buy a package, you travel on your own, just as though you had planned the trip yourself. Fly/drive packages, which combine airfare and car rental, are often a good deal. In cities, ask the local visitors' bureau about hotel packages that include tickets to major museum exhibits or other special events.

EMERGENCIES

1–800–DOCTORS is a referral service that locates doctors, dentists, and urgent-care clinics in the greater Washington area. The D.C. Dental Society operates a referral line weekdays from 8 to 4.

➤ DOCTORS & DENTISTS: **1–800–DOCTORS** (☎ 800/362–8677). **D.C. Dental Society** (☎ 202/547–7615).

➤ EMERGENCY SERVICES: Dial 911 for **police, fire,** or **ambulance** in an emergency.

➤ HOSPITALS: **Children's National
Medical Center** (✉ 111 Michigan
Ave. NW, ☎ 202/884–5000). **George
Washington University Hospital**
(✉ 901 23rd St. NW, ☎ 202/715–
4911 emergencies only; 202/715-
4000 non-emergencies). **Georgetown
University Medical Center** (✉ 3800
Reservoir Rd. NW, ☎ 202/342–2400
or 202/687–2000). **Washington Hospital Center** (✉ 110 Irving St. NW,
☎ 202/877–7000).

➤ 24-HOUR PHARMACIES: **CVS Phar-
macy** (✉ 14th St. and Vermont Ave.
NW on Thomas Circle, ☎ 202/628–
0720; ✉ 7 Dupont Circle NW, ☎
202/785–1466 or 202/833–5704).

GAY & LESBIAN TRAVEL

There's a gay and lesbian presence in
the Dupont Circle area as well as in
Adams-Morgan, Mount Pleasant, Logan Circle, and Capitol Hill. Residents
of the District tend to be tolerant, but
the millions of visitors who come each
year may not be; exercise good judgment. And despite all the political
activism, gay Washingtonians have a
reputation for being conservative, so
something unobjectionable in San
Francisco's Castro or New York's
West Village might draw stares at the
local bars, stores, and restaurants. For
details about the gay and lesbian
scene, consult *Fodor's Gay Guide to
the USA* (available in bookstores
everywhere).

➤ GAY- & LESBIAN-FRIENDLY TRAVEL
AGENCIES: **Different Roads Travel**
(✉ 8383 Wilshire Blvd., Suite 902,
Beverly Hills, CA 90211, ☎ 323/
651–5557 or 800/429–8747, FAX 323/
651–3678, leigh@west.tzell.com).
Kennedy Travel (✉ 314 Jericho Turn-
pike, Floral Park, NY 11001, ☎ 516/
352–4888 or 800/237–7433, FAX 516/
354–8849, main@kennedytravel.com,
WEB www.kennedytravel.com). **Now
Voyager** (✉ 4406 18th St., San Francisco, CA 94114, ☎ 415/626–1169
or 800/255–6951, FAX 415/626–8626,
WEB www.nowvoyager.com). **Skylink
Travel and Tour** (✉ 1006 Mendocino
Ave., Santa Rosa, CA 95401, ☎ 707/
546–9888 or 800/225–5759, FAX 707/
546–9891, skylinktvl@aol.com,
WEB www.skylinktravel.com),
serving lesbian travelers.

GUIDEBOOKS

Plan well and you won't be sorry.
Guidebooks are excellent tools—and
you can take them with you. You may
want to check out pocket-size *City-
pack Washington, D.C.,* which includes a foldout map; *Fodor's
Flashmaps Washington D.C.,* with
full-color theme maps; and *Fodor's
CITYGUIDE Washington D.C.,* for
residents. All are available at on-line
retailers and bookstores everywhere.

HOLIDAYS

Major national holidays include New
Year's Day (Jan. 1); Martin Luther
King, Jr., Day (3rd Mon. in Jan.);
Presidents' Day (3rd Mon. in Feb.);
Memorial Day (last Mon. in May);
Independence Day (July 4); Labor Day
(1st Mon. in Sept.); Thanksgiving Day
(4th Thurs. in Nov.); Christmas Eve
and Christmas Day (Dec. 24 and 25);
and New Year's Eve (Dec. 31).

INSURANCE

The most useful travel insurance plan
is a comprehensive policy that includes coverage for trip cancellation
and interruption, default, trip delay,
and medical expenses (with a waiver
for preexisting conditions).

Without insurance you will lose all
or most of your money if you cancel
your trip, regardless of the reason.
Default insurance covers you if your
tour operator, airline, or cruise line
goes out of business. Trip-delay
covers expenses that arise because
of bad weather or mechanical
delays. Study the fine print when
comparing policies.

British and Australian citizens need
extra medical coverage when traveling overseas.

Always **buy travel policies directly
from the insurance company**; if you
buy them from a cruise line, airline,
or tour operator that goes out of
business you probably will not be
covered for the agency or operator's
default, a major risk. Before making
any purchase, **review your existing
health and home-owner's policies**
to find what they cover away
from home.

➤ TRAVEL INSURERS: In the U.S.: **Access America** (✉ 6600 W. Broad St., Richmond, VA 23230, ☎ 804/285–3300 or 800/284–8300, FAX 804/673–1583, WEB www.previewtravel.com), **Travel Guard International** (✉ 1145 Clark St., Stevens Point, WI 54481, ☎ 715/345–0505 or 800/826–1300, FAX 800/955–8785, WEB www.noelgroup.com). In Canada: **Voyager Insurance** (✉ 44 Peel Center Dr., Brampton, Ontario L6T 4M8, ☎ 905/791–8700; 800/668–4342 in Canada).

➤ INSURANCE INFORMATION: In the U.K.: **Association of British Insurers** (✉ 51–55 Gresham St., London EC2V 7HQ, ☎ 020/7600–3333, FAX 020/7696–8999, info@abi.org.uk, WEB www.abi.org.uk). In Australia: **Insurance Council of Australia** (☎ 03/9614–1077, FAX 03/9614–7924).

FOR INTERNATIONAL TRAVELERS

CAR TRAVEL

In the D.C. area, gasoline cost $1.60–$2 a gallon at press time. Most gas stations stay open late (24 hours along large highways and in big cities), except in rural areas, where Sunday hours are limited and where you may drive long stretches without a refueling opportunity. Highways are well paved. Interstate highways—limited-access, multilane highways whose numbers are prefixed by "I–"—are the fastest routes. Interstates with three-digit numbers encircle urban areas, which may have other limited-access expressways, freeways, and parkways as well. Tolls may be levied on limited-access highways. So-called U.S. highways and state highways are not necessarily limited-access but may have several lanes.

Along larger highways, roadside stops with rest rooms, fast-food restaurants, and sundries stores are well spaced. State police and tow trucks patrol major highways and lend assistance. If your car breaks down on an interstate, pull onto the shoulder or as far off the road as possible and wait for help. Put your hazard lights on and, if possible, set up flares or reflecting triangles about 100 ft

behind your car. Note your location on the small green roadside mileage markers. If you have a cell phone, call for help right away.

Driving in the United States is on the right. Do **obey speed limits** posted along roads and highways. Watch for lower limits in small towns and on back roads. On weekdays between 6 and 10 AM and again between 4 and 7 PM **expect heavy traffic.** To encourage carpooling, some freeways have special lanes for so-called high-occupancy vehicles (HOV)—cars carrying a minimum of 2 or 3 passengers. *See also* Car Travel.

Bookstores, gas stations, convenience stores, and rest stops sell maps (about $3) and multiregion road atlases (about $10).

CURRENCY

The dollar is the basic unit of U.S. currency. It has 100 cents. Coins include the copper penny (1¢); the silvery nickel (5¢), dime (10¢), quarter (25¢), and half-dollar (50¢); and the golden $1 coin, replacing a now-rare silver dollar. Bills are denominated $1, $5, $10, $20, $50, and $100, all green and identical in size; designs vary. The exchange rate at press time was $1.58 US per British pound, $0.70 US per Canadian dollar, $0.57 US per Australian dollar, and $0.44 US per New Zealand dollar.

CUSTOMS & DUTIES

When shopping, **keep receipts** for all purchases. Upon reentering the country, **be ready to show customs officials what you've bought.** If you feel a duty is incorrect or object to the way your clearance was handled, note the inspector's badge number and ask to see a supervisor. If the problem isn't resolved, write to the appropriate authorities, beginning with the port director at your point of entry.

➤ IN AUSTRALIA: Australian residents who are 18 or older may bring home $A400 worth of souvenirs and gifts (including jewelry), 250 cigarettes or 250 grams of tobacco, and 1,125 ml of alcohol (including wine, beer, and spirits). Residents under 18 may bring back $A200 worth of goods. Prohibited items include meat products.

Seeds, plants, and fruits need to be declared upon arrival.

Australian Customs Service (Regional Director, ⊠ Box 8, Sydney, NSW 2001, ☎ 02/9213–2000, FAX 02/9213–4000).

➤ IN CANADA: Canadian residents who have been out of Canada for at least 7 days may bring home C$750 worth of goods duty-free. If you've been away less than 7 days but more than 48 hours, the duty-free allowance drops to C$200; if your trip lasts 24–48 hours, the allowance is C$50. You may not pool allowances with family members. Goods claimed under the C$750 exemption may follow you by mail; those claimed under the lesser exemptions must accompany you. Alcohol and tobacco products may be included in the 7-day and 48-hour exemptions but not in the 24-hour exemption. If you meet the age requirements of the province or territory through which you reenter Canada, you may bring in, duty-free, 1.14 liters (40 imperial ounces) of wine or liquor *or* 24 12-ounce cans or bottles of beer or ale. If you are 16 or older you may bring in, duty-free, 200 cigarettes and 50 cigars. Check ahead of time with Revenue Canada or the Department of Agriculture for policies regarding meat products, seeds, plants, and fruits.

You may send an unlimited number of gifts worth up to C$60 each duty-free to Canada. Label the package UNSOLICITED GIFT—VALUE UNDER $60. Alcohol and tobacco are excluded.

Revenue Canada (⊠ 2265 St. Laurent Blvd. S, Ottawa, Ontario K1G 4K3, ☎ 613/993–0534; 800/461–9999 in Canada, FAX 613/957–8911, WEB www.ccra-adrc.gc.ca).

➤ IN NEW ZEALAND: Homeward-bound residents 17 or older may bring back $700 worth of souvenirs and gifts. Your duty-free allowance also includes 4.5 liters of wine or beer; one 1,125-ml bottle of spirits; and either 200 cigarettes, 250 grams of tobacco, 50 cigars, or a combination of the three up to 250 grams. Prohibited items include meat products, seeds, plants, and fruits.

New Zealand Customs (Custom House, ⊠ 50 Anzac Ave., Box 29, Auckland, New Zealand, ☎ 09/359–6655, FAX 09/359–6732).

➤ IN THE U.K.: From countries outside the EU, including the U.S., you may bring home, duty-free, 200 cigarettes or 50 cigars; 1 liter of spirits or 2 liters of fortified or sparkling wine or liqueurs; 2 liters of still table wine; 60 ml of perfume; 250 ml of toilet water; plus £136 worth of other goods, including gifts and souvenirs. If returning from outside the EU, prohibited items include meat products, seeds, plants, and fruits.

HM Customs and Excise (⊠ Dorset House, Stamford St.; Bromley, Kent BR1 1XX, ☎ 020/7202–4227).

ELECTRICITY

The U.S. standard is AC, 110 volts/60 cycles. Plugs have two flat pins set parallel to each another.

EMERGENCIES

For police, fire, or ambulance, **dial 911** (0 in rural areas).

INSURANCE

Britons and Australians need extra medical coverage when traveling overseas.

➤ INSURANCE INFORMATION: **Association of British Insurers** (⊠ 51–55 Gresham St., London EC2V 7HQ, ☎ 020/7600–3333, FAX 020/7696–8999). **Insurance Council of Australia** (☎ 03/9614–1077, FAX 03/9614–7924).

MAIL & SHIPPING

You can buy stamps and aerograms and send letters and parcels in post offices. Stamp-dispensing machines can occasionally be found in airports, bus and train stations, office buildings, drugstores, and the like. You can also deposit mail in the stout, dark blue, steel bins at strategic locations everywhere and in the mail chutes of large buildings; pickup schedules are posted.

For mail sent within the United States, you need a 34¢ stamp for first-class letters weighing up to 1 ounce (23¢ for each additional ounce) and 21¢ for domestic postcards. For overseas mail, you pay 80¢ for 1-ounce airmail letters, 70¢ for airmail postcards, and 35¢ for surface-rate postcards. For Canada and Mexico you need a 60¢ stamp for a 1-ounce letter and 50¢ for a postcard. For 70¢ you can buy an aerogram—a single sheet of lightweight blue paper that folds into its own envelope, stamped for overseas airmail.

To receive mail on the road, have it sent c/o General Delivery at your destination's main post office (use the correct five-digit zip code). You must pick up mail in person within 30 days and show a driver's license or passport.

PASSPORTS & VISAS

Visitor visas are not necessary for Canadian citizens or for citizens of Australia, New Zealand, and the United Kingdom staying fewer than 90 days.

➤ AUSTRALIAN CITIZENS: **Australian Passport Office** (☎ 131–232). The **U.S. Office of Australia Affairs** (✉ MLC Centre, 19-29 Martin Pl., 59th floor, Sydney NSW 2000).

➤ CANADIAN CITIZENS: **Passport Office** (☎ 819/994–3500 or 800/567–6868).

➤ NEW ZEALAND CITIZENS: **New Zealand Passport Office** (☎ 04/494–0700 for application procedures; 0800/225–050 in New Zealand for application-status updates). **U.S. Office of New Zealand Affairs** (✉ 29 Fitzherbert Terr., Thorndon, Wellington).

➤ U.K. CITIZENS: **London Passport Office** (☎ 0990/210410) for application procedures and emergency passports. **U.S. Embassy Visa Information Line** (☎ 01891/200290). **U.S. Embassy Visa Branch** (✉ 5 Upper Grosvenor Sq., London W1A 1AE); send a self-addressed, stamped envelope. **U.S. Consulate General** (✉ Queen's House, Queen St., Belfast BTI 6EO).

TELEPHONES

All U.S. telephone numbers consist of a three-digit area code and a seven-digit local number. Within most local calling areas, dial only the seven-digit number. Within the same area code, dial "1" first. To call between area-code regions, dial "1" then all 10 digits; the same goes for calls to numbers prefixed by "800," "888," and "877"—all toll-free. For calls to numbers preceded by "900" you must pay—usually dearly.

For international calls, dial "011" followed by the country code and the local number. For help, dial "0" and ask for an overseas operator. The country code is 61 for Australia, 64 for New Zealand, 44 for the United Kingdom. Calling Canada is the same as calling within the United States. Most local phone books list country codes and U.S. area codes. The country code for the United States is 1.

For operator assistance, dial "0". To obtain someone's phone number, call directory assistance, ☎ 555–1212 or occasionally 411 (free at public phones). To have the person you're calling foot the bill, phone collect; dial "0" instead of "1" before the 10-digit number.

At pay phones, instructions are usually posted. Usually you insert coins in a slot (25¢–35¢ for local calls) and wait for a steady tone before dialing. When you call long-distance, the operator will tell you how much to insert; prepaid phone cards, widely available in various denominations, are easier. Call the number on the back, punch in the card's personal identification number when prompted, then dial your number.

LODGING

Washington hotels equip their rooms to please their guests. And because Washington is an international city with a diverse population and variety of visitors, many hotel staffs are multilingual. The lodgings we list are the cream of the crop in each price category. We always list the facilities that are available—but we don't specify whether they cost extra: when pricing accommodations, always ask what's included and what costs extra. Properties indicated by an ✕▣ are lodging establishments whose restaurant warrants a special trip.

Price categories are as follows:

CATEGORY	COST*
$$$$	over $270
$$$	$205–$270
$$	$145–$205
$	under $145

All prices are for a standard double room, excluding room tax (14.5% in D.C., 12% in MD, and 9.75% in VA). A $3.44 per night energy charge is also applied to the total.

Assume that hotels operate on the **European Plan** (EP, with no meals) unless we specify that they use the **Continental Plan** (CP, with a Continental breakfast), **Breakfast Plan** (BP, with a full cooked breakfast), **Modified American Plan** (MAP, with breakfast and dinner), or the **Full American Plan** (FAP, with all meals).

APARTMENT RENTALS

If you want a home base that's roomy enough for a family and comes with cooking facilities, **consider a furnished rental.** These can save you money, especially if you're traveling with a group. Home-exchange directories sometimes list rentals as well as exchanges. The on-line databases of local newspapers are the best place to look for rentals and sublets. Try www.washingtonpost.com or www.washingtoncitypaper.com.

➤ LOCAL AGENT: **Apartment Finders** (✉ 291 S. Van Dorn St., Alexandria, VA, ☎ 703/379–3733).

B&BS

Bed & Breakfast Accommodations, Ltd. and the Bed & Breakfast League and Sweet Dreams and Toast are both booking agencies that can help match you with an appropriate B&B.

➤ RESERVATION SERVICES: **Bed & Breakfast Accommodations, Ltd.** (☎ 202/328–3510, www.bedandbreakfastdc.com). **Bed & Breakfast League and Sweet Dreams and Toast** (☎ 202/363–7767).

HOME EXCHANGES

If you would like to exchange your home for someone else's, **join a home-exchange organization,** which will send you its updated listings of available exchanges for a year and will

include your own listing in at least one of them. It's up to you to make specific arrangements.

➤ EXCHANGE CLUBS: **HomeLink International** (✉ Box 650, Key West, FL 33041, ☎ 305/294–7766 or 800/638–3841, FAX 305/294–1448, usa@homelink.org, WEB www.homelink.org; $98 per year). **Intervac U.S.** (✉ Box 590504, San Francisco, CA 94159, ☎ 800/756–4663, FAX 415/435–7440, WEB www.intervac.com; $89 per year includes two catalogues).

HOSTELS

No matter what your age, you can **save on lodging costs by staying at hostels.** Hostelling International-Washington, D.C., a member of Hostelling International, the umbrella group for a number of national youth-hostel associations, offers dorm-style beds and, if the hostel is not full, couples rooms and family accommodations. Membership in any HI national hostel association, open to travelers of all ages, allows you to stay in HI-affiliated hostels at member rates; one-year membership is about $25 for adults (C$26.75 in Canada, £9.30 in the U.K., $30 in Australia, and $30 in New Zealand); hostels run about $10–$25 per night. Members have priority if the hostel is full; they're also eligible for discounts around the world, even on rail and bus travel in some countries.

➤ ORGANIZATIONS: **Hostelling International—American Youth Hostels** (✉ 733 15th St. NW, Suite 840, Washington, DC 20005, ☎ 202/783–6161, FAX 202/783–6171, WEB www.hiayh.org). **Hostelling International—Canada** (✉ 400–205 Catherine St., Ottawa, Ontario K2P 1C3, ☎ 613/237–7884, FAX 613/237–7868, WEB www.hostellingintl.ca). **Youth Hostel Association of England and Wales** (✉ Trevelyan House, 8 St. Stephen's Hill, St. Albans, Hertfordshire AL1 2DY, ☎ 01727/855215 or 01727/845047, FAX 01727/844126, WEB www.yha.uk). **Australian Youth Hostel Association** (✉ 10 Mallett St., Camperdown, NSW 2050, ☎ 02/9565–1699, FAX 02/9565–1325, WEB www.yha.com.au). **Youth Hostels Association of New Zealand** (✉ Box 436, Christchurch,

New Zealand, ☎ 03/379–9970, FAX 03/365–4476, WEB www.yha.org.nz).

HOTELS

All hotels listed have private bath unless otherwise noted.

➤ TOLL-FREE NUMBERS: **Best Western** (☎ 800/528–1234, WEB www. bestwestern.com). **Choice** (☎ 800/221–2222, WEB www.hotelchoice. com). **Clarion** (☎ 800/252–7466, WEB www.choicehotels.com). **Colony** (☎ 800/777–1700, WEB www.colony. com). **Comfort** (☎ 800/228–5150, WEB www.comfortinn.com). **Days Inn** (☎ 800/325–2525. WEB www.daysinn. com). **Doubletree and Red Lion Hotels** (☎ 800/222–8733, WEB www. doubletreehotels.com). **Embassy Suites** (☎ 800/362–2779, WEB www. embassysuites.com). **Fairfield Inn** (☎ 800/228–2800, WEB www.marriott. com). **Four Seasons** (☎ 800/332–3442, WEB www.fourseasons.com). **Hilton** (☎ 800/445–8667, WEB www. hiltons.com). **Holiday Inn** (☎ 800/465–4329, WEB www.holiday-inn. com). **Howard Johnson** (☎ 800/654–4656, WEB www.hojo.com). **Hyatt Hotels & Resorts** (☎ 800/233–1234, WEB www.hyatt.com). **Inter-Continental** (☎ 800/327–0200, WEB www.interconti. com). **La Quinta** (☎ 800/531–5900, WEB www.laquinta.com). **Marriott** (☎ 800/228–9290, WEB www.marriott. com). **Quality Inn** (☎ 800/228–5151, WEB www.qualityinn.com). **Radisson** (☎ 800/333–3333, WEB www.radisson. com). **Ramada** (☎ 800/228–2828. WEB www.ramada.com). **Renaissance Hotels & Resorts** (☎ 800/468–3571, WEB www.hotels.com). **Sheraton** (☎ 800/325–3535, WEB www.sheraton.com). **Sleep Inn** (☎ 800/753–3746, WEB www. sleepinn.com). **Westin Hotels & Resorts** (☎ 800/228–3000, WEB www. starwood.com). **Wyndham Hotels & Resorts** (☎ 800/822–4200, WEB www. wyndham.com).

MAIL & SHIPPING

➤ POST OFFICES: **Main Post Office** (☎ 202/635–5300 for customer information).

MEDIA

NEWSPAPERS & MAGAZINES

Several publications have calendars of entertainment events. The *Washing-*

ton Post "Weekend" section comes out on Friday, and its "Guide to the Lively Arts" is printed daily. On Thursday, look for the *Washington Times* "Weekend" section and the free weekly *Washington CityPaper*. Also consult the "Where & When" section in the monthly *Washingtonian* magazine.

RADIO & TELEVISION

WAMU 88.5 FM has a public-radio format, with NPR programs and call-in shows. WPFW 89.3 FM, a non-commercial Pacifica station, broadcasts leftist news, jazz, and world music. WKYS 93.9 FM plays hip-hop and R&B. WMZQ 98.7 FM plays country. Mix 107.3 FM plays adult contemporary music. Z104.1 FM is a top-40 station. WGMS 103.5 FM is a classical station. WTOP 1500 AM has news, traffic, and weather.

METRO TRAVEL

The WMATA provides bus and subway service in the District and in the Maryland and Virginia suburbs. The Metro, opened in 1976, is one of the country's cleanest and safest subway systems.

FARES & SCHEDULES

Trains generally run weekdays 5:30 AM–midnight, weekends 8 AM–2 AM. On Friday and Saturday, some trains leave slightly before 2 AM, so you should plan to arrive at least 10 minutes before the last train is scheduled to leave. During the weekday rush hours (5:30–9:30 AM and 3–7 PM), trains come along every six minutes. At other times and on weekends and holidays, trains run about every 12–15 minutes. The base fare is $1.10; the actual price you pay depends on the time of day and the distance traveled. Children under age five ride free when accompanied by a paying passenger, and there is a maximum of two children per paying adult.

Buy your ticket at the Farecard machines; they accept coins and crisp $1, $5, $10, or $20 bills. If the machine spits your bill back out at you, try folding and unfolding it lengthwise before asking a native for help. The Farecard should be inserted into the turnstile to enter the platform. Make sure you **hang onto the card**—you'll need it to exit at your destination.

Some Washingtonians report that the Farecard's magnetic strip interferes with the strips on ATM cards and credit cards, so **keep the cards separated in your pocket or wallet.**

➤ SUBWAY INFORMATION: **Washington Metropolitan Area Transit Authority** (WMATA; ☎ 202/637–7000; 202/628–8973 or 202/638–3780 TDD).

DISCOUNT PASSES

For $5 you can **buy a pass that allows unlimited trips for one day.** It's good all day on weekends, holidays, and after 9:30 AM on weekdays. Passes are available at Metro stations and at many hotels, banks, and Safeway and Giant grocery stores.

MONEY MATTERS

Washington is an expensive city, comparable to New York. A big bonus to visitors is that most attractions in this city are free. A cup of coffee in D.C. costs $1 at a diner or $4 at an upscale café, a sandwich will set you back $4.50–$7. Taxi rides cost upward of $5 depending on your destination.

Prices throughout this guide are given for adults. Substantially reduced fees are almost always available for children, students, and senior citizens. For information on taxes, *see* Taxes.

ATMS

Most ATMs in the Washington, D.C., area are linked to national networks that let you withdraw money from your checking account or take a cash advance from your credit card account for an additional fee. ATMs can be found at most banks, in many grocery stores, and in some major tourist attractions. For more information on ATM locations that can be accessed with your particular account, call the phone number found on the back of your ATM or debit card.

CREDIT CARDS

Throughout this guide, the following abbreviations are used: **AE,** American Express; **D,** Discover; **DC,** Diners Club; **MC,** Master Card; and **V,** Visa.

➤ REPORTING LOST CARDS: To report a stolen or lost credit card contact: **American Express** (☎ 800/300–8765), **Diners Club** (☎ 800/234–6377), **Discover** (☎ 800/347–2683), **MasterCard** (☎ 800/826–2181), and **Visa** (☎ 800/336–8472).

PACKING

In your carry-on luggage, **pack an extra pair of eyeglasses or contact lenses** and **enough of any medication you take** to last the entire trip. You may also ask your doctor to write a spare prescription using the drug's generic name, since brand names may vary from country to country. In luggage to be checked, **never pack prescription drugs or valuables.** To avoid customs delays, carry medications in their original packaging. And don't forget to carry with you the addresses of offices that handle refunds of lost traveler's checks. For more tips, check *Fodor's How to Pack* (available in bookstores everywhere).

CHECKING LUGGAGE

How many carry-on bags you can bring with you is up to the airline. Most allow two, but not always, so make sure that everything you carry aboard will fit under your seat or in the overhead bin, and get to the gate early. Note that if you have a seat at the back of the plane, you'll probably board first, while the overhead bins are still empty.

If you are flying internationally, note that baggage allowances may be determined not by piece but by weight—generally 88 pounds (40 kilograms) in first class, 66 pounds (30 kilograms) in business class, and 44 pounds (20 kilograms) in economy.

Airline liability for baggage is limited to $1,250 per person on flights within the United States. On international flights it amounts to $9.07 per pound or $20 per kilogram for checked baggage (roughly $640 per 70-pound bag) and $400 per passenger for unchecked baggage. You can buy additional coverage at check-in for about $10 per $1,000 of coverage, but it excludes a rather extensive list of items, shown on your airline ticket.

Before departure, **itemize your bags' contents** and their worth, and label the bags with your name, address, and phone number. (If you use your home address, cover it so potential thieves can't see it readily.) Inside each bag, **pack a copy of your itinerary.** At check-in, **make sure that each bag is correctly tagged** with the destination airport's three-letter code. If your bags arrive damaged or fail to arrive at all, file a written report with the airline before leaving the airport.

PASSPORTS & VISAS

➤ CONTACTS: **U.S. Embassy Visa Information Line** (☎ 01891/200290; calls cost 49p per minute, 39p per minute cheap rate) for U.S. visa information. **U.S. Embassy Visa Branch** (✉ 5 Upper Grosvenor Sq., London W1A 1AE) for U.S. visa information; send a self-addressed, stamped envelope. **U.S. Consulate General** (✉ Queen's House, Queen St., Belfast BTI 6EO) if you live in Northern Ireland. **Office of Australia Affairs** (✉ 59th floor, MLC Centre, 19–29 Martin Pl., Sydney, NSW 2000) if you live in Australia. **Office of New Zealand Affairs** (✉ 29 Fitzherbert Terr., Thorndon, Wellington) if you live in New Zealand.

PASSPORT OFFICES

The best time to apply for a passport or to renew is in fall and winter. Before any trip, check your passport's expiration date, and, if necessary, renew it as soon as possible.

➤ AUSTRALIAN CITIZENS: **Australian Passport Office** (☎ 131–232, WEB www.dfat.gov.au/passports).

➤ CANADIAN CITIZENS: **Passport Office** (☎ 819/994–3500 or 800/ 567–6868, WEB www.dfait-maeci. gc.ca/passport).

➤ NEW ZEALAND CITIZENS: **New Zealand Passport Office** (☎ 04/494–0700, WEB www.passports.govt.nz).

➤ U.K. CITIZENS: **London Passport Office** (☎ 0990/210–410) for fees and documentation requirements and to request an emergency passport.

REST ROOMS

Rest rooms are available in hotels, restaurants, tourist attractions, and department stores. In upscale restaurants, ask before you enter.

SAFETY

D.C. is a fairly safe city, but as with any metropolitan area it's best to be alert and aware. Tourist areas and train stations are heavily patrolled by the city's numerous police affiliations. At night, stay in highly populated areas, and avoid dark streets and alleys. Panhandlers can be aggressive and may respond with verbal insults, but are otherwise usually harmless. If someone threatens you with violence for money, it's best to hand it over without a fight and seek police help later.

LOCAL SCAMS

The only likely scam you'll encounter in D.C. is an elaborate story from a panhandler. In order to evoke sympathy, a well-dressed panhandler may pretend to have lost his wallet and need money to get home or a woman may say she needs cab fare to take a sick child to the hospital. A simple, "I'm sorry," is usually enough to send them on their way, or you may suggest they call the police for help.

WOMEN IN WASHINGTON, D.C.

Women in D.C. should not encounter any hassles in areas that are most frequented by visitors.

SENIOR-CITIZEN TRAVEL

To qualify for age-related discounts, **mention your senior-citizen status up front** when booking hotel reservations (not when checking out) and before you're seated in restaurants (not when paying the bill). When renting a car, ask about promotional car-rental discounts, which can be cheaper than senior-citizen rates.

➤ EDUCATIONAL PROGRAMS: **Elderhostel** (✉ 75 Federal St., 3rd floor, Boston, MA 02110, ☎ 877/426–8056, FAX 877/426–2166, WEB www. elderhostel.org). **Interhostel** (✉ University of New Hampshire, 6 Garrison Ave., Durham, NH 03824, ☎ 603/862–1147 or 800/733–9753, FAX 603/862–1113, WEB www.learn.unh.edu).

SIGHTSEEING TOURS

BICYCLE TOURS

Bike the Sites Tours had knowledge-able guides leading daily tours of 35 Washington landmarks; these tours are geared to the occasional exerciser. Bicycles, helmets, snacks and water bottles are included. Prices are $40 for adults; $30 for children 12 and under. The national Adventure Cycling Association offers regional tours.

➤ CONTACTS: **Adventure Cycling Association** (☎ 800/755–2453, WEB www.adventurecycling.org). **Bike the Sites Tours** (☎ 202/966–8662, WEB www.bikethesites.com).

BOAT TOURS

The enclosed boat called the *Dandy* cruises up the Potomac to George-town. Lunch cruises board weekdays starting at 11 AM and weekends starting at 11:30 AM. Dinner cruises board daily at 6 PM. Prices are $35–$44 for lunch and $71–$85 for dinner. D.C. Ducks offers 90-minute tours in converted World War II amphibious vehicles from April–October. After an hour-long road tour of prominent sights, the tour moves from land to water, as the vehicle is piloted into the waters of the Po-tomac for a 30-minute boat's-eye view of the city. Tickets are $24.

Odyssey III, a long, sleek vessel specially built to fit under the Po-tomac's bridges, departs from the Gangplank Marina at 6th and Water streets SW. Lunch, dinner, or Saturday and Sunday brunch cruises are among the options. Prices start at $35 and go up to $86. This upscale, glass-en-closed vessel serves gourmet food; jackets are requested for men at dinner. The *Potomac Spirit* offers a variety of lunch and dinner cruises and sightseeing tours to Mount Vernon; prices range from $32 to $76 depending on the type of cruise and the time of year.

➤ CONTACTS: *Dandy* (✉ Prince St., between Duke and King Sts., Alexan-dria, VA, ☎ 703/683–6076 or 703/683–6090, WEB www.dandydinner.boat.com). **D.C. Ducks** (☎ 202/832–9800, WEB www.historictours.com). *Odyssey III* (✉ 600 Water St. SW,

☎ 202/488–6010, WEB www.odysseycruises.com). *Potomac Spirit* (✉ Pier 4, 6th and Water Sts. SW, ☎ 202/554–8000, WEB www.spiritcruises.com).

BUS TOURS

All About Town, Inc. has half-day, all-day, two-day, and twilight bus tours that drive by some sights and stop at others. Tours leave from various downtown locations and hotels. An all-day tour costs $36. Gray Line has a four-hour tour of Washington, Embassy Row, and Arlington National Cemetery that leaves Union Station at 8:30 AM and 2 PM (June 25–October 28; adults $28, children $14); tours of Mount Vernon and Alexandria depart at 8:30 AM and 2 PM (June 25–October 28; adults $28, children $14). An all-day trip combining both tours leaves at 8:30 AM (June 25–October 28; adults $48, children $24).

➤ CONTACTS: **All About Town, Inc.** (☎ 301/856–5556, aatc@aol.com). **Gray Line** (☎ 301/386–8300, WEB www.graylinedc.com).

ORIENTATION TOURS

Old Town Trolley Tours, orange-and-green motorized trolleys, take in the main downtown sights and also foray into Georgetown and the upper northwest. Tickets are $24. Tourmobile buses, authorized by the National Park Service, make 25 stops at more than 40 historical sites between the Capitol and Arlington National Cemetery. Tickets are $18 ($8 for children ages 3–11).

➤ CONTACTS: **Old Town Trolley Tours** (☎ 202/832–9800, WEB www.trolleytours.com). **Tourmobile** (☎ 202/554–5100, WEB www.tourmobile.com).

PRIVATE GUIDES

Private tours can be arranged through the Guide Service of Washington and A Tour de Force. Sonny Odom offers custom photography tours.

➤ CONTACTS: **Guide Service of Washington** (✉ 733 15th St. NW, Suite 1040, Washington, DC 20005, ☎ 202/628–2842, WEB www.dctourguides.com). **Sonny Odom** (✉ 2420F S. Walter Reed Dr., Arlington, VA 22206,

☎ 703/379–1633, WEB www. sonnyodom.photoreflect.com). **A Tour de Force** (✉ Box 2782, Washington, DC 20013, ☎ 703/525–2948, WEB www.atourdeforce.com).

SPECIAL-INTEREST TOURS

Special tours of government buildings—including the Archives, the Capitol, the FBI Building, the Supreme Court, and the White House—can be arranged through your representative's or senator's office. Limited numbers of these so-called VIP tickets are available, so **plan up to six months in advance of your trip.** Reservations are required for all the tours listed here. Government buildings and offices that have regularly scheduled tours include the Old Executive Office Building and the Bureau of Engraving and Printing, which offers free tours weekdays 9 AM–2 PM (5 PM–7 PM evening tours available June–August only. In addition, tours of the opulent 18th- and early 19th-century State Department Diplomatic Reception Rooms are given weekdays at 9:30, 10:30, and 2:45. The Voice of America offers free 45-minute tours weekdays at 10:30, 1:30, and 2:30; and the Washington, D.C., Post Office has free tours weekdays by appointment, and does not admit children under seven.

The Washington Post leads free 50-minute guided tours for ages 11 and up on Monday 10–3. (Reservations are necessary.) Every second Saturday in May, a half-dozen embassies in Washington open their doors as stops on a self-guided Goodwill Embassy Tour. The cost is $30, which includes a tour booklet and free shuttle bus between embassies.

Scandal Tours offers 75–90 minute tours of Washington's seamier locales. Tours leave from the Pavilion at the Old Post Office Building on Saturday at 1 PM (April 1–Labor Day only). The cost is $35 per person and reservations are required.

➤ CONTACTS: **Bureau of Engraving and Printing** (✉ 14th and C Streets, SW, ☎ 202/874–3188, WEB www.bep. treas.gov). **Goodwill Embassy Tour** (☎ 202/636–4225, WEB www. dcgoodwill.com). **Old Executive**

Office Building (✉ Pennsylvania Ave. and 17th St. NW, ☎ 202/395–5895). **Scandal Tours** (☎ 202/783–7212, WEB www.gnpcomedy.com). **State Department Diplomatic Reception Rooms** (✉ 23rd and C Sts. NW, ☎ 202/647–3241). **Voice of America** (✉ 330 Independence Ave. SW, ☎ 202/619–3919, WEB www.voa.gov). **Washington, D.C., Post Office** (✉ Brentwood Rd. NE between Rhode Island and New York Aves., ☎ 202/636–2148). *The Washington Post* (✉ 1150 15th St. NW, ☎ 202/ 334–7969).

WALKING TOURS

The Guild of Professional Tourguides of Washington D.C. has information on specialized walking tours, bus tours, and customized tours available from its 450 members. Guided walks and bus tours of neighborhoods in Washington and communities outside the city are routinely offered by the Smithsonian Resident Associates Program. Tour D.C. specializes in walking tours of Georgetown and Dupont Circle, covering historical topics such as the Civil War and the underground railroad. Guided Walking Tours of D.C. leads anecdotal history tours of Georgetown, Adams Morgan, Capitol Hill, and the White House area.

The Black History National Recreation Trail links a group of sights within historic neighborhoods illustrating aspects of African-American history in Washington, from slavery days to the New Deal. A brochure outlining the trail is available from the National Park Service. Capital Entertainment Services also offers tours focusing on African-American history.

➤ CONTACTS: **Capital Entertainment Services** (✉ 3633 18th St., NE, Washington, DC 20018, ☎ 202/636– 9203, WEB www.washington-dc-tours. com). **Guided Walking Tours of D.C.** (✉ 9009 Paddock Ln., Potomac, MD 20854, ☎ 301/294–9514, WEB www. dcsightseeing.com). **Guild of Professional Tourguides of Washington D.C.** (✉ 1524 35th St. NW, Washington, DC, ☎ 202/298–1127). **National Park Service** (✉ 1100 Ohio Dr. SW, Washington, DC 20242, ☎ 202/

619–7222, WEB www.nps.gov).
**Smithsonian Resident Associates
Program** (☎ 202/357–3030, WEB
www.smithsonianassociates.org).
Tour D.C. (✉ 1912 Glen Ross Rd.,
Silver Spring, MD 20910, ☎ 301/
588–8999, WEB www.tourdc.com).

STUDENTS IN WASHINGTON, D.C.

To save money, **look into deals available through student-oriented travel agencies.** To qualify you'll need a bona fide student ID card. Members of international student groups are also eligible.

➤ I.D.s & SERVICES: **Council Travel**
(CIEE; ✉ 205 E. 42nd St., New
York, NY 10017, ☎ 212/822–2700
or 800/268–6245, FAX 212/822–2719,
customerservice@counciltravel.com,
WEB www.counciltravel.com) for mail
orders only, in the U.S. **Travel Cuts**
(✉ 187 College St., Toronto, Ontario
M5T 1P7, ☎ 416/979–2406 or 800/
667–2887, WEB www.travelcuts.com)
in Canada.

TAXES

SALES TAX

Sales tax is 5.75% in D.C., 5% in
Maryland, and 3.5% in Virginia.
Hotel tax is 14.5% in Washington,
12% in Maryland, and 9.75% in
Virginia.

TAXIS

Taxis in the District are not metered;
they operate instead on a zone system. **Before you set off, ask your cab
driver how much the fare will be.** The
basic single rate for traveling within
one zone is $4. There is an extra
$1.50 charge for each additional
passenger and a $1 surcharge during
the 7–9:30 AM and 4–6:30 PM rush
hour. Bulky suitcases are charged at a
higher rate, and a $1.50 surcharge is
tacked on when you phone for a cab.
Maryland and Virginia taxis are
metered but are not allowed to take
passengers between points in D.C.

➤ TAXI COMPANIES: **Diamond Cab**
(202/332–6200). **Taxi Dispatch** (☎
202/398–0505) is an affiliation of 14
cab companies. **Yellow Cab** (☎ 202/
544–1212).

TELEPHONES

Competitive long-distance carriers
make calling within the United States
relatively convenient and let you
avoid hotel surcharges. By dialing a
toll-free number, you can get connected to the long-distance company
of your choice.

➤ LONG-DISTANCE CARRIERS: **AT&T**
(☎ 800/225–5288). **MCI** (☎ 800/
888–8000). **Sprint** (☎ 800/366–
2255).

TIME

Washington, D.C., is in the eastern
time zone. It is 3 hours ahead of Los
Angeles, 1 hour ahead of Chicago, 5
hours behind London, and 15 hours
behind Sydney.

TIPPING

At restaurants, a 15% tip is standard
for waiters; up to 20% may be expected at more expensive establishments. The same goes for taxi drivers,
bartenders, and hairdressers. Coat-
check operators usually expect $1–
$2; bellhops and porters should get
50¢–$1 per bag; hotel maids in up-
scale hotels should get about $5 per
day of your stay. On package tours,
conductors and drivers usually get
$10 per day from the group as a
whole; check whether this has already
been figured into your cost. For local
sightseeing tours, you may individu-
ally tip the driver-guide a few dollars
if he or she has been helpful or informative. Ushers in theaters, museum
guides, and gas station attendants do
not expect tips.

A concierge typically receives a tip of
$5 to $10, with an additional gratuity
for special services or favors.

TOURS & PACKAGES

Because everything is prearranged on
a prepackaged tour or independent
vacation, you'll spend less time planning—and often get it all at a good
price.

BOOKING WITH AN AGENT

Travel agents are excellent resources.
But it's a good idea to collect
brochures from several agencies as
some agents' suggestions may be
influenced by relationships with tour

and package firms that reward them for volume sales. If you have a special interest, **find an agent with expertise in that area**; ASTA (☞ Travel Agencies) has a database of specialists worldwide.

Make sure your travel agent knows the accommodations and other services of the place they're recommending. Ask about the hotel's location, room size, beds, and whether it has a pool, room service, or programs for children, if you care about these. Has your agent been there in person or sent others whom you can contact?

Do some homework on your own, too: local tourism boards can provide information about lesser-known and small-niche operators, some of which may sell only direct.

BUYER BEWARE

Each year consumers are stranded or lose their money when tour operators—even large ones with excellent reputations—go out of business. So **check out the operator.** Ask several travel agents about its reputation, and try to **book with a company that has a consumer-protection program.** (Look for information in the company's brochure.) In the United States, members of the National Tour Association and the United States Tour Operators Association are required to set aside funds to cover your payments and travel arrangements in the event that the company defaults. It's also a good idea to choose a company that participates in the American Society of Travel Agents' Tour Operator Program (TOP); ASTA will act as mediator in any disputes between you and your tour operator.

Remember that the more your package or tour includes the better you can predict the ultimate cost of your vacation. Make sure you know exactly what is covered, and **beware of hidden costs.** Are taxes, tips, and transfers included? Entertainment and excursions? These can add up.

➤ TOUR-OPERATOR RECOMMENDATIONS: **American Society of Travel Agents** (☞ Travel Agencies). **National Tour Association** (NTA; ✉ 546 E. Main St., Lexington, KY 40508,

☎ 606/226–4444 or 800/682–8886, WEB www.ntaonline.com). **United States Tour Operators Association** (USTOA; ✉ 342 Madison Ave., Suite 1522, New York, NY 10173, ☎ 212/599–6599 or 800/468–7862, FAX 212/599–6744, ustoa@aol.com, WEB www.ustoa.com).

TRAIN TRAVEL TO AND FROM WASHINGTON, D.C.

More than 80 trains a day arrive at Washington, D.C.'s Union Station. For information on arrivals, departures, and fares, contact Amtrak, MARC (Maryland Area Rail Commuter Train), or the Metro. Acela, Amtrak's high-speed service, travels from D.C. to New York in 2½ hours and from D.C. to Boston in 6½ hours.

➤ TRAIN INFORMATION: **Acela** (☎ 800/872–7245, WEB www.acela.com). **Amtrak** (☎ 800/872–7245, WEB www.amtrak.com. **MARC** (☎ 800/325–7245, WEB www.mtamaryland.com). **Union Station** (✉ 50 Massachusetts Ave. NE; ☎ 202/371–9441). **Washington Metropolitan Area Transit Authority** (WMATA; ☎ 202/637–7000; 202/638–3780 or 202/628–8973 TDD, WEB www.wmata.com).

RESERVATIONS

Reservations are a good idea on Amtrak trains, especially the Metroliner or Acela. Plan to arrive early if you are traveling during holiday seasons; the trains can be *very* crowded.

TRAVEL AGENCIES

A good travel agent puts your needs first. Look for an agency that has been in business at least five years, emphasizes customer service, and has someone on staff who specializes in your destination. In addition, **make sure the agency belongs to a professional trade organization.** The American Society of Travel Agents (ASTA)—the largest and most influential in the field, with more than 26,000 members in some 170 countries—maintains and enforces a strict code of ethics and will step in to help mediate any agent-client disputes if necessary. ASTA (whose motto is "Without a travel agent, you're on your own") also maintains a Web site that includes a directory of agents. (If a travel agency is also acting as your tour operator, *see* Buyer Beware *in* Tours & Packages.)

➤ LOCAL AGENT REFERRALS: American Society of Travel Agents (ASTA; ☎ 800/965–2782 24-hr hot line, FAX 703/684–8319, WEB www.astanet.com). Association of British Travel Agents (✉ 68–71 Newman St., London W1P 4AH, ☎ 020/7637–2444, FAX 020/7637–0713, abta.co.uk, WEB www.abtanet.com). Association of Canadian Travel Agents (✉ 1729 Bank St., Suite 201, Ottawa, Ontario K1V 7Z5, ☎ 613/521–0474, FAX 613/521–0805, acta.ntl@sympatico.ca). Australian Federation of Travel Agents (✉ Level 3, 309 Pitt St., Sydney 2000, ☎ 02/9264–3299, FAX 02/9264–1085, WEB www.afta.com.au). Travel Agents' Association of New Zealand (✉ Box 1888, Wellington 10033, ☎ 04/499–0104, FAX 04/499–0827, taanz@tiasnet.co.nz).

VISITOR INFORMATION

➤ TOURIST INFORMATION: **D.C. Chamber of Commerce Visitor Center** (✉ Reagan Bldg., 1300 Pennsylvania Ave. NW, Suite 309, Washington, DC 20004, ☎ 202/328–4748, WEB www.dcvisit.com). **Washington, D.C., Convention and Tourism Corporation** (✉ 1212 New York Ave. NW, Suite 600, Washington, DC 20005, ☎ 202/789–7000 or 800/422–8644, WEB www.washington.org).

➤ EVENTS AND ATTRACTIONS: **White House Visitor Center** (✉ Baldridge Hall, Dept. of Commerce, 1450 S. Pennsylvania Ave. NW, ☎ 202/208–1631, WEB www.whitehouse.gov). **Dial-A-Museum** (☎ 202/357–2020). **Dial-A-Park** (☎ 202/619–7275).

➤ NATIONAL PARKS: **National Park Service** (✉ Office of Public Affairs, National Capital Region, 1100 Ohio Dr. SW, Washington, DC 20242, ☎ 202/619–7222, WEB www.nps.gov).

➤ STATE INFORMATION: **State of Maryland** (✉ Office of Tourist Development, 217 E. Redwood St., 9th floor, Baltimore, MD 21202, ☎ 410/767–3400 or 800/634–7386, WEB www.mdisfun.org). **Virginia Tourism Corporation** (Headquarters: ✉ 901 E.

Byrd St., Richmond, VA 23219, ☎ 804/786–4484 or 804/786–2051, WEB www.virginia.org; walk-in office: ✉ 1629 K St. NW, Washington, DC 20006, ☎ 202/872–0523 or 800/934–9184).

WEB SITES

Do check out the World Wide Web when planning your trip. You'll find everything from weather forecasts to virtual tours of famous cities. Be sure to **visit Fodors.com** (www.fodors.com), a complete travel-planning site. You can research prices and book plane tickets, hotel rooms, rental cars, vacation packages, and more. In addition, you can post your pressing questions in the Travel Talk section and, in the site's Rants & Raves section, read comments about some of the restaurants and hotels in this book—and chime in yourself. Other planning tools include a currency converter and weather reports, and there are loads of links to travel resources.

For more information specifically on Washington, you can visit the following sites:

www.americanparknetwork.com – Created by the publisher of visitor guide magazines for the national parks, this site has travel and safety tips, as well as environmental primers.

www.dcregistry.com – DC Registry has links to Washington-related Web sites.

www.vietvet.org – Poems, photographs, and personal stories pay tribute to the Vietnam Veterans Memorial and the lives it memorializes.

www.si.edu – The nation's largest museum provides a comprehensive guide to all things Smithsonian.

www.washingtoncitypaper.com – The *Washington CityPaper*'s site is a nifty and very selective guide to the best of D.C.'s happenings.

sc94.ameslab.gov – At this site, a detailed map shows the capital's major attractions.

www.washingtonpost.com – Like many big city newspapers, the *Washington Post* has an electronic edition.

www.washingtonian.com – *The Washingtonian* magazine's on-line version has upcoming events, restaurant reviews, and more.

WHEN TO GO

Washington has two delightful seasons: spring and autumn. In spring, the city's ornamental fruit trees are budding, and its many gardens are in bloom. By autumn, most of the summer crowds have left and you can enjoy the sights in peace. Summers can be uncomfortably hot and humid. Winter weather is often bitter, with a handful of modest snowstorms that somehow bring this southern city to a standstill. If you're interested in government, visit when Congress is in session. When lawmakers break for recess (at Thanksgiving, Christmas, Easter, July 4, the entire month of August, and other holiday periods), the city seems a little less vibrant.

CLIMATE

What follows are the average daily maximum and minimum temperatures for Washington.

➤ FORECASTS: **Weather Channel Connection** (☎ 900/932–8437), 95¢ per minute from a Touch-Tone phone.

WASHINGTON, D.C.

Jan.	47F	8C	May	76F	24C	Sept.	79F	26C
	34	– 1		58	14		61	16
Feb.	47F	8C	June	85F	29C	Oct.	70F	21C
	31	– 1		65	18		52	11
Mar.	56F	13C	July	88F	31C	Nov.	56F	13C
	38	3		70	21		41	5
Apr.	67F	19C	Aug.	86F	30C	Dec.	47F	8C
	47	8		68	20		32	0

FESTIVALS AND SEASONAL EVENTS

➤ MID-NOV.–LATE DEC.: *A Christmas Carol* returns each year to Ford's Theatre (☎ 202/347–4833, WEB www.fordstheatre.org).

➤ EARLY DEC.: The **National Cathedral Christmas Celebration and Services** (☎ 202/537–6200, WEB www.cathedral.org) has carols, pageants, and choral performances. The **Scottish Christmas Walk** (☎ 703/838–4200) salutes Alexandria's Scottish heritage with a parade, bagpipers, house tours, and crafts.

➤ MID-DEC.: **Old Town Christmas Candlelight Tours** (☎ 703/838–4200) visit Alexandria's Gadsby's Tavern Museum, the Lyceum, Lee-Fendall House, and Carlyle House. Included in the tour are music and refreshments. Military bands perform at the **People's Christmas Tree Lighting** (☎ 202/224–6645) on the west side of the Capitol.

➤ MID–LATE DEC.: *The Nutcracker* is performed by the Washington Ballet at Warner Theatre (☎ 202/362–3606).

➤ MID-DEC.–JAN. 1: The **National Christmas Tree Lighting/Pageant of Peace** (☎ 202/619–7222) is accompanied by music and caroling. In mid-December, the president lights the tree at dusk on the Ellipse. For the next few weeks the Ellipse grounds host choral performances, a Nativity scene, a Yule log, and a display of lighted Christmas trees representing each U.S. state and territory.

➤ LATE DEC.: **White House Christmas Candlelight Tours** (☎ 202/456–2200 or 202/208–1631) conducts evening tours of the White House, which is adorned with Christmas decorations. Tours, given from 5–7, are free but very popular; arrive early.

➤ MID-JAN.: **Martin Luther King Jr.'s birthday** is celebrated with speeches and dance and choral performances. For details contact the Martin Luther King Jr. Library (☎ 202/727–1186), the National Park Service (☎ 202/619–7222), or the Smithsonian (☎ 202/357–2700).

➤ LATE JAN.– EARLY FEB.: The **Chinese Lunar New Year Festival** (☎ 202/638–1041) explodes in Chinatown with firecrackers and a dragon-led parade.

➤ FEB.: **African-American History Month** (☎ 202/727–1186) features special events, exhibits, and cultural programs.

➤ MID-FEB.: On **Lincoln's birthday** (Feb. 12), a wreath-laying ceremony and a reading of the Gettysburg Address takes place at the Lincoln Memorial (☎ 202/619–7222). A wreath-laying ceremony is held at the Frederick Douglass National Historic Site (☎ 202/619–7222 or 202/426–5961) on **Frederick Douglass's birthday. George Washington's birthday** (☎ 703/838–4200) is celebrated over Presidents Day weekend with a parade and a reenactment of his farewell address in Old Town Alexandria, a Birthnight Banquet and Ball at Gadsby's Tavern Museum, a birthday celebration and wreath-laying ceremony at Mt. Vernon, and Revolutionary War reenactments at Ft. Ward Park.

➤ EARLY MAR.: The **Spring Antiques Show** (☎ 301/933–9433; 202/547–9215 during the show) at the armory hosts almost 200 dealers the first weekend in March.

➤ MID-MAR.: **St. Patrick's Day** (☎ 202/637–2474, WEB www.dcstpatsparade.com) begins with a parade down Constitution Avenue at noon. The following days feature theater, folk music, and dance concerts. **Alexandria's St. Patrick's parade** (☎ 703/838–4200 or 703/237–2199) usually takes place the weekend before the St. Patrick's Day parade in Washington. The **Bach Marathon** honors Johann Sebastian's birthday. Ten organists each play the pipe organ at Chevy Chase Presbyterian Church (☎ 202/363–2202) from 1 to 6.

➤ MAR. OR APR.: The **White House Easter Egg Roll** (☎ 202/456–2200 or 202/208–1631) brings children ages three to six to the White House lawn on Easter Monday.

➤ LATE MAR.–EARLY APR.: The **Smithsonian Kite Festival,** for kite makers and fliers of all ages, is held on the Washington Monument grounds (☎ 202/357–2700). The two-week-long **National Cherry Blossom Festival** (☎ 202/728–1137, WEB www.

gwjapan.com/parade) opens with a Japanese lantern-lighting ceremony at the Tidal Basin.

➤ MID-APR.: **Thomas Jefferson's birthday** (☎ 202/619–7222) is marked by military drills and a wreath-laying service at his memorial on April 13. The **White House Spring Garden and House Tours** (☎ 202/456–2200 or 202/208–1631) take in the Jacqueline Kennedy Rose Garden and the South Lawn; you can also visit public rooms in the White House.

➤ MID–LATE APR.: The **Georgetown House Tour** (☎ 202/338–1796, WEB www.georgetownhousetour.com) gives you the chance to view private homes. Admission includes high tea at historic St. John's Georgetown Parish Church. During the **Alexandria Garden Tour** (☎ 703/838–4200 or 703/370–1963, WEB www.vagardenweek.org), six private gardens and another half-dozen historical sights are open to the public, with afternoon tea at the Athenaeum.

➤ LATE APR.: The **Smithsonian Craft Show** (☎ 202/357–2700) exhibits one-of-a-kind, handcrafted objects by 120 top U.S. artisans.

➤ LATE APR.–EARLY MAY: The **D.C. International Film Festival** (☎ 202/724–5613) is where dozens of films premiere. Tickets are required.

➤ EARLY MAY: The **National Cathedral Flower Mart** (☎ 202/537–6200) salutes a different country each year with flower booths, crafts, and demonstrations. The **Georgetown Garden Tour** (☎ 202/333–3921) shows off more than a dozen private gardens in one of the city's most historic neighborhoods.

➤ EARLY–MID-MAY: Baltimore is all abuzz around the running of the Preakness Stakes, the middle jewel in horse racing's Triple Crown. The **Preakness Celebration** (☎ 410/837–3030, WEB www.preaknesscelebration.org) includes a balloon festival, parade, and music.

➤ EARLY MAY–MID AUG.: During the **Twilight Tattoo Series** (☎ 703/696–3399), the 3rd U.S. Infantry, the U.S. Army Band, the Drill Team, and the

Old Guard Fife and Drum Corps play on the Ellipse grounds Wednesdays at 7 PM.

➤ MID-MAY: The **Joint Services Open House** at Andrews Air Force Base in Maryland (☎ 301/568–5995 or 301/981–4424, WEB www.andrews.af.mil) has two days of static aircraft and weapons displays, parachute jumps, and the navy's Blue Angels or the air force's Thunderbirds aerobatic team.

➤ LATE MAY: The **Memorial Day Concert** (☎ 202/619–7222), by the National Symphony Orchestra at 8 PM on the Capitol's West Lawn, officially welcomes summer to D.C. **Memorial Day at Arlington National Cemetery** (☎ 703/607–8052) includes a wreath-laying ceremony at the Tomb of the Unknowns, services at the Memorial Amphitheatre featuring military bands, and a presidential keynote address. **Memorial Day at the U.S. Navy Memorial** (☎ 202/737–2300 Ext. 710) has wreath-laying ceremonies as well as an outdoor evening concert by the navy band. **Memorial Day at the Vietnam Veterans Memorial** (☎ 202/619–7222) is commemorated with a wreath-laying ceremony and a concert by the National Symphony. The **Memorial Day Jazz Festival** (☎ 703/883–4686) in Old Town Alexandria features big-band music performed by local musicians.

➤ EARLY JUNE: The **Alexandria Red Cross Waterfront Festival** (☎ 703/549–8300) promotes the American Red Cross and recognizes Alexandria's rich maritime heritage. Tall ships are open for visits, and there are arts-and-crafts displays, a 10K run, and a blessing of the fleet.

➤ JUNE: The **Shakespeare Theatre Free for All** is a series of free, nightly performances at the open-air Carter Barron Amphitheater, performed by the Washington Shakespeare Theatre (☎ 202/547–3230 Washington Shakespeare Theatre; 202/426–0486 Carter Barron Amphitheater, WEB www.shakespearedc.or).

➤ EARLY–MID-JUNE: The **Capital Jazz Fest** (☎ 301/218–0404 or 888/378–3378) is a weekend showcase for such contemporary performers as David Sanborn and Grover Washington Jr. in Manassas, Virginia.

➤ JUNE–JULY: The **National Cathedral's Summer Festival of Music** (☎ 202/537–6200) features everything from Renaissance choral music to contemporary instrumental fare.

➤ JUNE–AUG.: The **Military Band Summer Concert Series** (☎ 202/433–2525, 703/696–3399, 202/433–4011, or 202/767–5658), which runs from June 1–August 28, is held on Tuesday evenings at the Washington Monument and Friday evenings on the west steps of the Capitol at 8 PM. Every August the army band performs the *1812 Overture,* complete with real cannons at the Sylvan Theater at the base of the Washington Monument.

➤ LATE JUNE–EARLY JULY: The Smithsonian's **Folk Life Festival** (☎ 202/357–2700) is held on the Mall and celebrates the cultural traditions of communities across the United States and around the world with music, arts and crafts, and food.

➤ EARLY JULY: The **Independence Day Celebration** (☎ 202/619–7222) includes a grand parade past many monuments. In the evening, the National Symphony Orchestra gives free performances on the Capitol's West Lawn; this is followed by fireworks over the Washington Monument.

➤ LATE JULY: The **Korean War Armistice Day Ceremony** (☎ 202/619–7222) remembering the 1953 cease fire includes a formal wreath laying at the Korean War Veterans Memorial.

➤ LATE JULY: The **Virginia Scottish Games** (☎ 703/838–4200) include Highland dancing, bagpipes, a national professional heptathalon, fiddling competitions, animal events, and a British antique auto show on Alexandria's Episcopal High School grounds.

➤ EARLY SEPT.: The **Labor Day Weekend Concert** (☎ 202/619–7222 or 202/467–4600) by the National Symphony Orchestra takes place on the Capitol's West Lawn. At the free **John F. Kennedy Center's Open**

House (☎ 202/467–4600, WEB www. kennedy-center.org) there are musicians, dancers, and other performers on all five stages. The **National Black Family Reunion Celebration** (☎ 202/737–0120) includes free performances by nationally renowned R&B and gospel singers, exhibits, and food on the Washington Monument grounds. **Adams Morgan Day** (☎ 202/789–7000 or 202/234–4240, WEB www.adamsmorganday.org) celebrates family and community and cultural diversity with a large neighborhood street festival.

➤ MID-SEPT.: The **Constitution Day Commemoration** (☎ 202/501–5000 or 301/713–6000) observes the anniversary of the signing of the Constitution. Events include a naturalization ceremony, speakers, and concerts.

➤ LATE SEPT.: The **National Cathedral Open House** (☎ 202/537–6200) is a chance to share in cathedral-related crafts, music, and activities.

➤ EARLY OCT.: The **"Taste of D.C."** **Festival** (☎ 202/724–5430) presents dishes (and the chance to taste them) from a variety of D.C. eateries.

➤ MID-OCT.: The **White House Fall Garden Tours** (☎ 202/456–2200 or 202/208–1631) are an opportunity to see the White House gardens.

➤ LATE OCT.: The **Marine Corps Marathon** (☎ 703/690–3431) attracts thousands of world-class runners on the fourth Sunday in October. **Theodore Roosevelt's birthday** (☎ 703/289–2530) is celebrated on Roosevelt Island with tours of the island, exhibits, and family activities. The **Washington International Horse Show** (☎ 301/840–0281, WEB www.wihs.org) is D.C.'s major equestrian event.

➤ MID-NOV.: **Veterans' Day** services take place at Arlington National Cemetery (☎ 703/607–8052 Cemetery Visitors Center; 202/619–7222 National Park Service), the Vietnam Veterans Memorial, and the U.S. Navy Memorial, as well as an 11 AM wreath-laying ceremony at the Tomb of the Unknowns.

NW ◆ NE

T St.

S St.

R St.

Vernon Ave.

Ⓜ **SHAW/ HOWARD U.**

S St.

Florida Ave.

Lincoln Rd.

Rhode Island Ave.

Q St.

Q St.

R St.

Logan Circle

O St.

P St.

1st St.

O St.

9th St.

8th St.

7th St.

6th St.

5th St.

4th St.

3rd St.

New Jersey Ave.

N St.

N St.

M St.

13th St.

12th St.

11th St.

10th St.

L St.

New York Ave.

North Capitol St.

1st St.

Massachusetts Ave.

M St.

M St.

Mt. Vernon Square

MT. VERNON

Ⓜ

Washington Convention Center

I St.

H St.

Massachusetts Ave.

New Jersey Ave.

National Postal Museum

UNION STATION

Ⓜ

G St.

METRO CENTER

Ⓜ

F St.

Ⓜ **GALLERY PLACE/ CHINATOWN**

National Building Museum

JUDICIARY SQUARE Ⓜ

2nd St.

Columbus Memorial Fountain

E St.

FEDERAL TRIANGLE

Ⓜ

D St.

ARCHIVES/ NAVY MEMORIAL Ⓜ

Pennsylvania Ave.

Louisiana Ave.

NE

National Gallery Sculpture Garden

adison Dr.

National Museum of Natural History

National Gallery of Art

US Capitol

Supreme Court Building

Smithsonian Institution

T H E   M A L L

Jefferson Dr.

National Air and Space Museum

E. Capitol St.

SE

ISONIAN Ⓜ

Independence Ave.

Maryland Ave.

Canal St.

C St.

L'ENFANT PLAZA Ⓜ

D St.

D St.

Ⓜ

FEDERAL CENTER SW

Ⓜ **CAPITOL SOUTH** E St.

Southwest Fwy.

G St.

New Jersey Ave.

Virginia Ave.

Ave.

0 ——— 500 yards

0 ——— 500 meters

SW ◆ SE

Francis Case Memorial Bridge

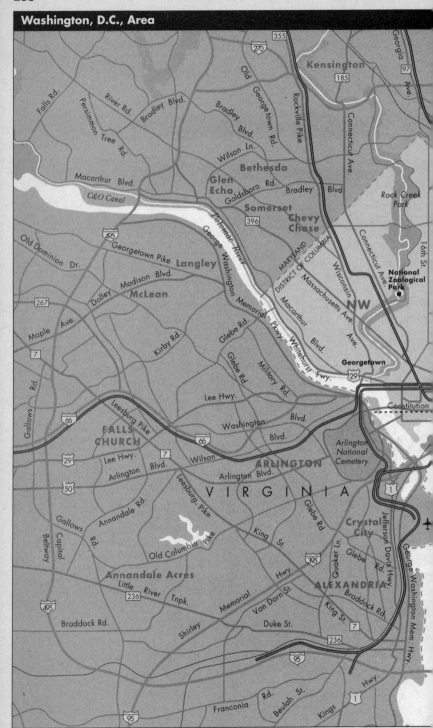

University

29

Capital Beltway

650

I-95

1

650

29

495

Silver Spring

193

Greenbelt

295

Greenbelt Rd.

Pkwy.

Capital Blvd.

193

College Park

University

Kenilworth Ave.

Baltimore-Washington

New Carrollton

I-95

Lantham-Severn Rd.

Takoma Park

650

Riggs Rd.

East-West Hwy

1

Riverdale Rd.

New Hampshire Ave.

M A R Y L A N D

Hyattsville

50

Georgia Ave.

DISTRICT OF COLUMBIA

NE

Rhode Island Ave.

Bladensburg Rd.

Landover Rd.

Cheverly

Landover Hills

29

1

50

New York Ave.

Sherrif Rd.

Martin Luther King Jr. Hwy.

Hill Rd.

Capital Beltway

Ritchie Rd.

I-95

Benning Rd.

Fairmont Heights

Ave.

US Capitol

Independence Ave.

RFK Stadium

E. Capitol St.

214

Capitol Heights

SW

River

SE

Anacostia

Pennsylvania

Marlboro Pike

Ave.

4

District Heights

Ritchie Rd.

Ritchie Rd.

395

Washington National Airport

I-95

Alabama Ave.

DISTRICT OF COLUMBIA

MARYLAND

Iverson St.

Morningside

4

Bolling Air Force Base

Wheeler Rd.

5

Forest Heights

I-95

Branch Ave.

Temple Hill Rd.

Andrews Air Force Base

N

Brinkley Rd.

210

KEY

Rail Line

Metroline

4 miles

6 km

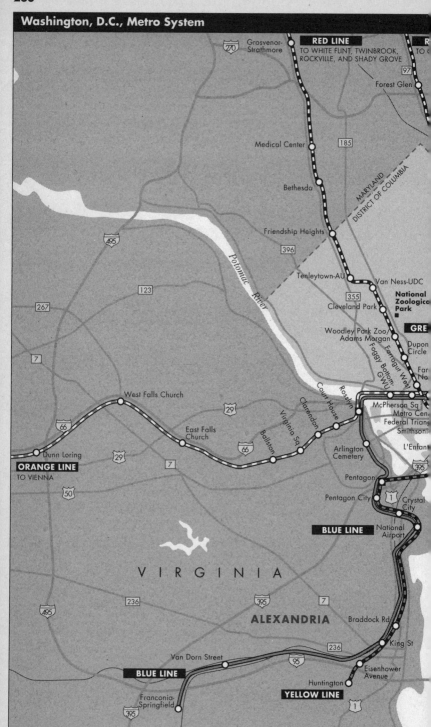

Grosvenor-Strathmore

RED LINE
TO WHITE FLINT, TWINBROOK,
ROCKVILLE, AND SHADY GROVE

Forest Glen

Medical Center

Bethesda

MARYLAND
DISTRICT OF COLUMBIA

Friendship Heights

Tenleytown-AU

Van Ness-UDC

**National
Zoological
Park**

Cleveland Park

Woodley Park Zoo/
Adams Morgan

GRE

Dupont
Circle

Far
No

McPherson Sq
Metro Cen
Federal Trian
Smithsoni

West Falls Church

Court House

Rosslyn

Clarendon

Virginia Sq

Ballston

East Falls
Church

Dunn Loring

ORANGE LINE
TO VIENNA

Arlington
Cemetery

L'Enfant

Pentagon

Pentagon City

Crystal
City

BLUE LINE

National
Airport

V I R G I N I A

ALEXANDRIA

Braddock Rd

King St

Van Dorn Street

Eisenhower
Avenue

BLUE LINE

Huntington

YELLOW LINE

Franconia-
Springfield

Potomac River

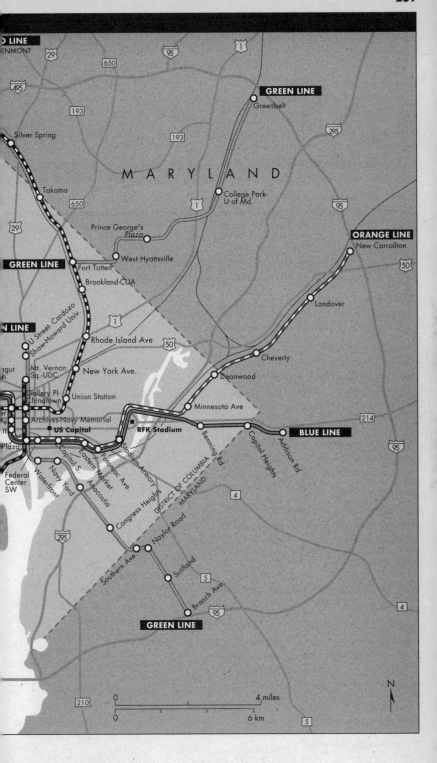

GREEN LINE

ORANGE LINE

BLUE LINE

GREEN LINE

ENMONT

Silver Spring

Takoma

Prince George's Plaza

West Hyattsville

Fort Totten

Brookland-CUA

U Street- Cardozo
Shaw-Howard Univ.

Rhode Island Ave

Mt. Vernon
Sq.-UDC

New York Ave.

Gallery Pl-
Chinatown

Union Station

Archives-Navy Memorial

US Capitol

Plaza

Eastern Market

Federal
Center
SW

Capitol S.

Waterfront

Navy Yard

Potomac Ave.

Stadium-Armory

RFK Stadium

Anacostia

Congress Heights

Minnesota Ave

Deanwood

Cheverly

Landover

New Carrollton

Benning Rd.

Capitol Heights

Addison Rd.

Naylor Road

Suitland

Branch Ave.

Southern Ave.

College Park-
U of Md.

Greenbelt

M A R Y L A N D

DISTRICT OF COLUMBIA
MARYLAND

N

0   4 miles

0   6 km

INDEX

NOTES

NOTES

NOTES

NOTES

FODOR'S WASHINGTON, D.C. 2002

EDITORS: Jane Driesen, Julie Mazur, Chris Swiac

Editorial Contributors: Robin Dougherty, Maureen Graney, Lisa Guttman Greaves, Thomas Head, Grace Hill-Putnam, John A. Kelly, Shannon Kelly, Karyn-Siobhan Robinson, Helayne Schiff, Mitchel Tropin, CiCi Williamson

Editorial Production: Taryn Luciani

Maps: David Lindroth, *cartographer*; Rebecca Baer and Bob Blake, *map editors*

Design: Fabrizio La Rocca, *creative director*; Guido Caroti, *art director*; Jolie Novak, *senior picture editor*; Melanie Marin, *photo editor*

Cover Design: Pentagram

Production/Manufacturing: Colleen Ziemba

COPYRIGHT

ISBN 0–676–90184–0

ISSN 0743-9741

SPECIAL SALES

Fodor's Travel Publications are available at special discounts for bulk purchases for sales promotions or premiums. Special editions, including personalized covers, excerpts of existing guides, and corporate imprints, can be created in large quantities for special needs. For more information, contact your local bookseller or write to Special Markets, Fodor's Travel Publications, 280 Park Avenue, New York, NY 10017. Inquiries from Canada should be directed to your local Canadian bookseller or sent to Random House of Canada, Ltd., Marketing Department, 2775 Matheson Blvd. East, Mississauga, Ontario, L4W 4P7. Inquiries from the United Kingdom should be sent to Fodor's Travel Publications, 20 Vauxhall Bridge Road, London SW1V 2SA.

PRINTED IN THE UNITED STATES OF AMERICA

10 9 8 7 6 5 4 3 2 1

IMPORTANT TIP

Although all prices, opening times, and other details in this book are based on information supplied to us at press time, changes occur all the time in the travel world, and Fodor's cannot accept responsibility for facts that become outdated or for inadvertent errors or omissions. So always confirm information when it matters, especially if you're making a detour to visit a specific place.

PHOTOGRAPHY

ABOUT OUR WRITERS

The more you know before you go, the better your trip will be. The city's most fascinating small museum (or its newest monument or most creative restaurant) could be just around the corner from your hotel, but if you don't know it's there, it might as well be on the other side of the globe. That's where this book comes in. It's a great step toward making sure your next trip lives up to your expectations. As you plan, check out the Web as well. Guidebooks have been helping smart travelers find the special places for years; the Web is one more tool. Whatever reference you consult, be savvy about what you read, and always consider the source. Images and language can be massaged to make places appear better than they are. And one traveler's quaint is another's grimy. Here at Fodor's, and at our on-line arm, Fodors.com, our focus is on providing you with information that's not only useful but accurate and on target. Every day Fodor's editors put enormous effort into getting things right, beginning with the search for the right contributors—people who have objective judgment, broad travel experience, and the writing ability to put their insights into words. There's no substitute for advice from a like-minded friend who has just come back from where you're going, but our writers, having seen all corners of Washington, D.C., are the next best thing. They're the kind of people you'd poll for tips yourself if you knew them.

Robin Dougherty, a native Washingtonian, moved back to D.C. after living in Miami and Boston. Updating the Lodging and Shopping chapters, in addition to parts of the Exploring chapter, helped her to become reacquainted with the city again. A longtime arts writer and former critic for the *Miami Herald,* she also reviews books for the *Boston Globe.*

Maureen Graney, a freelance editor and book producer who updated much of the Exploring D.C. chapter, regularly makes the rounds of Washington's top sights with her two young sons. The transplanted New Yorker loves her family's Capitol Hill townhouse.

Dining-chapter reviewer **Thomas Head** is the executive wine and food editor at the *Washingtonian* magazine. This resident of the Dupont Circle neighborhood also writes about travel.

A stickler for details who loves to explore, **Grace Hill-Putnam** updated Smart Travel Tips A to Z, to make your trip even easier. She's called Washington home for 13 years, and has explored most every nook and cranny. Before becoming a freelance writer, she worked for the *Washington Post* for 12 years.

Karyn-Siobhan Robinson, who checked out the nightlife and arts scenes for this book, is a freelance writer, poet, part-time actor, and essayist. She has lived in the Dupont Circle neighborhood since 1991 and is working on her first novel.

Native Washingtonian **Mitch Tropin,** who updated the Outdoor Activities and Sports chapter, has been a dedicated runner for 25 years. A senior editor for a news organization, he spends lunch hours running the streets and parks of D.C. in search of new routes. Mitch has written for a number of running publications.

CiCi Williamson has been a food and travel writer and syndicated newspaper columnist for almost two decades. She updated the Maryland and Virginia portions of the Exploring chapter and the Side Trips chapter with her husband and writing partner, **John A. Kelly.** They live in McLean, Virginia, and their travels have taken them to more than 70 countries on six continents.

Don't Forget to Write

Keeping a travel guide fresh and up-to-date is a big job. So we love your feedback—positive and negative—and follow up on all suggestions. Contact the Washington editor at editors@fodors.com or c/o Fodor's, 280 Park Avenue, New York, NY 10017. And have a wonderful trip!

Karen Cure
Editorial Director